The First
Christian Histories

The First
Christian Histories

Eusebius, Socrates, Sozomen,
Theodoret, and Evagrius

GLENN F. CHESNUT

Second Edition, Revised and Enlarged

MERCER UNIVERSITY PRESS

PEETERS

ISBN 0-86554-164-7 (cloth)
ISBN 0-86554-203-1 (paper)

The paper used in this publication meets
the minimum requirements of American National Standard
for Information Sciences—Permanence of Paper
for Printed Library Materials, ANSI Z39.48-1984.

Library of Congress Cataloging-in-Publication Data

Chesnut, Glenn F.
    The first Christian histories.

    Bibliography: p. 259
    Includes index.
    1. Church history—Primitive and early church,
ca. 30-600—Historiography. I. Title.
BR166.C49   1986   270.1'072   85-28515
ISBN 0-86554-164-7 (alk. paper)
ISBN 0-86554-203-1 (pbk. : alk. paper)

Contents

CHAPTER 11

To my father

Abbreviations

Amm. Marc.	Ammianus Marcellinus
Aug.	Augustine
Conf.	*Confessions*
De civ. Dei	*De civitate Dei*
Dio Cass.	Dio Cassius
Eus.	Eusebius of Caesarea
Armen. Chron.	*Chronicle*, Armenian translation
Chron.	*Chronicle*, Jerome's translation
Contra Hier.	*Contra Hieroclem*
De laud	*De laudibus Constantini*
DE	*Demonstratio Evangelica*
HE	*Historia Ecclesiastica*
PE	*Praeparatio Evangelica*
Theoph.	*Theophania*
VC	*Vita Constantini*
Evag.	Evagrius Scholasticus
HE	*Historia Ecclesiastica*
GCS	*Die griechischen christlichen Schriftsteller*
Greg. Nyss.	Gregory of Nyssa
Or. cat.	*Oratio catechetica magna*
Her.	Herodotus
Iren.	Irenaeus
Adv. haer.	*Adversus haereses*
Jos.	Josephus
Ant.	*Antiquitates Judaicae*
BJ	*Bellum Judaicum*
LCL	*Loeb Classical Library*
Migne	Migne
PG	*Patrologia Graeca*
NEB	*New English Bible*
OCT	*Oxford Classical Texts*

Polyb.	Polybius
Sall.	Sallust
Cat.	*Bellum Catilinae*
Jug.	*Bellum Jugurthinum*
Socr.	Socrates Scholasticus
HE	*Historia Ecclesiastica*
Soz.	Sozomen
HE	*Historia Ecclesiastica*
Stob.	Ioannes Stobaeus, *Anthologium*
Tac.	Tacitus
Ann.	*Annales*
Ger.	*Germania*
Hist.	*Historiae*
Theod.	Theodoret of Cyrrhus
Epist. Sirm.	The epistles of the *Collectio Sirmondiana*
HE	*Historia Ecclesiastica*
Thuc.	Thucydides
Xen.	Xenophon
Hell.	*Hellenica*
Zos.	Zosimus, *Historia Nova*

Preface to the Second Edition

I greatly appreciate the opportunity given me by Mercer University Press for the publication of a second edition of this work. I must also thank Éditions Beauchesne, the publisher of the first edition, for allowing Mercer to reissue it in this revised form, and I am especially grateful to Professor Charles Kannengiesser, director of Beauchesne's Théologie Historique series, for his good offices in making the necessary arrangements.

There are many small changes and additions throughout this second edition, for which the type has been completely reset. The most important addition, however, is a new chapter, "Eusebius: From Youthful Defender of Religious Liberty to Spokesman for the Constantinian Imperial Church." The portrayal of the young Eusebius as one who believed in toleration, nonviolence, and religious pluralism may be quite startling to those familiar with most of the treatments of Eusebius's ideas about church and state that have appeared over the past century and a half. Most of the first seven books of his *Church History*, however, clearly shows such a position, and the chronology of Eusebius's writings is on much firmer ground now than it was when I was writing the first edition, allowing far more to be said than previously. I have also attempted to give my own interpretation of the likely nature of the first edition of the *Church History*, and have gone on in that chapter to show how Eusebius's elevation to the episcopacy and the necessity he then had for negotiating with the subsequent emperors under whom he lived, and his attempts to influence their religious policies, eventually led him to the quite different position on church and state that he espoused in the *Life of Constantine* at the very end of his life.

The Prix de Rome awarded in 1978 allowed me a year as a Fellow of the American Academy in Rome, where I carried out some of the research now included in this second edition. My articles in *Anglican Theological Review* and *Religious Studies Review* in 1983 permitted me to explore some of these new ideas in print. That excellent Eusebian scholar, Robert M. Grant, and the other members of the Chicago Patristics Seminar, gave me many opportunities as well over the past years for trying out ideas, and in turn learning from them. Indiana University at South Bend supplied research and development funds to aid partially in typesetting costs. A Visiting Professorship in History and Theology at Boston University has given me the time this academic year to carry out the actual revision of the first edition and see the new text through the press. Boston University also very graciously subsidized the entire typing of the manuscript, which was very ably done by John Pearson, who had to cope with altering French typographical style to American under intense time pressure.

Special thanks are also due to Dennis E. Groh, Michele Salzman, and J. Patout Burns for reading through the typescript of chapter six shortly before it went to press and giving me both pertinent comments and useful additional information. I must also express my very special gratitude for the care that Mercer University Press put into the preparation and editorial revision of this volume at every point in the process.

May I conclude by simply saying, blessed be God whose providence has led me thus far, and thanks to everyone who has rendered me kindnesses along the way.

Boston   G. F. C.
May 1985

Preface to the First Edition

The need for a study such as this was first suggested to me by one of my early and influential teachers, Albert C. Outler. I was later able to spend three years at Oxford University, at Linacre College, devoting my full time to the early church historians, thanks to several grants. A Fulbright Fellowship (1965-1966, 1966-1967) initially brought me over to England. I also held a Moore Fellowship from Perkins School of Theology (1965-1966), a Dempster Fellowship (1966-1967), and finally a Rockefeller Doctoral Fellowship during my last year there (1967-1968).

I wish to thank S. L. Greenslade, who so patiently and carefully read the earliest versions of this work and was always available for help and counsel through the whole time at Oxford. My good friend Peter Brown also encouraged me and advised me at several critical points while I was at Oxford, and has continued to discuss the work with me through the years that have followed.

Since I came back to the States a number of people in this country have been helpful in a variety of ways. I wish to pay special thanks, however, to Joseph D. Quillian, Jr., Albert C. Outler, Van A. Harvey, Robert M. Grant, and Dennis E. Groh; their kindness has meant a good deal to me at various stages of my research. Jean Laporte was of great help in the final revision of the book for publication. I must also thank a number of people at Indiana University at South Bend. The university has supported my research in every possible way. Summer faculty fellowships in 1972 and 1975 provided me time to write. Donna B. Harlan and her library staff obtained obscure books from all corners of the country. By their friendship and kindness my colleagues in the history department provided a congenial place to work and teach. I must also express my appreciation to Richard Bondi, who compiled the index at the end of this volume.

Chapter 3 of this book first appeared as an article entitled "Fate, Fortune, Free Will and Nature in Eusebius of Caesarea," in *Church History* in June 1973. The latter part of chapter 8 also appeared as an article, "Kairos and Cosmic Sympathy in the Church Historian Socrates Scholasticus," in the same journal, in June 1975. The first half of chapter 7 will appear in a slightly more detailed version as "The Ruler and the Logos in Neopythag-orean, Middle Platonic, and Late Stoic Political Philosophy," in Hildegard Temporini and Wolfgang Haase, eds., *Aufstieg und Niedergang der Römischen Welt: Geschichte und Kultur Roms im Spiegel der neueren Forschung.* My article on "The Pattern of the Past: Augustine's Debate with Eusebius and Sallust," which was published in J. Deschner, L. T. Howe, and K. Penzel, eds., *Our Common History as Christians: Essays in Honor of Albert C. Outler* (New York, 1975), dealt with the relationship between Augustine's and Eusebius's theology of history from the Augustinian, not the Eusebian side. Various parts of the article, however, have been drawn on in a number of places in the present book where the material seemed useful.

Last I must attempt, however inadequately, to express my thanks to my wife, Roberta. She has given me the use of her own knowledge of theology and patristic thought, but even more importantly, she has helped to shape my own understanding, over the years, of that divine reality to which we all owe honor. Of all debts of gratitude which should be declared in the preface to a book, my debts to her are the greatest.

Indiana University   G. F. C.
South Bend
August 1976

CHAPTER 1

Introduction

Eusebius of Caesarea's *Church History* was the first full-length, continuous narrative history written from a Christian point of view. It thereby became one of the four or five most important and seminal works in the history of Western historiography. His work, and that of his immediate successors and imitators, determined to a large degree the way history was written for a thousand years afterward.

Eusebius's *Church History*, in its final edition, gave an account of the history of Christianity in its first three centuries of trial and persecution, from the coming of Jesus to the final triumph of Constantine. Several generations later, two lawyers in Constantinople, Socrates Scholasticus and Sozomen, and Theodoret the bishop of Cyrrhus in Euphratensis, each wrote a history continuing Eusebius's narrative from the time of Constantine down to the early fifth century. In the next century, yet another lawyer, Evagrius Scholasticus in Antioch, put himself in the tradition of these preceding figures, and continued the history of the Christian church down to 594 C.E. These five historians, put together, gave a connected account of the truly formative years of Christianity, when the early church was working out its basic understanding of such fundamental issues as Bible, canon, hermeneutics, Christology and Trinitarian theology, doctrine of the church, and relationship between church and state.

In addition, Eusebius prepared a *Chronicle* that endeavored to lay out a scientific, comparative chronology for all of ancient Near Eastern, Greek, Roman, and biblical history (the latter, with good critical sense, attempted only from the time of Abraham). The tradition of the medieval chronicle was built on its basis.[1] His *Martyrs of Palestine* must also be included in a list of his historical works, as well as the *Life of Constantine*.[2]

---

[1] The *Chronicle* of Hydatius, from fifth-century Visigothic Spain, is an excellent case in point. See Hydace, *Chronique*, ed. Alain Tranoy (Paris, 1974); reviewed by Glenn F. Chesnut, *Church History* 45 (1976): 375.

[2] On the authorship and authenticity of the *Life of Constantine*, see the extended footnote at the beginning of chapter 7.

Eusebius had of course inherited an already established theological tradition that contained in nucleus a theory of history. The ideas of earlier Christian thinkers like Justin Martyr, Clement of Alexandria, and Origen gave him solutions already at hand for many issues.[3] In his massive reading, Eusebius had also learned much from the Greek philosophical tradition— from Plato himself, the Aristotelians and the Stoics, the Neopythagoreans and, most important of all, the Middle Platonists. He drew on this already existing theological and philosophical material to help in his theoretical solutions to historiographical problems. Nevertheless, the problem of working out a method for applying those ideas to the actual writing of an extended historical narrative was left for Eusebius himself to resolve. Moreover, the principal problems that he had to solve were primarily created by his predecessor historians, the great pagan authors like Herodotus, Thucydides, and Polybius, not the subsequent commentaries of theologians or philosophers. So the chapters that follow will concentrate when possible on comparing historians with historians—that is, comparing the understanding of history held by Eusebius and his successors with that of the classical authors who preceded them.

This book deals with a number of topics, but in one way or another they tend to focus on two principal centers of interest: on the one hand the motifs of fate and fortune that so preoccupied the pagan Graeco-Roman historians (and continued to dog their Christian successors), and on the other hand the issue of Rome and its emperor. As part of the first focus, this work will show how the rejection of the classical historians' understanding of fate, and the defense instead of a vigorous doctrine of free will, fundamentally shaped the narrative style and explanatory methods of the first Christian historians. In addition several of the following chapters will attempt to trace both the open and covert ways in which the classical Graeco-Roman understanding of the fortuitous nature of human life was

---

[3]It would have been an impossible task even to begin to note all the echoes in Eusebius of second- and third-century theologians. It must be assumed at many points in the following pages that the reader will be able to recognize the commonplaces of early patristic theology as such. But see Robert M. Grant, "The Appeal to the Early Fathers," *Journal of Theological Studies* new series 11 (1960): 13-24; and "The Uses of History in the Church before Nicaea," in F. L. Cross, ed., *Studia Patristica* 11 = *Texte und Untersuchungen* 108 (Berlin: Akademie-Verlag, 1972) 166-78.

preserved, in one way or another, in each of the Christian histories studied.

The other focus of the present study will be Rome and the Roman emperor. In the histories of this period, the ruler of the Roman state, due to his enormous power, often played the single most important role in determining the course of human events. He had traditionally been regarded by many ancient men and women as a divine being, who was god on earth for the rest of the human race. Earlier pagan thinkers, like Plato, had dreamed of a philosopher-king who would possess the wisdom and self-denial of a sage as he ruled the royal realm he had been granted. It will be necessary to explore the attempt of the first Christian historians to deal with both the sacred king and the philosophical king, and the gradual emergence in their writings of a combination of the old pagan theory of rulership with a new, medieval understanding of the ideal monarch as a pious, ascetic soldier-monk. Furthermore, the Roman state itself embodied certain concepts that also had to be transmuted in Christian hands. It was necessary to confront the pagan idea of Eternal Rome with some more Christian concept, while dealing as well with the quite different pagan historiographical motif of the decline and fall of the Roman empire. This of course in turn raised more basic issues about historical progress and degeneration, and the widespread pagan notion of history as cyclical. Since all of these ideas presented major problems for the creators of the first Christian histories, the present study must also investigate the manner in which these issues were confronted and resolved.

This book is therefore an attempt to deal with the broadest issues of historiography. It is an endeavor to explore how five ancient authors, brought up in a society in which the ancient pagan classics were still alive, tried to write a new kind of history. It is an attempt to be sensitive to the kind of intellectual issues of which they themselves were most acutely conscious. And in the process, I hope, a world of thought can be revealed. Late Antiquity was not an age of sterility and decay. In the fourth century there was a new Roman resurgence, accompanied by a mutation in thought that broke in many basic ways with the classical past even while attempting to preserve it. In the process, a fair amount of creativity touched several areas of human life and thought—law, political theory, religion, art and, of course, the writing of history. The strength of the new Christian-Roman synthesis was shown by the way it survived the barbarian invasions and the eventual Dark Age that followed, to serve as the seed, in Western Europe, for a new, dynamic society that eventually began to blossom there.

Working as they did in that crucially formative transitional era between the classical world and the middle ages, these five historians have become important to modern scholars in a variety of areas. They are used as sources, not only by Late Roman historians, but also by scholars in Early Medieval and Early Byzantine studies. In addition, Eusebius's work has been important to New Testament scholars because of his preservation of so many early traditions that may still be used, with the aid of modern critical methods, to help in the reconstruction of earliest Christian history. The present study, with its account of the methodology used by these historians and its examination of their historical presuppositions, biases, and tendencies, will be of importance therefore to those who must use these ancient works as sources.

One must also remember the crucial role that Eusebius in particular played in the development of Western political thought. The reformulation of Christian political theory necessitated by the legitimation of Christianity under Constantine was given official form in the writings of Eusebius, and further developed by his successors. The Roman empire suddenly became a government within which Christians could take more active part, but for which they had to take more active responsibility. Some set of ideals for the Christian monarch had to be developed and given shape, by which men and women could live their lives in the new Christian world. The results were passed down, in both Western European and Byzantine political theory, through the entire Middle Ages. Not until the English Civil War and, on the Continent, the French and Russian revolutions, was this tradition of political thought brought to an end.

Finally, the theological significance of Eusebius's thought in particular is of the greatest importance, because it stood as the only serious ancient alternative to Augustine's theology of history. Augustine's doctrine of predestination and grace effectively denied what would today ordinarily be called free will. His doctrine of the two cities rejected any possibility of genuine historical progress, and at least called into question the possibility of any fundamental Christianization of the secular order. Eusebius stood over against him as the most thoughtful ancient spokesman for a different view of history, one that was founded on a Christian humanism committed to achieving the full positive interaction of reason, religion, morality, voluntarism, and the power of civilization. For Eusebius, human beings in history had free will, and the social order could be reformed from a Christian perspective. Even today it is theologically instructive to analyze the issues that actually separated him from the Augustinianism that appeared (in partial reaction to his ideas) in the century after his death.

All five of these historians, and especially Eusebius, have been of enormous importance in the intellectual history of the West. They were nevertheless sadly neglected in modern scholarship in many ways up until the past decade or so. The present volume may aid in the current task, in which increasing numbers of excellent scholars have now become involved, of recalling to the attention of the modern age the significance of these truly formative works of historiography.

CHAPTER 2

The Pagan Background

It is impossible to comprehend the full set of problems confronting the first Christian historians without understanding the background that lay behind them. History writing in the early Christian period was dominated by the pagan Graeco-Roman historiographical tradition that went back to Herodotus. Within that tradition various historians held that the historical process was controlled by acts of Fortune, that human free will was under the rule of Fate, and that the gods intervened in history with omens, retribution, and vindictive acts of jealousy. In order to work out a coherent Christian understanding of history and the forces that shaped it, Eusebius and his successors first of all had to deal with those overwhelming issues. Fortune, Fate, omens, retribution, and the envy of the gods were discussed so often and played such a major role in Greek and Roman historiography that a Christian historian was almost forced to make some explicit statement about these issues and either attack them as pagan or adapt them to Christian purposes. Because of the importance of these ideas, it will be useful to begin with a brief survey of their varied roles in Greek and Roman history writing through the centuries.

The concept of Fortune (Τύχη) in particular lay at the very center of traditional pagan thought about history. It could be regarded in either supernatural or natural terms. Herodotus believed that the gods intervened in history to control the course of the fortunes of human beings.[1] Even

---

[1] Her. 1.124, 1.32; see also 1.126, 3.139. J. L. Myres (*Herodotus: Father of History* [Oxford: Clarendon Press, 1953] 48-49, 55) discusses the degree to which Herodotus personified Fate and Fortune. He feels this to have been slight. For an even more impersonal interpretation, see R. G. Collingwood, *The Idea of History* (Oxford: Clarendon Press, 1946) 22-23. Nevertheless, Fortune and Fate were for Herodotus clearly manifestations of the *divine*. For discussions of this, see Harry Elmer Barnes, *A History of Historical Writing* (New York: Dover, 1962) 29; Joseph Wells, *Studies in Herodotus* (Oxford: Basil Blackwell, 1923) 194; R. W. Macan, "Herodotus and Thucydides," in *Cambridge Ancient History* (1927) 5:407; W. C. Greene, *Moira: Fate, Good, and Evil in Greek Thought* (New York: Harper and Row, 1963) 270.

though his successor Thucydides completely rejected any notion of divine intervention in history, he also used the word τύχη—twenty-eight times in his speeches, and eleven times in his narrative sections.[2] In contrast to Herodotus, clearly, he did not imply anything supernatural by his use of the word; rather, he simply identified unforeseen chance occurrences that disrupted human plans. Later on, in the Hellenistic period, Polybius's use of the concept of Fortune was particularly notorious, and a vast modern, scholarly literature discusses the question of what this historian in fact meant by the term, and whether he thought of Fortune in different ways at different stages in his own intellectual development.[3] Polybius proclaimed that Fortune had directed the overall historical process whereby Rome had gradually conquered the entire Mediterranean world.

> I therefore thought it quite necessary not to leave unnoticed or allow to pass into oblivion this the finest and most beneficent of the performances of Fortune. For though she is ever producing something new and ever playing a part in the lives of men, she has not in a single instance ever accomplished such a work, ever achieved such a triumph, as in our own times.[4]

In at least some passages he seems to have spoken of Fortune as itself a personified divine power deliberately guiding the course of world events. This development is not strange, since in the Hellenistic period Tyche was

---

[2] Plus one use in a treaty (4.118.11). See M. H. N. von Essen, *Index Thucydideus* (Berlin: Weidmannos, 1887).

[3] See for example, Rudolf von Scala, *Die Studien des Polybios* (Stuttgart: Kohlhammer, 1890) 1:159ff., 167-68, 174-81; Otto Cuntz, *Polybius und sein Werk* (Leipzig: Teubner, 1902) 43-45; J. B. Bury, *The Ancient Greek Historians* (London: Macmillan, 1909) 200-203; Richard Laqueur, *Polybius* (Leipzig: Teubner, 1913) 250-60; Walter Siegfried, *Studien zur geschichtlichen Anschauung des Polybios* (Leipzig: Teubner, 1928) 1-7, 37-39, and 47-67; F. W. Walbank, *Historical Commentary on Polybius* (Oxford: Clarendon, 1957) 1:23-26; Paul Pédech, *La méthode historique de Polybe* (Paris: Les Belles lettres, 1964) 331-38. Unfortunately, this work has not usually been done with sufficient sensitivity to the textual problems in some of the crucial passages most often cited. For a modern survey of the state of the text of Polybius's history, see John M. Moore, *The Manuscript Tradition of Polybius* (Cambridge: Cambridge University Press, 1965).

[4] Polyb. 1.4.3-5.

widely worshiped as a goddess, sometimes as a sort of tutelary genius of a particular city, and her statues are found in great number.

When the Romans began to write history, they took over the concept of Fortune as an intrinsic part of the Greek models they were following. As Sallust put it, "Fortune" (*fortuna*) is she "whose irrational whim [*lubido*] controls the nations."[5] Fortune's personification grew as one passed further into the Roman imperial period. In Dio Cassius (late second and early third century C.E.) Fortune had become personified so completely that an individual worshiper could now devote his life to this goddess and receive special revelations from her. In his dreams, Dio tells us, the goddess Fortune commanded him to write his history, and he wrote of her with admiration in that work: "This goddess gives me strength to continue my history when I become timid and disposed to shrink from it; when I grow weary and would resign the task, she wins me back by sending dreams. . . . I have dedicated myself to her."[6]

In short, hardly any pagan historian in the Graeco-Roman world could have conceived of writing a history in which the concept of Fortune did not play some role. It intruded into every sort of historical circumstance. It could be interpreted as a personal deity, or as a mechanical combination of natural circumstances, or anything in between, depending on the degree of piety in the historian.

But even if we find differing opinions on the question of whether or not acts of Fortune were ultimately controlled by some supernatural power, on a more phenomenological level it is possible to describe clearly the sorts of historical events that were apt to be called "acts of Fortune" by ancient historians, and explain why these particular events were so regarded. Basically, Fortune to them meant the way in which history was dominated by combinations of forces outside any single human being's prediction or control. On the one hand it meant the *conjuncture* of two or more independent chains of historical events—independent in that no one single human being was in control of all the important factors involved, nor were all the events part of some single, simple natural process. On the other hand there was usually some element of the *unexpected* involved, so that the final turn of events came as a surprise and a shock to the human actors involved.

---

[5]Sall. *Cat.* 51.25. Compare *Jug.* 102.9, *Cat.* 8.1, and so forth.

[6]Dio Cass. 73(72).23.2-4.

Herodotus tells us that at the very point when Croesus had temporarily disbanded most of his army, Cyrus decided to make a sudden attack on Sardis. This conjuncture of events was an act of Fortune, and it proved disastrous for Croesus, whose kingdom was consequently destroyed.[7] Polybius tells us that Hannibal's one attempt to make a surprise attack on Rome itself happened to come on the very day when Gnaeus Fulvius and Publius Sulpicius had ordered the recruits for two newly formed legions to assemble there in the city. One chain of events began when Hannibal secretly began moving towards Rome; the other, originally unconnected, chain of events began when the two Roman officials published that particular date as the time for the new recruits to report for enrollment and active duty. They had no idea that Hannibal was planning an attack. The conjuncture of these two chains of events was entirely an act of Fortune, but Rome, which otherwise would have been undefended, was saved by it.[8] The concept of Fortune, as can be seen, in no sense implied the inability to give a complete causal explanation of the events involved; in this sense it was quite different from what a modern person often means by "chance." An act of Fortune was not "inexplicable" or "uncaused"; it was uncontrollable, which is a quite different kind of statement.

An act of Fortune was also usually unpredictable. It was the element of the unexpected in history. However carefully human plans for the future were laid, unforeseen factors continually cropped up to produce results different from those that were planned or expected. As we find the idea expressed in Thucydides' history, "We commonly lay upon fortune (τὴν τύχην) the blame for whatever turns out contrary to our calculations

---

[7]Her. 1.77, 79.

[8]Polyb. 9.6.5-7. Compare the passage in J. B. Bury's historiographical essay, "Cleopatra's Nose" (in *Selected Essays* [Cambridge: Cambridge University Press, 1930] 60-69): "I visit Paris. I meet an American friend, whom I had not seen for years, in the Rue de la Paix. We were mutually ignorant of each other's presence in Paris, and we describe our meeting as a happy chance. My visit to Paris and my walking in the Rue de la Paix at a particular hour were the result of a sequence of causes and effects. His visit to Paris and his presence in the same street at the same hour followed upon another sequence of causes and effects. The collision, as we may say, of these two independent chains made what we call the chance of our meeting."

(παρὰ λόγον)."[9] Polybius regarded this as the principal fascination of the topic he had chosen for his great historical work: "the very element of un-expectedness (τὸ παράδοξον) in the events I have chosen as my theme will be sufficient to challenge and incite everyone, young and old alike, to peruse my systematic history."[10] Even with the greatest wisdom and prep-aration, a finite human mind could never calculate all the possible avenues for catastrophe. By repeated bitter experience, history taught "a lesson to humankind never to discuss the future as if it were the present, or to have any confident hope about things that may still turn out quite otherwise. We are but human beings, and should in every matter assign its share to the unexpected (τῷ παραδόξῳ)."[11]

One of the most useful and sensitive analyses of Fortune in ancient Greek thought was drawn up by Aristotle in one section of the *Physics*.[12] A man went to the market, he said, on an unusual errand (he did not usually go to that part of the market) and unexpectedly met a man from whom he wanted to collect some money. The successful collection of the money was not due to some intentional choice of a particular course of action (προαί-

---

[9]Thuc. 1.140.1. Compare 6.23.3 and 7.67.4, where Fortune is contrasted with those factors that the human actors have knowingly prepared for in advance. F. M. Cornford (*Thucydides Mythistoricus* [London: Routledge and Kegan Paul, 1965] 167-68, 222) emphasized this aspect of Fortune: "The future is dark and uncertain, and although rational foresight (γνώμη) can see a little way into the gloom, For-tune, or Fate, or Providence, is an incalculable factor which at any moment may reverse the purposes and defeat the designs of man." "Not only in the great catas-trophes, in flood and avalanche and earthquake, but again and again in the turns of daily experience, man finds himself the sport of an unseen demon. Now, by some unforeseen stroke, his long-cherished design is foiled; now, with equally un-intelligible caprice, goods are heaped on him which he never expected."

[10]Polyb. 1.1.4. In his history, words meaning "unexpected," like παράδοξος and παράλογος, occur with almost wearisome repetition, for example 1.6.8, 24.1, 44.5, 54.8, 58.1-2, 58.3, 61.7, 82.3-8. 87.1 (connected with περιπέτεια); 2.17.3, 18.6, 37.6, 70.2-3; 9.6.5-7, 16.2-4; 15.15.5; 30.10.1-2.

[11]Polyb. 2.4.3-5. Compare 2.7.1-2, "For we are but human beings, and to meet with some unexpected (παραλόγως) blow is not the sufferer's fault, but that of Fortune (τῆς τύχης) and those who inflict it on him."

[12]2.4.195b-6.198a. Compare the discussion in John Herman Randall, *Aristotle*, 182-84.

ρεσις) based upon intelligent planning (διάνοια) and directed to the end of collecting the money. The man did not go to the market with any idea or expectation of finding the one from whom he wanted money, but, while there on some other purpose, just happened to run into him. In normal Greek usage, one would say that it was simply a matter of fortune (τύχη), Aristotle said. "Clearly, therefore, fortune is an accidental cause affecting those happenings which are for the sake of some purpose or end, and which also involve free choice."[13] Only human beings could experience fortune, Aristotle said, and indeed only human beings out of infancy and old enough to form purposeful plans and to decide on courses of action by rational choice. Fortune was a much more highly specialized concept than the sort of crude mechanical principle of chance that governed whether a tossed coin, for example, came down heads or tails. Inanimate objects could not suffer Fortune, only human beings. Fortune, Aristotle said—using one of his most important philosophical terms—was "the accidental," τὸ κατὰ συμβεβηκός, which made human purposeful action produce results different from those that were planned and expected. This exact technical phrase[14] was to be used more than six centuries later by Eusebius, the first Christian historian, in his own analysis of the fortuitous, so Aristotle's discussion of this issue must be carefully noted.

One finds a similar definition from Eusebius's own century in Nemesius of Emesa. One should note the way both sides of the idea are brought out, Fortune as conjuncture of two or more independent chains of historical events, and Fortune as the unexpected in history.

For fortune is defined as the coincidence and concurrence (σύμπτωσιν καὶ

---

[13]*Physics* 2.5.197a: δῆλον ἄρα ὅτι ἡ τύχη αἰτία κατὰ συμβεβηκὸς ἐν τοῖς κατὰ προαίρεσιν τῶν ἕνεκά του.

[14]Mediated perhaps through Middle Platonic sources. One sees Tyche referred to as τὸ κατὰ συμβεβηκός for example, in works like the essay "On Fate" in Plutarch's *Moralia*, 571e-572c. See vol. 7 of the LCL edition of the *Moralia* (where Plutarch's authorship of the piece is, however, questioned, 303), trans. P. H. De Lacy and B. Einarson (London: Heinemann, 1959) 303-59. We also find here succinct descriptions of both aspects of Fortune. For Fortune as the unexpected we get the classic Stoic definition of it as "a cause unforeseen and not evident to human calculation" (572a). For Fortune as historical conjuncture we have a Platonic example in which we are told that "the outcome resulted from a concourse of causes (ἐκ συνδρομῆς τινος αἰτίων), each of them having a different end" (572c).

συνδρομὴν) of two actions each of which arises from some particular purpose, to produce something quite different from what was intended by
either, as when a man digs a ditch and finds a buried treasure. For one man
buried the treasure, but not that the other man might find it. Nor did the
other man dig for the purpose of finding treasure. The first intended, in
his own time, to dig the treasure up again, while the second intended to
dig a ditch. What fell out was something different from what either had
intended. [15]

The Stoics also had a famous definition of Fortune. "Chance is a cause obscure to the human mind," they said, "and thus the same event appears to
one as chance and to another not, depending on whether one knows the
cause or does not know it." [16] But this definition did not give a true picture
of all that Greek historians had meant by the term. It was distorted by Stoic
metaphysics, which insisted that the universe was completely deterministic. Unlike Aristotelians or Platonists, Stoics had no room for genuine
chance or accident in their philosophy, and so they had to "explain away"
part of what a Greek historian would usually have meant by the word Fortune. Aristotle, and the Middle Platonist Nemesius, are therefore better
guides to usual Graeco-Roman historical practice.

But it is important to remember that "Fortune" was not just an abstract
concept to be discussed and defined at the academic, philosophical level.
Within Greek culture especially, this motif was an expression of a basic,
fundamental attitude toward life. [17] It dominated Greek drama as much as

---

[15]Nemesius of Emesa, De natura hominis 39 (Migne PG 40, cols. 761b-764a) trans.
by W. Telfer in the Library of Christian Classics.

[16]Alexander Aphrodisiensis, De anima 179.6, quoted in S. Sambursky, Physics
of the Stoics (London, 1959) 76, 135.

[17]As Collingwood said (The Idea of History, 22), the Greek historical consciousness was one "of violent περιπέτειαι, catastrophic changes from one state of
things to its opposite, from smallness to greatness, from pride to abasement, from
happiness to misery. This was how they interpreted the general character of human life in their dramas, and this was how they narrated the particular parts of it
in their history. The only thing that a shrewd and critical Greek like Herodotus
would say about the divine power that ordains the course of history is that it is
φθονερὸν καὶ ταραχῶδες: it rejoices in upsetting and disturbing things. He was
only repeating (i. 32) what every Greek knew: that the power of Zeus is mani-
fested in the thunderbolt, that of Poseidon in the earthquake, that of Apollo in
the pestilence, and that of Aphrodite in the passion that destroyed at once the
pride of Phaedra and the chastity of Hippolytus."

Greek history. Human beings were never in complete control of their lives or their futures. Powerful forces were at work in history that could destroy the strongest king as quickly as the poorest member of his kingdom. No person ever enjoyed a life of good unmixed with evil. The wise person accepted every good event with a certain tincture of sadness and pessimism; in some way, unforeseeable at the present, what he enjoyed would eventually be taken away, or counterbalanced with some terrible misfortune, unless death first brought him an escape of sorts. "Count no man blessed until he is dead" was one of the most famous summaries of classical Greek pessimism about the world. [18] A wise person set his plans for the future with a mixture of pragmatic precaution and humility. The use of reason and caution would sometimes lead to ruin, but the failure to do so would nearly always bring destruction. A refusal to acknowledge in his heart the inescapability of uncertainty and death was what was truly at the core of the tragic hero's self-willed drive towards his own tragic downfall. These widespread assumptions about the nature of life were so much a part of Greek culture that the first Christian historians were practically driven by necessity to thinking about these issues.

But we must not minimize the role of human decisions. History to the Greeks was a complicated interplay between the power of Fortune and the willful actions of hundreds of individual human beings. If the classical Greek history was an account of the disrupting power of the fortuitous, it was equally a history of decisions. The ancient historians analyzed these decisions in terms of motives and purposes; they illustrated the consequences of each decision; they discussed the alternative possibilities open to the decision makers. One need only think of the marvelous speeches in Thucydides here. This emphasis upon human decisions as the basic stuff of history is one of the features that give ancient Greek histories their characteristic flavor. It is the thing that makes them look so different from those histories of our own period that put such a stress on impersonal social and economic forces. Even those caught in a situation like the Spartans at Thermopylae could still make certain basic choices, and Herodotus in typical Greek fashion focused carefully on these men caught in the ultimate

---

[18]Her. 1.32; Aeschylus, *Agamemnon* 928-929; Aristotle, *Nicomachean Ethics* 1.10(1100a-1101a).

hour of decision and recorded how they chose between death and dishonor. [19]

Although the power of Fortune held sway over most of history, it was nevertheless true that Fortune herself could create a certain exceptional situation—the καιρός or "critical moment"—in which a single decision by a single human being affected the whole subsequent course of history. Graeco-Roman historians lovingly analyzed such crucial events. [20] Herodotus wrote that the decision of a single man, Callimachus, made the Greeks stay and fight at Marathon. [21] On five different occasions, he tells us, Themistocles took actions that determined the whole subsequent course of the Persian war. [22] Thucydides ascribed an even greater importance to Pericles—had he lived, the Peloponnesian war would not have caused the Athenian spirit to fall apart. [23] Polybius prefaced his account of the great battle between Hannibal and Scipio at Zama with the statement that "Fortune" had never "offered to contending armies a more splendid prize of victory," since the victor in this single battle in Africa would win as a reward the entire world. [24] Sallust turned this idea of the key man who knew how to seize the opportune moment into a generalized theory of the great man in history. At times he almost approached the hero worship of a Thomas

---

[19]Her. 7. 201-233.

[20]See again Bury's amusing historiographical essay, "Cleopatra's Nose," for a series of examples of such key figures and key events drawn from history at large: Antony and Cleopatra, the invasion of the Huns, George III and the American Revolution, Napoleon's military genius, and Constantine's decision to support Christianity.

[21]Her. 6. 109-110.

[22]Whether there would be any Greek resistance to the Persians depended on whether the Athenians decided to fight or to give in (Her. 7. 139), and Themistocles also played a key role in the development of the Athenian decision to fight at sea (7. 140-144). Three times, Themistocles alone got the Greeks to stand and fight instead of fleeing (8. 4-5, 56-64, 74-76).

[23]Thuc. 2. 65. Note especially 65. 9: Pericles kept the spirits of the Athenian people at all times in line with reason and the καιρός of the moment.

[24]Polyb. 15. 9. 2-5. Compare 9. 22. 1, "of all that befell both nations, Romans and Carthaginians, the cause was one man and one mind—Hannibal."

Carlyle. Sallust used his "great man" theory to explain, for example, why
the early Romans had been able to carry out their magnificent deeds.

> After long reflection I became convinced that it had all been accomplished
> by the eminent merit of a few citizens; that it was due to them that poverty
> had triumphed over riches, and a few over a multitude. But after the state
> had become demoralized by extravagance and sloth . . . for a long time,
> as when mothers are exhausted by child-bearing, no one at all was pro-
> duced at Rome who was great in merit. But within my own memory there
> have appeared two men of towering merit, though of diverse character,
> Marcus Cato and Gaius Caesar.[25]

But it was rare to displace this theory of the great man, as Sallust did, so
completely from its roots. The great man existed, in usual Graeco-Roman
historiographical practice, only because a καιρός had occurred—an "opportune moment" or "critical moment"—in which one human decision had
a shaping effect on all subsequent history. This basic concept of the καιρός was everywhere present in Graeco-Roman histories. In Polybius one
finds it in passage after passage;[26] Thucydides[27] and Sallust[28] both invoked
it. But even though it raised human decision making to ultimate historical
significance, the important point was that the καιρός was simply another
face of Fortune.[29]

As I shall later demonstrate, the second major Christian historian, Socrates Scholasticus, used this word καιρός as a way to talk about the for-

---

[25]Sall. *Cat.* 53.2-6. Thomas Carlyle's work *On Heroes, Hero-Worship, and the Heroic
in History* (1841) was very influential on the more popular nineteenth-century English historical literature, and had a profound indirect effect on the writing of standard textbooks for schools.

[26]For example, Polyb. 3.109.12; 5.101.5-10, 104.2-4, and 104.7-8; 7.12;
9.2.5, 12.3-5, 13.7, 15.1; 10.5.8; 15.14.7, 16.1; 18.22.8, 24.7, 26.2 (three critical moments in the course of the same battle), 36.8; 27.20.1-2; 29.27.8; 32.13.4.

[27]See Thuc. 2.42.4, where it is connected with τύχη.

[28]See Sall. *Jug.* 6.3 (*opportunitas*), 56.4 (*fortunam, casum*).

[29]In Polybius for example, see 2.49.7-8 (τύχη); 5.26.12-13 (sudden reversals
of fortune, that is, περιπέτειαι); 34.2-3 (τύχη); 9.6.5-7 (παράδοξος,
τυχικός, αὐτομάτως); 11.24a.3 (τύχη); 15.29.5 (synergesis of ταὐτόματον
at the proper καιρός).

tuitous in history without bringing in all of the pagan associations that the word τύχη raised. Well before Socrates' century, Tyche had become a widely known goddess whom many pagans worshiped; but Kairos (in spite of one altar to him at Olympia) never developed a widespread cult. The word καιρός could be used by a Christian in a way that the word τύχη could not.

On a simple phenomenological level, an act of Fortune did not involve miracles. A straightforward account of historical events would not show any laws of nature being broken. But in other situations (where the word Fortune significantly was *not* used) some Graeco-Roman historians would tell miracle tales. An ancient historian would call such an event an act that went "against nature." The ancient world did not think in terms of a highly articulated set of "laws of nature" such as we assume in our own scientific age. The scale of our knowledge today is so much greater that it is different in kind. But the Graeco-Roman period did have a clear concept, in its own way, of φύσις or "nature." At roughly the same time Herodotus was producing the first piece of Greek history writing, the medical scholars of the Hippocratic school at Cos were trying to give more precise theoretical form to the concept of φύσις.[30] The island of Cos was situated within eyesight of Herodotus's birthplace, Halicarnassus, and the possible connections have been noted by modern scholars.[31] At any rate, Herodotus's own writing gives ample evidence as to what he understood by the term "nature." When he said, for example, that he was going to tell the reader about the φύσις of the crocodile, he talked about its body, scales, and jaws; the way it lived its life along the riverbanks; its reproductive cycle; and the way it related to other animals and birds of its region.[32] The word φύσις, in other words, implied normal process, growth, functioning, and behavioral patterns.[33] One would say that a crocodile acted "against nature" if it had two heads,

---

[30]W. H. S. Jones, introduction to the LCL edition of Hippocrates, 1: xvi.

[31]Joseph Wells, *Studies in Herodotus*, 188-89. See also Myres, *Herodotus*, 2-3; T. R. Glover, *Herodotus* (Berkeley: University of California Press, 1924) 14.

[32]Her. 2.68.

[33]John L. Myres, *Herodotus*, 47-48. It was this commonplace Greek idea that lay behind Aristotle's more technical definition, later on, of φύσις as something that grew, moved, or changed, and had within itself its own source of movement; see *Physics* Beta 1.192b and *Metaphysics* Delta 4.1014b-1015a.

flew through the air, lived in the middle of a desert, or spoke with a human voice. In that sense, one finds a number of "miracle stories" in Herodotus and some of the other Graeco-Roman historians. We are told that the dust and chanting of thousands marching in an Eleusinian procession was seen and heard after Attica had been completely evacuated of its people and lay vacant before the Persians; that when Darius conquered Babylon, a mule gave birth to a foal; that whenever disaster threatened the people of Pedasa, the priestess of Athene grew a long beard.[34]

But there was also a good deal of skepticism within the Graeco-Roman historiographical tradition. Even Herodotus showed this more than is frequently acknowledged. When he reported the story that the deep-sea diver Scyllias deserted the Persians and got safely over to the Greek side by swimming underwater from Aphetae to Artemisium without coming up for air, he immediately went on to poke fun at the tale: "It is my opinion, which I hereby declare, that he came to Artemisium in a boat!"[35] Herodotus gave ample warning to his readers in 7.152: "For myself, though it be my business to set down that which is told me, to believe it is none at all of my business; let that saying hold good for the whole of my history." Thucydides rejected the whole notion of miracle completely, and refused even to include such stories in his history at all. His scepticism is famous. In the introduction to his history he acknowledged that "it may well be that the absence of the fabulous from my narrative will seem less pleasing to the ear."[36] Polybius also said, in some very sharp and critical passages, that superstitious nonsense about miracles and the intervention of gods and demigods in human history had no place in an intellectually respectable historical work.[37] A crafty politician or general could use the credulity of the uneducated masses to manipulate them to his own advantage,[38] but woe to the statesman or military commander who, like Nicias, let superstition affect his own mind.[39] It was common in later historians for a few miracle stories

---

[34]Her. 8.65; 3.151-153; 1.175.

[35]Her. 8.8.

[36]Thuc. 1.22.4.

[37]Polyb. 3.47.7-9 and 48.7-10; 10.5.8; 12.24.5; 16.12.

[38]Polyb. 10.2.8-12; 10.4-5; 10.11.7-8; 10.14.

[39]Polyb. 9.19.1-3.

to be included in the narrative, but it was also quite customary for the miracle story to be prefixed with a phrase like "some people say" or concluded with a phrase like "let the reader judge for himself."[40]

The first Christian historians therefore found that the existing pagan historiographical tradition did give some room for miracles, but that this was mixed with a good deal of scepticism. In particular, even pagan historians who told large numbers of miracle stories would not usually claim that a miracle had itself altered the basic course of history at any point in their narratives. Consequently, the first Christian histories could defend the possibility of miracles on the grounds of Christian piety, but it did not help them any in solving the basic problem, that of giving God real, omnicompetent control over the fundamental course of human history. Appeal to the miraculous has never been a good theological device for introducing any continuous divine presence into human history. God is absent more often than he is present in that way. Furthermore the concept of miracles in the simple sense (men walking on water, and so forth) does not get a church historian very far in an analysis, say, of the course of the fourth-century Arian controversy. So even though the first Christian historians did believe in miracles, this was a suprisingly peripheral question in terms of the development from pagan to Christian historiography. They found the debate over Fortune and Fate moved one much closer to the central problem of God and history.

The matter of miracles was of great importance in pagan historiography in one regard, however. If one surveys a list of all the miracle tales that a pagan historian like Herodotus recorded in his history, one notes that the majority of them were either stories of omens and portents, or stories about acts of retribution against human beings who committed sacrilege against the gods who gave these omens and portents.[41] And in addition to miraculous signs such as water boiling without fire, horses eating snakes, and mules giving birth to foals, there were also other ways of predicting the future. The proclamations of the Delphic oracle and other such oracular

---

[40]See the comments, for example, on Dionysius of Halicarnassus, Josephus, and Lucian's *Quomodo hist. sit conscribenda* in H. St. John Thackeray, *Josephus: The Man and the Historian* (New York: Jewish Institute of Religion Press, 1929) 57-58.

[41]Omens and portents: Her. 1.59, 78, 175; 3.151-153; 8.65; 9.120. Other miracle tales: 1.19 and 22, 23-24, 86-87; 8.35-39; 9.65.

predictions played a prominent role in Herodotus's history.[42] The Athenians were told that their city would be saved by the Athenian fleet, the "wooden wall"; poor Croesus was told that if he attacked the Persians "he would destroy a mighty empire," and then forgot to ask whether it would be his or theirs.[43] Dreams were another important way of predicting the future. Croesus dreamed at one point that his son Atys would be killed by an iron spear, and in spite of all his precautions the terrible prophecy came true.[44] One important variety were "kingship dreams"—what Bischoff called *Dynastienträume*[45]—that foretold either the accession of a new king to the throne or the downfall of a king, or both.[46]

Portents, oracles, and dreams were dismissed as a matter of course by the most skeptical among the Graeco-Roman historians. Thucydides declared contemptuously that the only Greek oracle that ever came true in the whole Peloponnesian war was the one that predicted the number of years it would last![47] But Xenophon, his successor, took a position closer to that of the average person of that time. The ancient Greeks as a whole were a superstitious people in certain matters. An army, one remembers, did not go out of its home country or enter into battle or start any other major project without sacrificing animals and having a professional fortune-teller (μάντις) inspect the livers to see whether the future looked favorable.[48] Xenophon himself was a pious man,[49] and seems to have believed that this really worked.[50] It was the gods who revealed the future to

---

[42]Her. 1.13, 53-56, 62-63, 66, 91; 2.152; 3.57-58; 7.140-144, 220; 8.77, 96; 9.43.

[43]Her. 7.141; 1.53.

[44]Her. 1.34.

[45]Heinrich Bischoff, *Der Warner bei Herodot* (Borna-Leipzig: R. Noske, 1932) 41.

[46]Her. 1.107 and 108, 209; 3.30, 124; 7.19.

[47]Thuc. 5.26.3-4. Compare 2.21.3, 47.4; 5.103; 8.1.1.

[48]Among the many examples in Xenophon, see *Hell.* 3.1.17 and 19, 4.15; 4.1.22, 2.18, 4.5, 7.2 (at the frontier of one's home country), 7.7 (setting up a fortified post).

[49]See, for example, *Hell.* 3.4.18, and Xenophon's praise of Agesilaus in *Hell.* 4.3.20.

[50]*Anabasis* 7.8.8-10 and 21-22. *Hell.* 4.8.36-37, 7.2.20-23.

human beings, through the signs, the omens, the pronouncements of oracular shrines, and the inspection of the livers of sacrificial victims. For everything was known to the gods, "who see all things both now and forever."[51] In Polybius one found a more Thucydidean mood, so that classical Greek historiography ended on a skeptical note at the Roman conquest. But in the subsequent centuries of Roman historiography, the signs and portents and oracles and prophecies came back in again. Sallust, for example, made the accurate prediction of Marius's future by the haruspex play a key role in the development of the plot in the *Jugurthine War*.[52] Roman historiography was further affected by the new religious mood that began to take over the empire in the late second century C.E. The historian Dio Cassius actually produced as his first literary work a small book of dreams and signs predicting the rise to power of the then reigning emperor, Septimius Severus.[53]

In the fourth century C.E. Ammianus Marcellinus, the last great Latin historian, gave his readers a careful catalogue of the many different ways he approved for predicting the future. In Ammianus's work one had reached the twilight of paganism, and there one moved through a particularly dim and gloomy world, dark with foreboding, as signs and portents appeared to the horrified eyes of men abandoned by the guardian daemons to their Fate. By secret theurgic rituals, these last pagans tried to probe the future behind locked doors. "The elemental powers, when propitiated by divers rites, supply mortals with words of prophecy, as if from the veins of inexhaustible founts." Augury and auspice could also be used. "A god so directs the flight of birds that the sound of their bills or the passing flight of their wings in disturbed or in gentle passage foretells future events." The livers of sacrificial animals could also be inspected with the same intent. By this century, the rationale had begun to assume the forms of a Neoplatonized sun worship of the sort that one also sees in the writings of Ammianus's hero, the emperor Julian. "The Sun, the soul of the universe, sending out our minds from himself after the manner of sparks," is able to make the hu-

---

[51]*Hell.* 6.5.41.

[52]*Jug.* 63.1. See also 64.1; 90.1; 92.1-2, 6; 93.1; 94.6.

[53]Dio Cassius 73(72).23.1-2, 75(74).3. Dio was significant because he was a rather proto-Byzantine figure, pointing towards the ideas and attitudes of the future in many ways—see Fergus Millar, *A Study of Cassius Dio* (Oxford, 1964) vii.

man mind "blaze up" in ecstatic prophecy like that of the Sibyls. Other techniques of predicting the future involved observing thunder, or lightning, or the stars. "And dreams, as Aristotle declares, are certain and trustworthy, when the person is in a deep sleep and the pupil of the eye is inclined to neither side but looks directly forward."[54] Here in Ammianus one is in contact with an immediate contemporary, a pagan whose lifespan overlapped with those of most of the first Christian historians. This was the sort of paganism they had to argue against.

Implicit in the belief in omens, dreams, and portents was the doctrine of Fate. What the gods revealed of the future had necessarily to come true. "None may escape his destined lot, not even a god."[55] Sometimes an oracle was conditional, and provided an avenue of escape if certain actions were avoided. But often there was only inevitable doom, and as the Greeks knew, "it is the hatefulest of all human sorrows to have much knowledge and no power."[56] The oracle or omen was itself sent by the divine, but from that point on no miracle occurred. In some mysterious fashion the person's fate would be worked out in the natural course of events. The person went to his foreordained doom by a series of acts of his own free will. But his choices always seemed to conspire against him. Much as in acts of Fortune, the catastrophe normally broke upon the person in some unexpected conjuncture of events.

There was another current of thought also present in the classical concept of Fate. This was a particular kind of psychological theory used to explain certain types of self-destructive action. In the mechanism involved, the person's own free decisions produced consequences whose possibility he *ought* to have foreseen. He did not anticipate what he ought to have foreseen because he had fallen into a certain kind of dangerous state of mind, which made him act unreasonably in certain crucial situations. One could be suddenly overcome by a powerful emotional state. Blind rage, insane jealousy, or uncontrollable lust could make a person act in the heat of a sudden moment in foolish and tragic ways. Or a person could fall into a frame of mind that caused him consistently to make unwise decisions in certain kinds of situations, until he slowly but inexorably led himself to his

---

[54]Ammianus Marcellinus 21.1.8-12.

[55]Her. 1.91.

[56]Her. 9.16.

own doom. But there was no infringement of free will in the normal Greek understanding of the term. The unhappy consequences came as a result of the tragic victim's own decisions. It was not his will but his understanding that was the cause of his misfortune.[57] On the other hand, these dangerous states of mind tended to have a self-perpetuating component, in that a person caught up in such a frame of mind tended systematically to overlook or discount precisely that sort of information that could break him out of it. Only the experience of the traumatic act of self-destruction itself could clear the mind to reawakened self-knowledge. This was the standard *pattern of tragic downfall*. It was the basis, of course, of the Greek tragic drama, but it had an influence on Greek history writing as well.

One could have either or both aspects of Fate present in the story. Fate could mean the mysterious oracular prediction of some event long in advance, or it could mean only a kind of semideterministic psychological theory, but quite often it meant a combination of the two: the oracle spoke, but then the tragic flaw in the principal character actually produced the fated outcome. The story of King Croesus in Herodotus was an excellent example of the combination. The Delphic oracle foretold his end, but then his own character led him into the fatal decisions that destroyed his kingdom.[58] John L. Myres has argued that not only Croesus, but also Cyrus, Cambyses, Polycrates, Darius, Cleomenes, and Mardonius were all por-

---

[57]As Collingwood says (*The Idea of History*, 23-24), "This conception of history was the very opposite of deterministic, because the Greeks regarded the course of history as flexible and open to salutary modification by the well-instructed human will. Nothing that happens is inevitable. The person who is about to be involved in a tragedy is actually overwhelmed by it only because he is too blind to see his danger."

[58]Croesus's tragic character flaw was ἐλπίζειν, the pathological Hope of the compulsive gambler who squanders everything he or she has (and more) on foolish bets—Her. 1.54, 55-56, 75, 77, 80; also in Her. 1.30, where Bischoff, *Der Warner bei Herodot*, 32, speaks of "die Spannung, die zwischen der ἐλπίς des Fragers und den Antworten des Gefragten besteht." As Cornford points out (*Thucydides Mythistoricus*, 167-68), "Elpis had not to the Greeks the associations which Christianity has given to 'Hope'; she is not a virtue, but a dangerous passion. . . . Elpis is the passion which deludes man to count on the future as if he could perfectly control it."

trayed in Herodotus's history as tragic figures in the style of the Attic
drama.[59]

Thucydides' sceptical method naturally excluded all notions of oracular fatalism or supernatural guiding forces. But F. M. Cornford argued that
the purely *psychological* theory of tragic downfall influenced the basic plot
of his history. The power and might of Athens led it into a fatal hybris that
got the Athenian army destroyed on the foolish Sicilian expedition.[60] Later,
in Polybius, the pattern of tragic downfall showed up in its simplest form
in the story of Marcus Atilius Regulus and also in the story of Queen Teuta:[61]
good Fortune caused a person to start acting cruelly and arrogantly and un-
mercifully, and then a sudden reversal of Fortune in the other direction sent
the person to his or her destruction. When the Romans began to write history, Sallust for example took over this basic theme from the Greek world,
particularly the idea that extremes of prosperity or of poverty were a temp-
tation of Fortune that could lead men into the grips of overriding passions
that could destroy them. When Rome became prosperous and powerful,
he argued, the internal corruption began that would lead to her decline and
fall.[62] On the other side, the revolutionary Catiline had found his most
willing helpers among men rendered desperate by poverty, the other dangerous extreme.[63] In one form or another, therefore, the idea of Fate and
psychological patterns of tragic self-destruction influenced Greek and Roman history writing deeply. Even if it were only the trite statement that

---

[59]Myres, *Herodotus*, 77-78. "It is probably to Athenian influence that Herodotus
owes his debt to the literary technique of tragedy. His residence at Athens comes
midway in his career and affected him profoundly in other ways." See also 92, 137,
151, 169, and 218.

[60]Cornford, *Thucydides Mythistoricus*.

[61]Polyb. 1.31-35; 2.4.6-12.6.

[62]Sall. *Cat.* 10.1-3; 11; 12.2; 13.2-5; *Jug.* 41.1 and 3, 9 (vice leading to tragic
downfall). Changes occurred in the new Roman context. Sallust offered a rationale for this that had a Latin flavor quite different from the Greek psychological
theory of tragic downfall. To him, it was the vices of the flesh that led from prosperity to corruption and downfall. *Cat.* 13.2-5; 14.1-3; *Jug.* 1.1-4; 2.3-4.

[63]Sall. *Cat.* 14.1-3; 16.4; 18.4; 21.1-2; 37.

prosperity bred arrogance, it was a regular, frequent constituent of historical narratives in the pagan world.

In addition to this classical idea of Fate, with its Delphic oracles, and tragic heroes storming with majestic violence and passion against the onward sweep of destiny, there were other currents of fatalism present in the Roman world of the early Christian era. The practice of astrology began to invade the Roman empire from the East in the first century B.C.E. Astrologers taught that the position of the seven planets in the twelve signs of the zodiac and the twelve houses, together with the positive and negative aspects of the planets to one another, gave each person, at birth, a characteristic emotional signature. One could predict how that person would be angry, they said, and in what spheres of life; how the person would sense opportunity, and in what areas; the kinds of inner emotional turmoil the person would experience in certain situations; the person's ability to pursue long-term goals, and the style in which the person would pursue them (confrontationally, circuitously, analytically, intuitively, or whatever). In addition, the astrologers claimed that the planets in their circling set up cycles, spreading out over months and years of a person's life, in which the influence of Mars on anger, or Mercury on intellectual discrimination, or Saturn on defensiveness, would wax and wane in positive and negative fashion, and sometimes overlap disastrously, emotionally propelling the person uncontrollably into predictable actions in predictable directions. The ancient Graeco-Roman world was uncomfortable about the realm of the human emotions to begin with, and found the claims of astrology quite frightening. Astrology also exacerbated an already profound discomfort over the role of Fate in human life.

The first major discussion of astrology in a Graeco-Roman history was not until Tacitus, in the second century C.E., and the Christian historians later on rarely mention it explicitly. When Eusebius speaks of Fate, he usually chooses the oracles in Herodotus as his explicit target. But then one suddenly notes Eusebius claiming, in a quick aside, that the daemons who dwelt in the pagan oracular shrines, as at Delphi, actually gained their ability to predict the future from their knowledge of astrology, and one realizes that even when he seems to be using purely classical language about the role of Fate, he is doing this from the viewpoint of a postclassical world.[64] And even if the orthodox Christian theologians of the first several centuries did not obtain a fear of the possible influence of the stars directly from the astrologers themselves, they had always to deal with astrological beliefs at least secondhand, through the many heretical Christian gnostic systems that taught that the human ψυχή, the seat of the emotions, was enchained by the seven planetary archons and their rule of εἱμαρμένη. Astrology was an important and prevalent form of fatalistic belief that was often buried underground and not raised to the level of explicit discussion in orthodox Christian authors, but with which a Christian historian had to contend, at some level, in formulating his own understanding of history.

Another important form of fatalistic belief was the Stoic philosophical system, which had set up its own highly developed metaphysical view of the universe, in which Fate or εἱμαρμένη ultimately ruled the world. The

---

[64]Tacitus, *Annals* 6.20-22; Eus. *PE* 6.pref.1-3(236bc) and 6.1.6-7(237d-238a). Ancient horoscopes could be amusing. One was told that Sagittarians had square foreheads and profuse eyebrows, and that they were companionable people who were "jovial when they were drunk." Those born under Aries, on the other hand, were said to have contracted eyebrows and drawn cheeks, and had to be treated with caution since they were "quarrellers in a brawl" (Hippolytus, *Refutation of All Heresies* 4.23 and 4.15). A Gemini was promised (if other configurations did not interfere) "a life of ease and unfading youth spent in the arms of love" (Manilius, *Astronomica* 4.157). It must be remembered that astrology in the full sense, with mathematically calculated horoscopes, was a relatively new idea in the ancient world. The earliest known calculation of a horoscope based on all the planetary positions dates back only to 410 B.C.E., found on a cuneiform tablet referring to the positions of the stars on 29 April of that year (Cramer, *Astrology in Roman Law and Politics* 3-5). As can be seen from the systematic collection made by O. Neugebauer and H. B. Van Hoesen (*Greek Horoscopes* [Philadelphia: American Philosophical Society, 1959] vii) the earliest full horoscopes did not begin to appear in Greek texts until the first century B.C.E. Christian gnosticism quickly began to pick up astrological ideas in the next two centuries. On Jewish astrology and its connection with later Jewish angelology—another area in which Christians came into contact with astrological beliefs—see E. A. Wallis Budge, *Amulets and Superstitions* (New York: Dover, 1978) 386-89, 393-94. See also Pierre Boyancé, "La religion astrale de Platon à Cicéron," *Revues des Etudes Grecques* 65 (1952): 312-50; Leroy A. Campbell, *Mithraic Iconography and Ideology* (Leiden: Brill, 1968) 49, 54-55, 66-67, 261-63, 392; and Franz Cumont, *Les mystères de Mithra* (Brussels: Lamertin, 1913) 145.

Stoic Fate was equated with Zeus, and also with what we today would call the laws of nature. It was not quite what Herodotus or the Greek tragic dramatists had meant by Fate, but the Stoics did defend popular faith in oracles and the validity of oracular predictions of the future, partly as an attempted proof of their own philosophical theory of determinism. Stoicism was important from the Hellenistic period down to the second century of the early Roman empire. Even though it had no important supporters by the time of the first Christian histories, nevertheless Stoic ideas and terminology had entered the philosophical tradition of Middle Platonism, and in this indirect form, Stoicism still had to be confronted intellectually by Eusebius in the fourth century. Originally Stoic terms, like the distinction between τὸ ἐφ' ἡμῖν and τὸ οὐκ ἐφ' ἡμῖν ("what is in our power" and "what is not in our power," that is, what is fated), were used by Eusebius to set out his own quite different philosophy of free will.[65]

In the fourth century C.E., the oracular shrines experienced a resurgence as part of the new anti-Christian pagan revivals. It was the oracle of Apollo at Didyma near Miletus—in Classical times one of the most widely recognized oracular sanctuaries after Delphi itself—that commanded the Great Persecution under Diocletian and Galerius in 303.[66] Later in the century, the emperor Julian's attempt to revive paganism and push back Christianity involved massive support of the oracular shrines, such as that of Apollo at Daphne outside Antioch.[67] In the long battle in that century between Christianity and the new paganism (with its basically Late Neoplatonic inspiration), both sides regarded the use of oracles and other such fortune-telling techniques as a fundamental line of division between the two religions. What we could now call magical methods of predicting the fu-

---

[65]For example, Eus. PE 6.6.22(245c). There were also linkages between astrology and Late Stoicism, as one sees in more specialized works like Manilius's *Astronomica*, but also in widely read Late Stoic authors like Seneca, *Quaestiones Naturales* 3.29.1, 27.1, and 30.8.

[66]Eusebius VC 2.50-51; Lactantius, *On the Deaths of the Persecutors* 11. See Henry Chadwick, *The Early Church* (Harmondsworth, England: Penguin, 1967) 121; W. H. C. Frend, *Martyrdom and Persecution in the Early Church* (Oxford: Blackwell, 1965) 129.

[67]Socrates HE 3.18-19; Sozomen HE 5.19-20; Theodoret HE 3.10-11; Ammianus Marcellinus 22.12.6-13.3; 25.4.17.

ture were an intrinsic and important part of the new paganism, but feared
and rejected by orthodox and theologically sophisticated Christians. The
dividing line was not necessarily so clear, of course, to many ordinary, uneducated Christians, which made the issue even more important to bishops
and theologians who wanted to deliver their flocks from that evil.

When Eusebius therefore began writing the first Christian history, "Fate"
meant a variety of things. The classical histories, with their oracles, dreams,
and portents, were still read as masterpieces of literature, as were also the
classical tragedies. The oracles pronounced at Delphi and preserved in Herodotus were especially well known. The concept of the tragic hero struggling against destiny was an intrinsic part of Greek culture. Astrology and
gnosticism were also deeply fatalistic, though in a way different from the
classical understanding of Fate. Stoic ideas still had to be fought intellectually because of their role in the Middle Platonic philosophical tradition,
and the Stoics had supported oracular prediction of the future. Last of all,
the resurgent neopaganism of the fourth century revived the old oracular
shrines and eagerly supported various other methods of divination. It was
the combination of all these things that had to be combated in order to
develop a Christian view of history, but in particular it was the central role
of the concept of Fate in Greek and Roman historiography—a role it had
played from the very beginning—that made the issue almost unavoidable
for Eusebius.

A notion of retribution was sometimes involved in the classical doctrine of Fate. Herodotus recounted many stories in which a human being
was punished for having committed some enormous moral outrage. "The
gods do greatly punish great wrongdoing."[68] But even though Herodotus
said in one place that "no man on earth doth wrong but at last shall suffer
requital,"[69] it was not petty offenses that were at stake for him but only great
atrocities and infamous deeds of wanton cruelty and violence. A second
variety of retribution stories concerned cases in which human beings committed an act of sacrilege against something that had been dedicated to the
gods.[70] As Rudolf Otto pointed out, the "idea of the holy" in its primitive,

---

[68]Her. 2.120. For examples see 1.13, 86, 118-119 and 130, 166-167, 212-214;
4.202 and 205; 6.72, 75 and 84; 7.133-137; 8.105-106.

[69]Her. 5.56.

[70]Her. 1.105; 3.29-30, 33, 64; 6.75 and 84; 8.129.

original form conveyed the idea of mysterious power and danger completely divorced from any moral component, so this second variety of retribution story was very important, but more primitive than the more moralistically conceived type.

A third type of retribution story involved the widespread Ancient Near Eastern notion of the jealousy (φθόνος) of the gods. As Solon said to Croesus by way of warning, "Well I know how jealous is Heaven and how it loves to trouble us."[71] Any kind of human greatness or excellence or beauty was apt to arouse the irritation of some god. As Euripides pointed out in his *Hippolytus*, even piety towards the gods was dangerous if it caused one to stand out of the ordinary. An extreme, but widespread piece of advice throughout the general Ancient Near Eastern world was that the best way to get along with the gods was to avoid doing anything that would attract their attention. As Herodotus put it, in Greek fashion,

> You see how God strikes with his lightning those living beings who stand out above the rest, and does not permit them to make an ostentatious show, while the smaller ones do not irritate him at all. You see how it is always the biggest houses and the tallest trees at which he hurls his thunderbolts. For God loves to cut short everything that stands out above the rest. In the same way a large army is completely destroyed by a small one whenever God is jealous and sends them fear or thunder, by which they perish in a manner unworthy of themselves. For God does not permit anyone besides himself to have high and mighty ideas.[72]

This notion of the jealousy of the gods was a basic and characteristic mode of ancient thought.

Thucydides naturally rejected all ideas of divine retribution. He did not regard the fundamental structures of the universe as being either personal or moral. The plague at Athens showed, he believed, that moral constraints existed only on a surface layer even of the human psyche.[73] His successor Xenophon spoke more piously: "The gods do not overlook either those who act impiously or those who do wicked, unholy things."[74] Po-

---

[71]Her. 1.32.

[72]Her. 7.10. For examples, see 1.8-12, 34; 8.13, 109.

[73]Thuc. 2.52-53.

[74]Xen. *Hell.* 5.4.1. See also 2.4.14-15; 6.4.30-31.

lybius had two retribution stories, but in general did not think in those terms,[75] while Sallust went so far as to say that Fortune acted only *ex lubidine*, on the basis of arbitrary, irrational whim.[76] So as these examples illustrate, in the pre-Christian period historians were more apt to view the basic structures of history in fairly amoral terms, but the pious ones could and did introduce into their histories notions of moral judgment, or "jealous" retribution against human pride and presumption.

Ideas of divine moral retribution in history caused early Christians no trouble at all, of course—it fitted in smoothly with their own view of the divine justice. The concept of the jealousy of the gods raised more problems. This was a deeply felt expression of the general Greek pessimism towards existence. Joy over any kind of success or prosperity became tinged with apprehension that Fortune, or a jealous god, or some dark force intrinsic in the nature of things would strike in retribution. Over in the eastern, Greek-speaking half of the Roman empire, not even Christians could remove that dark fear completely from their minds. It was too fundamental a part of the Greek attitude towards life. Yet the Christian God could hardly be said to be an enemy of the good, the excellent, and the truly beautiful. So an interesting compromise was worked out, which the first Christian historians then used in their histories, as shall be seen in subsequent chapters. The idea of jealous supernatural powers was retained, but this function was assigned to daemons, who became totally evil beings in Christian teaching. The "jealousy" of "the daemons who hate the good" was then blamed in early Christian histories for certain kinds of events in a way closely analogous to earlier pagan teaching about the jealous and envious acts of the Olympian gods. The idea of the jealousy of the gods did not disappear; it was merely reinterpreted.

Ancient Graeco-Roman historiography therefore raised a series of serious problems for the first Christian historians. It was the intellectual tradition in which they had been cast. Yet it regarded the historical human being as one whose life was continuously at the mercy of the fortuitous. Oracles, dreams, and omens—as well as the stars—cast a web of fate upon

---

[75]Polyb. 1.84.9-10; 15.20.5-8.

[76]Sall. *Cat.* 8.1; 51.25.

the human future. The gods beheld the works of men and women through eyes of jealousy. This dark vision of reality was obviously alien to the Judaeo-Christian understanding of God and history, so that some sort of response was demanded, but various ancient Jewish and Christian historical thinkers developed quite different answers to this problem.

CHAPTER 3

Eusebius: Fate, Fortune, Free Will, and Nature

Eusebius developed his own distinctive philosophy of historical causation in order to deal with the great issues of Graeco-Roman historiography. Fatalism, the fortuitous, the concept of nature, and the problem of free will—all were tied together in the traditional pagan understanding of history. To reinterpret these basic ideas and reconstruct them into a coherent Christian interpretation of history, Eusebius therefore had to work out a sophisticated philosophical analysis of the human psyche's encounter with time, physical process, societal pressures, and the vision of the Good.

The pagan concept of Fate is an excellent place to begin. This idea played a part in Graeco-Roman history all the way back to Herodotus himself. The great Jewish historian Josephus, the first historian of the Judaeo-Christian tradition to wrestle with this issue, had simply taken the normal Greek words for Fate (εἱμαρμένη, χρεών, and so forth) and used them to talk about divine Providence, conceived in fairly deterministic fashion. Eusebius greatly admired Josephus's historical works but took a completely opposite approach: he attacked the pagan notion of Fate vigorously and affirmed instead a real concept of human free will that was quite different from the psychological determinism of Josephus (or for that matter, of Augustine).

On the surface, the kind of Fate against which Eusebius wrote appears primarily connected with oracular shrines, the same kind of Fate that had appeared in Herodotus's stories about the Delphic oracle.[1] This was partly

---

[1] See, for example, Books 4 and 5 of the *Praeparatio Evangelica*. In *PE* 5.18-27, he went back to Herodotus, the father of Graeco-Roman historiography, to obtain all but one of his examples of famous oracular predictions. He chose those particular oracles, he said, because they were the ones "which are repeated in the mouth of all Greeks, and are taught in the schools of every city to those who resort to them for instruction" (5.18.1[208bc]). The ancient figure of Herodotus himself was therefore a prime target in Eusebius's attack on the role of the oracle in the classical Graeco-Roman understanding of history.

true; Herodotus was a figure with whom he had to deal. But Eusebius believed that these oracular shrines were inhabited by daemons who gained what small knowledge of the future they had, he said, from the practice of astrology. He also claimed that the mathematical techniques that they used for their calculations were exactly the same as those used by human astrologers. [2] It is at this point that one realizes that one is not in fact totally in the world of Herodotus, surface appearances to the contrary, but at least partially in a quite different thought world, one centuries removed, in which the idea of a universe ruled by astrological fatalism preyed on people's minds. In Plotinus's tractate "Are the Stars Causes?" (Enneads 2.3), in the heretical gnostic belief in the seven planetary Archons, and in any number of other places, one sees a pervasive and widespread conviction in the early Christian period that the person who could read the stars properly could at least to some degree predict the human future. Eusebius, as a man of his time, also seems to have regarded astrology as a technique that could in fact forecast the future to a certain extent, but he denied the existence of a universal εἱμαρμένη and he refused to allow astrological fatalism the right to rule history completely. [3]

Nevertheless, in spite of his linkage of oracular fatalism with astrological fatalism, Eusebius chose to cast most of his argument in purely classical form: attacking the oracular shrines with traditional Greek arguments and denying the classical, Herodotean doctrine of history produced by belief in the ability of such oracles to foretell the future. [4] In his attacks on the

---

[2] Eus. PE 6. pref. 1-3(236bc), 6.1.6-7(237d-238a). Speaking of daemons as the authors of the oracles was Eusebius's usual practice (as in, for example, DE 5.introd.6-7[203c-204a], introd.17-19[206ac]), but in one passage he suggested that arguments could also be drawn from pagan sources to support the contention that sorcery (γοητεία) was the uncanny power at work (PE 4.2.12-14[136ad]).

[3] Eus.PE 6.6.5(242d). See Utto Riedinger, Die Heilige Schrift im Kampf der Griechischen Kirche gegen die Astrologie: Von Origenes bis Johannes von Damaskos (Innsbruck: Wagner, 1956). He discusses references to astrology in the writings of thirty of the Church fathers, and also describes the position taken by these Christians on such things as the problem of free will and the stars viewed as signs.

[4] Of course, most of Eusebius's own pagan contemporaries devoutly believed that the future could be foretold by what we today would call magical means—

oracles, Eusebius was then able to turn to the older pagan literature itself and draw plenty of ammunition for his cause, since there was a centuries-old tradition of debates among the philosophic schools on this subject. Eusebius therefore put himself on the side of the Aristotelians, Cynics, and Epicureans, in their attacks on the Stoics (who traditionally had brought up examples of oracular prediction of the future as a proof that the universe was deterministic).[5]

In addition, Eusebius said that the Christian God, unlike the deities of paganism, was above Fate, and was therefore the true Lord of history. Eusebius promised freedom from the bonds of Fate to those who turned and put their faith in the Christian God.[6] Given the success of the many vari-

---

see the list of different traditional pagan techniques familiar to Eusebius in DE 5.introd.3-5(202d-203b) and introd.29(209d). In their eyes this was a real science, an ἐπιστήμη in the full technical sense of the word (DE 5.introd.3-5[202d-203b]). Eusebius denied this: "For neither should we call an archer scientific (ἐπιστήμονα) who hit the mark once now and then, but missed many times; nor a physician who killed the greater number of those who were attended by him, but was able to save one sometimes" (PE 4.3.4[137c]). In many other passages Eusebius asserted that the oracular predictions were usually false. Ammianus Marcellinus (21.1.13) shows how a fourth-century pagan historian defended himself against this particular criticism.

[5]Eus. PE 4.2.12-14(136ad). Eusebius was also very strict in his historical writings about excluding stories in which pagan oracles were said to have been fulfilled, one exception being the oracle that had predicted that Maximinian would be put to death by being strangled, HE 8.appendix.3. Some of his successor church historians (Socrates, for example, in HE 4.8) did not abide so closely by this rule. Although many Christians, including notably the emperor Constantine (Oration of Constantine 18-21) and the great historical theoretician Augustine (De. civ. Dei 18.23) would quote avidly from the Sibylline oracles, Eusebius was too skeptical by nature, and too good a historian, to be taken in by such a forgery. Eus. De laud. 9.3-6 excluded their use. Pagan sceptics like Celsus also recognized as spurious the parts of the Sibylline oracles quoted by the Christians—see Origen, Contra Celsum 7.53.

[6]Eus. PE 6.3.5(240c); Theoph. 2.87. Of course, Eusebius took quite seriously the notion that the Old Testament authors were able to foresee the future (see the summary statement of the prophetic task of foresight in DE 1.introd.[2-3]), and this presupposed some sort of determinacy of the future, but Eusebius would have

eties of heretical gnosticism that also promised, as a major component of
their proffered salvation, freedom from the seven planetary Archons who
ruled this present cosmos according to an all-determining εἱμαρμένη, one
can see the widespread fear of Fate that existed in the early Christian period, and the eagerness with which men and women would turn to any system that promised some escape. There was a great difference between
Eusebius and the gnostics, however. In the typical gnostic system, the escape route led the human πνεῦμα through the heavens to another, completely spiritual realm, and left this present world still in the iron grip of
Fate. This kind of gnosticism was not an answer to the problem of history,
but an attempt to escape from history. Eusebius was immersed too deeply
in the tradition of Hebrew historiography to go along with that kind of
thinking; for him, the only acceptable solution to the problem of Fate would
have to be one in which the *present* world order was somehow under the
Savior God's control. Furthermore, Eusebius was also too much influenced
by the classical Greek tradition to accept a gnostic solution either. Though

---

refused to call it "Fate." In the early centuries of the Church, the argument from
fulfillment of biblical prophecy was one of the mainstays of Christian apologists
trying to prove the truth of Christianity, and Eusebius himself devoted many more
pages of his own writings to this kind of work than he did to the historical works
that earned him his place in the history of human thought. Although Eusebius did
believe that the Old Testament prophets had been able to predict certain far-off
future events in amazing fashion, he nevertheless insisted that the major role of
the biblical prophet was to teach about theology, the doctrine of creation, the
history of virtuous men and women, philosophy and ethics, and the new covenant
and the messianic age in which the gentiles would stream in to Mount Zion to
worship the God of Abraham, Isaac, and Jacob (*DE* 5. introd. 11-20[204d-207b]).
"The prophets," Eusebius wrote, "foretold some things incidentally to inquirers if
anything was asked relating to their daily life, but their prophecy in its main purpose was concerned with great issues. For they did not reckon it worthy of their
divine duty to deal with those who sought oracles about daily matters or that actual time, or about slight and trivial things, but the illumination of the Holy Spirit
in them including in its vast scope the whole race of humankind, promised no prediction about any particular person who was sick, nor about this present life so
open to accidents and sufferings, nor about anyone dead, nor, in a word, about
ordinary and common things, which when present make the soul no better and
when absent cause it no harm or loss. And, as I said, when their predictions referred to such things, it was not in the line of their main meaning, but as accompanying a greater conception" (*DE* 5. introd. 21-22[207bd]).

Herodotus had included the Delphic oracle in his history, he had also originated a historiographical tradition in which the flux of human events was described as a history of *decisions*. This was a point that affected Eusebius as deeply as anything in his intellectual makeup: above all, it seemed necessary to him to defend the efficacy of human decision making within the present historical world order. Therefore Eusebius had to work out his own nongnostic solution to the problem.

Now it is important to be completely clear about what Eusebius was denying. He wanted to reject, first of all, the notion that what appeared to be conscious, rational, personal decisions were actually determined by forces outside our control *in a way of which we were not directly conscious.*[7]

> For we plainly feel (αἰσθόμεθα) ourselves desiring this or that by our own impulse and motion (ὁρμῇ καὶ κινήσει). . . . So evident therefore is the argument for free-will, that in the same way as the feeling of pain and pleasure, and seeing and hearing this or that, is perceived not by reasoning but by actual sensation, so we consciously feel ourselves moving of ourselves and of our own purpose, and choosing some things and rejecting others.[8]

Eusebius's analysis of the nature of human decision was therefore based on immediate human awareness of the distinction between willing and being coerced,[9] and rejected any notion of *hidden* coercive forces, such as Fate or the stars, operating *secretly*. The only alternative to Eusebius's position is to treat normal human experience as an illusion. Eusebius said that the psyche was not like a puppet pulled by strings;[10] that is, that there were no hidden agencies acting as *efficient* causes to determine the will's decisions.

An entire tradition of standard arguments for and against the doctrine of Fate reappears time and time again in classical Greek and Roman literature. One of the regular attacks on the doctrine of Fate was the so-called "lazy argument," and this naturally appears in Eusebius.[11] If human beings

---

[7]Eus. *PE* 6.1.6-7(237d-238a), 6.5(242d), 6.13-14(243d-244a); *Contra Hier.* 41.

[8]Eus. *PE* 6.6.20-21(245ac).

[9]Eus. *PE* 6.6.8-12(243ad).

[10]Eus. *Contra Hier.* 41; *PE* 6.6.20-21(245ac).

[11]Eus. *PE* 6.6.8-12(243ad).

were to believe everything was fated, the argument runs, then it would cut
the nerve of their will to achieve when it came time to make hard decisions. There were, of course, traditional counterarguments to this (used
notably by the Stoics), which worked well as long as the force of Fate was
regarded as working through the natural operations of the causal order. Such
had been the case with the kind of oracular fatalism that Herodotus had
introduced into classical Greek history writing. But Eusebius seems to have
had in mind here another, more naive understanding of fatalism that was
current among some people, what one might call "the broken-legged marathon runner doctrine of Fate."

> He who is destined to become a carpenter, will become one, even though
> his hands have been cut off; and he who has been predestined to carry off
> the prize for running in the Olympic games will never fail to win, even
> though he break his leg; and the man to whom the Fates have decreed that
> he shall be an eminent archer, will not miss the mark, even though he lose
> his eyesight. [12]

It is immediately apparent, of course, how very different Eusebius's target
here was from the naturalistic concept of Fate found in the Graeco-Roman
historians. The nature of his illustrations suggests that he may have had in
mind the kind of forecasts found in Roman astrological writings and still
current on newsstands today which purport to predict the kinds of careers
most appropriate and congenial to each astrological sign.

Eusebius used a second argument against Fate, what one might call the
"moral argument," in conjunction with the lazy argument. [13] The argument
here was that, if a human decision were determined by a force outside that
person's control, then there could be no culpability or responsibility fastened on that person. (Over the past few years there has been a debate in
the United States over an issue very similar to this—that is, the question
of whether and how far insanity releases a person from criminal responsibility in a court of law.)

Most important of all, Eusebius regarded all full-fledged doctrines of
Fate as ἄλογος, insisting that any thoroughgoing fatalism would be unable
to do justice to the Logos structure of history. Eusebius believed that the

---

[12] Eus. *Contra Hier.* 39.
[13] Eus. *PE* 6.6.5(242d), 6.8-12(243ad); *Contra Hier.* 41.

human subject could, at any particular moment in time, analyze the particular historical situation in which he stood as the product of a set of external events that had taken place outside of his own personal control but in accordance with a natural causal order supplied by the universal Logos (the rational structure of the cosmos), so that the whole set of external events was amenable to rational investigation and explanation. "Providence" was simply identified, then, as the λόγος of those events that had taken place outside our own control. [14] The use of the word "providence" (πρόνοια) in this connection—a word whose more frequent reference in Christian writings of that period was not towards the historical per se, but rather an affirmation of the beneficence of the cosmos and its suitability for human life—shows that Eusebius regarded the Logos structure of history as displaying meaning and direction, and as a coherent part of a cosmos whose overall coherence was supportive of organized life and organized human activity. [15]

Even more important than the idea of Fate in classical Graeco-Roman historiography was the concept of Fortune. Thucydides, Polybius, Sallust, and the rest, had all used that word. Eusebius also had to deal with this aspect of the pagan historical tradition, and had partially to reject, partially to modify it, to fit the new Christian theology of history he was working out.

In the classical Graeco-Roman histories, an act of Fortune had meant an unexpected occurrence produced by the conjuncture of two or more independent chains of historical events. In particular, Fortune as "the unex-

---

[14]Eus. *PE* 6.6.22(245c). On the ancient Logos concept, see G. F. Chesnut, *Images of Christ: An Introduction to Christology* (Minneapolis: Seabury, 1984) 35-38, 44-47, 52-53, 92-93, 99, 139.

[15]In ancient Christian thought in general, the normal opposite of πρόνοια was conceived to be a universe displaying only Epicurean chance and accident. The standard Christian argument defending the doctrine of πρόνοια was then a list of examples, usually cosmological rather than historical, showing the marvelous intricacy with which each part of the world was perfectly adapted to the other parts, with the idea of showing that the entire universe was one completely harmonious whole, in its basic design at any rate. This was conceived to be a *benevolent* order, because it was what made human life possible, and therefore it was called πρόνοια, the divine "provision" for creaturely existence within the world. See Theod., *De providentia*, for an example of this kind of argumentation.

pected" was closely bound up with the ancient pagan Greek understanding of the eschatological character of human historical existence. "Count no man blessed until he is dead" was a succinct summary of the belief that human plans for the future had always to be projected upon uncertainty and death.

Eusebius in fact picked up a certain amount of this pessimistic Fortune language about uncertainty and death from the classical Graeco-Roman historiographical tradition, but he used that language only in company with a Platonic reinterpretation of its significance for human life. The future was indeed filled with perilous uncertainties as the Greek and Roman historians had pointed out, but the moral to be drawn from this, Eusebius said, was that it was necessary for human beings to recognize that their true home was in that hypercosmic realm where their souls would return at death. Even more important, one should not even concern one's mind with the question of what Fortune might bring, because these sorts of things did not affect the soul for either better or worse. [16] Eusebius inveighed against the Aristotelian notion that one had to have money, family, all four limbs and so on, before one could be a true philosopher, [17] because this made the possibility of the soul's acquiring saving virtue a matter dependent to some degree on Fortune. This was also a reason why he could discount astrological fatalism out of hand, insofar as it claimed to predict external changes in wealth, success in love, and so on. The soul gained neither profit nor harm from matters such as these, whether the astrologers could predict them or not, and so it was not even necessary to argue the matter.

The first-century Roman historian Sallust was significant in the development of ancient historiography because he rejected in part the dominant naturalistic, materialistic pragmatism of the Greek historical tradition he inherited, and moved at least a small distance in the direction of a Platonic soul-body dualism. [18] The effect of this was to cause him to deny any fundamental importance to the role of Fortune in human life, [19] although an interest in Fortune still ran through his histories. Eusebius was a far more

---

[16] Eus. DE 5. introd. 21-22(207bd).

[17] Cf. Aristotle's Nicomachean Ethics.

[18] Sall., Cat. 1-2.

[19] Sall., Jug. 1-2, esp. 1.3 and 2.3.

throughgoing Platonist, and although he would make general philosophical statements about the role of uncertainty and death in human life, there was almost nothing in the way of concrete application of these ideas at all. When it came to writing real historical narrative, Eusebius's Platonism had caused him to lose all interest in the concrete role played by Fortune as the unexpected element in particular historical situations.

Eusebius's Christianity pushed him in this same direction too, of course. The truly important thing was how people stood in the eyes of God, not their material successes and failures. Furthermore, at the fundamental level, even if the future were a largely unknown quantity as far as human knowledge went, it was not being left to the sway of blind chance, but was going to take place in accordance with God's direction and control. One did not await the future with the tense expectancy of those who had calculated the odds and now anxiously awaited the roll of the dice, but with the staunch confidence of those who knew that, no matter how bad a turn the future course of events might take, there was no situation which God could not, in his own mysterious way, redeem for those who loved him. Tyche was a goddess by whom Christians could not let themselves be captivated. [20]

But Fortune meant more than just the unexpected—as has already been noted, it also meant accidental conjuncture. In this second sense, Fortune was a motif used in the ancient histories to emphasize a basic element of the human condition—that no human being could ever get all the causal chains of history into his own grasp, but instead would continually find himself in situations created by cause-effect chains outside his own control.

Eusebius built this basic idea of Fortune as the conjunctures of history into the heart of his philosophy of history. He changed the name, and called it τὰ συμβεβηκότα, the "accidents" of history, instead of τύχη, but the idea was the same. Aristotle had already used the phrase τὸ κατὰ συμβεβηκός as a technical description of Fortune many centuries before.[21] This usage could have been mediated to Eusebius through Middle Platonic works.

---

[20]Eus. DE 2.3.141(80b)—Isa 65:11-12.

[21]Aristotle, Physics 2.5.197a: ἡ τύχη αἰτία κατὰ συμβεβηκός, "Fortune is an accidental cause."

Eusebius had to find some word to replace τύχη for a variety of reasons. He was interested in τύχη as the conjunctures of history but not in τύχη as the unexpected in history, for the reasons we have already discussed in detail. He needed a word that did not have the emotional connotations that τύχη had picked up from its continual usage in the classical Greek and Roman histories. He needed a word that had never been used to name a pagan success deity, or the tutelary spirit of a city, or any other object of pagan worship. He needed a word, in short, that had no prior religious associations and was emotionally neutral, and that could be used with narrow philosophical precision to state exactly what he wanted to say but no more. Τὰ συμβεβηκότα was just such a neutral term. A Greek who read Eusebius would probably have read it, at first glance, as meaning something like "chance events" or "accidents." But it was the perfect participle of the verb συμβαίνω so the participle could also be translated literally as "those things that have happened." Eusebius was probably consciously playing to a certain extent on this literal meaning when he used the term, since τὰ συμβεβηκότα were, to Eusebius, those aspects of the historical context in which a person found himself or herself at any given moment, *as that historical situation had been created by the sum of all the things that had happened in the past.* In every present moment one stands at the nexus of a set of converging cause-effect chains fanning back into the past like the tributaries of a mighty river. The further back one goes into the past the larger the set of causal antecedents responsible for the concrete present situation in which an individual finds himself. The situation in which each of us stands at any given moment was created in large part by the actions of innumerable people many generations back in the past. Furthermore, if the verb συμβαίνω is broken down to its root meaning, it can be seen that it means to "come together," and so a sense of the "conjuncture,"—that is, the "coming together"—of two or more cause-effect chains is also implied by the participle. Finally, the technical Aristotelian use of the term τὰ συμβεβηκότα meant that the phrase implied accident as opposed to substance; external impingement as opposed to the unimpeded self-unfolding of a single, simple natural process.

Before going into a more detailed explanation of what the phrase τὰ συμβεβηκότα meant to Eusebius, however, it would be well to explain something about this concept of "nature" and his idea of the cosmos as natural process. As early as Herodotus, the father of Graeco-Roman history, the word φύσις ("nature") was used to refer to the characteristic behavioral patterns and possible range of activities of a certain kind of creature or thing. This continued to be one of the basic meanings of the word in Greek thought all the way down to the fourth century C.E.,[22] when Eusebius also used it in this same sense. The requirements of his Logos theory caused Eusebius to stress that nature had "laws" and that these laws of nature applied universally to all things, specifying the course from beginning to end of each of the natural processes that made up the Being (οὐσία) of the universe. The universe as a whole was also conceived by Eusebius as a single great mechanistic and architectonic process taking place in accordance with the laws of nature.[23] It was, of course, the Logos (the rational structure of the universe) that supplied these natural laws, or to put it the other way round, the laws of nature were part of the Logos structure of the cosmos.[24]

Eusebius sometimes called them "laws" (νόμοι) and sometimes called them "limitations" (ὅροι). They were the rules that determined such things as the position of the earth in the universe, the regularly changing pattern of day and night, the regular motion of the sun, moon, and planets, the yearly cycle of the seasons, the geological structures that caused the continental masses to remain pushed up above the level of the water that filled the ocean basins, and the meteorological structures that provided for transfer of moisture through evaporation and precipitation.[25] Furthermore the physical limitations placed upon each kind of creature as part of its φύσις were also called νόμοι and ὅροι: fish could not live on the dry land because of their natural limitations, while the laws of nature likewise prevented land creatures from living permanently beneath the surface of the

---

[22]For example, compare Herodotus's description of the φύσις of the crocodile (2.68—τῶν δὲ κροκοδείλων φύσις ἐστὶ τοιήδε) with the set of rhetorical questions about the φύσις of the ant drawn up by one of the Cappadocian fathers in the fourth century C.E., a generation after Eusebius; see Basil, Letter 16; also occurring as a portion of Gregory of Nyssa, Contra Eunomium 10 (Migne, PG 45.828).

[23]Eus. Contra Hier. 6. The use of the words τέλη and τελεσιουργεῖτα shows that Eusebius was thinking of processes.

[24]Eus. PE 7.10.1-3(314bd); De laud. 12.5, cf. 11.17. For a more complete discussion of what the Logos concept meant in the ancient Christian world, see G. F. Chesnut, Images of Christ, 35-38, 44-47, 52-53, 92-93, 99, 139.

[25]Eus. PE 7.10.1-3(314bd).

water. In the same way, a limitation that was part of their nature prevented human beings from soaring aloft on wings like the eagle.[26]

The cosmos as a whole was made up of countless natural entities, each one attempting to carry out its own natural processes: acorns growing into oaks, fish swimming under the water, land animals breathing air, planets moving through the heavens. Insofar as each entity was following its own laws and limitations (νόμοι and ὅροι) the Logos formed a structure of universal specifications that unified the whole cosmos at an abstract level.[27] But the impingement of the concrete natural activity of one concrete natural entity on the concrete natural activity of another concrete natural entity was "accidental." If a squirrel came upon an acorn and ate it, this was an "accident," from the acorn's point of view at any rate. "Accident" (τὸ συμβεβηκός), defined in this way, was therefore as fundamental a part of the makeup of the universe as was "nature" or the "Logos structure." Since the cosmos was made up of these countless natural entities, each struggling to go its own way, according to its own natural behavioral patterns and sequences, the progress through time of the cosmos as a whole was constituted of the "accidental" interlacing of these countless individual natural processes.

The individual human psyche, with its body, is immersed at every moment in a universe of this sort. The individual person's psyche operates according to its nature, and his body carries out its own proper natural processes, but he is also continuously affected by the independent operations of all the other countless natural entities in the universe. Eusebius says that these effects are *accidents* (τὰ . . . συμβεβηκότα) with respect to . . . psyche and body, but are brought about by other things acting according to *nature* (κατὰ φύσιν)."[28] Man "is made to pass his time among wild beasts and venomous reptiles, and amid fire and water and the surrounding air, and the perverted and diverse natures in all these," so that his life is a continuing struggle

---

[26]Eus. *Contra Hier.* 6. Cf. *De laud.* 12.5, duplicated in *Theoph.* 1.23.

[27]Cf. Plutarch, "On Fate," 568cd and 569d-570a.

[28]Eus. *PE* 6.6.29-30(246d-247a). Cf. the use of "nature" and "accident" as technical terms in one section of Aristotle's *On the Soul* (1.3.406ab) where he is looking at other philosophers' ideas on the nature of the soul before laying out his own position.

against the countless accidents (τὰ . . . συμβεβηκότα) from without.
. . . Ere now, for instance, many such and such kinds of food, and such
and such temperatures of the atmosphere, and sudden frosts, and burning
heats, and very many other things, though moving naturally (φυσικῶς)
according to certain laws (λόγους) proper to them, yet by falling con-
jointly (συμβατικῶς) upon us, have caused no common disturbance of our
independence because of the connection with the body; for our bodily nature cannot withstand the assaults from without, but is overpowered and
conquered by these external things which are acting according to their own
proper natures (κατὰ φύσιν οἰκείαν).[29]

Eusebius continually speaks of τὰ συμβεβηκότα, the external accidents that impinge on our own nature from without, as factors that limit
human freedom. Τὰ συμβεβηκότα are the things that are "not in our own
power," the things that happen "against our will."[30] But this is simply another way of expressing one of the most important parts of the ancient idea
of Fortune: human beings as historical creatures are always immersed in situations that are not completely within their own control. Furthermore, even
though the συμβεβηκότα of the particular historical situation are not the
creation of the particular person caught in that situation, he or she is nevertheless obliged to struggle against them.[31] Eusebius may drop the word
τύχη then, but in the concept of the συμβεβηκότα, the "accidents" of
history, there is nevertheless a recovery of the Greek historical consciousness of the constant human struggle against forces one cannot control.

The struggle is not completely in vain because of one very important
difference between Eusebius's idea of natural law and ours. In the modern
understanding of natural law, the laws of nature are conceived as rigid, un-
bendable rules that completely specify every detail of every happening and
that cannot be violated or modified in the slightest by any kind of being.
But the ancient Greek understanding of φύσις was, in the first place, often
conceived of as no more than a set of outside limits, beyond which a particular kind of creature could not go, and secondly, and even more im-

---

[29]Eus. *PE* 6.6.39-40(248bd). Cf. also *PE* 6.6.22(245c)—we must recognize that
the "things happening to us (συμβαίνοντα ἡμῖν)" have a *nature*, and therefore
are taking place in accordance with the Logos structure of the cosmos.

[30]Eus. *PE* 6.6.22(245c).

[31]Eus. *PE* 6.6.39-40(248bd).

portantly, was often conceived of as no more than a directional tendency, an organic striving in a certain direction, which could be distorted and warped by an outside force. To give an example of the first sort of use of the term, φύσις was regarded as a set of outside limits when one said that human "nature" did not permit people to live in the sea like fish or fly in the air like birds. But the possibilities left open for a human being to choose among were still numberless even if the life of the trout or the lark had to be excluded. Similarly, though the "nature" of the crocodile was to have the upper jaw hinged instead of the lower (as was believed in the ancient world), this did not necessarily produce a deterministic view of the universe, since who was to say (on the basis of a knowledge of the "nature" of the crocodile) whether this particular crocodile would pick this particular moment to snap at my left leg?

It is the second sense of the word φύσις, however, φύσις viewed as an organic striving in a certain direction, that is a more important one for the purposes of our investigation. This is the sense of the word that lies behind so much of Aristotle's thought. A sapling by its nature tends to grow straight up. But an outside distorting force can cause the sapling to grow into a tree that is twisted and bent in an unnatural fashion. Or to use an example from biblical Greek of the same kind of concept of nature: human beings by nature form heterosexual pair-bonds for the purpose of child care and procreation but "their women have exchanged natural (φυσικήν) intercourse for unnatural (τὴν παρὰ φύσιν), and their men in turn, giving up natural relations with women, burn with lust for one another" (Rom 1:26-27 NEB). Eusebius says:

> If therefore anyone were to subject those things which happen according to nature (τὰ κατὰ φύσιν), either of the body or of the soul, to necessity as their cause, calling it "Fate," he would miss the proper name. . . . For if they say that Fate is unalterable and that nothing can happen contrary to it (because necessity is inexorable), and if, as I said, many things happen to both soul and body contrary to their natural functions (τὰ κατὰ φύσιν), a man would not use the right names, if he said that Fate and nature were the same. [32]

So the struggle of humanity against τὰ συμβεβηκότα can have a certain

---

[32]Eus. PE 6.6.27-28(246bd).

amount of success, because these external forces affecting them are simply natural processes, and if they apply enough counterforce of the right sort, they can distort and redirect them to their own advantage.

As long as one had a concept of what was natural, of course, one could also easily conceive of miracle—of something which was more than a slight bending of the rules of nature. Miracle was quite distinct, in Eusebius's system, from either the purely accidental or the willful, purposeful distortion of natural functions by the human actors in history. In truly miraculous intervention, God himself could be seen at work "changing many even of the events which take place according to nature (τῶν κατὰ φύσιν)." An example would be the story of the miracle that Bishop Narcissus was said to have performed when oil for the lamps ran out during the all-night Easter vigil. He sent for water, and by his miraculous power "its nature (τὴν φύσιν) was changed in quality from water into oil." In fact, there were very few miracles in Eusebius's historical writings. Miracles were viewed very suspiciously by his non-Christian contemporaries, as possible sorcery (γοητεία). Even Jesus had to be defended against the charge that his miracles had been worked by sorcery. Furthermore, the miraculous was of questionable intellectual respectability in the pagan historiographical tradition to which he looked in so many fundamental ways as his guide. Eusebius therefore did defend the basic possibility of miracles, as a divine suspension or modification of the normal workings of nature, but did so principally to justify the Christian's acceptance of biblical stories involving the miraculous. In Eusebius's accounts of postbiblical history, tales of the miraculous were almost nonexistent. A workable doctrine of providence, as he knew, simply had to go beyond that level if God was to be seen as directing not just a few extraordinary events in a far-off time but the everyday course of history. [33]

In order fully to introduce a sense of divine guidance into history—particularly the history of Christianity after the New Testament period—Eusebius therefore had to develop some device other than miracle. He turned to the distinction he had made between nature and accident, and developed a parallel differentiation between two different kinds of divine providence, much like the distinction between "general" and "special" providence made by later theologians. Since τὰ συμβεβηκότα ("the things that hap-   ·

---

[33] Eus. *PE* 6.6.45(249cd); *HE* 6.9.1-3; *DE* 3.5.110(125b).

pen to us," συμβαίνοντα ἡμῖν) take place in accordance with nature (τὴν φύσιν), and the course of natural events is prescribed by the laws of nature contained in the Logos,[34] this means that a sort of "general providence" specifies the *general* possibilities within which the events of history are allowed to unfold. But there is also a "special" providence, because at every historical conjuncture God also chooses exactly which *particular* set of concrete events is going to take place within the manifold set of abstract, purely formal possibilities laid out by the Logos. That is, in every historical conjuncture we see God's providence arranging τὰ συμβεβηκότα into whatever order (τάξις) he wishes.[35]

Eusebius himself points out clearly in *PE* 6.6.29-30(246d-247a) that it is the doctrine of creation that stands at the foundation of his concept of providence. If *everything* derives its being, metaphysically speaking, from the Being of God, then the entire course of events that we call history must be given not only its general structure but also its individuality by the Source of its being. Therefore God is not only the giver of the laws of nature but also the creator of the accidents of history (ὁ . . . τῶν κατὰ συμβεβηκὸς δημιουργός). The distinction between a sort of general providence and a sort of special providence unfolds very neatly because of this, since Eusebius held that the *form* of the cosmos was supplied by the Father's *Logos*, and the *matter* by the Father's *will*.[36]

---

[34]Eus. *PE* 6.6.22(245c).

[35]Eus. *PE* 6.6.45(249cd)—we see the πρόνοια (providence) of God "assigning their proper place (τὴν . . .τάξιν) to external circumstances (τοῖς ἐκτὸς . . . συμβαίνουσι)."

[36]The Logos is the ἀρχή or metaphysical first principle of the universe (Eus. *PE* 7.12.1-2[320c]) because "it carries in itself . . . the invisible and incorporeal ideas (τὰς . . . ἰδέας) of visible things" (*DE* 5.5.10[230c]). With Philo, Eusebius says that the Logos *is* the noetic world (τὸν νοητὸν κόσμον) that contains the archetypal Idea of the ideas (ἀρχέτυπος ἰδέα τῶν ἰδεῶν) (*PE* 11.24.1-3[546d-547a], cf. 11.23.3-6[545bd]). Had it not been for the Logos, the universe would have remained as unorganized matter without form or structure (ἄμορφός τε καὶ ἀνείδος) (*De laud.* 11.12-13, see also 12.8). The Father's will then serves as a sort of matter and substance (ὕλη and οὐσία) out of which the universe is constituted (*DE* 4.1.7[145c]). For a more general discussion of the early Christian Logos doctrine, see Chesnut, *Images of Christ*, 35-38, 44-47, 52-53, 92-93, 99, 139.

In this sense then the Father is seen, by a direct act of his will, "assigning their proper place (τὴν . . . τάξιν) to external circumstances (τοῖς ἐκτὸς . . . συμβαίνουσι)."[37] That is, God manipulates τὰ συμβεβηκότα to carry out his purposes, and Eusebius gives a number of examples of such divine manipulation of the accidents of history. Events worked out so that Constantine was able to be present at the death of his father Constantius, with the result that he was the one who took the throne as his father's successor.[38] The emperors who persecuted Christianity found τὰ συμβεβηκότα stacked against them in divine punishment.[39] The troubles that came upon the Jews, from the time of Pontius Pilate on up to the reign of Caligula, are described as συμβεβηκότα and συμφοραί.[40] The troubles that struck the Jews during the siege of Jerusalem by the Romans—the work of such things as famine and the sword—are described as συμβεβηκότα.[41] The events that befell the Christian church in Lyons and Vienne, described in the famous account of the martyrdoms there in 177 C.E., are called συμβεβηκότα.[42] The fact that an eyewitness had put an account of these martyrdoms down in writing, and that a copy of this had survived the vicissitudes of a century and a quarter of rather chaotic Christian history, was described by Eusebius as a συμβεβηκός.[43] (Here one is especially reminded of Sallust's statement about the role Fortune plays in preserving the glorious memory of some historical events and not others.)[44]

In each case there was a historical event or circumstance that a classical Graeco-Roman historian would have ascribed to Fortune. On the level of particular causes and effects each event or circumstance was completely explainable in terms of natural cause-effect relationships. It was not nec-

---

[37]Eus. *PE* 6.6.45(249cd).

[38]Eus. *VC* 1.18.

[39]Eus. *VC* 1.23.

[40]Eus. *HE* 2.5.6 and 6.3.

[41]Eus. *HE* 3.5.7.

[42]Eus. *HE* 5.pref.1 and 5.2.1.

[43]Eus. *HE* 5.pref.1.

[44]Sall. *Cat.* 8.

essary to appeal to *miracles* in order to account for the course of events.[45]
Eusebius's word for describing these phenomena was almost perfect: they
were produced by a combination of συμβεβηκότα, a technical term implying, not some concept of a completely lawless chance, but the combination of two or more natural processes by an impingement of one upon
the other in a matter dictated by certain particularities of time and place
and individual idiosyncrasies—a conjuncture that was perfectly explainable, but only by referring to the particular details of the particular case.

The place where Eusebius stretched his point is the same place at which
the ancient Greeks had often been tempted to stretch it. Having characterized an event as an act of Fortune, and therefore perfectly explainable
in terms of natural cause-effect relationships, they would then sometimes
go further and state that the act of Fortune was also part of a cause-effect
relationship in the supernatural realm: the human victims of Fortune had
offended some god or goddess, and their misfortune was an act of divine
retribution. The same historical event was "doubly determined" or "over-
determined," to use E. R. Dodds's terminology.

> For Herodotus, history is overdetermined: while it is overtly the outcome
> of human purposes, the penetrating eye can detect everywhere the covert
> working of *phthonos*. In the same spirit the Messenger in the *Persae* attributes
> Xerxes' unwise tactics at Salamis to the cunning Greek who deceived him,
> and simultaneously to the *phthonos* of the gods working through an *alastor*
> or evil daemon: the event is doubly determined, on the natural and on the
> supernatural plane.[46]

Eusebius did something very similar to this. To him, certain kinds of events
that seemed to be pure "accidents" when one looked only at proximate
causes in fact fell into empirically observable patterns when one looked at
the overall course of history over the centuries. Those who persecuted
Christianity always came to bad ends, for example. Eusebius wanted to account for this by postulating a second network of empirically observable
cause-effect relationships, separate from yet somehow involving the same

---

[45]We must remember again the sharp distinction, in Eusebius's system, between miracle and accident.

[46]E. R. Dodds, *The Greeks and the Irrational* (Berkeley: University of California
Press, 1951) 30-31.

objects as the network of ordinary cause-effect relationships. An event like Constantine's victory at the battle of the Milvian bridge or the fall of Jerusalem in 70 C.E. was caught up in both these interpenetrating networks of cause-effect relationships—the network of cause-effect chains exposed by ordinary historical analysis, in which human beings contended with each other and with the elements, and a second, separate network of interrelationships in which a human being stood before a personal deity as a free and morally responsible agent. Within each network it was possible to give a complete (but different) explanation of why the same particular event had occurred: the same event that appeared as a clear-cut instance of divine punishment or reward within the "theological" cause-effect network appeared as an "accident" within the cause-effect networks explored by the pragmatic causal analysis of Polybian naturalistic empiricism. The same event was therefore "doubly determined"—determined by a set of pragmatic causes, but also determined by a set of theological causes.

The modern empiricist would usually try to reject Eusebius's scheme of double determination on philosophical grounds by invoking Ockham's razor: If a historical accident could be, by definition, completely accounted for in terms of the laws of nature and the particularities of the situation in question, then talk about a second set of causal explanations in terms of divine retribution and such like was superfluous material, *entia multiplicanda praeter necessitatem*. Back in the patristic period, Augustine rejected the Eusebian scheme because it involved the claim that there was an empirically observable pattern to the divine manipulation of the accidents of history. Even if the Old Testament had sometimes seemed to proclaim such to be the case, Augustine declared on the basis of the empirical evidence of history that there was in fact no such simple pattern to history in which the wicked regularly received earthly retribution and the innocent won earthly rewards (or even peace). Eusebius on this issue perhaps failed to follow out the logic of his own doctrine of free will: If freedom of the will was the ability to decide for or against the Good itself (and, as shall be discussed later, this was his position), then the providential pattern of history should have been interpreted in terms of the moral imperative felt by the deciding subject, in the light of the Good, at the time of moral decision. That is, providence is not a mechanical, deterministic formula of reward and punishment, but the moral burden that the past lays upon the present, when the present (and the future) are seen as the arena in which free will must be exercised in the light of the Good. Such an interpretation would be workable—note Herbert Butterfield in our own century—and one cannot help thinking that it would have better suited Eusebius's otherwise almost total rejection of mechanistic and deterministic interpretations of history.

With these comments, the question of providence must now be set aside to return to the question of human freedom. As has already been pointed out at the beginning of this chapter, in Eusebius's firm rejection of any kind of doctrine of Fate he affirmed the reality of human free will. It is now necessary to consider some other aspects of this freedom of self-determination, and the limitations placed upon it by the nature of human historical existence.

As an Origenist Eusebius believed that the first Fall, the cosmic Fall in which humankind was thrown into historical time,[47] left human beings exiled here on earth, cast into bodies. These bodies acted as the first great hindrance to the exercise of human free will. Eusebius held to an extreme soul-body dualism. He even took Plato to task for not being dualistic enough! Plato had made a tripartite division of the soul, into a rational part (τὸ λογιστικόν), a courageous or spirited part (τὸ θυμοειδές), and an appetitive part (τὸ ἐπιθυμητικόν);[48] and Eusebius pointed out that though this meant "that one part of the soul is divine and rational (θεῖον καὶ λογικὸν)," it also meant that another part of the soul was "irrational and the seat of emotions (ἄλογον καὶ παθητικὸν)."[49] In some passages, Eusebius said, Plato seemed to regard the soul as a composite entity, partly divine but partly partaking of the nature of bodies (τὰ σώματα).[50] but the true doctrine (which Plato had only partially recognized) was that the soul was "like God (τῷ θεῷ ὁμοίαν)"[51]—divine and rational, completely a member of the transcendent and noetic realms, neither itself the seat of emotions nor itself a member of the realm of bodies apprehended by sense impression.

---

[47]Eusebius held to the Origenist doctrine of preexistence of souls: Armen. *Chron.* 36; *PE* 7.18.7-10(332cd).

[48]There is a good summary account of Plato's idea of the soul in Frederick Copleston, *A History of Philosophy* (Westminster MD: Newman, 1959) 1:chapter 21, sections 1-3.

[49]Eus. *PE* 13.16.18(700b).

[50]Eus. *PE* 13.16.1-2(696bc); Plato, *Timaeus* 34c.

[51]Eus. *PE* 13.16.1(696b); cf. *PE* 7.18.6(332bc).

Eusebius therefore affirmed, against Plato, a starkly dualistic system—
human beings were composed of two "natures," body and soul, and the
emotions were to be identified solely as *bodily* drives and warning signals:
physical pain, the sexual drive, hunger, thirst, the awareness of cold or fatigue.[52] This was also perhaps the most important reason why Eusebius felt
he could reject the astrologers' claims that the stars controlled the lives of
human beings. The truly frightening aspect of astrological teaching to the
ancient world was the assertion that all the powerful human emotions ebbed
and flowed at the total mercy of the configurations of the planets. Eusebius's answer was in one way similar to the common gnostic approach—
one identified the true seat of human selfhood with a level of the psyche
that was above the purely emotional level and, in essence, denied that the
emotions that a human being felt were his or her "true" self.

For Eusebius, therefore, the split between body and soul, emotion and
reason, was extreme and fundamental. The soul or psyche, he said, was
one "nature" (φύσις) and the body was another. One must at this point
recall that the idea of φύσις often meant, to an ancient Greek, a directional tendency, an organic striving in a certain direction, which an outside force could distort and warp to a certain extent.[53] This meant that

---

[52]Eus. *PE* 6.6.31-38(247b-248a). The overall context of Eusebius's argument
here can be seen by referring to Origen's *De principiis* 3.4. Origen was trying to
refute, first, the Platonic tripartite division of the soul by interpreting internal
mental conflict in terms of a more idealistic philosophy, as consideration and de-
liberation by the rational free will over two mental images, each suggesting a rational choice whose probable outcome required time and thought to calculate. But
Origen was even more concerned to refute another position, the gnostic notion
that there were two souls in the same human body, a heavenly soul and a fleshly
soul. Human sin then followed from the war of the flesh against the spirit, seen
quite literally as a battle between two different entities, the true self fighting against
an alien being locked within the same mind. This position required God to have
created something (the fleshly soul) that was necessarily and inherently at enmity
with himself, which would be absurd. And Origen concluded by warning that this
gnostic position led inevitably to the classic gnostic predestination into pneu-
matic, psychic, and hylic human beings, thereby destroying free will. Eusebius's
concept of soul-body dualism is therefore in continuity with a basic Origenistic
position designed to defend free will and directed originally against the gnostics.

[53]See Eus. *PE* 6.6.27-28(246bd).

Eusebius regarded the psyche and the body as two striving forces, each with its own natural directional tendency, but locked by their mutual relationship in a continuing struggle that resulted in a distortion, sometimes of one and sometimes of the other. In the same way that human beings can domesticate a wild animal, and distort and redirect its natural tendencies (its φύσις) into ways useful to humans, so also the psyche should try to domesticate the body by partially bending the force of the bodily φύσις in directions contrary to its inherent natural tendencies. [54] That is, the psyche can keep the body from acquiescing to its feelings of hunger, thirst, cold, and fatigue, for a time at any rate. The psyche can also redirect the body's natural libidinal drives (presumably directed by φύσις toward male-female sexual intercourse) into homosexual patterns, to give one example, or into the sublimated form of monastic asceticism, to give another. The psyche can even overcome the body's natural survival instinct by committing suicide. [55] On the other hand, a large enough amount of bodily pain can cause the psyche to depart from its natural inclinations, and physical illness or the physical breakdown of the body with old age can seriously distort the natural rational workings of the psyche (that is, in delirium or senility). [56]

Eusebius's picture of the struggle between these two "natures," the rational psyche and the bodily emotions and drives, was in certain ways like Freud's psychological conception of the conflict between the ego and the id (the conscious self and the primitive instinctual drives). In both systems there is a continuous, dynamic struggle between two driving forces, the force of conscious rationality, and the amoral, irrational force of emotion and desire. Sometimes one force is able to bend the other to its will, and sometimes the reverse takes place. But conscious rationality can never simply annul the dynamic, forcelike character of its opponent, it can only, at best, redirect the force of emotion and desire into more domesticated pat-

---

[54]Eus. *PE* 7. 18. 6(332bc).

[55]Eus. *PE* 6. 6. 34-38(247c-248a). Unlike later Christianity, which regarded suicide as an unforgivable sin, Eusebius held to the classical Roman view, that suicide was the honorable course when one was trapped in a position that led to irreparable shame and disgrace. See Eus. *VC* 1. 34.

[56]Eus. *PE* 6. 6. 31-33(247bc).

terns. In Eusebius's language, the body always remained a φύσις, an organic striving in a certain direction. By practicing the ascetic life one could harness this natural force and control it to an amazing extent. But in Eusebius's system, as in Freud's, the contest between the ψυχή and the bodily φύσις, the ego and the id, had always the character only of a temporary compromise, a temporary working accommodation, a temporary balance point that would shift as the two great competing forces shifted the direction and pressure of their demands. In spite of this the basic goal for both Freud and Eusebius was the same: to achieve insofar as was possible a compromise between the two sets of forces, a compromise nevertheless marked by the essential dominance of the ego over the id, of rational awareness over the emotions and bodily drives. Eusebius was simply more optimistic than Freud about the character of the compromise that could be achieved.

Unfortunately, the body was not the only hindrance to human free will. An individual's freedom of self-determination could also be limited in a second way, namely by the force of society. In some passages it seems as though Eusebius was holding up the mental image in his own mind of one of those decision scenes in Thucydides, where a spokesman for each side stood up in his turn and presented the arguments in favor of his proposed course of action in a carefully reasoned speech: "The rational faculty of the soul is carried this way and that by the arguments of those who encounter it from without."[57] But in other passages Eusebius seems to have been thinking more in terms of a general and pervasive social pressure; at times, he thought,

> our will . . . being disturbed by a thousand external wills, is induced by its own independent decision to give itself up to the external forces; and sometimes is rendered better, and sometimes worse: since bad company is apt to corrupt, just as on the contrary the intercourse of honorable men makes us better.[58]

One is strongly reminded of one of the central themes in Sallust's historical

---

[57]Eus. *PE* 6.6.43(249ab).

[58]Eus. *PE* 6.6.41-42(248d-249a).

works, the corruption of a good individual by a corrupt society.[59] Eusebius used the idea to interpret the Christian theme of the Fall (not the first, cosmic Fall, but the second, sociological-historical Fall). This Fall had taken place gradually as corrupt men and women managed progressively to corrupt the human societies they lived in, and it was extraordinarily difficult to reverse, because of the way in which, as the quotation from Eusebius noted, a thoroughly corrupt society would tend eventually to corrupt every good man or woman who ever appeared in it.

On the other hand, as Eusebius also stated firmly in the passage quoted, the will "is induced . . . to give itself up to the external forces" of those "thousand external wills" only *by its own independent decision.* Eusebius was attempting carefully to walk the delicate theological tightrope of the doctrine of original sin. He did not want to deny human free will and hence human moral responsibility. But on the other hand, he did not want to suggest that human beings could pull themselves out of the universal corruption by their own unaided efforts, because then there would be no need for God's grace, and no necessity for the sending of Jesus as the savior of humankind. He therefore painted the picture of a corrupt society working with a high degree of success at the task of pulling every good person into corrupting himself by an act of his own free will. And Eusebius portrayed the self-perpetuating powers of this societal corruption as so tenacious that only a series of theophanies of the Logos—Holy Reason, Divine Rational Structure itself—culminating in the incarnation of the Logos in the form of a historical human life, could break the power of the forces that used the free decisions of a society of free human beings to keep them perpetually in bondage.

---

[59]Sallust interpreted his own youth in these terms (*Cat.* 3.3-5). He portrayed Catiline as an archetypal example of the corrupt man pulling others down into his own corruption (*Cat.* 14.4-5 and 16.1-2). Jugurtha started out as an outstandingly virtuous man, but turned off down the road to moral degeneration with help supplied by the influence of corrupt elements within Roman society (*Jug.* 8.1: *Romae omnia venalia esse,* 13.5-8; 20.1). Marius also began as an exceptionally virtuous man, but fell into vice in a slightly different way. Nevertheless, the influence of a corrupt society was still at work, because it was the *superbia* of the nobility, as represented especially in Metellus, which broke Marius's virtuous self-restraint (*Jug.* 64.1-6).

The important point is that whether accepting or rejecting the everyday fallen world of normal human society, the human psyche does so freely, and in a way that is impenetrable to human analysis. To Eusebius the psyche is placed completely within the realm of the divine.[60] (Eusebius's critique of Plato on this point was discussed earlier.) To him the human psyche is a transcendent mystery, unknowable in the same way that God the Father is unknowable. But its hiddenness is above all the seat of decision and will. "The invisible and unseen mind within us, the essence of which no one has ever known, sits like a king in his secret inner chambers and alone considers what things are to be done."[61]

The options that a human being is allowed to choose between are created by God[62]—the actual choice is left up to the person. There is a ὁρμή (impulse or desire)[63] within the human psyche, a ὁρμή that determines the fundamental direction of each person's life, whether it will be directed toward the good or toward the bad. "With respect to things which are in our control, each person possesses in the will itself a ὁρμή towards one of the pair, virtue or vice."[64] This ὁρμή is determined by the individual human beings themselves, and not by Moira, or εἱμαρμένη, or Ananke, or even God.[65] For each person was created "free and having within his own power the tipping of the balance (τῆς . . . ῥοπῆς), either towards the good and beautiful or towards the opposite."[66] Hence "free will" is at its heart a *moral* issue, based upon the human ability to apprehend, to seek, or to reject what

---

[60]See for example Eus. *PE* 6.6.26(246a).

[61]Eus. *De laud.* 12.3-4. See also *HE* 10.4.21-22, the metaphor in which the inmost recesses of the human soul are compared to the Holy of Holies, the innermost shrine of the Temple, whose mysteries were penetrated only by the High Priest of the Universe (and perhaps, partially, by a worthy Christian bishop, who might be given the right to look into another person's soul as part of pastoral duties).

[62]Eus. *PE* 6.6.29-30(246d-247a): ὁ . . . τῶν ἐφ᾽ ἡμῖν . . . δημιουργός.

[63]Originally a Stoic term, but part of the general philosophical coinage by the fourth century.

[64]Eus. *Contra Hier.* 42.

[65]Eus. *Contra Hier.* 42, compare *PE* 6.6.47-56(249d-251d).

[66]Eus. *DE* 4.6.6-10(155c-156a).

Plato called the Good. It is the *moral* component in decision-making that makes it different from a mechanical selection device. Furthermore, this analysis of human free will adds a dimension of depth to Eusebius's understanding of evil. Evil is not merely error, it derives its fundamental power from some elemental, either-or choice made in the depths of the human heart.

The question of "free will," in other words, did not refer to normal everyday decisions about what to eat for dinner, or how much to pay for a cloak in the market. Although in principle the problem of freedom could arise in any decision, in practice it arose only in those exceptional situations in which the vision of the true good, and the whole question of morality itself, was at stake. Later in the fourth century, Gregory of Nyssa developed this interpretation of free will further, and in his *Catechetical Oration* laid out two different mechanisms by which human beings could turn away from the vision of the true good. God as the Good was like the sun shining down from the sky. But by an act of free will a person could deliberately shut his or her eyes and live in inner darkness. This was what the Greeks called φθόνος or "envy." The English word in its normal usage does not mean quite the same thing—the Greek word meant hatred of the good and a deliberate attempt to blot out its manifestations. That was the way Satan fell, and human beings could fall into "envy" also. In the other mechanism Gregory used to explain moral evil, "pleasure" was the key instead of "envy." By nature human beings desired the good. But "the good is of two kinds: what is really good in the nature of things, and what is not such, but has only an outward and artificial appearance of the good." Gregory repeated the well-known story of the dog who leaned over the edge of the water with a bone in his mouth. He saw the reflection of the bone in the water, tried to snap at the reflected image, which looked even juicier, and ended up losing the real bone and the illusory one as well. The false good that human beings were regularly lured into following was *pleasure*—sense pleasure, hedonism. Pleasure, Gregory said in a colorful metaphor, was the bait wrapped around the fishhook of evil.[67]

In defending his own particular doctrine of free will, Eusebius holds that the psyche itself moves (a Platonic doctrine that Aristotle argued against

---

[67]Greg. Nyss. *Or. cat.* 6-7, 21.

in the *De anima* 1.3).[68] For Eusebius, the psyche is a self-moved mover, which can serve as the *first* link in a causal chain. It is therefore to be distinguished from those things that move only because they make up one of the intermediate links of a causal chain.[69] The psyche therefore acts in the present tense moment of decision, not as an effect completely determined by the causal forces making up the historical context of decision, but rather in such a way as to introduce an element of genuine novelty into the situation.[70]

Since human free will was inviolable, the only way that God's providence could relate to the human will in history was through synergism:[71] God's providence "working with and cooperating with our wills (συνεϱ-γοῦσά τε καὶ συμπϱάττουσα τοῖς ἐφ' ἡμῖν)."[72] "Synergism" in this case obviously did not mean the Lutheran heresy by that name![73] It was a standard patristic idea: The Alexandrian tradition, beginning with Clement and Origen, had used the term συνεϱγία (working together, cooperation) to describe the way that God's grace was at work sanctifying the Christian ascetic who was struggling on towards Christian perfection. After Eusebius's time, the Cappadocian fathers continued this teaching.[74] Euse-

---

[68]See Copleston, *History of Philosophy* 1:328n.

[69]Eus. *Contra Hier.* 41.

[70]Compare Whitehead's philosophy in our own century.

[71]We have already seen, earlier in this study, three other ways that God's directing providence could enter the realm of history. Eusebius believed that God's providence controlled the course of history principally through the Logos (which laid down the general laws of nature and universal categories within which all events had to take place) and by manipulation of τὰ συμβεβηκότα (the accidents of history). Miracles represented a third way that God could act in history, but Eusebius made little use of the miraculous as an explanatory device in church history per se (in spite of his pious defense of the biblical miracles). Synergism was a fourth way that the divine purpose could enter into and shape the course of human history, and it was a quite important mode to Eusebius.

[72]Eus. *PE* 6.6.45(249cd).

[73]As advocated by the "Philippists," associated with the name of Philip Melanchthon.

[74]For a statement of the role the concept of synergism played in Clement, Origen, and the Cappadocians, see Werner Jaeger, *Two Rediscovered Works of Ancient Christian Literature: Gregory of Nyssa and Macarius* (Leiden: Brill, 1954) 85-109.

bius adapted the idea so that he could talk, not in this case about sanctifying grace, but about the way God's providence was at work in history.
The word συνεργία itself shows up a number of times in his writing about
historical events,[75] but the basic belief—that is, that God's providence could
not override, but only work synergistically along with the free, uncoerced
cooperation of the human actors in his history—was a basic presupposition
of every part of his historical writing even when the term συνεργία or
its equivalent did not appear.

In conclusion therefore one can say that for Eusebius providence means
God's control over the whole fabric of history, with its interlacing pattern
of nature, accident, and free will.[76] The fact that human beings have been
given free will does not produce any fundamental threat to God's control
over the essential course of history. God is omnicompetent, and no matter
what human beings do to try to thwart the divine plans, even to the point
of raising the sword against the Church, God is competent to reorder history according to his original project. Eusebius says at one point that providence is a kind of ἀνακεφαλαίωσις, a recapitulation or summary of the
entire course of human history and all the events that have made it up—
things that involve free will, things that involve natural process, and things
that involve historical accident—in the one Logos, the rational structure
of creation and history.[77] Seemingly disparate events, seeming accidents,
seeming setbacks to God's intentions in history suddenly fall into a larger
pattern when seen in the light of the divine plan for human history as a
whole.

> He has made known to us his hidden purpose—such was his will and plea-
> sure determined beforehand in Christ—to be put into effect when the time
> was ripe: namely, that the universe, all in heaven and on earth, might be
> brought into a unity (ἀνακεφαλαιώσασθαι) in Christ (Ephesians 1:9-10
> NEB).

How did these theories affect the actual writing of history? Eusebius's
rationalism, coupled with his strong body-soul dualism, meant that he der-

---

[75]Eus. HE 3.24.3, 37.2-3; 6.3.6-7. DE 3.7.22-29(138c-139d). VC 2.4, cf. also
3.12.

[76]Eus. PE 6.6.45(249cd).

[77]Eus. PE 6.6.46(249d).

ogated the emotions to the role merely of physical urges tending to lead
the psyche astray. Hence in his historical narratives one finds almost no
recording of human emotion at all except for such passages as the triumphant stories of the martyrs who overcome their emotions. Eusebius describes the pain and suffering that they felt only in order to show how their
rational psyches refused to give in to those "bodily passions." A history
written on Augustinian principles, to draw a helpful contrast, would have
been quite different. In the *City of God* (14.6-8) Augustine turns the basic
structure of Greek psychological theory completely on its head. It is difficult to exaggerate the revolutionary character of his thought at this point.
Even Plato himself had barely allowed the human emotions any honorable
place within the soul, and then always in subjection to a totally nonemo-
tional, rational center of the soul. Most later Greek philosophical systems
(including the later Platonists) had gone much further in their rejection of
the emotions, and regarded human emotionality as profoundly dangerous—as the enemy to be totally conquered if one were to achieve true wisdom. Even the Epicureans taught that the goal was to achieve a quiet
ἀταραξία, or serene, untroubled enjoyment of a few simple pleasures
that minimized the feeling of any strong emotions. But Augustine makes
the emotions the very core of the human psyche. Using Stoic nomencla-
ture to emphasize his point—terminology that would have been recognizable to every well-read man or woman in antiquity—he turns the four
passions (desire, joy, fear, sadness) from which the Stoic wise man was
supposedly free into the very fabric of human willing. The direction of the
human will, for sinner or saved, was in fact still nothing other than the direction of those emotions, and from this arose Augustine's whole theory of
the Two Cities and the Two Loves. [78] Hence in an Augustinian history (the

---

[78]Even for a nonphilosophical Greek thinker, "will" still typically meant delib-
erative decision making by conscious weighing of options, as for example in the
speeches in Thucydides. For Augustine, whose saints are as passionate as his sinners, "will" instead referred more to the spontaneous welling up of deep emotions
in the heart—he tells us, for example, how in his own schooling he had instinc-
tively loved Latin and utterly detested Greek. It was his observation of the totally
spontaneous quality of most of our emotional reactions that ultimately caused Augustine to deny any freedom for the will at the basic level, and thereby to break
with the usual Greek Christian theological affirmation of uninfringed free will even
in the fallen.

Confessions illustrates the point even though it is not a history but an auto-
biography) it would be not only legitimate but also necessary to record the
emotions that affected the historical character at each stage of his or her
life. The affects of the historical subject *were* the willing subject in action.

Eusebius held strongly to a doctrine of free will, but in the precise form
in which he set it out it permitted no greys, only black and white. It was
based at bottom on a naked either/or: the ὁρμή or impetus that energized
all an individual's actions could be only good or evil. The atmosphere created by the Great Persecution certainly must have done its part also in polarizing Eusebius's judgments—when one's friends and teachers and the
people everywhere who are associated with one's cause are being executed,
jailed, and driven into the wilderness, it soon becomes difficult indeed to
avoid saying "he who is not with us is against us." In this sort of situation,
it is the sheep and the goats, the good fish and the bad fish, the wheat and
the tares.

But the combination of the two tendencies—the lack of interest in the
emotions and the polarizing doctrine of free will—resulted in a history filled
with characters who did not have much complexity compared to those described in Augustine's *Confessions,* for example—although here Augustine had
the advantage of privileged access to the mind of his principal character!
On that ground, and others, it is probably not really fair to compare Augustine's *Confessions* to the church histories written by Eusebius and his continuators and successors.[79] The scattered references to the Roman emperors
in the *City of God,* for example, suggest that Augustine would not have read
their deeds and characters much differently from the way Eusebius or Socrates Scholasticus did—there is no more depth or profundity in Augustine's
pious description of the emperor Theodosius in *De civ. Dei* 5.26 than what
we find in Socrates, for example. The practical difficulties have to be taken
into account here too—who could possibly have written an account of, say,
Irenaeus's life, given the historical sources left to Eusebius—and to us—
that would have compared with Augustine's *Confessions?*

The doctrine of free will also required that a free human decision could
not be "explained" by the historian, that is, shown to be the effect of cer-

---

[79]These historians—Socrates Scholasticus, Sozomen, Theodoret of Cyrrhus,
Evagrius Scholasticus—all wrote history in basically Eusebian rather than Augustinian fashion.

tain specifiable causal factors. Insofar as a causal explanation could be given for a decision it was not free but determined by factors from the external environment or the past. The historian who assumed free will had to insist on principle that every meaningful human decision could only be judged as good or evil. Hence, a history written along these lines would have to show a dearth of causal explanation coupled with a strong element of moral judgment, whenever free will was supposed to be at work. This is in fact the case most of the time in Eusebius and his successors and continuators, Socrates Scholasticus, Sozomen, Theodoret of Cyrrhus, and Evagrius Scholasticus.

There were a few causal explanations. A historical figure could be described as being misled by, for example, being given false information (as when Constantine was supposedly misled about Arius's theological views by the presbyter in Socrates, *HE* 1.25). But in general in the histories written by Eusebius and his successors one must look, not at what is there, but at what is not there, to see the effect of theory on practice. One can run through a lengthy list of deterministic theories that were absent from the historical narratives. Unlike Josephus, there were no references to an individual person's invariant "nature" as a psychological determining factor. National character, invoked again and again in the classical histories, was not used to explain human behavior in the church histories looked at in this work (with one interesting exception in Socrates *HE* 4.28). Although Herodotus had spoken of the force of sociological determinism in the behavior of the Spartans, such ideas do not show up in the church histories— Christianity was supposed to free one from the traditional laws and customs of one's social group, so that one could live according to a purely rational ethic. The notion that climate was a deterministic cause of human character, found in the Hippocratic corpus in such works as *Airs, Waters, Places*, had a few faint echoes in historians like Herodotus ("soft lands make soft peoples") but none in the church historians. Although Thucydides had been no Marxist, the introductory parts of his history (see, for example, Thuc. 1.2-13) were deeply marked by a rather materialistic conception of history. But here too, no references to gross economic forces as determinative of human action play any important role in the church histories. There was no use made of the Greek medical theory according to which human behavior could be affected by the balance of the four humors, nor was astrological determinism invoked to explain the motivating character of any historical figures.[80] In short, one of the most important effects of historical theory on historical practice in Eusebius and his successors was the way they so carefully avoided the most common varieties of determinism found in their thought world, even though this forced them to give few causal explanations when compared with the usual practice of our own period.

The theoretical structure of Eusebius's thought was therefore not just an intellectual construct to answer problems debated among philosophers. It actually had a profound effect on the style and method of explanation and characterization that he used throughout the narrative portions of his purely historical work. Consciously or unconsciously, his followers in the next two centuries modeled their narrative styles on his, and the same fundamental understanding of the nature of human freedom can be seen equally at work there as well.

---

[80]In the English Renaissance there were attempts to use these two devices at least for fictional purposes. Ben Jonson's *Every Man in His Humour* in 1598, for example, played on the typology of the sanguine, the phlegmatic, the choleric, and the melancholic "humors" or personality types (compare also the masque, the *Hymenaei*, performed at the marriage of the Earl of Essex and Lady Frances Howard in 1606). In Chaucer's *Troilus and Criseyde* many of the major turns of the plot were explicitly linked to the precise configuration of the planets at that point in the tale. Compare also his astrological explanation of the character of the lusty Wife of Bath in her prologue in the *Canterbury Tales*: her Mars and her ascendant both in conjunction in earthy, sensuous, stubborn Taurus, and apparently her Venus so placed as to produce her unquenchable lecherousness.

CHAPTER 4

Eusebius:
The History of Salvation
from the Garden of Eden
to the Rise of the Roman Empire

Eusebius's *Church History* began its truly detailed historical narrative only with the birth of Christ, but his overall theory of history tried to accommodate all of world history, stretching as far back into the past as could be known to a Roman of his time. In order, therefore, to give a total picture of Eusebius's thought at the historical-theoretical level, this chapter is a prolegomenon of sorts, devoted in the main to exploring Eusebius's understanding of pre-Christian history: the creation and fall into superstition and savagery of the human race at the beginning of time, the period of the Old Testament patriarchs, the significance of Moses, and the implications of the rise of the Roman empire. Some of Eusebius's beliefs about the early Christian period itself and the church's relationship to the Roman emperors will also be noticed at one point.

Although Eusebius discusses pre-Christian history briefly in the introductory section of his *Church History* (1.1.7-1.4.15) in a sort of condensed summary, one must look elsewhere in his writings—including not only the *Chronicle* but also works like the *Praeparatio Evangelica* and the *Demonstratio Evangelica*—to obtain any detailed view of his picture of the pre-Christian world and the way this affected the later period about which he then wrote in such detail in his *Church History*. A Christian historian must always form some sort of opinion about Judaism and the world of the Old Testament in order to develop any overarching theory of history, and Eusebius was no exception here. Also, a historian living in the Roman empire at that time had to deal with the classical tradition as well, and the world that created the bright gods and goddesses who inhabited the pages of Homer, Hesiod, and Herodotus. If these beings did not truly exist as meaningful objects of worship, then one had to explain why so many people over so many centuries had thought so. A careful look at all of Eusebius's writings finds a coherent, comprehensive theory, affecting his understanding of the pre-Christian period and, as well, the early part of the subsequent era, when Christianity was an unlicensed sect dealing with often hostile emperors. Many of the ideas and presuppositions developed in that context affected Eusebius's thought through all the editions of his *Church History*, and even in the *Life of Constantine* that he wrote at the very end of his life, albeit with a conclusion to the story that the young Eusebius could never even have imagined.

The typical classical Greek or Roman historian did not have to contend, as Eusebius did, with a story whose overall historical sweep extended back to the very creation of the world. But Eusebius clearly felt that he had to do so, at least in outline, and in his own mind. From his Christian perspective, world history had had an overall pattern and design that had stretched over the centuries and that gave some explanation, in the process, to the historical role of the Christian religion whose story he then so carefully narrated in his *Church History*.

The history of the world, seen in this context, appeared to him as a sequence of stages: it had begun with a cosmic Fall into the world of history and temporality, then had come an era of superstition and savagery (broken only by the appearance of the Old Testament patriarchs), next had come the age dominated by the figure of Moses, and finally the period that began with the nearly simultaneous appearance of Christ and Augustus (the foundation of Church and Empire). Within the world thus created, the young Eusebius believed, Christianity was to carry out its missionary enterprise, until the Roman empire, the last of the great universal empires, became the complete agent of Satan in the last battles at the end of the world, and was destroyed in the second coming of Christ.

The whole story was a "salvation history" that set the Christian experience of grace and the Christian hope of the future into a context of historical knowledge shared by all educated people in the ancient world. In spite of the rather grim ending to the story, with apocalyptic destruction raining down as the history of this universe reached its final end, it was for most of its length a rather optimistic view of the world, seeing real, continuous progress in all areas—civilization, culture, morality, and religion. It was important not only to Eusebius's understanding of history, but also to his political thought. He used this theory of universal history both to justify the unique power of the Roman state over the Mediterranean world and to explain the proper function of the Roman emperor. When Eusebius was compelled, later on in his life, to insert the fully developed, post-Nicene figure of the Christian emperor Constantine into this story, it added some novel features that he had surely never even imagined in his youth, and it demanded that he reverse himself almost totally on the question of religious liberty, but it did not require him to alter the basic views of the structure and meaning of history, particularly in the pre-Christian period. Constantine gave him a triumphant conclusion to the story in the period that fell, Eusebius thought, just before the end of the world, but the clear success of Christian missionary efforts in the later third century would have given him a victory to proclaim whether there had been a Christian emperor or not.

In his basic understanding of pre-Christian history, one must not of course portray Eusebius as totally innovative by any means. The broad outlines of a Christian picture of world history had already been laid out by Christian theologians of the second and third centuries,[1] by writers such as Justin Martyr, Irenaeus, Clement of Alexandria and Origen. Eusebius took basic themes from them—the role of the daemons, the priority of Moses to Plato, Origen's theory of free will and the fall—and wove these traditional statements into a continuous account, bolstered by the best historical scholarship of the time (and in particular a detailed knowledge of the history of Graeco-Roman thought). He accompanied this with a full exposition of the theoretical consequences, for a practicing historian, of

---

[1]Anyone familiar with the second-century apologists, for example, will immediately recognize the elements in Eusebius's system that came originally from that source. Justin, for one, taught that at the beginning of history the daemons tricked human beings into regarding them as gods (*First Apology*, chapter 5), that Abraham and other Old Testament figures should be regarded as Christians before Christ (chapter 46), that Plato plagiarized his best ideas from Moses (chapters 44, 59-60), and that later on, in the Christian period itself, it was the daemons who were responsible for the rise of heresy (chapter 26). One could at length cite further references. On the general relationship of Eusebius to the second-century fathers, see Robert M. Grant, "The Appeal to the Early Fathers," *Journal of Theological Studies* new series 11 (1960): 13-24; and "The Uses of History in the Church before Nicaea," in F. L. Cross, ed., *Studia Patristica* 11 = *Texte und Untersuchungen* 108 (Berlin: Akademie-Verlag, 1972) 166-78.

such a view of history. Eusebius was insightful and brilliant, a creator of
new genres and a follower of the most radical philosophical theology of
his time, but most of the pieces out of which he constructed his total picture of pre-Christian history had already been developed before his time.

Origen, the great radical theologian, gave Eusebius some of his most
unusual ideas. Eusebius was a devoted follower of Origen's thought,[2] and
his theology of history is colored by an especially rationalistic variety of
Origenism from one end to the other. For Eusebius, following Origen, the
"Garden" of Eden had been a realm outside this present space-time continuum, and "Adam" had been the totality of humankind. All our souls preex-
isted before this earth was ever created.[3] An act of disobedience on the part
of some of those unembodied noetic beings caused God to cast them into
human bodies and imprison them on earth for a period of discipline, as-
sailed by death and corruption.[4]

This cosmic Fall was a fall into *historical time*. Eusebius the historian was
interpreting Origen's theological ideas here. Chronology—a necessary and
integral part of historiography—could not begin until Adam had already
fallen and been driven out of that hypercosmic realm, the "Garden," with
its quite different temporality,[5] and had been cast down into the world τῶν
πραγμάτων, of *history*, which was ceaselessly driving onwards towards its
final eschatological destruction.[6]

But even after their souls had been cast down into bodies on this earth
human beings still retained their freedom of will, which in fact was never
lost even in the most fallen. The contrast with the Augustinian doctrine of
original sin, developed a century afterwards, appears at every stage of Eusebius's doctrine of the first things. Due to this freedom of will, once hu-

---

[2]For the historical background of Eusebius's dependence on Origen, see Robert M. Grant, "Early Alexandrian Christianity," *Church History* 40 (1971): 133-44.

[3]Eus. Armen. *Chron.*, Karst edition, 36; *PE* 7.18.7-10(332cd).

[4]Eus. *PE* 7.18.7-10(332cd); *DE* 4.1.4(144d-145a). But also note *PE*
7.17.3(330d), where Eusebius used a different theory: humans were *created* as
dwellers on earth, and for a positive function, that is, so that the universal worship
service (the cosmic liturgy) would extend all the way down to the earth.

[5]Eus. Armen. *Chron.*, Karst edition, 36-37.

[6]Eus. *DE* 1.9.3-4(30d-31a).

manity had entered this present worldtime a further, progressive Fall was able to take place. Most of those first human beings at the beginning of history soon fell into what Eusebius regarded as a subhuman, animal-like existence[7]—the life of desert nomads, he called it (his urban Palestinian prejudices showing up here), without πόλις or πολιτεία, without τέχνη or ἐπιστήμη, without legal system or any concept of ἀρετή or philosophy (his thoroughly Greek prejudices appearing in his choice of words here).[8] This second fall was the fall of human society as such; the social structure of humankind, with all its social institutions, degenerated and disintegrated over a period of time.[9] The lack of real knowledge of God condemned them to the lowest sort of existence even on earth; conversely, any widespread growth of civilized human community would have to take place in company with the appearance of some sort of renewed knowledge of God.

To make matters more difficult, God and the members of the human race were not the only figures who were taking part in the history of events on earth. After humanity had fallen completely and human beings were living like animals, God divided the human race into nations and put one of the angels in charge of each nation as a shepherd.[10] But there were other incorporeal spirits also abroad in the world—the daemons—who promptly set to work to upset God's plan. These daemons lured men and women into wickedness and disrupted every human community, until they had oblit-

---

[7]Eus. DE 4.6.6-10(155c-156a), see also 8.introd.5-12(363c-365b).

[8]Eus. HE 1.2.18-19; DE 8.introd.5-12(363c-365b).

[9]Compare Eus. HE 1.2.18-21. Eusebius was convinced that it took a span of generations for the historic Fall to work its way to the lowest depths. His historical investigations, for example, seemed to show that human beings in the earliest age had not worshiped man-made idols, so that this aspect of humanity's historic Fall had taken time to grow up—see Eus. DE 4.9.10(160bc); also Theoph. 1.42.

[10]The one exception was the Friends of God, who were put under the direct care of the Logos himself; Eus. DE 4.6.6-7.3(155c-157a). See G. B. Caird, Principalities and Powers (Oxford: Clarendon Press, 1956) 5. The idea is based on one reading of Deut. 32:8-9; the form quoted for example in Eus. DE 4.7.1(156bc). Compare also the story in Daniel 10:13 of the archangels Gabriel and Michael battling for twenty-one days against the angel who had been placed in charge of the nation of Persia.

erated the boundaries that God had set up for the nations. Most of the human race came into the power of the daemon-overlords, and remained under their control until Jesus' resurrection broke their power.[11]

The original religion designed by God for the majority of fallen humanity was a sort of astral piety. The angel-guardians were instructed by God to allow the nations they were caring for to worship the sun, moon, and stars. The human beings under their care were intellectually incapable of conceiving of anything that transcended the visible, material world.[12] It was therefore better for these early men and women to worship "the best of things visible in heaven" than to turn towards something daemonic.[13] Eusebius was here following an earlier tradition, but it also perhaps helps explain his unwillingness to write off astrology as totally nonsense. The prominence he gave to this theory suggests also that he may have sensed the value of the good feelings that had existed for a while between the sun-worshiping emperor Aurelian and the Christian church during his own adolescent years, and that he may have hoped for some possibility of restoring such a modus vivendi between Christianity and the more tolerant and enlightened Neoplatonic sun-worshipers. Clearly a bishop holding Eusebius's views would not have worried overmuch about the precise mixture of Christianity and sun worship that might still have existed in the emperor Constantine's mind immediately after the battle of the Milvian bridge. H. A. Drake has argued that, as late as his *Panegyric to Constantine* in 336, Eusebius was still on occasion trying to bridge the gap between Christianity and the sort of Middle Platonic quasi-monotheism in which the supreme God was mediated to the rest of the universe through his Logos. The ac-

---

[11]Eus. *DE* 4.9.1-9(158c-160b), 10.1(161a), 10.9-10(162d-163a); *Theoph.* 4.8.

[12]Eus. *DE* 4.8(157c-158b); *PE* 1.9.15(30ab). The one exception to this astral piety, of course, was the Hebrew nation, which worshiped the true transcendent God.

[13]Eus. *DE* 4.8(157c-158b). In Plato's *Timaeus* the heavenly bodies were regarded as alive, and in Eusebius's respected master Origen (*De principiis* 1.7) there was a long discussion of this. Origen said that the sun, moon, and stars were preexistent souls clothed with their present visible bodies in order to give light to the human race. These lights above the earth were hence living, rational beings with the power of free will with respect to good and evil.

ceptance of the sun as a tolerated non-Christian symbol of the supreme God and his manifestation to us would have furthered this cause. [14]

Astral piety had therefore been God's original design, Eusebius said, for the majority of the human race. But the daemons were hard at work, and as the angel guardians lost control of the human beings under their charge, God's original plan for the fallen human race was to be disrupted here also. The first nations where the pure, primitive astral piety disappeared were Phoenicia and Egypt. This lapse into a more superstitious form of polytheism, Eusebius tells us, soon spread to other nations as well. Both the Phoenician and the Egyptian mysteries were brought to the Greeks, for example, the former by Cadmus and the latter by Orpheus. [15] Eusebius was here drawing on an important tradition within pagan Greek thought that held that the anthropomorphic gods and special cults of classical Greek religion had been of late and derivative origin. [16] It was a rationalizing ap-

---

[14]The idea that astral piety was better than idolatry could be found for example in Wisdom of Solomon 13-14; as G. B. Caird points out (*Principalities and Powers*, 13), "The author regards the worship of the heavenly bodies as misguided but pardonable, whereas 'the devising of idols was the beginning of fornication, and the invention of them the corruption of life.' " This general idea is very important for the light it throws on the problem of the "conversion" of Constantine. Many modern historians have been greatly puzzled by the confusing mixture of both solar monotheism and genuine Christianity in the historical data about Constantine. But it is clear that Eusebius, as one very influential church leader, would not have objected overmuch on principle to a slight admixture of solar monotheism in the imperial Christianity. Solar monotheism saw only the shadow, from his point of view, while Christianity saw the substance, but the sun worshipers were, nevertheless, quite literally "on the side of the angels" in the conflict with the daemons and their idolatrous human minions. On other attempts to build a bridge between Christianity and the more "enlightened" forms of paganism, see H. A. Drake, *In Praise of Constantine: A Historical Study and New Translation of Eusebius' Tricennial Orations* (Berkeley: University of California Press, 1976) chapter 4. Drake's book has a number of excellent insights from a classicist sensitive to what a non-Christian of the fourth century would have heard Eusebius saying, and can add something to the perspective of the more typically Christian-oriented patristics scholar.

[15]Eus. *PE* 1.6.4(17d-18a).

[16]Compare Eus. *PE* 1.9.13-14(29d-30a); see also *DE* 4.9.10(160bc). An account with slight differences is given in *PE* 1.6.1 and 3 (17b and d).

proach to the Greek religious tradition, seen among the classical Greek historians, for example, in Herodotus.[17]

In spite of all the evils that had developed, however, even in the first primitive centuries of this earth's history the picture was not entirely without redeeming figures. Amidst the mass of fallen men and women were some of a quite different sort—Enosh, Enoch, Noah, Seth, Japheth, Abraham, Isaac, Jacob, Job, and Joseph—a whole series of figures from early biblical history.[18] These were the θεοφιλεῖς, the "Friends of God." They formed a small minority of good and virtuous human beings, worshipers of the true God. Their religion was based upon knowledge of the Logos, the rational structure of reality as a whole.[19] It was natural religion which they had— that is, one based on "natural concepts" (φυσικαῖς ἐννοίαις),[20] a piece of (originally) Stoic phraseology that Middle Platonism had taken over by Eusebius's time. Even though the Friends of God lived centuries before the coming of Jesus, and practiced a religion based on reason alone, Eusebius believed that they were properly to be described as "Christians in fact, if not in name."[21]

These Friends of God were called into being by a series of theophanies of the divine Logos. This distinct second person of the Trinity was the necessary intermediary between the world of history and the transcendent, unknowable Father. Through his "Word" or Logos, God the Father called out these great Old Testament figures and taught them those vital truths about God and human life that had been suppressed and forgotten by sinful men and women after the Fall. It was the Logos, in Eusebius's interpretation, who appeared to Abraham at the oak of Mamre, and to Jacob when he saw the ladder stretching up to heaven. The Old Testament recorded a whole series of such theophanies or divine manifestations.[22] In this way,

---

[17]Her. 2.49-58, 81; 5.57-61.

[18]Eus. *PE* 7.8.4-36(306d-312b); *DE* 1.2.3-7(12-13) and 5.7(10b).

[19]Eus. *HE* 1.4.

[20]Eus. *HE* 1.4.4; *DE* 1.5.2-4(9cd).

[21]Eus. *HE* 1.4.6.

[22]Among the Old Testament theophanies Eusebius mentions are the two already cited—the appearance to Abraham at the oak of Mamre (Gen 18) and Jacob's ladder (Gen 28:10-15)—along with Jacob's dream (Gen 31:10-13), Jacob

the divine Logos became the agent through which the human race was to be lifted out of savagery and superstition and was to be led gradually, over the centuries, to civilization and a rational religion. This was God's way of helping humankind when the fallen race, at the beginning of history, had almost been completely swallowed up in evil.

The period of the great pre-Mosaic theophanies was followed by the period dominated by Moses himself. In order to justify Christianity's rejection of the law of Moses, Eusebius naturally had to portray this as in some way a step backwards. According to his explanation, when the Hebrew people took up residence in Egypt, they eventually found the Egyptian moral climate so enervating that they were no longer able to rise to the level of those virtues that had been practiced by the Friends of God among their foreparents. God therefore sent Moses to give the Hebrew people a different religious system—Judaism—that presented the truths of religion in riddles and symbols to this people grown too weak to face the naked reality.[23] This was a standard patristic argument. The law of Moses thereby became only an *Interimsethik*, so to speak, designed to care for the Hebrew people until the coming of Jesus, when it could be discarded.[24]

Eusebius then developed in greater detail another argument that had also already been used in earlier Christian apologetic—the claim that Plato had borrowed his best ideas from Moses. The Christians had the basic chronology on their side. The oldest books of the Old Testament antedated by several centuries the rise of classical Greek culture, and lack of

---

wrestling (Gen 32:24-30), Moses and the burning bush (Exod 3:1ff.), the pillar of smoke and the pillar of fire (Exod 13:21-22), the soldier with the drawn sword who appeared to Joshua (Jos 5:13ff.), and the Lord speaking to Job out of the whirlwind (Job 38ff.); see Eus. *HE* 1.2.6-16; *PE* 7.12.8(321d); *DE* 1.5.10-18(10d-11d); 5.19.4-5(246d-247a). The series finally culminated in the appearance of Jesus of Nazareth, when the Logos used an actual human life as the vehicle for revealing God to the human race. There were also postbiblical theophanies in Eusebius's system, namely to Constantine; this, of course, was not part of the traditional Logos theology that Eusebius had inherited from his predecessors; see Eus. *VC* 1.28-29, 32, 47; 2.12.

[23]Eus. *PE* 7.8.37-40(312b-313a). See also *HE* 1.2.22—Moses' teaching contained "icons and symbols . . . but not clear and distinct initiations into the mysteries themselves." Compare *DE* 4.10.4-8(161c-162d).

[24]Eus. *DE* 1.6.31-32(16d-17a), compare 2.1-10(11-14).

knowledge of cuneiform and hieroglyphics kept educated people of Eusebius's period from any real knowledge of the magnificent sweep of Egyptian and Mesopotamian civilization in the second and third millennia B.C.E. So Eusebius adopted a diffusion theory of civilization and argued that all the world's knowledge of philosophy and ethics had spread outward from a Palestinian center by ordinary transcultural intellectual contacts during the millennium following Moses, that is, roughly the first millennium B.C.E.[25] This theory was presupposed in the important introductory section of his *Church History*. The law of the Hebrews, Eusebius said (1.2.23),

> became famous and spread among all human beings like a fragrant breeze. Beginning with them the arrogance of most of the nations was tamed by the lawgivers and philosophers who arose everywhere. Savage and unbridled brutality was changed to mildness, so that deep peace, friendship, and mutual dealings with one another obtained.[26]

As civilization slowly spread over all the world through the course of the first millennium B.C.E., Eusebius pointed proudly to the savage and barbaric practices that were eradicated: murder, cannibalism, incest, killing aged parents after they became senile and burdensome, putting human corpses out to be eaten by dogs and carrion-eating birds, burning the living

---

[25]There was an important pagan countertheory that held that the city of Athens instead was the source and foster parent of all true civilization and all truly civilized human beings. It was this single city that had brought humanity out of the life of savagery. See James H. Oliver, *The Civilizing Power: A Study of the Panathenaic Discourse of Aelius Aristides*, in *Transactions of the American Philosophical Society* new series 58 (1968) Part 1. The Panathenaic discourse was composed shortly before 167, while Aristides was professor of rhetoric at Smyrna, an important Christian center in the second century (Oliver, 34-35). Oliver further states that Aristides was attacking both the Christian assertion that Plato had gotten his ideas from Moses, and also the Christian claim that Christians were the true possessors of the Logos (36).

[26]See also *DE* 8.introd.5-12(363c-365b). Eusebius makes the point repeatedly that Moses came earlier than any Greek thinker—*HE* 6.13.7; Armen. *Chron.*, Karst edition, 1. "The Greeks . . . borrowed all their philosophy from barbarians," and therefore probably from Hebrew sources among others—*PE* 11.pref.1-2(507d-508a). "The philosophy of Plato in very many points contains a translation, as it were, of Moses"—*PE* 13.pref.(639ab).

relatives of a dead person on his funeral pyre, and human sacrifice.[27] It can be noted that some of the items on Eusebius's list simply represented societal customs that normally differ from culture to culture—burial practices, for example, and the exact specification of the persons within the kinship system with whom sexual relations would be called incestuous. On the other hand, he never criticized accepted Roman customs such as, for example, the practice of judicial examination under torture, even though this went against Old Testament and rabbinic law. Eusebius's notions of "natural morality" were in fact very much conditioned by the standards of his own age and culture. What he was in fact celebrating was in large part simply the Hellenization and Romanization of the Mediterranean world over the preceding six centuries. But the historical myth made this the final triumphant reversal of a dreadful and long-lasting primeval fall that had occurred back at the beginning of history.

In Eusebius's theory, civilization was therefore spread from its Palestinian center over the entire inhabited world by the first century B.C.E. For the next era of history to dawn, this Palestinian center then had to be destroyed. Following the traditional Christian interpretation, Eusebius regarded the first-century Roman takeover as the end of Jewish Palestine. It was regarded as an act of God's hand, the necessary prelude to the appearance of the Messiah, who would then call in the Gentiles to the worship of the God of the Hebrews.[28]

History was now finally ready to receive the final and highest revelation of God, the incarnation. The Logos therefore entered human history once again, but in a new way, in the life of Jesus of Nazareth.[29] Shortly afterwards, the priestly religion of Old Testament Judaism was brought to an end by the destruction of Jerusalem and the Temple in 70 C.E.[30] Like

---

[27]Eus. *HE* 1.2.19; *DE* 4.10.1-3(161bc); *De laud.* 13.6-8, 13.14; *Theoph.* 2.81-82.

[28]Eus. *DE* 7.introd.1(308).

[29]Eus. *HE* 1.2.23; *DE* 8.introd.5-12(363c-365b); *De laud.* 13.15. Christ did not come to all the peoples of the earth until so late in the world's history, because the proper historical preparation had not yet been made—*DE* 8.introd.5-12(363c-365b); *HE* 1.2.17.

[30]As Eusebius describes in gory detail in his *Church History*. See also *DE* 1.1.7(5-6); 8.introd.2-3(363ab). By the fourth century there was little left even of the ancient ruins, *DE* 8.3.9-15(406b-407b).

Josephus, Eusebius held that this had been the result of divine wrath, but in a Christian interpretation of the event said that the killing of Jesus and three of his apostles had been the culpable deed.[31] Eusebius was no ancient anti-Semite; he held that the responsibility had been placed completely upon the heads of that one particular generation that met death and ruin at Jerusalem in 70 C.E.[32] There was no notion in Eusebius's philosophy of history of any supposed "racial guilt" of the Jews.

With the coming of Christ came the creation of the Church. And closely connected with this in God's plan for history came another event that happened at roughly the same time: the final collapse of the Late Roman Republic and its conversion, under Augustus, into the Early Empire. In Eusebius's theology of history, Church and Empire shared a common birth and (ultimately) a common destiny, "two great Powers sprung fully up, as it were, out of one stream."[33] In Eusebius's *Chronicle*, the multiple columns displaying the parallel histories of the various nations of the world (Assyria, Egypt, the Hebrews, Athens, Sparta, and so on) were reduced to only two columns for the period after Christ—one for the history of the Roman empire and one for the parallel history of the growth of Christianity. For Eusebius, these two columns summed up all that was significant in the history of the centuries after the birth of Jesus.

With the final, firm establishment of the Roman empire at the time of Christ, the political history of the world entered a completely new phase according to Eusebius's scheme of history. Before the coming of Christ, the world was filled with "polyarchy." The inhabited world was split up into a number of states, some ruled by democracies, others by tyrannies. Egypt, Arabia, Idumaea, Phoenicia, Syria, and many other states were ruled by kings. People who belonged to one state had no mutual dealings with people from other states.[34] "Hence wars of all kinds naturally arose," Eusebius wrote, "nations clashing against nations, and constantly rising up against their neighbors, ravaging and being ravaged, and making war in their sieges one against another, so that from these causes the whole population, both

---

[31]Eus. *DE* 1.1.7(5-6); *Theoph.* 4.14 and 16.

[32]Eus. *Theoph.* 4.17.

[33]Eus. *Theoph.* 3.2.

[34]Eus. *PE* 1.4.2-4(10ad); *DE* 7.2.20-22(344c-345a); *Theoph.* 2.67-68. See also *De laud.* 13.9-10, 16.1-5; *Theoph.* 2.69, 71-72, 78.

of dwellers in the cities, and laborers in the fields, from mere childhood were taught warlike exercises, and always wore swords both in the highways and in villages and fields."[35] Eusebius suggested that those who wanted to see what life was like in that period of history should read the records of butchery and carnage contained in the classical Greek and Roman histories. It was this continual strife that Augustus ended when he made himself sole ruler of the Roman empire in 31 B.C.E. The "monarchy" of Augustus replaced the wartorn "polyarchy" of the ancient Mediterranean world with a new era of peace.

To Eusebius, it was not chance that made Christ and Augustus historical contemporaries—their lives were inextricably linked in God's providential plan for history.[36] Christ came to save human beings from the idolatry of polytheism and bring them to the true monotheistic worship of the one true Church in the same way that Augustus had come to save human beings from the strife of polyarchy and bring them to the true monarchical government of the universal human State. In Eusebius's thought, *poly*theism and *poly*archy were linked together as necessarily as were *mono*theism and *mon*archy.[37] In good Platonic fashion, one level of reality was merely the icon or image of the next higher level: the organization of humanity's secular political life simply mirrored on a lower plane the organization of its spiritual life. The extreme monarchical nature of Eusebius's political ideas is discussed in almost every comprehensive history of the development of Western political thought; as can be seen here, it was linked in his own mind with a particular kind of philosophy of history that in fact used the defense of absolute monarchy in reverse as a sort of indirect, Platonizing argument in defense of Christian monotheism.

To Eusebius, polyarchy was linked with strife and warfare, while monarchy meant peace.[38] The primary example he gave of what would happen

---

[35]Eus. *PE* 1.4.2-4(10ad), perhaps an echo of Thucydides 1.6.1, "Indeed, all the Hellenes used to carry arms because the places where they dwelt were unprotected, and intercourse with each other was unsafe; and in their everyday life they regularly went armed just as the Barbarians did."

[36]Eus. *PE* 1.4.2-4(10ad); *DE* 3.7.30-31(139d); 7.2.20-22(344c-345a); *Theoph.* 3.1.

[37]Eus. *De laud.* 16.1-5; *Theoph.* 2.67-68, 76.

[38]"The deepest peace" (εἰρήνη) resulted when polyarchy and "piecemeal rule of the earth" was replaced by the rule of a single imperial authority, Eus. *DE* 8.3.9-15(406b-407b). Compare *DE* 9.17.14-15(457d-458a).

if the Roman imperial government broke down completely was drawn from
the period before the triumph of Augustus in 31 B.C.E. But one cannot help
wondering how much one is also hearing an echo here of more contemporary fears. The assassination of the emperor Severus Alexander in 235
C.E. had produced what is called the crisis of the third century. For nearly
fifty years a string of barracks emperors reigned, each one rising briefly to
power and then confronting mutiny and assassination as he strove to reas-
semble a disintegrating empire. At Palmyra in Syria and at Trier in Gaul,
rival Roman empires were centered for part of this anarchic period. Real
stability did not return until Diocletian was proclaimed emperor in 284 C.E.
Eusebius had lived through some of the worst of this himself. Born around
260 C.E., he lived in an area that was under the control of Queen Zenobia
of Palmyra when he was around ten years old. [39] When he was just beginning his adolescence, the emperor Aurelian was crushing the rival imperial
power at Palmyra and returning the eastern Mediterranean world to Roman control. To Eusebius, a strong monarchy was the only alternative to
a kind of suicidal civil warfare that he himself had experienced; the word
"peace" (εἰϱήνη) meant the stability of the reconstructed Late Empire, put
together during his lifetime by the emperors Diocletian and Constantine.
Even in the next century, Eusebius's successor church historians were still
holding absence of civil strife as the central goal of both ecclesiastical and
secular government, [40] a rather Byzantine attitude that placed "peace" of this
kind above either personal liberties or freedom of self-expression.

---

[39]Eusebius was probably born in Palestinian Caesarea; it is known that he developed his massive scholarship in the libraries of the presbyter Pamphilus in Caesarea and Bishop Alexander at Jerusalem (only fifty miles away), and that he spent
all his later life in Caesarea. There is no suggestion in any ancient work that he
originally came from elsewhere.

[40]Socrates, for example, at the conclusion of his history, *HE* 7.48: "But we shall
here close our history, praying that the churches everywhere, with the cities and
nations, may live in peace. For as long as peace continues, those who desire to
write histories will find no materials for their purpose." As the chapter about Socrates will explain in more detail this historian also believed that the secular political sphere and the spiritual sphere were necessarily linked together. A disruption
of "peace" in one area would produce, by a kind of cosmic "sympathy," a parallel
disruption in the other (Socr. *HE* 5.introd.).

Another important reason why the concept of εἰρήνη was given such importance in Eusebius's political thought was his equation of the Pax Romana with the eschatological Kingdom of Peace prophesied in Isaiah 2:4 and Micah 4:1-4,[41] when swords were to be beaten into plowshares, and spears into pruning hooks, and nation was not to lift up sword against nation any more.[42] To Eusebius, the fulfillment of those prophecies was not to be seen in the miraculous future kingdom of the millennialists, in which grapevines gave 225 gallons of wine from each grape,[43] but in the Roman rule he himself lived under. This claim was not mere rhetorical hyperbole on his part, but as will be seen in chapter 7, a consistent part of his overall treatment of the problem of eschatology.

In the period after Christ, just as had been the case in the period before his coming, there was still, of course, a celestial dualism intruding as a disturbing force into the events of human history: the battle between the Logos and the daemons, a cosmic struggle between Good and Evil personified. In the Preface to Book Five of his *Church History*, Eusebius tells us that all church history was the history of a war against the invisible daemons.[44] The daemons were the Old Gods, the gods whom the pagan persecutors worshiped.[45] The evil daemon used these men as his agents. He had Licinius persecute Christianity in the East and start a war with Constantine, for example.[46] The evil daemon could "raise up" individual human beings as his personal agents,[47] and single out individual Christians for special attack,[48] or when God let him he could raise a wholesale persecution against the entire Church, as in the Great Persecution that Eusebius had lived

---

[41]Also, in Eusebius's interpretation, such passages as Micah 5:4-5a and Psalm 72(71):7, where the exegetical focal point was the word "peace."

[42]Eus. *PE* 1.4.2-4(10ad); *DE* 7.2.20-22(344c-345a); 8.3.9-15(406b-407b); *De laud.* 16.7-8; *Theoph.* 3.2.

[43]Irenaeus, *Adv. haer.* 5.33.3.

[44]Eus. *HE* 5.pref.3-4.

[45]Such as the persecutors of Eusebius's own time, Licinius and Maximin, Eus. *VC* 1.54, 58; 3.1.

[46]Eus. *VC* 1.49; *HE* 10.8.2.

[47]Eus. *HE* 5.21.1-2 (ἐγείρας).

[48]Eus. *HE* 6.39.5.

through.[49] The evil daemon preferred to use persecutors to attack the Church, but when he was prevented from doing this he would use heretics instead:[50] Simon Magus, Menander, the Ebionites, Saturninus, Basilides, Carpocrates, the Montanists, Florinus, Blastus, Mani, the Donatists, and those who started the Arian controversy.[51] In fact, any kind of violent internal dispute in the Church, such as the turbulent Synod of Tyre in 335 that condemned Athanasius, was blamed on the evil daemon[52]—although one may wonder which people in particular Eusebius thought were daemon-inspired in that council!

The daemons were not always successful in turning Roman emperors against the Christians, so that the history of the first three centuries of Christianity was in fact marked by long periods of relative toleration. As a result, Eusebius in his young years divided all Roman emperors into two classes—those who had and those who had not persecuted the church. He believed that the history of the previous centuries proved that God gave success to the good emperors who were tolerant towards Christianity, whereas the bad, persecuting emperors always came to bad ends.[53]

By the end of his life, by which time the Christian Constantine had gained total control over the entire empire, Eusebius had decided that the good emperor henceforward had to be more than simply a tolerant, liberal pagan. Sanction of polytheism and participation in pagan sacrifice in themselves made a bad emperor, whether the monarch persecuted Christians or not. Nevertheless, Eusebius made no changes in the nature of the this-worldly rewards promised the good emperor, or the character of the

---

[49]Eus. *HE* 10.4.13-16.

[50]Eus. *HE* 4.7.1-3.

[51]Eus. *HE* 2.14.1-3; 3.26, 27.1; 4.7.1-3, 7.10-11, 5.14.1-16.1; 7.31.1. *VC* 1.45, 2.73.

[52]Eus. *VC* 4.41. Compare 3.1, 59.

[53]The phrase "the divine δίϰη" was the standard term for divine retribution in Eusebius's writings (he used the word even more often than Josephus). It was the "divine δίϰη" that struck down the persecuting emperors, we are told continually: Eus. *HE* 7.30.20-21; 9.7.2, 9a.12; 10.4.29; *VC* 1.58 (Maximian), 58-59 (Maximin). Of course, the divine δίϰη would strike down not only emperors, but other persecutors and enemies of Christianity as well; Eus. *HE* 2.6.8 and 3.5.6; 2.7.1, 10.1; 9.11.5-6. Compare *HE* 6.9.4-8; *VC* 1.12.

this-worldly punishments with which the bad emperor was threatened. He simply set higher requirements for gaining these rewards.

There were at least eight separate factors involved in the "success" granted the good emperor under Eusebius's theory, factors worth listing because of the insight they give into the ideas and values of the ancient world for which the church historian was writing. First, Eusebius believed that, in time of war, God gave success in battle to the good emperor,[54] and defeat to the bad.[55] Second, he believed that having a good emperor on the throne would result in general prosperity for the empire,[56] whereas having a bad emperor would produce hard times for the entire realm: civil war, famine, and pestilence.[57] Furthermore, "peace"—that ideal that so deeply affected the hopes and dreams of all the church historians investigated here—would reign everywhere when a good emperor was in command,[58] whereas war would be sent in divine retribution if a bad emperor gained control.[59] The good emperor himself was given a long reign,[60] and a happy end to his life, still in possession of his throne.[61] The bad emperor found his reign cut off short,[62] and went to an unhappy end, having lost all his power, or having been forced to resign the throne, or meeting death by violence or loathsome disease, or being defeated in battle and captured, or something else of this sort.[63] The good emperor was honored both during his life and after death.[64] The bad emperor's memory was dishonored

---

[54]Eus. VC 1.27.

[55]Eus. HE 7.13; 9.9.2-8; 9.10.

[56]Eus. De laud. 3.

[57]Eus. HE 8.14.18-15.2; 9.7.3-14 and 7.16-8.3.

[58]Eus. HE 8.13.9. Compare Rudolph H. Storch, "The 'Eusebian Constantine,'" Church History 40 (1971): 145-55.

[59]Eus. HE 8.14.18-15.2; 9.8.2.

[60]Eus. HE 8.13.9; De laud. 3, 9.18.

[61]Eus. HE 8.13.12-13; 8.appendix; VC 1.3, 17.

[62]Eus. HE 7.1, 30.20-22.

[63]Eus. HE 7.1, 10-13; 8.13.9-11, 13.15; 8.appendix; 9.9.2-8; 9.10. VC 1.27; Theoph. 5.52.

[64]Eus. HE 8.13.12; VC 1.27; 4.75.

after his death, his inscriptions and statutes torn down and mutilated[65]—surely a dire thought, given the nature of Roman emperors and their desire to become an "honored ancestor" to their posterity. The good emperor was given many children,[66] while the bad emperor would either be unable to beget children who would grow to maturity, or his children, relatives, and associates would all be put to death as soon as he himself was dead.[67] Furthermore, the good emperor would be permitted by God to leave the throne to his rightful heir,[68] whereas the bad emperor's line would come to an end with his own death.[69]

Hence the principle was asserted that the emperor's religious stance was the determinant of the course of imperial history. This same basic principle was taken over and enlarged upon, as shall be seen later, by Eusebius's fifth- and sixth-century successors. As the standards of Christian orthodoxy became more firmly set, and as the public's moral and personal expectations of a Christian monarch became progressively higher, these historians laid out more complicated requirements for becoming a "good emperor," but they promised essentially the same providential rewards to the emperors who fulfilled their standards: success in battle, prosperity and peace for the empire, a long reign, a happy end to his life, an honored memory, children, and a rightful heir as his successor on the throne. In the eastern half of the Roman empire there were to be no serious problems raised for this understanding of history until the rise of Islam in the early seventh century.[70]

The most important thing to note, however, is that implicit in Eusebius's whole treatment of the problem of Church and Empire, even in his younger years, was the assumption that the two were necessarily tied together at the deepest level: Christianity as the ultimate world religion and Rome as the ultimate world state. In his scheme of universal history, the

---

[65]Eus. *HE* 8.13.15; 9.11.2; *VC* 1.27.

[66]Eus. *VC* 1.18; *De laud.* 3, 9.18.

[67]Eus. *HE* 7.1; 9.11.3-7; *VC* 1.27.

[68]Eus. *HE* 8.13.12-13; 8. appendix; *VC* 1.18.

[69]Eus. *HE* 7.1; *VC* 1.27.

[70]See Walter Emil Kaegi, Jr., "Initial Byzantine Reactions to the Arab Conquest," *Church History* 38 (1969): 139-49.

nearly simultaneous appearance at the end of the first century B.C.E. of Christ and the emperor Augustus created these two forces, and both the Christian religion and the Roman empire were the culmination of all the millennia of history that had gone before. Even before Constantine's conversion to Christianity had become a believable factor to be reckoned with, Eusebius seems to have understood that Rome's destiny and the Church's divine calling were somehow to be intertwined in any future he could foresee.

Eusebius therefore saw the major events of world history as a connected sequence, beginning with the creation itself and the original cosmic fall of the human race, and culminating in the emergence of early Christianity in the newly created Roman Principate. The remainder of this chapter must discuss the significance of a historian's seeing this kind of overall pattern in history. What kind of patterns had his pagan predecessors seen, or thought they saw? How did Eusebius's views fit into the historiographical traditions of the ancient world?

In attempting to discuss the long-term patterns of world history, the Graeco-Roman tradition before Eusebius had explored all three of the basic alternatives: theories of historical progress, theories of historical decline, and theories of repeating historical cycles.[71] The first to raise the issue had been Hesiod, around 700 B.C.E., with his famous account in the *Works and Days* of the Five Ages of Man.[72] He presented human history as one of decline, from a blessed Golden Age at the primordial beginning, to the fifth and present age, the Age of Iron, where "human beings never rest from labor and sorrow by day, and from perishing by night." Over against this there were also, from earliest times, Greek theories of historical progress. The pre-Socratic philosopher Xenophanes, for example, displayed the Ionian Enlightenment's obvious pride in its scientific discoveries.

Not from the beginning did the gods reveal everything to humanity,
But in course of time by research human beings discover improvements.[73]

---

[71]One of the best recent studies of these themes is E. R. Dodds, "The Ancient Concept of Progress," in his *Ancient Concept of Progress and Other Essays* (Oxford: Clarendon Press, 1973) 1-24. Another important work is Ludwig Edelstein, *The Idea of Progress in Classical Antiquity* (Baltimore: Johns Hopkins University Press, 1967).

[72]Hesiod, *Works and Days,* 106-201.

[73]Diels, *Fragmente der Vorsokratiker,* fifth ed., frag. 18; trans. from E. R. Dodds, "The Ancient Concept of Progress."

On the other hand, both Hesiod and Xenophanes combined their theories of decline and progress, respectively, with cyclic views of history. It appears quite probable that Hesiod used a myth of eternal recurrence to set his theory of historical decline into a larger cyclic pattern, in which the destruction of the race of iron would allow a new golden age to emerge from the ruins. There seems to be no other way to explain the poet's cryptic remark at one point that he wished he had either "died before" the present dismal age of iron, which Zeus was going to destroy by abandoning it to an almost apocalyptic time of tribulation, "or been born *afterwards*" (174-175). Xenophanes thought that at long periodic intervals the sea rose and covered all the earth and destroyed all human life, thus introducing a cyclic element into his thought as well.

Cyclic elements of one sort or another appeared in most of the classical Greek historians. Herodotus, for example, emphasized the way the cyclic rise and fall of empires repeated itself incessantly through dreary centuries and millennia, and held that this was one of the basic structures of history. "For many states that were once great have now become small, and those that were great in my time were small formerly."[74] Characteristic Greek pessimism also made him certain in his heart that individual human prosperity would always be followed eventually by evil. "Men's fortunes are on a wheel, which in its turning suffers not the same man to prosper forever."[75] Thucydides said that he wrote his history in the belief that the sort of internal disintegration that the Athenian body politic suffered during the Peloponnesian war would be repeated again in some other nation in some later period of history.[76] To him, the historian's task was to study the pathologies of human societies, and like the Hippocratic school of Greek physicians, he thought of himself as cataloguing the progressive symptoms of a kind of political "disease" that would surely be met in human history again.

---

[74]Her. 1.5. One sees an awareness of this inevitable cyclic pattern even in Polybius, who presented Rome's rise to power so triumphantly. The Persians had fallen, to be replaced by the Macedonians as rulers of the world. Then the Macedonians fell in their turn, to be replaced by the Romans (Polyb. 29.21). And the Carthaginians also fell, and were also replaced by the Romans. Some day, even Polybius admits, it would happen to Rome, too (38.21-22).

[75]Her. 1.207.

[76]Thuc. 1.22.4.

In this sense he might be spoken of as thinking in cyclic terms, but only in a mild way.

In Polybius the cyclic element was much more important. He laid out an involved series of constitutional changes that in one tradition of Greek political thought (compare Plato) were supposed to take place in recurrent cycles in the history of an individual city-state. The force of nature (φύσις) kept a city-state from remaining for any long stable period in any one simple political system. Forces inherent in that system inevitably worked towards a degeneration or mutation into a different kind of government, in a perpetual repeating sequence: monarchy to kingship to tyranny to aristocracy to oligarchy to democracy to mob-rule to savagery and back around again. [77] This particular kind of cycle applied per se only to the individual city-state, and not to world history as a whole. But Polybius also believed in one version of that persistent Greek theme of the periodic world-destroying catastrophe, and so he was committed to a cyclic theory of history at the world-historical level on these grounds: "Floods, famines, failure of crops or other such causes" could produce "such a destruction of the human race as tradition tells us has more than once happened, and as we must believe will often happen again." In the catastrophe one had "all arts and crafts perishing at the same time," so that the pitifully few survivors had to build civilization and human society completely anew, out of savagery and total anarchy. [78]

---

[77]Polyb. 6.3-9; Plato, *Republic* 8.1(544c)-9.6(580c).

[78]Polyb. 6.5.5. On the other hand, even Polybius did not teach the extreme Stoic view of time. Many modern writers have used as their primary example of the "Greek cyclic view of time" this early Stoic theory in which exactly the same sequence of historical events was supposed to occur again and again into infinity, with an identical Socrates drinking an identical draught of hemlock once every world-cycle, an identical wooden horse being brought within the walls of an identical Troy, and so on, down to the last detail of world history. The principal surviving Graeco-Roman historians certainly did not teach this sort of extreme theory. Even Polybius, though he spoke of natural catastrophes, nowhere taught of the great World-Conflagration in which, according to early Stoic theory, everything—earth, human beings, and even the gods (except for Zeus himself)—would be consumed in flames as each world-cycle came to an end. On the contrary, in 4.40.4-7, Polybius asserted the infinity of time.

Against this background of cyclic theories, the Greek historians (as opposed to the Roman historians later) generally believed strongly that the history of their own immediate past, extending back for several centuries even, had been one of continuous historical progress, and their viewpoint was basically cheerful and optimistic on these grounds. They developed this positive attitude by emphasizing the history of progress in technology, scientific knowledge, and the general civilized arts. Herodotus's history as a whole was a celebration of the military superiority of Greeks to barbarians, yet his experience in Egypt[79] gave him a vivid sense of how young Greek civilization was in comparison with other peoples. He knew quite well how important a role progress had played in recent Greek history. Thucydides, writing from a slightly later period of history, spoke with even more civilized amazement of "the weakness of olden times," when the soldiers of a Greek army had to row themselves across the sea in little undecked pirate boats in order to do battle with the enemy. Then came the invention of the trireme, which gave the technological basis for great ocean battles. But even the Athenian navy that triumphed at sea in the Persian war looked primitive from the viewpoint of his own time.[80] In Polybius, this sense of "modern superiority" was even more pronounced. He was extremely proud of the rapid technological progress that had taken place in his own day,[81] by which he meant the various sorts of modern inventions and developments discussed so much through the course of his history: improvements in the design of hand weapons and armor, the replacement of the Macedonian phalanx by the Roman legion as the lord of the battlefield, the Roman development of the "crow" for use in sea-battles, Polybius's own invention of a long-distance signalling device, Archimedes' wonderful machines used in the defense of Syracuse, the increase in the number of banks of oars used on warships from three, as in the trireme (the classical warship of an earlier period), to five and even higher, and so on.[82]

Unlike these earlier Greek historians, the Roman historians who followed them were more apt to view the history of the immediately preced-

---

[79]Her. 2.142-143.

[80]Thuc. 1.3.1, 10.4, 13.2-4, 14.3.

[81]Polyb. 9.2.5, the rapid progress in the ἐμπειρίαι and τέχναι.

[82]See for example Polyb. 1.20.9-16; 1.22-23; 8.3-7; and 18.28-32.

ing period as one of decline. Sallust gave the classical account of this.[83]
The early Roman republic had been filled with people of primitive virtue,
who preferred hardship, discipline, and victory with honor, over all the
lures of riches, revelry, and harlotry. But "by gradual changes" over the
hundred years preceding his own time, Rome had "ceased to be the noblest
and best" and had "become the worst and most vicious."[84] The final victory
over her mortal enemy Carthage in 146 B.C.E. released all external pressure,
and with that, self-discipline relaxed,[85] and the vice of *ambitio* sprang up.[86]
The next step in Rome's moral downfall took place during the reign of the
dictator Sulla. The license he gave his troops introduced the vice of *luxuria*
into the Roman national spirit,[87] and the mass proscriptions that followed
his complete takeover of the Roman state in 83 B.C.E. brought the further
vice of *avaritia*, the "desire for money, which no wise person covets."[88] Forty
years later, at the time Sallust was writing, Rome was fallen, he felt, into
a permanent and irreparable state of decadence and moral corruption.

Tacitus also adopted a theory of historical decline from an original state
of primitive perfection, but he pushed the golden age much further back
into the past. "Mortals of the primeval age, untouched as yet by criminal
passion, lived their lives without reproach or guilt," in a tribal society where
the force of traditional custom meant that "good was sought instinc-

---

[83]See especially the first thirteen chapters of his *Bellum Catilinae*.

[84]Sall. *Cat.* 5.9.

[85]"Those who had found it easy to bear hardship and dangers, anxiety and ad-
versity, found leisure and wealth, desirable under other circumstances, a burden
and a curse"—Sall. *Cat.* 10.2.

[86]A vice of "craft and deception," which found "one thought locked in the breast,
another ready on the tongue"—Sall. *Cat.* 11.1-2; 10.5.

[87]When Sulla billeted his troops in the homes of private citizens in the recon-
quered province of Asia, "those charming and voluptuous lands . . . easily demoralized the warlike spirit of his soldiers," as they learned too great a love of
women, drink, and classical Greek *objets d'art*—Sall. *Cat.* 11.5-6. Sallust does not
say which of these three vices he considered the gravest sign of total moral de-
generacy!

[88]Sall. *Cat.* 11.3.

tively."[89] Government was by the sort of primitive democracy typically found in the tribal stage.[90] The fall came when kings arose and destroyed the ancestral customs of that primitive social system with their despotism. Formal codes of law, like the laws of Lycurgus in Sparta or Solon in Athens, were attempts to curb the power of those kings and tyrants, and also attempts to replace vanished customs with new, consciously organized standards of behavior. Rome had followed this standard historical pattern; it had overthrown its kings and instituted government by law, but Tacitus dourly remarked that the Twelve Tables were "the last instance" in Roman history of truly "equitable legislation."[91] The lawmaking process became entangled in class warfare.[92] Then at the final desperate end of the Republic complete chaos resigned for twenty years during which there was neither law *nor* custom—"villainy was immune, decency not rarely a sentence of death."[93] Order was finally restored by Augustus, who gave Rome peace, but also the Principate.[94] He took complete control of the state, and all opposition quickly vanished. The surviving members of the senatorial aristocracy "found a cheerful acceptance of slavery the smoothest road to wealth and office."[95] The remainder of Tacitus's *Annals* and *Histories* was devoted to cataloguing the tyranny, cruelty, depravity, and paranoiac insanity of the line of emperors that followed. Tacitus's theory of Rome's decline and fall was joined to an antimonarchical zeal quite the opposite of Eusebius's glorification of the imperial power.

Tacitus's theories were based on a kind of romantic primitivism. Civilization was evil and corrupting. The *Annals* and the *Histories* used Rome as

---

[89]Tac. *Ann.* 3.26—behavior guided by *mos* (traditional custom) rather than by *ius* (formally enacted law).

[90]Tac. *Ger.* 11. This primitive democracy Tacitus called *aequalitas* (*Ann.* 3.26), that is, "political equality" in the sense of the Greek ἰσοτιμία.

[91]*Finis aequi iuris*—Tac. *Ann.* 3.27.

[92]*Dissensione ordinum*—Tac. *Ann.* 3.27. Each social class battled to distort the laws in its own favor, and as one might say today, class interest came to dictate the ideological structure of the state.

[93]Tac. *Ann.* 3.28.

[94]*Pace et principe*—ibid.

[95]Tac. *Ann.* 1.2.

the example of this, while his *Germania* showed by the strongest possible contrast the virtues of the noble savage. The primitive Germanic tribesmen whom he described were still in the seminomadic stage, and he romanticized their bravery in battle, faithfulness in marriage, and simplicity in clothes and dwellings. There were many varieties of romantic primitivism in the ancient world—the philosophy of the wandering Cynic with his staff and single cloak and knapsack, the bucolic poetry of writers like Theocritus, Ovid's theory of the Golden Age, Seneca's description of the noble savage—and as can be seen in Tacitus, it was quite possible to write history from this perspective. [96]

Eusebius's historical theories made an interesting contrast with these Greek and Roman ideas that had come before. The life of savages was never romanticized by him. The Edenic life was lifted by him to a nonphysical, precosmic, spiritual realm. He had much more in common with positive Greek ideas of historical progress than he had with Latin ideas of corruption and decline, even though he placed a fall into immorality at the beginning of history. Although Hesiod's account of the end of the Age of Iron had had faintly apocalyptic overtones, and although orthodox Stoics believed that this present cosmos would end in a World Conflagration, Eusebius (as shall be seen in more detail in chapter 7) had a much keener sense, not only that this world would come to an end some day, but that he himself was living well towards the end of historical time. [97] Although theories

---

[96]An especially important study of the history of romantic primitivism in the Graeco-Roman period is Ragnar Höistad, *Cynic Hero and Cynic King: Studies in the Cynic Conception of Man* (Uppsala: C. Bloms, 1948). See also Donald R. Dudley, *A History of Cynicism, from Diogenes to the Sixth Century A.D.* (London: Methuen, 1937). Tacitus's description of primeval humanity is very similar to Ovid's account of the Golden Age at the beginning of his *Metamorphoses*. The human race's fall into corruption is attributed by the latter to the invention of the ship, and to the consequent beginning, not just of warfare abroad, but also of maritime commerce—surely an aristocratic senatorial bias at work! In Seneca, see the tragic hero's description of his earlier virtuous and idyllic life in *Hippolytus* 483-564, where again the development of shipbuilding and maritime commerce are said to have produced the fall of the human race.

[97]Eusebius seems to have believed, at all points in his life, that history would be brought to its final end with the full paraphernalia of apocalyptic horrors falling

of historical cycles were fairly common in Greek speculation about history especially, there were clearly no important cyclical elements in Eusebius, at least as far as the this-worldly sequence of events was concerned. The history of this world for him was a line with a beginning and an end, not a circle.[98]

The question of whether Eusebius believed in some larger hypercosmic cycle still remains. He did reject that early Stoic cyclic theory of time that held that the historical events stretching from any one World-Conflagration to the next were exact duplicates of the events that had taken place in every previous cycle, and that would take place in every subsequent cycle.[99] On the other hand, he was an Origenist, and could easily have been influenced by the well-known theory of transmigration, espoused by some of the radical Origenists, which held that the soul was reincarnated in different bodies in different circumstances, in an endless series of existences.[100]

---

on earth. Christ would come for the second time, to battle the Antichrist and defeat him. The earth would be destroyed, all the stars extinguished, and then the Last Judgment would take place. Eus. DE 3.3.14-15(106ab), 3.17(106d); 9.15.6-8(453ac); 15. fragments 5 and 6. De laud. 12.5. Theoph. 4.29. The total story of the world's history, for him, ran from the primordial fall into time and space at the beginning to this final cataclysmic termination of all earthly things at the end. Although I suggested the possibility of showing development in Eusebius's eschatological ideas in my article in Religious Studies Review 9 (1983): 118-23, I have subsequently rejected that hypothesis. Eusebius's writings seem to show a mixture of apocalyptic and Platonizing elements at all the stages of his life that can be reconstructed. This negative conclusion about any fundamental philosophical development in no way, of course, implies a rejection of Robert M. Grant's quite different observation, that Eusebius changed his mind about the book of Revelation and Papias. Grant is certainly correct on this point.

[98]But see the warnings against the overenthusiastic speculations of many modern theologians on the "Greek mind's" understanding of time as a circle, and the "Hebrew mind's" understanding of time as a line, in Arnaldo Momigliano, "Time in Ancient Historiography," History and Theory Beiheft 6, History and the Concept of Time (1966): 1-23.

[99]Eus. Theoph. 2.21. Augustine rejected Stoic cyclicism in similar fashion several generations later, in De civ. Dei 12.14(13).

[100]One must be careful about attributing this doctrine to Origen himself, as Henry Chadwick has warned in his chapter on "Origen" in The Cambridge History of Later Greek and Early Medieval Philosophy, ed. A. H. Armstrong (Cambridge: Cambridge University Press, 1967) 190-92.

Eusebius did not teach such a cyclic theory in the surviving parts of his writings, [101] but on the other hand never condemned such an opinion either. Such an argument from silence is a weak one, but it is still difficult to avoid being suspicious when Eusebius condemns Plato's doctrine of transmigration of souls only because it asserted that human souls could be reborn in the bodies of *animals*—"dogs, hedgehogs, ants, horses, donkeys."[102] Since the Origenistic theory spoke of transmigration only by ascent and descent up and down the great chain of rational being (daemons, human beings, sun, moon, planets, and angels), Eusebius's violent attack on Plato begged the important question too neatly.

Even if he did have some hidden sympathy with the radical Origenistic theory of multiple reincarnations, nevertheless Eusebius's basic view of temporality was linear and not cyclical. In his metaphysics, the basic ground of the universe itself was said to be pure, undifferentiated, unidirectional, linear temporal process. [103] His technical term for this was ὁ αἰών; in English, "aeon." This pure temporal flow, or better, this mysterious ground on which we construct our human concept of temporal sequence, was "stretched out in a straight line and stretches onward into infinity."[104] The Greek word αἰών is often translated into English as "eternity," but since the Platonic Ideas are also, in a different way, αἰώνιαι (eternal), the use of the word eternity can suggest a static view of the ground of the universe that is quite misleading. Eusebius used the word αἰών to mean eternity in the same sense as the famous passage from Marcus Aurelius: "As a river consisting of all things that come into being, aye, a rushing torrent, is eternity (ὁ αἰών). No sooner is a thing sighted than it is carried past, and lo, another is passing, and it too will be carried away."[105]

On the other hand, the aeon, for Eusebius, was not the same as χρόνος. The latter word is usually translated into English as "time," but

---

[101]Eus. *De laud.* 1 is ambiguous, and could have been intended to be read in an orthodox manner as simply a rather luxuriant liturgical hyperbole—"The timeless aeons before this heaven and earth, and others of these, infinite aeons of aeons, before all subsistence of visible things, acknowledge Him the sole and supreme sovereign and Lord." The passage about aeons in *De laud.* 2 is similarly ambiguous.

[102]Eus. *Theoph.* 2.44.

[103]Eus. *De laud.* 6.4-5.

[104]Eus. *De laud.* 6.4.

[105]Marcus Aurelius, *Meditations* 4.43.

Glenn F. Chesnut

frequently had a far narrower and more specific meaning in Greek philosophical language, so that this common translation also can be misleading
to the average English reader. "Chronological time" might be a better
translation of the word. When Eusebius speculated on the true meaning of
χϱόνος, he pointed out that what one meant by the present, that is, "the
now," was always given its conceptual meaning by the human mind in the
context of memory images of the past, and mental constructs embodying
calculations and expectations for the future. But all the meaning was coming from purely mental constructs of what we imagined the past-present-
future sequence to be, so that χϱόνος, "chronological time," was a construct of the human mind that only interpreted what the mind thought the
onward flow of the aeon to be at the moment. The aeon was what was truly
real; chronological time (past, present, and future) was the human mind's
interpretation of it. [106] So the aeon was not the same as time, but it also
must be pointed out that it transcended the realm of unchanging formal

---

[106]Eusebius had a well-developed metaphysical theory of χϱόνος or "time."
The temporal creature who was actually immersed in the flow of time could not,
from his position *in medias res*, perceive any beginning to time or any other limitation to time's extent. And not only were the limits of time inaccessible to human
thought, there were also epistemological and metaphysical problems attached to
the simple division of time into past, present, and future. The past is not (οὐκ ἔστιν) because it is already gone, and the future also is not (οὐδ' ἔστιν) because
it has not yet arrived. Although past and future therefore had the ontological status of nonbeing, this did not mean that one could fall back on the present (τὸ
νῦν) to find true reality. There was a necessary time lag between the actual occurrence of the present and thinking about the present, such that the present could
never be grasped by the mind while it was still present. Therefore one was thrown
back on the unreality of the past or the unreality of the future if one attempted to
grasp any object of thought, either in expectation of events in the future or in a
synoptic view of events in the past. Therefore "the aeon," that is, pure temporal
process itself, or one might say the ground on which we construct our human conception of "before" and "after," was totally resistant in all parts to any true com-
prehension by the human reason—Eus. *De laud.* 6.3. On the impossibility of
conceptualizing the present tense as genuinely present reality, and its conceptual
absorption into the nonbeing of the future and the past, one might compare the
treatment of the distinction between past, present, and future in the Stoic idea of
time; see S. Sambursky, *Physics of the Stoics* (London: Routledge and Kegan Paul,
1959) 103-104.

knowledge in the same way that it transcended the realm of χρόνος, so to view it as static is also totally misleading. [107]

Eusebius said that God created the universe by hypostatizing it upon the fabric of this pure undifferentiated flow ("the aeon") like embroidery sewn on a long piece of ribbon. [108] First God created matter (ὕλη) and placed it in the already existing flow of the aeon, and than added form (εἶδος), and then created three-dimensional space by combining matter and form into body (σῶμα). Then came the four elements, and the numerical basis for the chronological division of time into days, months, and years. [109] But since the basic flow of the aeon on which this creation was grounded was linear and not cyclic, whatever Eusebius's position on any Origenistic ideas of possible multiple reincarnations of all the human souls in that universe, there was no idea in his thought of endless cycles simply going nowhere. The life of the universe moved forward and onward continuously with meaning and purpose.

Eusebius did not basically view time and history as cyclical. His view of the overall pattern of history in fact placed him closer to those Greek historians who had believed in progress in history than to the typical Latin historians. Unlike these Latin writers, he rejected any notion that the Roman empire was declining and falling into moral corruption and decadence. He rejected the basic premise of romantic primitivism, which held that civilization was necessarily evil and corrupting in itself. In opposition

---

[107]See G. F. Chesnut, *Images of Christ: An Introduction to Christology* (Minneapolis: Seabury Press, 1984) 52-53. The popular interpretations of the modern philosopher and historian of philosophy, Charles Hartshorne, who argues that the ancients viewed eternity as static and refused to accept that temporal process was the truly concrete and real, can be very misleading if read back into the Greek patristic period; whether he is basically correct on Western medieval philosophy, the primary target of his attack, is a different question that I am less qualified to judge.

[108]Eus. *De laud.* 6.4.

[109]Eus. *De laud.* 6.5 Beyond this present aeon there will be another life or existence (ζωή, βίος) where the good will be rewarded and the wicked punished. This will be a realm of "nonchronological time (χρόνος ἄχρονος)" that is "not defined by intervals of days and months, the revolutions of years, or the recurrence of times and seasons" (Eus. *De laud.* 6.9, 6.19), but instead presumably some sort of pure noetic existence.

both to this and to the later view that Augustine was to take in his *City of God* roughly a century later, Eusebius held that the growth of civilization and the growth of true religion necessarily went hand in hand.[110] To Eusebius, the history of the preceding thousand years had been one of continual progress in both,[111] a position that he had held even before Constantine supplied him with a truly dramatic conclusion to that story.

The idea that real historical progress was possible, and the idea that true religion had the responsibility for creating civilized life itself, were among the most important things that Eusebius bequeathed to the middle ages. In spite of Augustine's attempt to provide a different understanding of history for the West at the time of the fifth-century collapse,[112] one of

---

[110]In his *City of God* Augustine held that the Two Cities had always existed, since the beginning of life on earth. Whatever growth there had been in knowledge of the civilized arts, the tension between those two bodies of people had never been affected. At the fundamental moral level, there had been neither progress nor decline. There had been as many people who truly loved God in primitive times as there were in his own time, while the opportunities for the subtler sins of pride and power in a sophisticated civilization made the Romans of his own day as liable to sin as any naked savage.

[111]Walter Goffart, "Zosimus, the First Historian of Rome's Fall," *American Historical Review* 76 (1971): 412-41, esp. 432, describes this "Christian theory of progress elaborated by Eusebius and expressed by the other Church historians," and then explains the pessimistic reaction to it that eventually came in the early sixth century.

[112]Eusebius may also of course have been partly responsible for creating one of the major problems that Augustine had to resolve in his *City of God*. For Eusebius, the Four Kingdoms in Daniel 2:31-45 were the Assyrian, Persian, Macedonian, and Roman empires (Eus. *DE* 15.fragment 1), which unfortunately implied that the inevitable collapse of the Roman government that Augustine saw coming after the sack of Rome by the Visigoths in 410 was the immediate precursor to the apocalyptic end of the world itself. This may well have been an important hidden agenda that Augustine had to accomplish in writing a "survival manual" for Christians caught in the fall of the Roman empire. For influences on Augustine's interpretation of biblical apocalyptic ideas, see also the Tyconius literature, for example, J. Haussleiter, "Die lateinische Apokalypse der alten Afrikanischen Kirche" in T. Zahn, *Forschungen zur Geschichte des neutestamentlichen Kanons und der altkirchlichen Literatur* (Erlangen: A. Deichert, 1891) 4:1-244; T. Hahn, *Tyconius-Studien*, Studien zur Ge-

the forces that eventually gave Western Europe the courage to pull itself out of the dark age into which it began to fall was perhaps the implicit optimism of Eusebius's account of the possibilities of history. He gave the middle ages a positive vision of what humans could do to create civilization out of savagery.

schichte der Theologie und der Kirche 6, 2 (Aalen: Scientia Verlag, 1971); and E. Dinkler, "Ticonius," in Pauly-Wissowa, *Real-Encyclopädie*, Zweite Reihe 6, 1 (1936) cols. 849-56.

CHAPTER 5

Eusebius:
The Rational
and the Irrational
in Human Motivation

The forces that motivate human beings in history are a complex mixture of rational and irrational impulses. Any well-developed theory of history has to take account of both kinds. Eusebius's understanding of this problem came out especially clearly in his "salvation history" discussed in the previous chapter. His description of the various stages through which world history had passed and the forces operating at each stage delineated more clearly than in any other part of his thought what he considered to be the true driving and motivating forces within human life.

From one point of view, Eusebius's philosophy of history appeared to be a rather optimistic rationalism. Human beings were created by God as rational creatures possessing free will. In fact, as has often been pointed out, in Greek thought what was normally meant by rationality necessarily implied the faculty of choice. By proper exercise of their reason and their freedom, human beings had the inborn power to build an ideal world for themselves. Eusebius's emphasis on free will and rationality caused him to insist that even fallen human beings still retained this all-important freedom of the will. In this he maintained the tradition that Eastern theology in general has always followed. In the fall from their preexistent state, human beings had been given bodies and cast into history, but in spite of this, there were still authentic human possibilities within this historical existence that were well worth struggling to attain. Like many other Eastern theologians, Eusebius in his understanding of history showed no trace of that fundamentally tragic view of fallen humanity's irrevocable brokenness such as is found to a certain extent in Augustine, and carried out even further in Luther and Calvin—that is, that brooding sense of men's and women's utter inability to achieve even their full, natural *historical* possibilities after the Fall. Over the first few centuries of human life on earth, early humanity had gradually descended into savagery, ignorance, and superstition; but this decline had taken place by acts of free will within this historical dimension of existence, and by acts of free will it could be reversed. To Eusebius (unlike Augustine a century later), a perfected human society, built around true dedication to God, was fully possible on this earth.

The rationalistic side of this understanding of the human possibility was seen especially clearly in Eusebius's picture of the Old Testament patriarchs who lived in the first stage of the world's history in his schematization. These pre-Mosaic "Friends of God," who practiced a purely natural religion based on "natural concepts" alone, and who lived centuries before the coming of Jesus, were nevertheless acclaimed by Eusebius as "Christians in fact, if not in name."[1] He described their religion in the language—often slightly incongruous—of Greek rationalism. He said that Noah, Abraham, Jacob and the others devoted themselves to the study of "physics," which he used in the classical Greek sense to mean questions about cosmogony, attempts to identify the first principle of Nature, and other such problems; and that they saw that "the order of the whole cosmos" required them to look higher, to a Creator God. They learned to make the body-soul distinction, Eusebius said, and saw that the rational soul was the highest and best part of humankind. They also saw that knowledge of God, and friendship with him, was the proper eudaemonistic end of human life.[2] They possessed every virtue (ἀρετή) in the Greek sense of the word. Their religion was a pure and rational one because it was based upon knowledge of the Logos, the rational structure of reality as a whole.[3]

Eusebius was rather like an eighteenth-century Deist in that he believed that the basic truths of religion—the immortality of the soul, morality based on natural law and right reason, and so on—were easily demonstrable to any intelligent, intellectually free, educated person. In this kind of Logos theology there was no Thomistic distinction between "truths of reason" and "truths of revelation": *all* truths were basically truths of rea-

---

[1]Eus. *HE* 1.4.4-6.

[2]Eus. *PE* 7.3-4 and 6(301b-303c and 304a-305a).

[3]Eus. *HE* 1.4.

son.[4] Eusebius did not believe that by his period of history an educated person required any appeal to faith or the authority of the Church. His whole historical method, for example, was an attempt to demonstrate the correctness of the Christian historical record on purely natural historical grounds. Hence he appealed to Josephus and other non-Christian witnesses, written documents, relative chronology, and so forth—sometimes naively from a modern point of view, but perfectly scientifically in basic intent.

Eusebius's rationalism was created by the Logos theology that lay at the heart of his entire understanding of religion and history. The centrality of this idea was the reason why his *Church History*—which was mostly devoted to pure narrative history—nevertheless began with a short theological dissertation on the nature of the Logos. In his scheme for world history, as has been seen, the Logos appeared as a central concept again and again. Eusebius's Logos theology was the thing that most set him off, not only from the pagan Graeco-Roman historians and Josephus, but also from the other great Christian theorizer about history, Augustine.[5]

Eusebius derived his Logos theology from the heritage of second- and third-century Christian thought. It came ultimately from Middle Platonic and Philonic combinations of the Stoic divinized World Soul with Platonic

---

[4]Revelation was historically necessary because fallen humanity had gone astray into error and had been caught up in a vicious circle of self-perpetuating ignorance. But revelation in this sort of Logos theology was a revealing of truths that could be demonstrated rationally once knowledge of them had been reintroduced into the body of human knowledge.

[5]Compare for example *De civ. Dei* 16.29, where Augustine mounted a direct attack on the Logos-theology interpretation of one Old Testament passage that was a major foundation stone in the Logos-theophany schematization of history. In the *City of God*, God was generally described as acting immediately in history by directly manipulating the created things that he had made (10.15), or as acting indirectly through angels (4.17). In the *City of God*, Augustine never spoke of God the Father acting in history by using the Logos as His intermediary. Albert C. Outler has discussed Augustine's use of the Logos doctrine at various points in his intellectual development in an essay on "The Person and Work of Christ" in *A Companion to the Study of St. Augustine*, ed. Roy W. Battenhouse (New York: Oxford University Press, 1955) 343-70.

idealism.[6] Ultimate reality as it was in itself—God the Father—was an un-knowable, unfathomable abyss. But the Logos, which *was* knowable, was an icon or image of the Father. Ontologically, the Logos was related to the Father as a painted portrait was related to the human being of whom it was a likeness. In more specific terms, the Logos was the formal, rational con-tent of all human knowledge. In a Platonic context that meant that it in-cluded archetypes of all human virtues, since to a Platonist the virtues (such as justice, for example) were the most important of the eternal forms. As was discussed in the previous chapter, the Logos also included what today would be called the laws of nature.[7] This was also a highly significant theo-logical statement. God was not completely "out there" in some transcen-dent heaven, totally separated from life on earth. Instead, Eusebius's world was continually lit with the light of the divine. In the natural growth of a flower or tree, or in the natural fall of raindrops from the clouds, the hand of God was seen immediately at work. Nature was the theophany of God. Last of all, the Logos was πρόνοια or "providence" in the ancient Stoic sense. Over and over Stoic writings insisted that nothing that happened to human beings, whether good or bad, was accidental in any ultimate sense. Whatever happened was part of God's deliberate plan for that particular person. The universal Logos, in that sense, was therefore God's plan for human history. Conversely, to say that history had a λόγος was to say that history had a "plot." It was a meaningful story, with an inherent system of values that separated out good characters and bad. As these characters re-acted to one another in a chronological series of incidents, each incident led in some way naturally and logically into the next. To say that human history had a λόγος was therefore to say that there was a meaning to his-

---

[6]A preceding chapter discussed the role of the Logos in Eusebius's understand-ing of providence. See also G. F. Chesnut, *Images of Christ: An Introduction to Chris-tology* (Minneapolis: Seabury Press, 1984) 35-38, 44-47, 52-53, 92-93, 99, 139.

[7]Νόμος, ὅρος, and λόγος ("law," "limitation," and "rational structure") were used by Eusebius as roughly equivalent terms when he was describing those reg-ular behavioral patterns and sequences that human beings discovered in their ob-servation of Nature. These rules were part of the overall Logos-structure of the cosmos and defined the physical limitations placed upon each kind of creature as part of its nature. See Eus. *PE* 7.10.1-3(314bd); *De laud.* 11.14; 12.5 (duplicated in *Theoph.* 1.23); *DE* 4.2.2(146cd).

tory. It was susceptible to human analysis, both logically and morally. It was not a meaningless, directionless struggle of purely amoral forces.

Eusebius's thesis that the good emperors had been rewarded by God's providence while the bad emperors had all been punished paralleled the general Old Testament understanding that the religious policy of the Hebrew king determined the treatment both king and nation received from God's hand. But it was also in fact an assertion that there were "laws of history" in the same way that there were laws of nature.[8] Eusebius claimed that this was an empirically observable pattern in history, which an emperor could take advantage of on pragmatic grounds.[9] This raised the important theological question of whether divine providence was something that could really be "proven" in the same way that a scientific hypothesis in chemistry or physics could be proven. In the ancient period, Augustine rejected this Eusebian theory that providence was an empirically observable, objective pattern in the *external* course of events, and held instead that providence appeared in the *inner* history of the human subjects involved. For Augustine "the meaning of history" lay "not in the flux of outward events, but in the hidden drama of sin and redemption."[10] Sometimes the good prospered, but often they suffered misfortune; sometimes the wicked suffered misfortune, but often they prospered. The true meaning of history, Augustine asserted, was not to be sought in any simple-minded, externalized calculation of materialistic success and prosperity; instead, it was to be sought in the inner spiritual history of each individual human soul, as God providentially arranged each external historical situation in which the soul found itself in order to chasten it, comfort it, reward it, warn it, and divert it from

---

[8]See the contemporary philosophical discussion of whether there are "laws of history" in the collection of articles assembled by Patrick Gardiner, ed., *Theories of History* (New York: Free Press, 1959) in his section on "Explanation and Laws," 344-475. Representative articles by Carl G. Hempel, Morton White, Ernest Nagel, and others are reprinted there.

[9]Eusebius's emphasis on deliberate, pragmatic calculation became especially prominent after 324 C.E., when Constantine had conquered both East and West and had become sole ruler of the Roman world; see *HE* 10.8.2, 9.5. See also *VC* 1.3, 23; 4.74-75 (the conclusion to the *Life of Constantine*).

[10]Henry Chadwick, *The Early Church* (Harmondsworth, England: Penguin, 1967) 226-27.

future spiritual dangers.[11] The important thing to Augustine was a person's subjective reaction to the situation in which he was placed.

> For as the same fire causes gold to glow brightly, and chaff to smoke . . .
> so the same violence of affliction proves, purges, clarifies the good, but
> damns, ruins, exterminates the wicked. And thus it is that in the same af-
> fliction the wicked detest God and blaspheme, while the good pray and
> praise.[12]

For Eusebius, this by itself would have been too subjective an approach; the idea of providence had to have an objective, verifiable component. Otherwise the skeptics who regarded the Old Testament understanding of history as "mythical" could not, he believed, be refuted.

In all the foregoing ways, Eusebius was a thoroughgoing rationalist. On the other hand, he was a Greek, and he was not so naive as to believe that a simple, rational counterargument would stop a person hell-bent for the destruction of himself and those around him. Eusebius had a Euripidean sense of the daemonic. As the old Greek tragedies showed, there were strange powers that could destroy human beings. When Aphrodite crept into her heart, Phaedra in blind passion eventually killed not only herself, but indirectly her stepson as well; at the very moment when Heracles had triumphantly rescued his wife and sons, Hera sent madness into his mind, and in his insanity he turned and slaughtered those he had come to save; it was Apollo who drove Orestes to the murder of his mother Clytemnestra; the maenads tore King Pentheus into pieces with their bare hands under the inspiration of Dionysus.[13] From the time of Homer, these strange

---

[11]The *Confessions* is the account of one human soul's inner spiritual history written along those general lines. It is often a drama of irony, as Augustine makes the
right decisions for the wrong reasons, is led in the proper paths by people acting
out of improper motives, and gradually makes his progress *toward* his conversion
by struggling as hard as he can to *renounce* Christianity. See, for example, *Conf.*
1.9.14-10.16, 12.19; 5.6.10-7.13, 8.14, 12.22-13.23; 7.9.13. The overall effect
is to deny any value to human pragmatic calculations when dealing with God's
providence, a point of view that sets Augustine at odds with Eusebius (as well as
the later church historians who wrote in the Eusebian tradition).

[12]Aug. *De civ. Dei* 1.8, compare 18.54.

[13]Euripides, *Hippolytus* 26-28; *Heracles* 815-873; *Electra* 1266-1267 and 1296-
1297; *Bacchae* 1074-1152.

mental occurrences were ascribed to "gods" or "daemons"—external forces that sometimes brought a sudden flash of insight or recognition, but equally often brought foolish refusal to understand, or pounding emotion that blocked the clear perception of sanity and reality. [14]

The Greek historians knew about the daemonic also. As Herodotus said, "a large army is completely destroyed by a small one whenever God is jealous and sends them fear [φόβος] or thunder." [15] The strange dreams that drove Xerxes and Artabanus to march against the Greeks were an even more primitive intrusion of the bullying, menacing divine force that suppressed human rationality. [16] In Xenophon there were two examples of the daemonic, in one case suddenly filling a whole army with overwhelming panic, in the other driving a state to start a war. [17] Demonology could be seen all the way down to the end of pagan historiography, as in Zosimus's early sixth-century account of the decline and fall of Rome. By this late period, the daemons were probably rather more Neoplatonic than Homer's and Herodotus's, [18] but they still appeared as agents in his history. [19]

In Homeric Greek there had been no clear-cut distinction between "gods" and "daemons." By Plato's time however, daemons had come to be regarded in a more specific sense as those beings who stood halfway be-

---

[14]This psychological aspect to divine or daemonic intervention was well characterized by E. R. Dodds, *The Greeks and the Irrational*, 3-12. An excellent summary of the various senses of the word δαίμων and their historical development is given in Arthur Darby Nock, "The Emperor's Divine Comes," *Journal of Roman Studies* 37 (1947): 102-16. For a fuller account, see the article on "Geister (Dämonen)," *Reallexikon für Antike und Christentum* 9, Lieferung 68 (1974) and 69 (1975), cols. 546-797. This extensive survey includes studies of demons in ancient Egypt, Mesopotamia, Syria, Asia Minor, Israel, Iran, pre-Hellenistic Greece, the Hellenistic world, Judaism, the imperial Roman world, the New Testament, and the early church fathers, with bibliographies for each major section.

[15]Her. 7.10.

[16]Her. 7.12-18.

[17]Xen. *Hell.* 4.4.12; 6.4.3.

[18]So James J. Buchanan and Harold T. Davis, in their translation of Zosimus's *Historia Nova* (San Antonio TX: Trinity University Press, 1967) ix, 232n.

[19]Zosimus, *Historia Nova* 5.35 (τὸν . . . δαίμονα) and 41 (ὁ . . . ἀλιτή-ριος δαίμων).

tween gods and human beings in nature, and served as mediators between the two sides.[20] This remained the standard Greek idea: Eusebius characterized the pagan doctrine of daemons of his own time in much the same way.[21]

A Jewish tradition also lay in the background here, of course. Old Testament figures like the *bene elohim* who formed the council of the gods, and *hasātān*, "the satan," originally a title of office held by a "public prosecutor" in the divine court, gradually developed over the centuries into the hostile thrones, lordships, principalities, and authorities who were portrayed in the Pauline writings of the New Testament as the world-rulers of this aeon of darkness.[22] Early Christian theologians like Justin Martyr turned this set of New Testament ideas into a polemic doctrine of daemons directed explicitly against the pagan world, and it was the daemons of this antipagan polemic who appeared in large part in Eusebius's own thought.

Following what had therefore become the traditional account by the fourth century C.E., Eusebius said that what the Christians called δαίμονες were once angels, but that they had fallen. The majority of οἱ δαίμονες were thrown into Tartarus, but a small portion were left to haunt the earth and fly about in the sublunar air.[23] Since they had once been angels, they were noetic and spiritual beings,[24] but they "love to dwell in graves and monuments of the dead and in all loathsome and impure matter, and delight in bloodshed and gore and the bodies of animals of all kinds, and in the exhalation from the fumes of incense and of vapors rising out of the earth."[25] Pagan sacrifices were actually sacrifices to these daemons, who delighted in them.[26] The daemons were not in fact gods, but they wanted

---

[20]*Oxford Classical Dictionary* (1949 ed.,), s.v. "Daimon"; Plato, *Symposium* 202E; G. B. Caird, *Principalities and Powers* (Oxford: Clarendon Press, 1956) 12-13.

[21]See for example Eus. *PE* 4.5(141a-142c).

[22]For a complete account of this development, see Caird, *Principalities and Powers*.

[23]Eus. *PE* 7.16(328a-330b); *DE* 3.3.18-19(106d-107b).

[24]Eus. *DE* 2.3.116(75d-76a) νοητούς . . . καὶ πνευματικούς.

[25]Eus. *PE* 5.2.1-2(181[bis]ad).

[26]Eus. *VC* 1.13 and 16; *De laud.* 2. Psalm 95(96):5 said, in the Septuagint version, "All the gods of the nations are daemons." See Eus. *PE* 4.16.20(161d); 7.16(328a-330b); and note the comment in Caird, *Principalities and Powers*, 12-13.

to be regarded by human beings as gods and honored as gods. [27] The daemons tempted men and women with the licentious myths of polytheism, [28]
and gave the illusion of divine support to idol worship by causing the idols
to move, by giving oracles, by causing apparitions or portents, and by
healing people (which they could easily do, since these were people whom
the daemons themselves had first made ill). [29]

Eusebius's daemons were also, even more significantly, a very vivid and
striking personification of three important psychological forces. They were
first the power of Πλάνη (Error). [30] In the ancient world, Error could refer
to something much more powerful than a merely subjective human psychic
state. It could be regarded as a personal force at work in the universe, attacking human beings from without, as an external power, and bringing
them under its control. [31] Eusebius's daemons were Error in this sense. [32] Eusebius also spoke of οἱ δαίμονες in terms of that very ancient personification, Ἀπάτη (Deception), [33] who, in the classical pattern of tragic
downfall, blinded men and women with Hope or Desire so that they would
plunge irretrievably to their ruin. The irrationality of the tragic hero, one
remembers, was rooted in his or her mind in a deadly sort of way that was
self-perpetuating and normally invincible against rational evidence and arguments. For Eusebius to have appropriated this language of tragedy meant
that he was portraying the majority of the human race as caught up in some

---

[27]Eus. PE 7.16(328a-330b); DE 3.3.18-19(106d-107b).

[28]Eus. DE 4.9.1-9(158c-160b).

[29]Eus. PE 5.2.1-2(181[bis]ad); 7.16(328a-330b); De laud. 2. See also Contra Hier.
31, where Eusebius asserts that Apollonius's miracles were only the work of daemons.

[30]A word that occurs again and again when Eusebius is talking about the daemons, see for example HE 2.3.2, 4.11.3, 10.4.13; De laud. 6.21.

[31]One sees Πλάνη personified under its own name in the gnostic Gospel of
Truth, for example. See The Gospel of Truth (17:14-18:38), trans. and commentary
by Kendrick Grobel (Nashville: Abingdon Press, 1960) 42-54.

[32]And could therefore be overturned only by the personified cosmic power of
Truth (Ἀλήθεια) itself, that is, the divine Logos—Eus. HE 2.14.1-3; 4.7.1-3,
7.12-13, 7.15; 5.pref.3-4, 14.1-16.1; 6.18.1.

[33]Eus. HE 4.7.10-11; 10.4.16; De laud. 13.6.

racial drive toward tragic doom. Men's and women's reasons appeared
blinded by some uncanny power that had crept over them. Finally, the
daemons were the personification of Φθόνος (Envy or Jealousy). The classical idea of the jealousy of the gods was thoroughly pagan, but it had been
ingrained so deeply in the Greek consciousness that Eusebius as a matter
of course believed that the very existence of human prosperity could in some
perverse way be responsible for arousing the agents of its own destruction.
As a Christian, however, he could not believe that this was malicious action on the part of *God*. Furthermore, the Hebraic tradition had always
stressed the goodness of the material creation and the goodness of prosperity (*shalom*). For this reason, the divine envy was fastened onto οἱ δαίμονες instead.

Whenever affairs in the Church reached a state of prosperity, for example, the φθόνος of the daemons was always aroused.[34] But Eusebius went
much further than the ancient Greeks, and accused οἱ δαίμονες not only
of a desire to disrupt prosperity, but also of a hatred of the fair and the
beautiful itself and an active desire for evil for its own sake: he speaks of ὁ
μισόκαλος φθόνος of ὁ φιλοπόνηρος δαίμων.[35] In the classical Greek
period, φθόνος (as a divine motive) had been able to range in meaning all
the way from displeasure at excessive human arrogance to petty jealousy,
but in Christian usage the word was not only denied all its positive range
of meaning but also extended in meaning to signify an active hatred of the
Good-and-the-Beautiful (καλοκἀγαθία) itself, a motivating emotion which
to a Greek would have seemed perverse indeed. In Eusebius's theory of free
will, as observed in chapter 3, this daemonic will was the diametric opposite of that fundamental act of will that brought salvation.

In other contexts as well, Eusebius continually described the daemonic
as μισόκαλος,[36] "hater of the good," and φιλοπόνηρος,[37] "lover of evil."
It was an attempt to deal with the same dark part of the human personality
with which Augustine tried to struggle, more than two generations later,

---

[34]Eus. *HE* 8.1.6. *VC* 2.61; 73; 3.59.

[35]Eus. *HE* 10.4.14, 4.57, 8.2; *VC* 4.41; compare *DE* 4.9.1-9(158c-160b), envy
of humanity's salvation.

[36]Eus. *HE* 2.14.1; 4.7.1; 5.14.1; 21.2; 10.4.14, 8.2. *VC* 3.1, 4.41.

[37]Eus. *HE* 5.14.1; 10.4.14, 4.57, 8.2.

in his account of the pear-stealing incident in the *Confessions*.[38] Augustine searched his memory of those adolescent years to try to analyze the motives that drove him to that act of pure vandalism, and finally decided that the major component was a love of evil itself—not a selfish desire to gain any material thing that he needed or wanted, nor a thirst for revenge, nor a fear of losing anything he already had, but seemingly a desire of evil for evil's own sake. For Eusebius, this was a basic part of the character of the fallen human soul,[39] and so it can be seen that even though Eusebius credited salvation to rationality and gnosis, he did not make the simpleminded rationalist's equation and say that sin was only ignorance, nothing more. Eusebius was well aware of the dark depths of the fallen soul and saw within it a frightening, uncanny, willful volition for the evil that he could only display in its full horror by calling upon the mythological concept of the demoniacal. One of the most important aspects of Christ's saving work was his coming to defeat these daemons and to free human beings from their grasp.[40]

The crucial attribute that separated the saved from the damned in Eusebius's system was also something more than simply rationality; it was εὐσέβεια, "piety." It was the great fundamental criterion that served to separate the sheep from the goats, and therefore played the same kind of role as *caritas* in Augustine's system, or "faith" in sixteenth-century Reformation thought.[41] When Eusebius explained what the word "gospel" meant in *PE* 1.1.2-5(2ad), he defined it as the opportunity to turn to God in εὐσέβεια, graciously given now to all humankind. In what can be recognized as a foretaste of later Byzantine spirituality, Eusebius regarded εὐσέβεια basically as human participation in the cosmic liturgy. All rational creatures, from the lowliest human being to the highest rank of angel, were supposed to be engaged in a continual, harmonious hymn and prayer to the God above the cosmos.

Eusebius noted how, thanks to the missionary success of Christianity, assemblies of people from all nations had been formed over the entire in-

---

[38]*Conf.* 2.4(9)-9(17).

[39]Eus. *HE* 10.4.57.

[40]Eus. *HE* 10.4.13-16; *PE* 7.16(328a-330b); *DE* 7.3.50-51(359c).

[41]*Eusebeia* was a distinguishing mark, for example, of the ancient, pre-Mosaic "Friends of God."

habited earth to raise up hymns to God.[42] The singing of hymns also went on in the superhuman levels of reality; God the Father was hymned by the Son and the Holy Spirit, and by all the angels, archangels, spirits, and heavenly hosts. He was worshiped by the principalities, powers, thrones, and dominions who played such an important role in Pauline theology. He was praised in hymnody by the sun, moon, and stars (rational beings possessing free will in Eusebius's thought world). He was blessed by the invisible powers of the sublunary sphere, who flew through the air on wings.[43] After the Christian emperor Constantine had become sole ruler of the entire Roman world, Eusebius could also extend this hierarchy of worship downwards in continuous order on earth as well: it started with the Augustus, and went down through the Caesars, the provincial governors, the army, and finally the private citizens.[44] Eusebius visualized all these beings united in one universal worship service, in which "the voice of mortal man is blended with the harmony of the angelic choirs in heaven."[45] This universal worship service took place on two ontological levels simultaneously, Eusebius said, in language frequently found also in later Eastern Orthodox thought: in a realm of Platonic transcendence was the paradigmatic worship service, while down in the Church ἐπὶ γῆς a worship service went on as a "noetic icon" (νοερὰν . . . εἰκόνα) of the transcendent paradigm above.[46] Participation in the cosmic liturgy was the proper end of human life; Eusebius's whole theology of history and doctrine of man were centered around this idea. Indeed in one place he said that humanity was expressly created by God so that the universal worship service would extend

---

[42]Eus. HE 8.1.5; PE 7.16.11(330ab).

[43]Eus. PE 7.15.15-17(327ad); Theoph. 1.41.

[44]Eus. De laud. 1.

[45]Eus. De laud. 10.5-6; see also Theoph. 1.39-40.

[46]Eus. HE 10.4.69-71. Compare the Cherubic Anthem, one of the most important points in the Eastern Orthodox liturgy of St. John Chrysostom, where the choir sings οἱ τὰ χερουβὶμ μυστικῶς εἰκονίζοντες, "we who allegorically [or symbolically] serve as an icon [or holy image] of the cherubim, sing the thrice-holy hymn to the life-giving Trinity."

all the way down to earth.[47] This was what εὐσέβεια or "piety" meant to Eusebius.

It was only εὐσέβεια that kept humanity in the saving awareness that its ultimate concern was with the God above the cosmos, and not with this-worldly security, material prosperity, and success. The only ultimate alternative to εὐσέβεια, Eusebius therefore believed, was *hedonism*, a captivity to physical pleasure.[48] This produced a vivid dichotomy in his doctrine of sin and salvation: The saved worshiped God as Lord of all, while the damned lived an animal-like existence, captive to the pleasure principle in its most crudely physical sense—like white rats, one would say today, running mazes so that the psychologist will reward them with a piece of cheese.

In conclusion, one might say that Eusebius's understanding of salvation and of history left room for *both* elements of human behavior, the rational and the irrational. For him and for the Logos tradition in which he stood, salvation was a return from the delusions of destructive, emotional, compulsive behavior to the clear light of conscious rationality. The fallen human being was a figure from Greek tragedy: blind, raging, destroying himself and those around him as he obstinately refused to listen to his fellow men and women who tried to bring him back to reason. The agent of salvation for these Christian heirs to Homer and Euripides was fittingly said to be the divine Logos, Holy Reason itself. But even then there was an element beyond the purely rational in salvation itself—εὐσέβεια, a total reabsorption into the cosmic hymn of joy and praise from which humanity in its mythical beginnings had so tragically fallen, and a putting aside of all humanity's lower cares in the vision of God himself.[49] This vision was

---

[47]Eus. *PE* 7.17.3(330d). In connection with the entire preceding discussion of Eusebius's understanding of εὐσέβεια, one might compare the closely similar concept of the "cosmic eucharist" of praise and thanksgiving in Philo's thought: Jean Laporte, *La doctrine eucharistique chez Philon d'Alexandrie* (Paris: Beauchesne, 1972).

[48]Those who lived their lives in this way ought properly to be spoken of as animals rather than human beings, Eusebius said. No one should be called a *true* human being but the true gnostic who was also a person of piety (τὸν ἀληθῶς γνωστικὸν ὁμοῦ καὶ εὐσεβῆ)—Eus. *PE* 7.8.4-7 and 11(306d-307b and 307d).

[49]G. F. Chesnut, *Images of Christ*, chapter 4, "The Vision of God," gives some of the larger context of this way of viewing Christian salvation.

above reason, but by reflection downwards, supportive of reason. The history of the world, to Eusebius, had been a mixture of passionate criminality and the serene bravery of the godly; of tragic alienation from the true vision of God, and heroic return. But through all the centuries of that story, the rational and the irrational had always been equally involved.

CHAPTER 6

Eusebius:
From Youthful Defender
of Religious Liberty
to Spokesman for the
Constantinian Imperial Church

Eusebius's life spanned a period of so many crises for the church that it is not surprising that his ideas on certain issues underwent striking changes. In particular, the triumph of Constantine forced him to deal with a different relationship between church and state than he could probably even have imagined in his youth. His early ideas of religious tolerance, nonviolence, and the peaceful spreading of the gospel by preaching and teaching the truth of God's goodness underwent a forced metamorphosis as he witnessed the incredible brutalities and atrocities committed against innocent human beings during the great persecution. He saw the Christians saved from that onslaught only by a warrior who, in the name of Christ, resorted to force of arms. By the end of his life, the aged Eusebius was preaching to Constantine's sons that they must see that the imperial throne remained at all costs in Christian hands, that they must support the decisions of the church's bishops with all the machinery of the Roman government, and that paganism and all its rites must be extirpated from the empire by force of law and all the power of the state. Much of the literature on Eusebius over the past hundred years has shown such revulsion at the principles he espoused at the very end of his life that even the possibility that earlier stages of his thought might exist was not often assumed.

The young Eusebius was very different, however, from the aged Eusebius. He lived in a totally different world. When he was born, around 260 or shortly thereafter, the midcentury persecutions under Decius and

Valerian had already ended.[1] For about the first forty years of his life, he lived in what modern church historians have sometimes called "the great peace of the church," a long period of open tolerance and freedom such as Christians had never seen before. The emperor could be appealed to openly, as an ally to help resolve Christian disputes.[2] There were Christians in the army, Christian provincial governors, and Christians in the imperial palace itself.[3] One could admit openly that one was a Christian. By 303 C.E., a cathedral had been situated, rather brazenly, immediately opposite the imperial palace in which Diocletian himself sat in state. Church building programs were going on in cities all over the empire, where ever larger structures had to be constructed to hold the increased number of converts.[4] It appeared that Christianity might become a triumphant major religious component of the Roman world by the sheer power of its faith, with full honor and acceptance alongside all the traditional faiths and cults. Even majority status was not unthinkable in some cities and areas.[5]

The beginning of the Great Persecution in February of 303 C.E. was a trauma whose magnitude to the Christians of that time is difficult to exaggerate. Eusebius must have been in his early to mid-forties, a fully trained scholar and theologian by that age. The persecution went on in the East, where Eusebius lived, for eight years without a real break. Constantine did not fight the battle of the Milvian bridge until 312, when Eusebius was in his early fifties and a man of some maturity. Eusebius did not himself come under the rule of a Christian emperor until Constantine defeated Licinius in 324, when he was actually in his sixties.[6] One must always remember

---

[1]Eusebius begins to refer to events in his *Church History* as contemporary with himself in the early part of the reign of Gallienus, who became sole emperor after the capture in 260 of his father, the emperor Valerian, by the Persians. He speaks of Dionysius, who became bishop of Alexandria in 247, and who died in 264 or 265, as of the previous generation. See *HE* 7.14 and 7.26.3.

[2]Eus. *HE* 7.30.19.

[3]Eus. *HE* 8.1.1-5.

[4]Ibid.

[5]See the data, for example, in Timothy D. Barnes, *Constantine and Eusebius* (Cambridge MA: Harvard University Press, 1981) 191.

[6]A point made skillfully by Barnes, *Constantine and Eusebius*, 104; see also 136, 142, 146-47, 162, and 191.

that Eusebius could in no way be construed as acting as a spokesman for Constantine until the very end of his life. Even at that point, as shall be discussed later, there is the question of who was attempting to use whom, since the aged Eusebius had purposes for Constantine's sons that Constantine himself may in no way have shared.

Eusebius's *Church History* was published in a series of different editions during some of the more traumatic decades of that period. He was forced both to add to the work and to edit earlier sections to meet the alternating ebb and flow of persecution and changes in imperial politics. The work of numerous scholars over the past hundred years makes it possible to reconstruct the stages by which these different editions of the *Church History* were put together.[7]

To give a simplified version of the basic sequence of development: In late 313 or fairly soon thereafter, there was an edition of the *Church History* with a version of Book 8 quite different from the present text (incorporating the entire short recension of the *Martyrs of Palestine*) and with Book 9 as the concluding book. This edition can be dated to the fall of Maximinus in 313 and the resulting cessation of persecution in the East and, by indirect reference, to the death of the retired emperor Diocletian in that same year.

The next edition came around 315, when Book 8 was completely revised into almost its final state, Book 9 was retained basically as it was, and Book 10.1-7 was then created to conclude the whole work. The dating of this edition is established by the inclusion of imperial legislation up to the synod of Arles (1 August 314) and by the presence of material favorable to Licinius, which presumably antedated the war which broke out between him and Constantine in 316.

---

[7]D. S. Wallace-Hadrill, *Eusebius of Caesarea* (London: Mowbray, 1960) 39-43, gives a useful summary of the previous work. The most recent studies are Robert M. Grant, *Eusebius as Church Historian* (Oxford: Clarendon Press, 1980) and Timothy D. Barnes, *Constantine and Eusebius*. See also H. J. Lawlor, *Eusebiana* (Oxford: Clarendon Press, 1912) 243ff.; E. Schwartz, in his *GCS* edition of Eusebius's *Church History* (Leipzig: J. C. Hinrichs, 1903-1909) 2.3, lvi-lix; R. Laqueur, *Eusebius als Historiker seiner Zeit* (Berlin: de Gruyter, 1929); and Kirsopp Lake, introduction to the first *LCL* volume of Eusebius's *Ecclesiastical History* (London: Heinemann, 1926) xix-xxiv.

Shortly after Licinius's final defeat by Constantine in 324, the last major edition was produced by removing or altering material too favorable to Licinius in Books 8 and 10, and an account of Constantine's victory over him was added at the end to conclude Book 10. This edition should therefore be dated probably early in 325.

After Constantine executed his son Crispus in 326, the son's name was removed from the *Church History*, but this was simply a minor change not involving a new edition in the proper sense.

Changes were also made in the first seven books of the *Church History*. Robert M. Grant has skillfully identified some of these,[8] which are clearly editorial revisions made by Eusebius at some point, though most of them cannot be dated as to the precise edition in which they were made. One exception to the latter part of this statement may be Grant's argument dating the entire present preface of the *Church History* (1.1-1.4) specifically to the 315 edition.[9] Grant's is not the only possible reading here, but this also does not mean that it could not be the correct one.[10] This is important, because this means a caveat must be placed on using the present preface to the *Church History* as any kind of firm tool to establish the answer to the next question that must be raised, about when Eusebius wrote the *first* edition of his *Church History*. Was it the well-established edition of 313, or was there a yet earlier one?

The contemporary debate over the date and nature of the first edition of the *Church History* goes back almost sixty years to Richard Laqueur, the first scholar to look at the preface truly critically. Laqueur pointed out that the passage in *HE* 1.1.2 usually translated as speaking of "the martyrdoms of our own time and the gracious and kindly help of our savior at the end

---

[8]Grant, *Eusebius as Church Historian* (Oxford: Clarendon Press, 1980). See G. F. Chesnut, review essay on Eusebius in recent scholarship, *Religious Studies Review* 9 (1983): 118-23 for a discussion of Grant's method and results.

[9]Grant, *Eusebius as Church Historian*, 34-35, 142.

[10]Some counterarguments to Grant's reading are given by G. F. Chesnut, *Religious Studies Review* 9 (1983): 122. But Grant's is still a possible reading that cannot be excluded.

of it all," must be an interpolation,[11] since it introduced a totally foreign chronological element into what was otherwise a long, nonchronological list of very general subject areas and broad topics.[12] If the first edition of the *Church History* did not conclude with a description of the end of the persecution then it could have been written well before 311, and it did not need to have included anything in Books 8ff.[13] Laqueur therefore argued that the first edition was composed only of Books 1-7, and that it could have been published as early as 303.

Carrying this sort of argument further, Grant then pointed out in his recent careful study that Books 1-7 of the *Church History* are quite different in structure from the following three books. In their present form they present a connected treatise, ending quite smoothly at the conclusion of Book 7 with a discussion of events centering on the beginning of the great persecution under Diocletian in 303. On form-critical grounds, Grant says, the literary form of Book 7 is that of the final, concluding book of a longer work.[14] He adds that there is "no special reason to hold that Books I-VII came into existence as late as 311 or 312 . . . . The seventh book did not take long to produce, whenever it was written." The bulk of the material could have been written even before 303, since regular references to the great persecution did not begin to occur until close to the end of Book 7. On the other hand, Grant argues, "there is no special reason to date" Books

---

[11]See reference in preceding note. The phrase ἐπὶ πᾶσιν has many possible translations, including "in them all" or "overall." If the clause was meant to read something like "and the gracious and kindly help of our savior in all the matters described in the entire preceding part of the introduction," then the only interpolation may be the reference to "the martyrdoms of our own time."

[12]Richard Laqueur, *Eusebius als Historiker seiner Zeit*, 210-12.

[13]One might contrast H. J. Lawlor and J. E. L. Oulton, *Eusebius Bishop of Caesarea: The Ecclesiastical History and the Martyrs of Palestine*, 2 vols. (London: SPCK, 1928) 2:4-5. They argue, one year before the publication of Laqueur's book, on the strength of the reference to "the gracious and kindly succour of our Saviour at the end of all" (their translation) in *HE* 1.1.2, that the first edition consisted of Books 1-8 and was published in the latter half of the year 311.

[14]Grant, *Eusebius as Church Historian*, 31-32.

1-7 "much earlier" than 311 or 312.[15] This leaves one with a form-critically unified work of seven books, but with no date firmly specified for this first edition except to state that it could have been completed any time between 303 and 311 or 312.

Almost simultaneously with the appearance of Grant's book, Timothy D. Barnes published his *Constantine and Eusebius,* arguing for a far more radical solution to the problem.[16] Barnes believes that the first edition was written extremely early, around 295 C.E., and that it consisted of Books 1-7, but with the conclusion falling earlier than in the present Book 7, at the point (7.32.6-21) where the material appears on Bishop Anatolius of Laodicea and the Easter cycle that Anatolius devised to begin in 276/277 C.E.[17] To do this, Barnes also has to put extremely early dates on Eusebius's *Chronicle, Onomasticon,* and *Prophetic Eclogues.* This would be a fairly substantial output for a young scholar only barely into his thirties, particularly given the groundbreaking nature of some of that research.

Also, Barnes's contention that the first edition of the *Church History* ended precisely at 7.32.6-21 (with reference to an event that took place in 276/277 C.E., enabling one therefore to date the first edition quite early) perhaps attempts more precision than is possible.[18] His attempt to push the

---

[15]Ibid., 14.

[16]The debate had been going on between Grant and Barnes for some time previously, via journal articles and papers delivered at scholarly conferences, so each was already well aware of the other's position.

[17]Timothy D. Barnes, *Constantine and Eusebius,* 145-46, 346 n10.

[18]Barnes (111, 145-46) puts the conclusion to the first edition at this point, where Eusebius was discussing Bishop Anatolius of Laodicea, largely because he believes he can demonstrate that the first edition of Eusebius's *Chronicle* (the source of his dates for the first edition of his *Church History*) ended at 276/277 C.E., at which point that bishop's name was mentioned, and at which time the bishop's revised method of calculating the date of Easter took its starting point. Assuming parallelism between the chronological structure of the first edition of the *Chronicle* and the first edition of the *Church History,* both should originally have ended in 276/277, Barnes argues, and both could have been written very early indeed. Grant, however, shows (*Eusebius as Church Historian,* 7-8) that the special entry in the *Chronicle* at the year 276/77 C.E. (the second year of Probus) is more likely to have been a refutation of a contemporary Jewish claim that the Jewish Messiah would appear

composition of both the *Church History* and the *Chronicle* back to a very early date by dating Eusebius's *Onomasticon* (*On the Place-Names in Holy Scripture*) quite early, also rests on evidence that may not be that firm and unequivocal.[19]

Barnes's most important contribution to the debate, however, is his perceptive observation that the material even in the seventh book of the *Church History*, almost to the very end of the book, would have to have been written before the great persecution started in 303. Here he seems certainly correct. Even as late in Book 7 as 7.30.22, for example, the phrase "under whom was accomplished the persecution in our time and the destruction of the churches during it" seems clearly to have been a later editorial addition, implying that the preceding material existed before 303.[20] There is no reason why the section which Barnes cites only two chapters further along, that is, *HE* 7.32.6-21, could not also have been part of the material composed before 303. In fact, Barnes's excellent textual instincts are surely correct here, at one basic level, in that *HE* 7.32.6-21 must be the last material, in the *Church History* as we have it today, that could have come from a pre-303 edition. But that does not mean that this section was, as he seems to argue, the original *conclusion* to the first edition of the *Church History*. Eusebius had a sense of drama, and knew how to write a powerful con- ·

---

during the eighty-fifth jubilee, because Eusebius not only elaborately established that date by a synchronism with the calendars of Antioch, Tyre, Laodicea, Edessa, and Ascalon, but then carefully pointed out that the year in question was "the beginning of the 86th jubilee according to the Hebrews." The special form of the entry at the year 276/277 in the *Chronicle* was therefore more likely due to anti-Jewish polemic, rather than being the mark of the conclusion of a first edition.

[19]Barnes's argument (110-111) rests on Jerome's statement that Eusebius's *Onomasticon* was written after both the *Chronicle* and the *Church History* had been composed, and on Barnes's own dating of the incorporation of Arabia Petraea into the Roman province of Palestine, which would force us, on the surface at least, to date certain passages in the *Onomasticon* quite early. But Barnes himself admits that the crucial entries in the *Onomasticon* could have been the anachronistic result "of mere habit, carelessness, or inattention" on the part of a writer working at a much later date.

[20]Everything after the statement that Aurelian reigned for six years and then was succeeded by Probus at the beginning of *HE* 7.30.22 is in fact probably part of this editorial addition made after 303; cf. Barnes, 346 n10.

clusion. Bishop Anatolius's method of calculating the date of Easter on the basis of a repeating nineteen-year cycle of full moons, with full astronomical supporting data, hardly makes a dramatic finale to a work on church history. In form-critical terms this text exhibits none of the characteristics of passages that show "closure" in longer literary works.

An explanation of what may have happened, which at least accounts for all of the data, can be given. It is possible that there was no true "first edition" of the *Church History* in the same sense as the editions of 313, 315, and 325. The latter were all finished works, with true conclusions, which were circulated and read. But one could easily suppose Eusebius having been caught by the beginning of the great persecution in 303 with a first edition almost but not quite finished.

In his customary style, using the sequence of Roman emperors to provide his basic chronological framework, Eusebius had just finished his section on the reign of Aurelian, who was murdered in 275.[21] He had more than a quarter of a century left to cover to bring his history up to his own time.[22] He had begun doing research into the period right after Aurelian's death, and had already composed sections on Bishop Anatolius of Laodicea[23] and perhaps also on Mani.[24] It was at this point that Eusebius first learned of the persecution that had been proclaimed at Nicomedia on 23 February 303. The edict required not only the demolition of all churches but also the surrender and burning of all Christian scriptures and liturgical books. All Eusebius's research had to be set aside as the struggle began to save the most severely threatened portions of the library at Caesarea. It is still unknown how this was accomplished, whether by removing and hiding the especially valuable critical editions of the Bible that had been laboriously prepared there, or by appealing privately to sympathetic government officials to overlook the existence of these volumes.

----

[21]Through *HE* 7.30.22a, "At all events, when Aurelian had reigned for six years, he was succeeded by Probus."

[22]A period that Eusebius never did fill in with the same kind of detail as preceding periods, even in later editions of his history. That work, once stopped, apparently was never resumed.

[23]*HE* 7.32.6-21.

[24]*HE* 7.31.

The first edition, as it had been written up to that point, clearly reflects the period before 303, in which Christianity was normally tolerated and was operating openly and quite successfully. It assumed that the emperor would be a pagan, and argued only for religious toleration at the official level. It presupposed the continuation of a religiously pluralistic society in the Roman empire, and assumed that Christianity would make ever increasing numbers of converts by the peaceful preaching of the gospel and by the power of truth, ultimately, to triumph over error.

There was no Constantine in that first edition, no Christian emperor, no triumph of the cross at the battle of the Milvian bridge. But if the first edition was not a celebration of the victory of Constantine and the triumphal Christianization of the imperial government, one must ask what purpose it could have been written to accomplish. One must remember that Eusebius's position in Caesarea before the persecution was probably a post as what one should today call a librarian. Pamphilus, a very wealthy native of Berytus, had decided to use his fortune to create a large library—of 30,000 volumes, according to one ancient source—in the city of Caesarea in honor of the Christian teacher Origen, who had spent the last years of his life researching and writing there. Eusebius was what one should now call a research librarian, of course, in addition to his other librarian's tasks. He not only helped produce good, new, corrected manuscripts of biblical texts for the library, but also prepared research tools and library reference works like the *Chronicle*, the *Onomasticon*, and the *Eusebian Canons*. There were, of course, extremely important theological and apologetic implications in the way the latter three works were put together,[25] but one must never forget the extent to which a purely utilitarian aim shaped their basic structure. We still use them for their original purpose today.

---

[25]See Dennis E. Groh, "The *Onomasticon* of Eusebius and the Rise of Christian Palestine," forthcoming in *Studia Patristica*. On the library, see Barnes, *Constantine and Eusebius*, 333 n110; see also 93-94. Also see Alden A. Mosshammer, *The* Chronicle *of Eusebius and Greek Chronographic Tradition* (Lewisburg PA: Bucknell University Press, 1979) 31-32; H. A. Drake, *In Praise of Constantine: A Historical Study and New Translation of Eusebius' Tricennial Orations* (Berkeley: University of California Press, 1976) 5. Compare the role of scholar librarians in the modern period at the British Museum in London and at Pusey House in Oxford. Eusebius can also be seen as the precursor of the scholar monks in the monastic libraries of the middle ages.

There are good reasons to believe that the *Church History* may have at least been started as simply another such librarian's research aid. An ancient library had neither a card catalogue nor reference works like the *Oxford Dictionary of the Christian Church* or Quasten's *Patrology*. The *Church History* gave, in handy form, a careful outline of which authors wrote at which times, which authors and works were orthodox, which authors and works gave helpful material for the kinds of research which could be carried on at the library at Caesarea (with excerpts and examples), and, most importantly, complete lists of each author's works so the reader would know what to look for on the shelves. Today one might entitle such a work "Introductory Guide for Research Scholars Visiting the Patristics Collection of the Library at Caesarea."

As many authors find, however, a book, once begun, often takes on a life of its own. Eusebius seems to have had this experience as well. By the time he came to begin Book 5, and started writing the preface to that section, he seems to have realized that what he was creating was really something quite different and extraordinary: a totally new kind of historiography, completely different from the pagan Graeco-Roman tradition of politico-military historiography, but real history nevertheless. [26]

It would be fascinating to know how the first edition of the *Church History* was originally designed to conclude, but there is probably no way of firmly ascertaining this any longer. One assumes that passages striking themes similar to those in *HE* 8.1.1-2 and 2.3.1-2 would have been in the conclusion, proclaiming the spread of Christianity over all the known world, its acceptance by the Roman government as an honorable and tolerated religious sect, and the attainment by some Christians of relatively high-ranking positions in the government and the imperial palace. [27] This may have been all that was ever intended.

---

[26]Eus. *HE* 5.pref. *HE* 1.1.3-7, interrupting the flow of thought from 1.1.2 to 1.1.8, was then a retrospective addition made later, acknowledging this discovery.

[27]If a bit of further speculation is permitted, *HE* 8.1.1-2 could even be a reworking of material originally designed to be read at the end of the seventh book, split off and rewritten in 315 to form the introduction to the new eighth book.

But the first edition might also have been designed to conclude, in addition, with some encomiastic material praising Pamphilus and his work in establishing the magnificent research library at Caesarea, to which the *Church History* served as a reference guide. Eusebius's style in the *Church History* was quite hagiographic in dealing with such figures as Justin, Irenaeus, and particularly Origen, in whose memory the library had been founded. He admired Pamphilus so strongly that he took his name as his own surname, "Eusebius τοῦ Παμφίλου." It would have been stylistically consistent for Eusebius and quite appropriate to his manner of working had such a rather hagiographical and encomiastic section on Pamphilus been a conclusion to that first edition.

Since Eusebius seems rarely to have thrown away anything that he had written or researched, it is possible that this material, with considerable expansion, was split off and published later as the separate work called the *Life of Pamphilus*. A work by Eusebius with such a title did exist, but it is unfortunately now lost, except for a few fragments, so that there are no means of reconstructing the exact tone and tenor of the way such a conclusion to the *Church History* would have read.

There is no necessary reason, however, to believe that the conclusion to this "first edition" was ever written in anything like finished form, or had even gotten beyond the planning stages for most parts. This would explain the present state of the final chapters of Book 7. When Eusebius came to write the "second edition" in 313, he had an unfinished history with a seventh book going only a little past the reign of Aurelian, and a new idea for how to conclude the history, starting with a detailed look (Book 8 in the 313 edition form) at the persecution and martyrdoms that began in 303. He therefore rather hurriedly completed that unfinished seventh book, carrying it up to 303 (which was possibly fairly close to the stopping point he had originally intended years earlier) before going on to the newly composed Books 8 and 9, which were quite different in style and concerns from the first seven books. This is why Books 1-7 in a certain sense do form a closed form-critical unity. A careful look at the end of Book 7 will show, however, that there was no serious attempt to cover the last quarter century that stretched from a little past the end of Aurelian's reign in 275 to the great persecution in 303, other than to give episcopal lists. Eusebius was no longer interested in carrying his initial project to its originally intended completion; he had far more important things to write about now, in his own estimation, and a totally different kind of conclusion to write, which would not fit the former style.

At approximately the same time as he was preparing this second edition (that is, the one published in 313 or fairly soon thereafter), Eusebius also became bishop of Caesarea. The circumstantial evidence indicates that his immediate predecessor, whom he never names, had lapsed under persecution and renounced his Christianity.[28] Caesarea may have been with-

---

[28]Theotecnus, bishop of Caesarea in the 260s (HE 7.14.1 and 30.2) was succeeded by Agapius, bishop during Eusebius's youth (HE 7.32.24). Agapius did not live to see the persecution in 303 and there was then a total gap in Eusebius's record, until the time of his own episcopacy, with no bishop of Caesarea mentioned in either the *Church History* or *Martyrs of Palestine* for that period of more than a decade at least. (Cf. *Martyrs of Palestine* 1.3, short recension, for the pointed lack of such reference, HE 8.2.3 for the probable reason why that bishop's name was never mentioned, and the discussion by Lawlor and Oulton [2:263] in their notes and commentary on the HE). Eusebius was still Pamphilus's research assistant during the latter's long imprisonment from late 307 to early 310, and based on the same dates, Barnes (*Constantine and Eusebius*, 148-49) puts Eusebius's extensive travels in Egypt and Phoenicia during the second round of persecution in 311-313. Eusebius could only have copied the public inscription of the rescript of Maximinus (HE 9.7.3) if he had been in Tyre at some time between June 312 and ca. July 313. Paulinus was probably already bishop of Tyre by that point (cf. HE 10.4.24, Lawlor and Oulton 2:306, and the note at 2:413 of the LCC edition of HE).

On the other hand, Eusebius was already a bishop when he gave the speech in HE 10.4 at the dedication of the new church built at Tyre after the persecution had ended, a speech that must be dated at some point between midsummer of 314 and 8 October 316 (cf. Lawlor and Oulton 2:307 and Barnes, 67). This extremely long speech was the rhetorical conclusion to the third edition of HE, Eusebius as a new bishop was clearly publicly portraying himself in this fashion as the protégé of Bishop Paulinus of Tyre (note also HE 10.1.2). Had Paulinus consecrated Eusebius when the latter was in Tyre, at the end of persecution in 313, and sent him back to Caesarea to rebuild the leaderless and persecution-torn community there? The second edition of the HE, published ca. 313, was clearly in style and tone the work of either a bishop or someone soon to be one. Compare the effect on Augustine of his elevation to the episcopacy, discussed very sensitively in Peter Brown, *Augustine of Hippo: A Biography* (London: Faber and Faber, 1967) 193-210. Eusebius had to undergo the same inner changes as he came under the same pressures.

out a recognized bishop for a number of years before Eusebius was elected. He was finally totally forced out of the world of the quiet research scholar in the cloistered library at Caesarea into a post where he was confronted with the task of renewing the spirit and optimism of a scattered and demoralized flock. He also had to act as its spokesman, defender, and protector in dealings with the two rival emperors who had just now tentatively allied themselves with the Christians, but whose sincerity and long-term dependability Eusebius could in no way trust at that point. This edition of 313 and all subsequent editions of the *Church History* reveal Eusebius's new awareness of broader responsibilities, and, interestingly enough, from the beginning a real self-confidence and awareness of his own rhetorical and political skills in this new leadership role.

By the early 330s, Eusebius had become one of the four or five most influential and powerful bishops in the entire Mediterranean world. In 330 and 335 he demonstrated that he could even topple a patriarch of Antioch or of Alexandria; in 331 he was himself offered the patriarchate of Antioch although he refused the honor. He was a key spokesman for a large and essentially still defenseless Christian community that had little direct political power, but he was no more the servile tool of a Roman emperor than was Athanasius or Ambrose. His goal was always to control Licinius, Constantine, and the latter's sons as much as possible in matters affecting the Christian community, and to avoid being controlled by them. When he flattered an emperor in public, Eusebius had either just obtained something he wanted for the Christians or was moving strategically toward some deliberate future goal.

There was therefore a major shift in Eusebius's style and in his concerns between the first edition of the *Church History*, which puts one into Eusebius's mind in the period before 303, and the second edition, which appeared in 313 or shortly thereafter. Books 8 and 10 of the *Church History* enable one also to discover how Eusebius was thinking over the twelve years or so immediately following his rise to the episcopacy, in the editions of ca. 315 and ca. 325.

For the very last period, toward the end of his life, other works are useful. The document that today is called the *De laudibus Constantini* is actually two separate works. *De laud.* 11-18 is the *Treatise on the Church of the Holy Sepulcher* that Eusebius delivered in September 335 in Jerusalem. The first part, *De laud.* 1-10, is the *Panegyric to Constantine* that Eusebius delivered on 25

July 336 in Constantinople.[29] Eusebius was by then in his mid-seventies. He had a long and eventful life behind him, and had now been under the direct rule of a Christian emperor himself for more than a decade.

Finally there is the *Life of Constantine* itself. Eusebius seems to have begun this almost immediately after the emperor died on 22 May 337. He was an elderly man himself and died only two years after the emperor; he may well have been almost eighty at that point. He was a very different person from the young man who had lived and worked in those much more optimistic times back in the late third century, when Christians had believed they could evangelize the world simply by appealing to truth and goodness.

The *Life* was a book, not just about Constantine, but about Christian princes in general. It was far more a work on political theory than a real biography, cast in extremely idealistic form, in many ways more like the genre called the "Mirror of Princes."[30] Every *Fürstenspiegel* or Mirror of Princes is apt to contain a hidden, prescriptive message. Sometimes it is a statement of ideals so different from the ruling monarch's actual actions that they are a *de facto* criticism of them, made in the only safe way in a totalitarian society. But Constantine was dead, so the prescriptive message, if any, had to have been aimed at Constantine's sons. It was the beginning of their reign, so it may not have been critical of their behavior at that time, but merely an attempt to point out firmly to them the way in which they should conduct their reigns. Any historical distortions of the way their father had actually behaved were therefore probably prescriptive messages directed at his sons—pious frauds if one wishes to be harsh—which Eusebius either hoped to slip over on the dead emperor's sons, or which they knew as well as he were not totally true. The true message would have gotten through

---

[29]See Barnes, *Constantine and Eusebius*, 187, 238, 253-55, 278, 282-83; Drake, *In Praise of Constantine*, chapter 3.

[30]See P. Hadot, "Fürstenspiegel," *Reallexikon für Antike und Christentum*. The custom of writing about political theory from a totally idealistic perspective rather than from the standpoint of practical political realities was also typical of most later medieval political thought, as in, for example, Thomas Aquinas and Dante. The shift to the modern way of writing about political theory did not truly begin until Machiavelli's *The Prince*, the entry into an entirely new era (one in which we are still largely dwelling). Eusebius's *Life of Constantine* offends the Machiavellian instinct at its deepest level.

either way, without violating the tacit rules for criticizing or advising an absolute monarch.[31]

One therefore has documents permitting insight into Eusebius's thought about church and state at a number of periods in his life, stretching over at least three and a half decades.

before the beginning of persecution in 303	*The "first edition" of the* Church History: Most of Books 1-7, excluding the preface at the beginning of the history at least in its present form, but going at least as far as the present *HE* 7.30.22a and probably including also *HE* 7.31 and *HE* 7.32.5-21. Nothing past that point could be first edition material.
ca. 313	*The second edition:* Books 1-7. An eighth book incorporating the entire short recension of what is now called the *Martyrs of Palestine*. Book 9.
ca. 315	*The third edition:* Books 1-10.7 (including the present Book 8, newly written to replace the older eighth book).
ca. 325	*The fourth edition:* Books 1-10 (with any older material favorable to Licinius altered or removed).
ca. 326	*A minor additional reediting:* Removal of any reference to the name of Constantine's son Crispus.
335	*Treatise on the Church of the Holy Sepulcher* = *De laud.* 11-18.
336	*Panegyric to Constantine* = *De laud.* 1-10.
337-339	*Life of Constantine*

With this material in hand, it is possible to see how Eusebius's mind changed quite remarkably on some important issues.

---

[31]The antipagan law in *Codex Theodosianus* 16.10.2, issued shortly after Eusebius's *VC* was finished and invoking Constantine's memory, was pointed out to me by Professor Michele Salzman. Eusebius's message may well have been heard, exactly as he intended it.

In the first edition of his *Church History* (written before the persecution that began in 303) Eusebius on occasion toward the end of his history invoked his theory that the "good emperor" would receive earthly rewards and the "bad emperor" would receive such earthly punishments as a short reign, defeat in battle, a bad end to his life, the deaths of his children, and no heir to inherit the throne.[32] Eusebius seems to have picked up this idea from the letters of Dionysius of Alexandria, which he seems to have discovered and begun using and quoting as a historical source as he came to the end of his work on Book 6 of the *Church History*.[33] In the earlier parts of his history, Eusebius did not invoke in any explicit fashion the idea of God's providence bringing bad emperors to bad ends even when it would have been very easy to have done so, as for example with Nero[34] or Domitian.[35] This was therefore a new idea for him, a new way of interpreting events.

But an even more important observation is that the "bad emperor" for Eusebius in the first edition was a persecuting emperor, and that this was the only criterion used. Gallienus, for example, was a "good emperor," even though a pagan, and described as avoiding the providential fate that God had meted out to his father, because he had stopped the persecution of Christians.[36] In the period when Eusebius was writing the first edition, he assumed that the emperor would normally be pagan, and asked only for toleration for Christians. He did not find it unbelievable that, on occasion, a Roman emperor or members of his immediate family could be converted

---

[32]Eus. *HE* 7.1; 7.10-13; 7.30.20-22.

[33]See *HE* 7.pref. and 1. He used a quotation from Melito of Sardis much earlier in his history (4.26.7) that was moving in that direction but was not yet a true good emperor/bad emperor theory.

[34]Eus. *HE* 2.25.1-5; 3.5.1. Eusebius says that Nero was morally despicable and that he was the first emperor to persecute Christians, but draws no explicit moral, either when describing Nero's end or the chaos of the year of the four emperors that followed.

[35]Eus. *HE* 3.17-20; 3.20.8. Eusebius says that Domitian was cruel and a persecutor, and was officially dishonored after his death, but again no explicit moral is drawn. Trajan, the third traditional persecuting emperor, of course would have caused problems for this theory, see *HE* 3.32.1ff. and 4.3.1.

[36]Eus. *HE* 7.13.

to Christianity.[37] The crucial point is that he did not push for this or set it as a goal toward which the Christian church should work, nor did he seem at all to have envisioned an empire in which each ruler in the succession of emperors would have to be Christian in order to don the purple. There is a total contrast between his position here, before the great persecution began in 303, and his position a third of a century later, when he was at the end of his life and was writing the *Life of Constantine*.

Even in the first edition of his *Church History*, the young Eusebius believed that one of the central threads of Christian history should be the record of the triumph of an unchanging orthodoxy over the attempts by heretics to introduce change and novelty. He was severely criticized for this by Adolf von Harnack.[38] Even the title of Eusebius's work, Ἐκ-κλησιαστικὴ ἱστορία, indicates the importance of orthodoxy to him, for the "ecclesiastical" writers, in Eusebius's Greek usage, were the orthodox Christian theologians as opposed to nonorthodox, heretical thinkers.[39] It was a "History of Orthodoxy" as the title itself indicated.

---

[37]Eusebius did believe this had happened in the first half of the third century. He asserted that Origen had preached to Julia Mamaea, the mother of the emperor Alexander Severus, at her request (*HE* 6.21.3-4), and that "the house of Alexander . . . consisted for the most part of believers" (6.28.1). Eusebius also claimed that the emperor Philip the Arabian was a Christian believer who had attended at least one Easter vigil, standing in the part of the church reserved for penitents (*HE* 6.34). He had a letter, he said, written by Origen to Philip, and another to his wife Severa, that he felt corroborated this assertion (6.36.3). He further argued that it was the strength of the alliance between Philip and the Christians that caused Philip's successor Decius to persecute them (6.39.1).

[38]Harnack, *History of Dogma*, trans. N. Buchanan (New York: Dover, 1961) 1:23. Compare Ferdinand Christian Baur, *Die Epochen der kirchlichen Geschichtschreibung*, ed. and trans. Peter C. Hodgson in *Ferdinand Christian Baur on the Writing of Church History* (New York: Oxford University Press, 1968) 59-60; also 57-58 and Hodgson's introduction, 12-16. See also Robert L. Wilken, *The Myth of Christian Beginnings: History's Impact on Belief* (Garden City: Doubleday, 1971).

[39]See, for example, *HE* 3.3.2, where the term is parallelled to "in Catholic tradition"; 4.7.5, where it is contrasted to "the heresies," namely of Saturninus and Basilides; 7.27.2, where it is contrasted to the heretical teaching of Paul of Samosata; and 5.27.1 and 6.18.1, where it is also clearly treated as synonymous or nearly synonymous with ὀρθόδοξος and ὀρθοδοξία.

But the word orthodoxy has such a different flavor to the present-day church historian that it can cause one seriously to misunderstand what it meant to Eusebius. The Council of Nicaea was not held until 325, Chalcedon was a century and a quarter later, the Fourth Lateran Council came in 1215 in the high middle ages; the Augsburg Confession, Formula of Concord, and the Thirty-Nine Articles of Religion were products of the sixteenth century. What Eusebius called orthodoxy in his *Church History* denoted none of the detailed, technical dogmas and excruciatingly precise definitions that the word conjured up in the pages of Harnack's *History of Dogma*.

When Eusebius wrote of orthodoxy in his *Church History* (all of which was written before the Council of Nicaea began the process of tightening the lines of permitted belief) the principal issues were quite simple: Against the somewhat paranoid picture of the universe given by the gnostics, the true Christian tradition had maintained since the time of Jesus himself that the material world was a creation of the one supreme God who was both loving and just. Against Paul of Samosata (and also against the gnostics), orthodox Christians had traditionally maintained that Jesus Christ was the real, divine incarnation of God's Word in the life and work of a genuine historical human being. As a final, vitally important issue, those "catholic" Christian congregations that had maintained communication with one another all around the Mediterranean world had by this time reached a fair consensus on the extent of the New Testament canon, fairly close to the canon for Christianity today. Eusebius also insisted (against the Montanists, against the more extreme of the apocalyptically oriented literalists, and against other similar groups) that these scriptures had to be interpreted in some reasonably sophisticated fashion, with no subsidiary bodies of later inspired writings or prophecies allowed to detract from the centrality of the New Testament scriptures themselves.[40] Even those modern Christians

---

[40]Argued at greater length, with full citations from Eusebius, in G. F. Chesnut, "Radicalism and Orthodoxy: The Unresolved Problem of the First Christian Histories," *Anglican Theological Review* 65 (1983): 295-305. See also Dennis E. Groh, "Hans von Campenhausen on Canon: Positions and Problems," *Interpretation* 28 (1974): 331-43; Robert L. Wilken, "Diversity and Unity in Early Christianity," *The Second Century: A Journal of Early Christian Studies* 1 (1981): 101-10, and the discussion of the problem of the canon in G. F. Chesnut, "From Alexander the Great to Constantine: Supplying the Context," *The Second Century: A Journal of Early Christian Studies* 1 (1981): 43-49. See also the article by G. F. Chesnut on Eusebius in the supplementary volume of the *Interpreter's Dictionary of the Bible*.

who scorn dogmas and creeds and stale orthodoxies would have to admit
that Eusebius was fairly close to a bare minimum of doctrinal guidelines in
many, if not most, areas.

Furthermore, in the first edition of his *Church History*, Eusebius nowhere
sanctioned physical violence or persecution against those regarded as heretics. [41] His model throughout was the defeat of heresies by verbal and
written argument alone. The true defenders of the church dealt with heretics, he said, "at one time by rebukes and exhortations to the brethren, at
another time by their more complete exposure by unwritten and personal
inquiry and conversation, and ultimately corrected their opinions by accurate arguments in written treatises."[42] These disputations, according to
Eusebius, ideally concluded in the free conversion of the heretic back to
the correct faith, an accomplishment in which he believed that Origen, for
example, was successful on occasion. [43] The orthodox were able to achieve
victory by verbal and written argument alone, because they possessed the
power of truth (ἡ ἀλήθεια) itself, and truth would always ultimately pre-
vail over error. [44]

On the more negative side, Eusebius believed that one could associate
with the nonorthodox when necessity required, but never pray with them. [45]
It was permissible for church councils to depose bishops, and in the one
case of Paul of Samosata, which set enormous precedents for the future,
Eusebius spoke approvingly of the church's action in appealing to the emperor Aurelian to evict Paul from possession of the church building at An-

---

[41] Again see Chesnut, "Radicalism and Orthodoxy," for a discussion of this and
the later move towards greater harassment and persecution of Christian "heretical"
groups as documented in the church histories of Eusebius's successors.

[42] Eus. *HE* 4.24; see also 8.1.7 from the third edition of the *HE*, which was published in 315.

[43] Eus. *HE* 6.18.1; 6.33.1-3; 6.37.

[44] Eus. *HE* 4.7.15 (note the way in which ὑπερμάχους and στρατευομέ-
νους are turned totally into metaphors); 6.18.1. With the lapse of time, Eusebius
held, heresies mutated into multiple forms and eventually withered away by themselves (an argument often repeated in subsequent eras of the church). They did
not have the power to endure through the centuries like the orthodox faith, "for
it ever held to the same points in the same way" (*HE* 4.7.10-14). Cf. also *HE* 7.23.4.

[45] Eus. *HE* 6.2.13-14.

tioch and of Aurelian's action in doing so.[46] But on the other hand, Eusebius insisted that not even the Montanists had been persecuted by the orthodox or subjected to violence.[47] In all, Eusebius recommended no actions that could not have been taken under the laws and ethos of a modern, tolerant, post-Enlightenment, religiously pluralistic, secular state like the United States.

So in the first edition of Eusebius's *Church History* one finds a strictly limited set of guidelines for orthodox belief, and an aversion to persecution and violence.[48] He assumes that the Roman empire will remain a religiously pluralistic society, and believes that Christianity will spread by the pure preaching of the gospel alone.

When Eusebius described the emergence of Christianity in the first century as the appearance of a new ἔθνος (ethnic group, nation, people) he may therefore have been arguing for the official acceptance of Christianity by the Roman government as a group similar in some ways to the Jews.[49] With this as a precedent, they could be given a special status, with some legal exemptions and privileges to allow them to follow their religious rules where they deviated from normal Roman custom as, for example, in refusing to sacrifice to the image of the emperor. This was the real problem to be overcome. It would have done the Christians no good to have been given the status of the worshipers of Mithras, for example, or of Athena or Hercules. It tends often to be forgotten that for genuine toleration and freedom from the threat of persecution, and access to all the occupations and positions in Roman society (especially the army and the

---

[46]Eus. *HE* 7.29-30, esp. 7.30.19.

[47]The Montanists apparently accused the orthodox of being "murderers of the prophets," Eus. *HE* 5.16.12-13.

[48]Note the emphasis on nonviolence, for example, in Eus. *HE* 5.pref.3-4.

[49]Eus. *HE* 1.4.2. His emphasis in regularly describing Abraham and the other pre-Mosaic Jewish patriarchs as "Christians in fact if not in name" may therefore have been part of an interesting legal argument, since the Roman government on principle tended to leave ancient traditional religions alone, no matter how bizarre some of their beliefs might seem to the Romans themselves. A historically rooted, clearly defined ἔθνος with religious practices dating back for two millennia or more might have some claims for special status.

government) Christianity had to have more than the legal status of a *religio licita* or authorized private club.[50]

Another point that emerges in surveying the first edition is that Eusebius seems throughout to have been committed to nonviolence.[51] The only slip was in one story contained in a long quotation from Dionysius of Alexandria (who had also introduced him to the theory of providential rewards and punishments for persecuting and nonpersecuting emperors). During the Decian persecution, as Bishop Dionysius relates in his story, he and all his companions but one were captured by Roman soldiers and held under arrest. The only Christian who escaped, a man named Timothy, ran down a country road, and told one of the rural folk what had happened. This man in turn went running to a place where they were holding an all-night wedding party, and all the rural folk jumped up immediately and in a violent mob stormed the place where Bishop Dionysius and the others were being held prisoner, sending the Roman soldiers fleeing for their lives. The bishop, who had a sense of humor, tells how he was wakened from sleep by the commotion. Thinking they were robbers, still in his nightshirt, he huddled in his bed and tried to give them all his clothes. The mob finally seized the bishop by force, dragging him along the ground by his hands and feet, threw him on a donkey's back, and got him to safety.[52] It is a marvelous tale, but a violent one—Christians taking up arms and attacking Roman soldiers to defend themselves. Eusebius included the story in his history without a word of protest about the violence done to the soldiers. Perhaps this tale had already planted a seed in his mind, enabling him later on to accept more easily the figure of Constantine as the warrior of God.

Eusebius's basic perspective was still, however, strongly antimilitaristic. In the preface to Book 5, he had described the great exploits of classical

---

[50]See the problem raised, for example, if a Christian soldier distinguished himself and was offered promotion to the rank of centurion (Eus. *HE* 7.15.1-2; *pace* Lawlor and Oulton [2:247], commentary on their translation of Eusebius). On the range of real and pressing problems faced by Christians, both theological and practical, see John Helgeland, "Christians and the Roman Army A.D. 173-337," *Church History* 43 (1974): 149-63, 200.

[51]For example, Eus. *HE* 5.pref.3-4.

[52]Eus. *HE* 6.40.4-9.

history—the last stand of Leonidas and his Spartans at Thermopylae, and similar tales of heroism and valor that all Greeks knew by heart—as in fact no more than the work of "men stained with blood and with countless murders for the sake of children and fatherland and that sort of thing."[53] Even as late as Book 7, Eusebius tells with pride how Theotecnus, who was the bishop of Caesarea during his childhood, had once brought a Roman soldier into his church and laid the gospel book down in front of him. He pointed to the sword buckled at the soldier's side and asked him to choose— the gospel or the sword.[54]

The beginning of the great persecution on 23 February 303 soon made that simple choice appear more complicated, particularly when one of the later coemperors began calling for support from the Christians in his bid for a takeover, military or (in the East) at least diplomatic, of other parts of the empire after he defeated a key rival at the battle of the Milvian bridge in 312. This was Constantine, of course, and the second edition of Eusebius's *Church History* appeared roughly a year later, in 313.

The idea of providential rewards and punishments meted out by God to "good emperors" and "bad emperors" was strongly developed by Eusebius in the new material that appeared in this second edition.[55] The preceding years of persecution had drawn the lines more strongly. Maximin, for example, was portrayed now not only as a persecutor but also as a man who had bragged, in "his zeal for the idols,"[56] that the worship of Zeus and the other immortal gods brought favorable weather, good crops, and freedom from war, earthquakes, and storms at sea, a claim that had manifestly been proven false.[57]

Constantine was depicted as calling upon "God who is in heaven" (the Christian God or the sun god?) and praying for Jesus Christ ("the Logos"

---

[53]Eus. *HE* 5. pref. 3.

[54]Eus. *HE* 7. 15. 4.

[55]Eus. *HE* 9.7.3-8.3, 9.2-8, 10.1-6 and 10.12-15, 11.2-7. *Martyrs of Palestine* (short recension, included in Book 8 of the second edition of the *HE*) 3.5-7; compare also 7.7-8, 13.9, and 13.14.

[56]Eus. *HE* 9.8.3.

[57]Eus. *HE* 9.7.3-8.2.

of the "Heavenly God") to be his "ally."[58] His opponent Maxentius was portrayed as a "tyrant" who had "enslaved" the people of Rome, and as a man who practiced "sorcery" (γοητεία).[59] Sorcery was considered an evil and despicable practice by the pagan majority, and in no way was equated with the practice of traditional Mediterranean polytheistic rituals. Constantine in turn was not said actually to be a Christian, but merely to have asked the Christians to be his *allies*. Eusebius's description of the god whom Constantine worshiped was studiously phrased to include within its terms, not only a Christian, but also a Middle or Neoplatonist who regarded the sun shining up in the sky as the earthly manifestation of Plato's Good, and who would speak of this divine power being mediated to the world of matter through the emanation of a Logos. Licinius was honored equally with Constantine for his "understanding and piety,"[60] although no one has ever tried to suggest that Licinius was anything other than a pagan. In no way did Eusebius portray Constantine as a devout, orthodox Christian monarch opposing an emperor whose only sin was polytheism.

Maximin was a persecutor, Eusebius wrote in 313, who included among his supporters Culcianus, "who gloried in the murder of countless Christians in Egypt," and Theotecnus, who had set up a statue of Zeus the Befriender in Antioch and claimed that the god was giving divine commands to persecute the Christians.[61] But he was also "mad" and "insane,"[62] and "a tyrant."[63] He "placed his hopes in demons, whom . . . he regarded as gods,"[64] and finally admitted, too late, the power of "the God of the Christians."[65] His opponent, Licinius, acted (along with Constantine) "in sobri-

---

[58]Eus. *HE* 9.9.2. Compare the pagan Middle Platonic philosopher Plutarch, *To an Uneducated Ruler* 781f-782a—in the world of nature the sun was the highest and most beautiful image of God, but in human life the divine image was mirrored in the Logos, which the wise learned about through the study of philosophy.

[59]Eus. *HE* 9.9.3.

[60]Eus. *HE* 9.9.1.

[61]Eus. *HE* 9.11.2-7, along with *HE* 9.3.

[62]Eus. *HE* 9.10.2.

[63]Eus. *HE* 9.9.13, 10.6, 11.2.

[64]Eus. *HE* 9.10.2.

[65]Eus. *HE* 9.10.6.

ety and piety towards the true God,"[66] which in context meant no more than that they were not persecuting emperors, since Licinius obviously was never a Christian, and Eusebius does not seem to have interpreted Constantine at this stage as any more than a friendly ally, such as the earlier emperor Philip the Arabian had been in his interpretation.[67]

Constantine, however, had won freedom from persecution for the Christians by armed force. Eusebius went back to his Old Testament, but still could not force himself totally to portray Constantine as "the Warrior of God." He instead seized upon the fact that Maxentius and his guard had been drowned, at the end of the battle of the Milvian bridge, when a pontoon bridge they were crossing collapsed and sank. He called up the image of Moses and the people of Israel crossing the Red Sea, and the drowning of Pharaoh's army.[68] But Moses and the Israelites had been a persecuted group who had not tried to fight back, and the death of Pharaoh's soldiers had not been by their hands.

Nevertheless, in one brief passage, Eusebius did remark, without condemnation, that when Maximin tried to force the Christians in Armenia "to sacrifice to idols and demons," the Armenians went to war against Rome.[69] The possibility of Roman Christians defending their lives by armed force was becoming more thinkable for him now.

Even in the third edition of his *Church History*, published in 315, Eusebius continued to stress the good emperor as the nonpersecuting emperor when he was describing the providential rewards that God would grant to such a ruler.[70] Although Eusebius was still praising Licinius as the best of monarchs, Licinius of course was not a Christian,[71] nor would Eusebius even

---

[66]Eus. *HE* 9.10.1.

[67]On Philip, see Eus. *HE* 6.34.1, 36.3, and 39.1.

[68]Eus. *HE* 9.9.5-8.

[69]Eus. *HE* 9.8.2.

[70]Eus. *HE* 8.13.9-11, 13.12-13, and 14.18-15.1.

[71]This is why one must be careful not to read too much into Eusebius's language when he seems to be portraying Constantine in very Christian terms at this point. In his sermon at the dedication of the new cathedral in Tyre in 315 (included in the *Church History* in *HE* 10.4) Eusebius says, of both Constantine *and* Licinius, that they "spit upon the faces of dead idols . . . and laugh at the old de-

yet have envisioned an empire where the Christians were totally in control. He did however use the good emperor/bad emperor doctrine to account for the death of Maximian in 310 by stating that he had been "discovered devising a plot to secure the death of Constantine."[72] This is a movement toward a very different kind of position, because it meant that enemies of Constantine were now automatically regarded as enemies of God.

Even in the fourth edition of the *Church History*, which appeared in 325, Eusebius usually felt more comfortable describing Constantine and his son Crispus not as Christians per se, but as rulers who publicly honored Christianity and were willing to "use an all-ruling god and son of a god, savior of all, as a guide and ally," that is, as rulers who were willing to ally themselves with the Christians.[73] Living in the East as he did, Eusebius would have found Constantine a totally new sovereign in 325, and perhaps he still did not trust the emperor's sincerity or his commitment to being a true Christian believer, as opposed to being simply a sympathetic sun worshiper.

It was not until the *Treatise on the Church of the Holy Sepulcher*, a speech Eusebius delivered at Jerusalem in 335 when he was in his seventies,[74] that the full heights of praise for Constantine came out. The emperor was now portrayed as the culmination of all human history, and the reality of his Christian faith was taken for granted.[75] The notoriously laudatory *Life of Constantine* that Eusebius began two years later, in 337, proclaimed a Christian emperor ruling by divine right over an empire where stern legal action was to be taken against the free practice of pagan religion. If Diocletian had ordered the destruction of Christian churches in 303, then the Roman government could now close down the idol temples in like manner.

---

ceits they inherited from their fathers." They "confess that Christ the Son of God is sovereign king of the universe" (*HE* 10.4.16). Timothy Barnes notes the incongruity of describing Licinius in this way, but gives a different interpretation in *Constantine and Eusebius*, 162-63, since he believes that Constantine was totally converted to Christianity at the battle of the Milvian bridge.

[72]Eus. *HE* 8.13.15.

[73]Eus. *HE* 10.9.4.

[74]That is, what is now *De laud*. 11-18.

[75]Cf. Barnes, *Constantine and Eusebius*, 187-88, 249-50.

In this *Life of Constantine*, Eusebius's final work, an emperor had to be far more than merely tolerant of Christianity to reap the providential rewards of being a "good emperor." Now he had to be a believing Christian. Perhaps it was the sort of retrospective falsification that this theory would require that caused Eusebius to portray Constantine's father Constantius Chlorus in the fashion he now did, as someone whose palace almost resembled a Christian church.[76] His throne would otherwise not have been passed on to his rightful heir Constantine, according to Eusebius's new version of the good emperor/bad emperor theory.[77]

A Roman emperor now had to be a practicing Christian, therefore, or the empire would suffer plague, invasion, crop failure, civil war, and dynastic struggles. The Roman emperor had to attack paganism vigorously, closing temples, turning statues of the gods into harmless museum pieces, and passing laws against pagan sacrifice. How had the young Eusebius, tolerant and a believer in freedom of religion, undergone such an extreme change of mind by his old age?

When one looks at the whole sequence of events, from the beginning of the great persecution in 303 to the publication of the *Life of Constantine* sometime after 339, the whole story of the development of the new role which Christianity would play in the Roman state becomes far more complex than is normally acknowledged. The pagan Diocletian (and his cohorts Galerius, Maximinus, and Licinius) become at least as responsible for the fourth-century mutation in Christian belief and practice as the Christian emperor from Britain. Put in other words, the Constantine we know from Eusebius's *Life* was thinkable—like modern Israeli Zionism—only in light of the preceding traumatic persecution. A docile religious group that had been traditionally harassed with local pogroms and legal disabilities for generations was suddenly turned completely away from its traditional long-suffering passivity by a neopagan revival and a persecution different in kind and magnitude from any that had been suffered before. The new breed of Christians who emerged seized the opportunity presented by Constantine and made the attempt for the first time to grasp the reins of

---

[76]Eus. *VC* 1. 17. Cf. *HE* 8. 13. 12-13 (from the third edition of the *HE* published in 315) where Constantine was a good emperor simply because he did not persecute Christians.

[77]Eus. *VC* 1. 18.

their own destiny. From the first realization that defending themselves against attack was possible and *thinkable*, they moved rapidly to a determination to prevent the forces of paganism from ever again being in a position to torture, maim, and drive countless numbers of Christians out to starve along the country roads, miles from home, as wandering refugees from the savagery of religious riots.

It is necessary to remember, though, that long before he had become a subject of the Christian emperor Constantine, Eusebius had regarded Christianity as the ultimate world religion and Rome as the ultimate world state. The reduction of his *Chronicle* to two parallel lines after the coming of Christ and Augustus (Christian history and Roman history) showed that even the young Eusebius regarded the two as providentially tied together. For the aged Eusebius, the victory of the emperor Constantine at the battle of the Milvian bridge in 312 had been simply the tying of the last knot. [78]

One must also remember that the Christianization of the empire had a significance for Eusebius that went far beyond the lifting of further threats of persecution. There was no modern map of the world in the library at Caesarea. As a good Roman, he thought of the empire naively, but quite literally, as embracing all significant portions of the entire inhabited world. Outside its immediate borders were only barbarians, and as for genuinely far-off lands like India, one heard only tall tales that scarcely demanded much credence. So in all good faith, Eusebius regarded the Roman empire as the truly ultimate World State, including the majority of the human race (and all civilized human beings!) under its government. This was the reason why he was able to regard the empire in an almost mystical sense: just as the Epistle to the Ephesians had spoken of the mystical body of the

---

[78]The battle of the Milvian bridge was quite important to Eusebius on other grounds as well. In a certain crucial statement, twice repeated, Eusebius said that *most* people of his time regarded the Old Testament account of God's mighty acts in history as merely "myths" (μῦθοι), and quite unbelievable; see Eus. *HE* 9.9.4; *VC* 1.38, compare 1.12; the word μῦθος is used in all three passages. This is a fascinating statement, showing a far deeper level of skepticism than one ordinarily associates with the fourth century. But Eusebius believed that the battle of the Milvian bridge conclusively refuted those who had regarded the Old Testament doctrine of history as mythological thinking. Constantine's triumph there was a mighty act of God, and proved, Eusebius believed, that God still came with a strong right hand and an outstretched arm to lead his chosen people to ultimate victory.

church whose head was Christ, so Eusebius spoke on the secular political level, of "the entire world as one immense body (ὥσπερ μέγα σῶμα τὸ πᾶν τῆς γῆς)" with the city of Rome as "the head of it all (τὴν τοῦ παντὸς κεφαλήν)."[79] With the Christian Constantine now the master of the imperial government, the secular and religious spheres were finally perfectly joined in a mystical union embracing all humanity.[80]

This linkage of Church and State in the Constantinian empire raised many new practical problems for Christian political theory. Especially in accounts of the historical development of the Christian attitude towards war and the magistracy, an analysis of Eusebius's ideas plays a major role. His views by the end of his life were quite different from those of earlier Christian figures like Tertullian, who demonstrated in detail why a scrupulous Christian might refuse to serve in the army or hold office in the civil government.[81] But this was because Eusebius had changed. As a young man

---

[79]Eus. VC 1.26.

[80]Eus. VC 2.19 and De laud. 8.9-9.2—the whole human race was united into a single body (σῶμα) with Constantine as its head (κεφαλή). Compare VC 4.14—on the metaphysical level, the harmony of the whole cosmos resulted from its guidance by a single steersman, the Christ-Logos, and in parallel fashion, on the politico-military level the Pax Romana resulted from the guidance of the whole world by a single steersman, the emperor who was the servant of God. The mystical solidarity of the entire human race was one important strand of fourth-century Eastern Christian thought, see for example, Gregory of Nyssa, To Ablabius, to Show that There Are Not Three Gods, where it is argued that "man" is used in the plural only by a misuse of language, since the nature of man is an indivisible unity, not a plurality. This was linked to the "physical theory of the atonement" that J. N. D. Kelly (Early Christian Doctrines [London: Adam and Charles Black, 1965] 377-82) finds prominently displayed in the writings of, especially, Gregory of Nyssa and Athanasius. Human nature was conceived as a sort of concrete universal, such that the incarnation of the divine Word in one human life produced the automatic deification of the entire race. See also G. F. Chesnut, Images of Christ: An Introduction to Christology (Minneapolis: Seabury Press, 1984) 108, 113-15.

[81]See, for example, Tertullian, De corona militum and De idololatria. Another oft-noted passage is that in which Origen defends Christians who refuse military and governmental duties in Contra Celsum 8.73-75. See Cecil John Cadoux, The Early Christian Attitude to War (London: Headley, 1919) and The Early Church and the World

he had been more like Tertullian (and Origen as well), showing a deeply
antimilitarist streak when he wrote in the first edition of his *Church History*
of the heroic generals and brave hoplites of the classical Greek histories,
fighting for fatherland and children, as murderers covered with gore—a
deliberately offensive juxtaposition of ideas.[82] But when the empire was
given a positive role in God's plan for history, and when an alliance of
Church and Empire was to be seen as the natural culmination towards which
the great currents of history had been providentially leading for three centuries, then those who worked to maintain and defend the social and legal
order of the state could justifiably claim some honorable recognition from
the church. Eusebius's device for doing this was to combine the idea of the
two ways of life (the ascetic life and the life in the world) with the Platonic
idea of hierarchies of Being. Those who wanted to tread the path to Christian perfection had to become monks. But there was a "secondary level of
piety" (δεύτερος εὐσεβείας . . . βαθμός) that was genuine, even if
it dealt only with the level of sense impressions and images—that is, with
the world of *history*. This allowed human beings "to join in pure nuptials
and to produce children, to undertake government, to give orders to soldiers fighting for the right; it allows them to have minds for farming, for
trade, and the other more secular interests as well as for religion."[83]

This Christianized imperial Roman regime, with its two levels of piety
and its mystical union of the entire human race, was then the universal goal,
at the end of time, towards which all preceding history had been directed.
It would reign over all the earth, till the end of the world.

In fact, even before the *Treatise on the Church of the Holy Sepulcher* or the
Life of Constantine, Eusebius had worked out at least the basic conclusion to
his story of the history of the world. In the concluding lines to the last real
edition of his *Church History*, published in 325, Eusebius was already sketch-
ing out that golden vision of the perfect human state that stood at the culmination and end of history. The Christian empire was the great Kingdom

---

(Edinburgh: T. & T. Clark, 1925); Adolf von Harnack, *Militia Christi: Die christliche
Religion und der Soldatenstand in den ersten drei Jahrhunderten* (Tübingen: J. C. B. Mohr,
1905) and *Mission and Expansion of Christianity in the First Three Centuries*, trans. James
Moffatt (London: Williams and Norgate, 1908) 52-64; John Helgeland, "Christians and the Roman Army," 149-63, 200.

[82]Eus. *HE* 5.pref.3.

[83]Eus. *DE* 1.8(29b-30b).

of Peace that had brought freedom from war to the whole ecumene. All humankind had been bound up into the cosmic liturgy, singing continuous hymns to God while the good emperor, the Friend of God, ruled with φιλανθρωπία and εὐσέβεια.[84] Those church historians who carried on Eusebius's work—Socrates, Sozomen, Theodoret, and Evagrius—continued to be haunted by that dream, and let it dominate some of their most basic historical judgments. This golden vision was the spiritual force that held the Byzantine Empire together for a thousand years. In spite of Augustine's attempt to provide a different understanding of history for the West at the time of the fifth-century collapse, as soon as Western Europe began to pull itself together again, there too (as medieval history illustrates) the dream of a Holy Roman Empire captured the human imagination at its deepest level once again.

---

[84]Eus. *HE* 10.9.6-9.

CHAPTER 7

Eusebius: Hellenistic Kingship and the Eschatological Constantine

In the final version of Eusebius's philosophy of history, as he had constructed it by the end of his life, Constantine had come to play the crucial role at one of the fundamental turning points of history. [1] But this was also a place at which philosophy of history lapped over into political philosophy. Eusebius's understanding of Constantine's imperial duties deeply influenced both Eastern and Western political thought for more than a millennium and a half afterward, as can easily be seen from a study of the history of political theory and the philosophy of kingship and also the ideology of millennialist movements from Eusebius's time all the way down to the French and Russian revolutions. Two major currents of thought were brought together in Eusebius's developed kingship theory: One was a particular tradition of Roman political thought rooted in early Hellenistic divine kingship ideology; the other was a more apocalyptic, Hebraic mode

_____

[1] The evidence for Eusebius's attitude toward Constantine is derived from the latter books of his *Historia Ecclesiastica*, from the two works found in what is now called the *De laudibus Constantini*, and from his *Vita Constantini*. An excellent discussion of the last work is found in Sabine MacCormack, "Latin Prose Panegyrics," in T. A. Dorey, ed., *Empire and Aftermath: Silver Latin II* (London: Routledge and Kegan Paul, 1975) 143-205, see esp. 168. She gives a detailed analysis of the relationship between panegyric and historiography at different periods of Greek and Roman history, and also describes the role of the emperor's religion in Late Roman panegyric, with useful comparisons between the official rhetoric of the Tetrarchy and (of great use in understanding Constantine) that which followed immediately upon its collapse.

of thought, dealing with the idea of Messianic deliverance and the role of God's chosen instruments in bringing about the eschatological kingdom at the end of world history.

It will be best to begin with the Romano-Hellenistic antecedents of Eusebius's thought. There was a particular tradition that developed within pagan Roman political theory of the very late Republic and early Empire that

---

The question of the authenticity of the *Vita Constantini* and its documents, and the possibility of later interpolations in the work, has produced an enormous body of literature in the past hundred years. A complete bibliography would take several pages; see the very thorough list in J. Quasten, *Patrology* (Utrecht: Spectrum, 1964) 3: 322-24. Some of the more important works include I. A. Heikel, Introduction to the GCS text of the *Vita* (Leipzig: J. C. Hinrichs, 1902); Giorgio Pasquali, "Die Composition der Vita Constantini des Eusebius," *Hermes* 45 (1910): 369-86; Norman H. Baynes, "Constantine the Great and the Christian Church," *Proceedings of the British Academy* 15 (1929): 341-442; Henri Grégoire, "Eusèbe n'est pas l'auteur de la 'Vita Constantini' dans sa forme actuelle et Constantin ne s'est pas 'converti' en 312," *Byzantion* 13 (1938): 561-83; Grégoire, "La vision de Constantin 'liquidée,'" *Byzantion* 14 (1939): 341-51; W. Seston, "Constantine as a Bishop," *Journal of Roman Studies* 37 (1947): 127-31; A. H. M. Jones, "Notes on the Genuineness of the Constantinian Documents in Eusebius's Life of Constantine," *Journal of Ecclesiastical History* 5 (1954): 196-200; Kurt Aland, "Eine Wende in der Konstantin-Forschung," *Forschungen und Fortschritte* 28 (1954): 213-17; F. Scheidweiler, "Nochmals die Vita Constantini," *Byzantinische Zeitschrift* 49 (1956): 1-32; K. Aland, "Die religiöse Haltung Kaiser Konstantins," *Studia Patristica* 1 = *Texte und Untersuchungen* 63 (Berlin: 1957) 549-68, first section of the study. More recently, see Andrew Alföldi, *The Conversion of Constantine and Pagan Rome*, trans. H. Mattingly (Oxford: Clarendon, 1969) "Note to the 1969 Impression," vii-x. And, of course, most recently of all, one may consult the material contained in the massive study by Timothy D. Barnes, *Constantine and Eusebius* (Cambridge MA: Harvard University Press, 1981) esp. 263, 265-71, and his bibliographies.

My position is that the *Life of Constantine* is by Eusebius, that it is an understandable development from the ideas expressed in his other works, and fits into both the rhetorical conventions of the time and the political situation of the period immediately after Constantine's death. It is as sound textually and correct in its assertions of historical fact as the *Church History*, which also has its problem passages, as anyone who has worked on it is well aware. But with the aid of modern critical scholarship both the *Life* and the *History* may be used to reconstruct the history of the later Roman empire, and both reflect quite accurately the ideas, prejudices, inconsistencies, and misconceptions of Eusebius himself.

tried to deal with the claims of Hellenistic divine kingship, which were making strong inroads into Roman political practice of that time by depicting the emperor as the incarnate Law or Reason or Logos of God.[2] By this time Hellenistic monarchs had been taking on some of the rituals and symbols of godhood for two or three centuries. The process had begun with Alexander the Great, when his divinity was proclaimed by the Greek cities of the Corinthian League after his return from India.[3] Later, when the Roman empire began spreading into the Eastern end of the Mediterranean world, many of these customs of divine kingship slowly but inexorably were transferred over into Roman practice as well. The extraordinary claims to divinity of two of the early emperors, Gaius Caligula and Nero, especially raised the intellectual issue of whether and how these imperial demands could be justified. Romans of philosophical bent were forced to consider the problem of whether a human being could in any sense be a god.

The particular philosophical tradition that is of concern here dealt with this issue by portraying the king or emperor as the Law or Reason or Logos of God. The ruler's soul was said to be the seat of Living Law, Sacred Thought, or Divine Logos—the precise term varied from author to author but the basic idea was much the same. The ruler's task was to be in his own life the ensoulment of cosmic order, and thereby bring it down to earth, so that the earthly state might mirror the cosmic harmony. The king or emperor was the supremely rational member of the human commonwealth, the ruling intelligence of the state. This was part of his divinity. It was necessary that he be a philosopher-sage, a wise man who could rule

---

[2]A slightly more detailed version of the present discussion may be found in Glenn F. Chesnut, "The Ruler and the Logos in Neopythagorean, Middle Platonic, and Late Stoic Political Philosophy," in Hildegard Temporini and Wolfgang Haase, eds., *Aufstieg und Niedergang der Römischen Welt: Geschichte und Kultur Roms im Spiegel der neueren Forschung*, II. Teil (Principat), Band II 16: Religion (Berlin: Walter de Gruyter, 1978) 1310-32. The Greek text of the material cited from Diotogenes and Ecphantus is also given there, from Delatte's critical edition (see note 4).

[3]And the roots of the idea extend back beyond Alexander into even earlier periods. L. Cerfaux and J. Tondriau give a thorough survey of this entire topic, with bibliography, from Homeric Greece down to the Late Roman Empire, in *Un concurrent du christianisme, le culte des souverains dans la civilisation gréco-romaine* (Tournai: Desclée, 1957).

others because he could rule himself. Rationality, and especially virtue, became the necessary medium whereby the earthly ruler established his divine likeness to God. Virtue was the hinge upon which the whole idea of
divinized humanity turned. Monarchy was above all the imitation of God:
the good ruler imitated God and thereby took on a kind of powerful reflected divinity himself. In this way the king or emperor was also turned
into a kind of savior figure. The common people were brought to salvation
by imitating the ruler, whose virtue, rationality, and very physical appearance were enough to reform the hearts and minds of the worst sinners
by giving a vision of a new and higher way of life. This particular philosophical tradition tended to weaken the claim of royal divinity to some degree—the earthly ruler was the image of God or the vicar of God, and
obviously not one of the Olympians pure and simple—but such ideas could
be used by those pagan intellectuals who moved in higher political circles
to justify some sort of acquiescence to the imperial demands for divine
honors and veneration.

This variety of political thought may have had its roots in Hellenistic
Neopythagorean speculation of the sort represented in the works attributed to Diotogenes and Ecphantus. Excerpts from treatises *On Kingship* ascribed to these two authors have been preserved in the *Anthology* of John
Stobaeus. [4] Diotogenes' political thought, for example, was based on a fun-

---

[4]Along with a fragment of a closely associated work *On Kingship* attributed to
Sthenidas of Locri. Ioannes Stobaeus, *Anthologium*, 5 vols., ed. C. Wachsmuth and
O. Hense (Berlin: Weidmannos, 1884-1912). The excerpts from Diotogenes are
found in Stobaeus, *Anth.* 4.7.61-62 (Hense, 263-70), the fragment of Sthenidas in
4.7.63 (Hense, 270-71), and the excerpts from Ecphantus in 4.6.22 (Hense, 244-
45) and 4.7.64-66 (Hense, 271-79). Erwin R. Goodenough, "The Political Philosophy of Hellenistic Kingship," *Yale Classical Studies* 1 (1928): 55-102, is a fundamental study. He gives an English translation of all the excerpts from Ecphantus,
Sthenidas, and Diotogenes in Stob. 4.7. A careful critical edition of the Greek text
has been prepared by Louis Delatte, along with a French translation, in *Les Traités
de la Royauté d'Ecphante, Diotogène et Sthénidas* (Paris: E. Droz, 1942). Delatte's Greek
text has been used in this present study; the English translations are mine.

The recent study by Holger Thesleff dates Diotogenes and Ecphantus to the
middle of the third century B.C.E. He believes that the works were composed in
Southern Italy, and that the Doric dialect in which they were written represented
a literary Italiote Koinē that developed in that area in the fourth and third cen-

damental analogy between the earthly monarch and the heavenly monarch.

> Now the king bears the same relation to the state as God to the world; and the state is to the world as the king is to God. For the state, made as it is by a harmonizing together of many different elements, is an imitation of (μεμίμαται) the order and harmony of the world, while the king who has an absolute rulership . . . has been transformed (παρεσχημάτισται) into a god among men.[5]

That is, just as the state by μίμησις copied the cosmic order, so the king took on at least the form (σχῆμα) of a god. The good king was asked to be like Zeus: beneficent, just, fair beyond the letter of the law, merciful, helpful to those who were in need, grateful, not burdensome to any human being, majestic and awe-inspiring, the punisher of evildoers, and the con-

---

turies B.C.E. He argues that Ecphantus's tract *On Kingship* was originally addressed to Hieron II, the powerful third-century king of Syracuse, since the work presupposed a strong Hellenistic monarchy. See Holger Thesleff, *An Introduction to the Pythagorean Writings of the Hellenistic Period* (Abo, 1961) 92-94, 65-66, 99-101. In the same year Walter Burkert ("Hellenistische Pseudopythagorica," *Philologus* 105 [1961]: 16-43, 226-46) also established an early dating (third century B.C.E.) for certain of the pseudepigrapha. The somewhat older work of Louis Delatte placed both Ecphantus and Diotogenes much later, but they were nevertheless clearly no later than the second century C.E. at most, and the importance of the material makes it worthy of careful study in spite of the difficulty of ascribing precise authorship and dating. In fact, the broadest possible limits, on both linguistic and philosophical grounds, would be third century B.C.E. to second century C.E. Diotogenes, the author of treatises both *On Kingship* and *On Piety*, is unknown outside the excerpts ascribed to those two works in Stobaeus. The second author is called Ecphantus the Pythagorean, but the real Ecphantus wrote in Attic Greek in the fourth century B.C.E., while the excerpts in Stobaeus are in Doric dialect (Goodenough, "Political Philosophy of Hellenistic Kingship," 75). Louis Delatte's position was that the language of the excerpts was "un dialecte dorien bigarré"—a mixture of Doric forms from various geographical areas, along with even Ionian, Attic, and Epic forms, producing a strange artificial language never spoken by any actual group of Greeks at any time in history. Delatte therefore assumed that it was the work of a late writer from the Koinē period who strove for an archaizing effect by using these old or exotic forms that had disappeared from normal usage (*Les Traités de la Royauté*, 85-87).

[5]Diotogenes in Stob. 4.7.61 (Hense, 265.6).

troller and ruler of all things.[6] For as Diotogenes declared, "in all these respects . . . royalty is an imitation of divinity" (θεόμιμόν ἐστι πρᾶγμα
βασιλεία).[7]

In another analogy, based on the Platonic doctrine of the tripartite division of the soul, Diotogenes said that the king was to his subjects as the
rational (λογικά) part of the human soul was to the lower parts (the spirited part, τὸ θυμοειδές, and the appetitive part, τὸ ἐπιθυμητικόν).[8]
This analogy therefore made rationality the distinguishing characteristic
that separated the true ruler from the ruled.[9] This attribute of the king was
stressed by Diotogenes in other passages as well. If the king was to be the
supremely rational member of the human commonwealth, then he had to
be completely freed from the passions,[10] and fortified by all the virtues that
gave self-control and prudence.[11] It was his surpassing virtue that distinguished the true king from the mere tyrant.[12] It was virtue and rationality
also that helped confer upon the king his divine fellowship with the gods.

> He must separate himself from the human passions and draw close to the
> gods [συνεγγίζοντα . . . τοῖς θεοῖς], not in arrogance, but in high-
> mindedness and in the exceeding greatness of his virtue.[13]

In other words, the king's supreme rationality was one important reason for
his reflected divinity.

---

[6]Diotogenes in Stob. 4.7.62 (Hense, 268.15, 269.10, 269.15, 270.1, 270.3).

[7]Diotogenes in Stob. 4.7.62 (Hense, 270.10).

[8]Diotogenes in Stob. 4.7.62 (Hense, 266.10). An analogy between the parts
of the soul and the divisions of the state was of course central to Plato's *Republic*.
See also Goodenough, "Political Philosophy of Hellenistic Kingship," 70.

[9]In the Cynic movement it was stressed that the true king by these lights might
actually be the wandering Cynic ascetic with his single cloak and staff, not the
purple-robed tyrant on the throne. See Ragnar Höistad, *Cynic Hero and Cynic King*
(Uppsala: C. Bloms, 1948).

[10]Diotogenes in Stob. 4.7.62 (Hense, 265.17).

[11]Diotogenes in Stob. 4.7.62 (Hense, 266.2): "he must excel the rest in virtue
(ἀρετᾷ) and on that account be judged worthy to rule."

[12]Diotogenes in Stob. 4.7.62 (Hense, 266.4).

[13]Diotogenes in Stob. 4.7.62 (Hense, 268.2).

The virtue of justice was one of the most important, and for this reason Diotogenes advised that "the king would begin by fixing in his own life the most just limitations and order of law."[14] As a respecter of law in his own person, and as creator of law and harmonious order for the state, the good king could be said to be νόμος ἔμψυχος, "Living Law."[15] His word became law in the earthly state because his superhuman role as king made him the embodiment of divine law on earth.[16]

As a final divine attribute, the king was required to display true "majesty [σεμνότας], a thing which imitates God [θεόμιμον]" and "can make him admired and honored by the multitude."[17] Diotogenes went on to explain that the king, by his very physical appearance, should have a beneficial effect on the souls of his admiring subjects.

He must wrap himself about with such decorum and pomp in his appearance, his calculations, his inferences, and the character of his soul, as well as in the actions, movements, and posture of his body, that he will put in order those who look upon him, amazed at his majesty, his self-control, and his attitude of decorum. For to look upon the good king ought to affect the souls of those who see him no less than a flute or harmony.[18]

In other words, the king was beginning to turn into a divine savior figure; he was expected to use his aura of divine majesty to lift the souls of his subjects out of improper thoughts and passions into the realm of right thought and tranquility.

---

[14]Diotogenes in Stob. 4.7.62 (Hense, 266.20).

[15]Diotogenes in Stob. 4.7.61 (Hense, 263.19, 265.11). The king is referred to as "Living Law" in a fragment attributed to Archytas of Tarentum, but the authenticity of this passage is questioned, and its dating not secure. The Stoic Musonius, writing in the first century C.E., said that the good king was "Living Law" as "the ancients" had also taught, so at the very least the phrase and the idea must go fairly far back into Hellenistic times. See Francis Dvornik, *Early Christian and Byzantine Political Philosophy* (Washington DC: Dumbarton Oaks, 1966) 1:245-48.

[16]Erwin R. Goodenough, *The Politics of Philo Judaeus* (New Haven: Yale University Press, 1938) 45.

[17]Diotogenes in Stob. 4.7.62 (Hense, 267.11; see also 267.5 and 267.16).

[18]Diotogenes in Stob. 4.7.62 (Hense, 268.5).

Ecphantus, who stressed the divinity of the ruler even more strongly than Diotogenes, began with the statement that humans were alien beings exiled on earth, part of the divinity mixed with earth.[19] He went on to say that the king had the same earthly matter in him that all human beings did, but that he had a larger portion of the divine than anyone else.[20] Furthermore, when God created the king he used himself as the archetype.[21] In this sense, then, Ecphantus could go on to say that "the king is an alien and foreign thing which has come down from heaven to human beings."[22]

A high standard of purity was required of the king so that he would not defile the divine light of royalty in which he stood.[23] But by achieving this purity for himself, he became a savior by example, the savior of the rest of the people from their sins. "If they sin [ἁμαρτάνωντι] their most holy purification is to make themselves like the rulers."[24] The king imitates God through virtue,[25] so that "both God and king are perfect in virtue."[26] Then

---

[19]Ecphantus in Stob. 4.6.22 (Hense, 244.14): "Upon earth, humanity is a thing in exile, greatly fallen from the purity of its original nature, and made heavy with much earth. Accordingly, humanity would scarcely have been elevated from Earth its Mother, if a portion of the divine had not been breathed into it to rejoin it to the eternal Living Being."

[20]Ecphantus in Stob. 4.7.64. In each separate part of the cosmos, "some one living being rules which is most suitable in its origin, and because it participates to a greater degree in the divine" (Hense, 272.3). Here on this earth, "the king, who possesses a greater share of the better portion of our common nature, is more divine than others" (Hense, 272.9).

[21]Ecphantus in Stob. 4.7.64 (Hense, 272.11): "His temporary dwelling place [τὸ σκᾶνος] is like the rest of humanity's, in that he is born from the same matter [τὰς ὕλας]; but he is fashioned by the supreme Artificer, who in making the king used himself as an archetype [ἀρχετύπῳ]."

[22]Ecphantus in Stob. 4.7.64 (Hense, 275.1).

[23]Ecphantus in Stob. 4.7.64 (Hense, 273.10): "Royalty is then a sure and incorruptible thing, very hard for a human being to achieve by reason of its exceeding divinity [θειότατος]. And he who stands in it must be pure and radiant in nature, so that he may not tarnish its exceeding brightness by his own blemishes, even as some people defile even the most sacred places."

[24]Ecphantus in Stob. 4.7.64 (Hense, 274.4).

[25]Ecphantus in Stob. 4.7.64 (Hense, 274.13).

[26]Ecphantus in Stob. 4.7.64 (Hense, 275.14).

the king's subjects in turn imitate him. This is the only way of developing virtue in humanity as a whole, so the king in his effect upon others necessarily becomes a savior figure. "The king alone," Ecphantus insists, "is capable of putting this good into human nature."[27]

Ecphantus carried this idea of the king as savior figure even further with an interesting version of the Stoic doctrine of the spermatic logos, a version in which the central role was transferred from God to the earthly monarch. The logos was in the king's mind, and was planted by him like a seed among his subjects, where it blossomed and saved them from their sins.

> His logos, if it is accepted, strengthens those who have been corrupted by evil nurture as if by drink, and who have fallen into forgetfulness; it heals the sick, drives out this forgetfulness which has settled upon them as a result of their sin, and makes memory live in its place, from which springs what is called obedience. Taking thus its beginning from seeds of trifling import [φαύλων σπερμάτων] this grows up as something excellent, even in an earthly environment, in which the logos, associating with humanity, restores what has been lost by sin.[28]

If the king was thus the bearer of the divine logos, it followed that the king's thoughts (ἔννοιαν) were themselves sacred and divine.[29] Just as God was the intelligence (φρόνασις) of the universe, so the king had to be the ruling intelligence of the earthly state. And all these attributes of the good king fitted together necessarily, since the incarnation of logos and divine thought and intelligence in the king was the font from which his saving virtues flowed: justice, self-control, and all the rest.[30]

A later, but better-known, representative of this tradition was the biographer and Middle Platonic philosopher Plutarch. He actually stood over on one extreme side of the tradition, because, in reaction perhaps to the excesses of the emperor Nero, he attacked or ridiculed quite a few of the claims of divine monarchs in many of his writings. "Is not almost any king called an Apollo if he can hum a tune, and a Dionysus if he gets drunk, and

---

[27]Ecphantus in Stob. 4.7.65 (Hense, 278.10). It is only "by imitation of him, their better," that "they will follow in the way they should go."

[28]Ecphantus in Stob. 4.7.65 (Hense, 278.12). See also Goodenough, "Political Philosophy of Hellenistic Kingship," 90.

[29]Ecphantus in Stob. 4.7.66 (Hense, 278.22).

[30]Ecphantus in Stob. 4.7.66 (Hense, 279.14).

a Heracles if he can wrestle? And is he not delighted, and thus led on into all kinds of disgrace by the flattery?"[31] To portray the monarch as a god, Plutarch insisted, or as a son of a god, was one of the frequent devices of the king's most dangerous flatterers. The ruler who listened overmuch to people like these, and allowed himself to be bowed down to "like a barbaric idol," was putting himself into the hands of persons who were not true friends, and who did not have his best interests at heart.[32] The greatest genuine honor that a Hellenistic king could receive from his subjects was not a title of divinity but the "noble yet human titles" like "Philadelphus or Philometor or Euergetes or Theophiles."[33] Plutarch especially poked fun at the practice of portraying earthly kings carrying such emblems of divinity as the trident or thunderbolt. "Cleitus, when he had scuttled three or four Greek triremes at Amorgos, caused himself to be proclaimed Poseidon and carried a trident!"[34] The gods punished nations, when they profaned their names by divinizing human kings in such ridiculous fashion.[35]

---

[31]Plutarch, *How to Tell a Flatterer from a Friend* 56f. A careful study of Plutarch's attitude toward divine kingship can be found in Kenneth Scott, "Plutarch and the Ruler Cult," *Transactions and Proceedings of the American Philological Association* 60 (1929): 117-35. Special attention to Plutarch's essay *To an Uneducated Ruler* is given in Goodenough, "The Political Philosophy of Hellenistic Kingship," 94-98.

[32]Plutarch, *How to Tell a Flatterer* 65d; *On the Fortune or the Virtue of Alexander* 331a.

[33]Plutarch, *On Praising Oneself Inoffensively* 543de.

[34]Plutarch, *On the Fortune or the Virtue of Alexander* 338ab; see also *Isis and Osiris* 360bd. In the latter passage Plutarch commented that wise rulers knew better than to believe in such pretensions to divinity: "The elder Antigonus, when a certain Hermodotus in a poem proclaimed him to be 'the offspring of the sun and a god,' said 'the slave who attends to my chamberpot is not conscious of any such thing!' "

[35]The divine honors given by the Athenians to Demetrius Poliorcetes were especially offensive to Plutarch; see esp. *Demetrius* 10.2-4; 11.1; 12.1; 13.1-2. They built an "altar of Demetrius Alighter" where he first stepped from his chariot onto Athenian soil, called their ambassadors to his court θεωροί (envoys to the gods), gave him the divine honors due to Demeter and Dionysus, and even sent to him for oracles. They put his picture (and his father's) along with those of Zeus and Athena on the sacred robe woven for the goddess and carried in the Panathenaïc procession every fifth year. But the gods, Plutarch tells us, were greatly offended, and as the robe was solemnly carried to the Acropolis it "was rent by a hurricane

But Plutarch certainly did not object on principle to the idea that human beings could in some way rise to deification. He was criticizing only what he regarded as gross abuses of the notion, particularly those ideas of divinization, common among the masses, that did not make a strong enough body-soul distinction, and that therefore frequently confused deity with the mortal and grossly physical aspects of human existence. A popular Roman legend, for example, said that Romulus at the end of his life on earth was caught up bodily to heaven in the presence of a group of Roman nobles, and there turned into a god. Plutarch presented this as typical of the "fables" told "by writers who unreasonably ascribe divinity to the mortal features in human nature, as well as to the divine."[36] Human beings did not go to heaven and become gods "by the law of a city" (νόμῳ πόλεως), and particularly not by bodily assumption. The divine element in humanity returned to the gods only after it had been separated from the body and purified as in the mystery cults.[37] This divine element was human virtue, not the physical body and its attributes. "To reject entirely the divinity of virtue were impious and base, but to mix heaven with earth is foolish."[38] In other words, for Plutarch there was a right way and a wrong way to talk about deification of human beings.

If understood properly, therefore, Plutarch was willing to speak of kingship as something "which makes human beings like to gods,"[39] but the true marks of divine kingship were the inner possession of virtue and the divine Logos, not the outward portrayal of the ruler holding thunderbolts and tridents in his hands in his official paintings and statues.[40] In the world

---

which smote it." Severe cold and frost halted the sacred procession for the Dionysia, ruined the grape and fig crop, and also destroyed most of that year's grain crop (*Demetrius* 12.2-3).

[36]Plutarch, *Romulus* 27.6-8, 28.6. Livy 1.16 tells the story less critically.

[37]Ibid., 28.7-8.

[38]Ibid. 28.6.

[39]Ἰσοδαίμονος; Plutarch, *On Brotherly Love* 479a, quoting Ariphron.

[40]Plutarch, *To an Uneducated Ruler* 780f-781a. The good ruler is the one who "has the Logos of God," not a thunderbolt or a trident. "God visits his wrath upon those who imitate his thunders, lightnings, and sunbeams, but with those who emulate his virtue and make themselves like unto his goodness and mercy he is well pleased."

of Nature the sun was the highest and most beautiful image of God, but in the State the divine image was mirrored in the Logos, which the wise learned about through the study of philosophy.[41] The good king especially had to enshrine this divine Logos within his mind so that he himself became the "Living Logos" (ἔμψυχος . . . λόγος), the incarnation of the divine Reason and the divine Law (νόμος) on earth.[42] The Logos was to be like a voice speaking within his mind and pointing out to him all his specific royal responsibilities.[43] The king furthermore had a duty to bring about the moral salvation of his subjects. His own thought and life had to be the pattern for the rest of humankind to model themselves upon. The king had to be their teacher and upholder.[44]

Plutarch listed three genuine attributes of divinity: incorruption (or deathlessness), power, and virtue. Human nature was not capable of the first and the second was in the hands of continually changing fortune, which left virtue as the only divine characteristic that human beings could truly have and hold as their own possession. Yet virtue, and above all justice, was the most divine attribute of all.[45] It was justice that one associated above all with Zeus, the ruler of the universe.[46] Therefore, by living a life of virtue and ruling with laws of justice, the earthly king could truly become "the image of God" (εἰκὼν θεοῦ) on earth.[47]

Of the three basic attributes of divinity, virtue was more important than incorruption or power, Plutarch tells us, since it required intelligent reasoning.[48] To say that virtue and justice required rationality was a Greek truism, but important nonetheless. The passions were much more dangerous in kings than in ordinary people, Plutarch said, because the enormous royal power quickly made "of anger murder, of love adultery, of covet-

---

[41]Ibid. 781f-782a.

[42]Ibid. 780c; see also 779df.

[43]Ibid. 780cd.

[44]Ibid. 780b.

[45]Plutarch, *Aristides* 6.

[46]Plutarch, *To an Uneducated Ruler* 781b.

[47]Ibid. 780ef.

[48]Plutarch, *Aristides* 6.3.

ousness confiscation."[49] The good king therefore had to be a perfect phi-
losopher, holding every passion in control by the strength of his reason.
Plutarch illustrated this standard Hellenistic equation of the king and the
sage with the classical locus—the legend of the confrontation between
Alexander the Great and Diogenes the Cynic. In Plutarch's interpretation,
Alexander was able, through the practice of philosophy, "to become Diogenes in disposition and yet to remain Alexander in outward fortunes."
And Alexander had to be an accomplished philosopher all the more, "since
for his great ship of fortune, tossed by high winds and surging sea, he
needed heavy ballast and a great pilot."[50] Plutarch was therefore willing to
give the Roman emperor a sort of reflected divinity, in spite of his distaste
for the more extreme pomp and imagery of Hellenistic sacred kingship.
The truly good emperor was divine in the same way that the sun was divine
(a point that would have been taken very seriously by ancient men and
women); he was the visible image of the god of cosmic Justice. Here the
heavenly Logos or Nomos was enshrined within a human soul, who ruled
the earthly state with godly wisdom and virtue.

One finds a variant of this teaching, not so thoroughly developed, in
the Stoic philosopher and moralist Seneca. His Stoic pantheism made it
easy for him to link the earthly with the divine. "All this universe which
encompasses us is one, and it is God; we are associates of God; we are his
members."[51] In the small epistolary essay "On the God within Us," Seneca
proclaimed the numinous presence of the divine in every truly wise person.[52] "God is near you, he is with you, he is within you."[53] The sage is

[49]Plutarch, *To an Uneducated Ruler* 782bc.

[50]Ibid. 782ab. The ideas that the good king must be a sage and that the pen-
niless sage was in reality the equal of a king, were widespread in the classical Greek
and Hellenistic world, running the gamut from Plato's highly trained philosopher-
king to the radical Cynic ideal of complete ascetic renunciation (on the latter see
Höistad, *Cynic Hero and Cynic King*). The equation of the true king and the true sage
went back in Stoic teaching all the way to Chrysippus certainly, and probably Zeno
also (see Diogenes Laertius 7.121-122; also von Arnim, *Stoicorum Veterum Fragmenta*
3.frags.617-622).

[51]Seneca, *Epistulae morales* 92.30.

[52]Ibid. 41.4. In 41.3 the true sage is said to display the same sort of awe-pro-
voking *numen* that is perceived in the deep forest or in a dark cavern in the moun-
tains.

[53]Ibid. 41.1.

someone who has genuinely become part of God (*qui dei pars est*).[54] It was Reason (the divine Logos) that above all bridged the gap between God and humanity. In good Stoic fashion, Seneca held that divine reason (*divina ratio*) ruled and controlled the universe. But human reason "is the same, because it is derived from the divine reason."[55] The divinity within humanity is not a mere shadow or copy of that possessed by the immortal gods— "reason [*ratio*] . . . is a common attribute of both gods and human beings."[56] By reason, and by virtue, a human being becomes "equal to the gods."[57]

Furthermore, in the same way that the individual human being's body was ruled by the mind or soul, so the state was ruled by the emperor. Seneca told the young emperor Nero that he was "the soul of the state" (*animus rei publicae*), the spirit or reason that guided and organized the enormous multitude of Roman subjects, "the great mind of the empire" (*mens illa imperii*).[58] Seneca encouraged Nero to recite to himself his list of godlike powers: "I am the arbiter of life and death for the nations; it rests in my power what each person's lot and state shall be; by my lips Fortune proclaims what gift she would bestow on each human being."[59] The good emperor served as "vicar of the gods" (*deorum vice*), and, within his powers, acted towards his subjects as a beneficent god.[60] His subjects elevated him to "a place second only to the gods" and treated him with the veneration and worship that would be due a god made visible.[61]

On the other hand, the savage satire on the deification of the emperor Claudius in the *Apocolocyntosis* shows that Seneca clearly wished to confine divinization only to those monarchs who had become true Stoic sages.[62]

---

[54]Ibid. 92.30.

[55]Ibid. 92.1.

[56]Ibid. 92.27: "in the gods it is already perfected, in us it is capable of being perfected." See also 41.8.

[57]Ibid. 92.27 and 29.

[58]Seneca, *De clementia* 1.3.5-4.1, 1.5.1.

[59]Ibid. 1.1.2. See also 1.5.7.

[60]Ibid. 1.1.2, 1.7.1.

[61]Ibid. 1.19.8-9.

[62]As pointed out by Marion Altman, "Ruler Cult in Seneca," *Classical Philology* 33 (1938): 198-204.

The Roman emperor was not automatically *ex officio* turned into a god, even after death. That Seneca regarded Nero as the more promising philosopher-king than Claudius certainly involved a rather inaccurate assessment of character; Seneca ultimately paid for it with his own life.

In Seneca therefore as in Plutarch, the same basic teaching appeared. The good ruler was the embodiment of the divine Reason or Logos. In this way the earthly king was to the state as God was to the world. Although the underlying metaphysics was different in Seneca—Stoic rather than Platonic—the same basic motif appeared in the political theory of both philosophers.

The motif was widespread and common. A surprising number of echoes appeared even in the writings of Cicero, even though the great orator's basic position was so antithetical to kingship of any sort, divine or otherwise. In the *Republic* Cicero actually agreed with the basic analogies that "kings, commanders, magistrates, senators, and popular assemblies govern citizens as the mind (*animus*) governs the body," and as God rules over the universe.[63] The good ruler was a person of virtue and reason, completely in control of his passions, who "puts his own life before his fellow-citizens as their law."[64] Since from Cicero's somewhat Stoicizing perspective, "true law is right reason in agreement with nature,"[65] he was not far from the idea of the good ruler as "Living Law" or "Reason Incarnate" even though he did not use that language explicitly. Cicero did toy with the arguments for kingship in his *Republic*,[66] and even said that it was the best of the three pure constitutional forms (better than aristocracy or democracy), but he also insisted that a mixed constitution was even more preferable.[67] So he was not a monarchist, and did not properly fall into the same political camp as Plutarch and Seneca.

---

[63]Cicero, *De re publica* 3.25.37.

[64]Ibid. 1.34.52.

[65]Ibid. 3.22.33: this is the "one eternal and unchangeable law . . . valid for all nations and all times," whose author is God himself.

[66]For example, in ibid. 1.36.56, the argument is repeated that just as the gods are ruled by a king, who is the divine Mind of the universe, so the earthly commonwealth ought to be ruled by one man. In 1.38.60, the king is said to be to the state as the rational part (*consilium*) is to the other parts of the soul.

[67]Ibid. 1.45.69.

This general pagan mode of thought was so widespread and influential within the early Roman empire that it affected contemporary Jewish ideas as well, particularly in the writings of Philo of Alexandria.[68] His religion of course made him sensitive to anything that even appeared to threaten monotheism. When attempts were made to put images of the emperor Gaius Caligula in the synagogues of Alexandria and then to place a colossal statue of him (to be worshiped under the name of Zeus) in the temple at Jerusalem itself,[69] Philo's position was clear: A good Jew could not possibly venerate the Roman emperor in this idolatrous fashion.[70] But when Philo came to set out his own theory of rulership, especially in his *Life of Moses* and his *Joseph*, many echoes of the more philosophical idea of sacred kingship still appeared.[71]

---

[68]See the study by Erwin R. Goodenough, *The Politics of Philo Judaeus.* There is also a very useful treatment of Philo's concept of Joseph as the "political man" in the introduction to Jean Laporte's edition of *De Iosepho* (Paris: Éditions du Cerf, 1964).

[69]Philo, *Legatio ad Gaium* 134, 188.

[70]Ibid. 114-18.

[71]Philo's lives of Abraham, Isaac, and Jacob represented the three paths to perfection. In contrast to them, Joseph was turned into an image, in the *De Iosepho*, of the "political man," and he was used to set forth many of Philo's views on the role of the good person put in a position of political power. Moses in the *De vita Mosis* then became especially the image of the ideal king, presented in very Hellenistic terms. See Laporte's edition of Philo's *De Iosepho*, 11, 31-32. It is important to note that for Philo, as for the pagan Hellenistic world, there was no possibility of a completely secular political philosophy. Philo insisted that Moses, as the ideal of true kingship, also had to have the two religious functions of priest and prophet before he could completely carry out his secular duties as king and lawgiver (*De vita Mosis* 2.2-6): "For it has been said . . . that states can only make progress in well-being if either kings are philosophers or philosophers are kings. But Moses will be found to have . . . combined in his single person, not only these two faculties, the kingly and the philosophical," but also the three necessarily accompanying functions of lawgiver, high priest, and prophet. In other words, Philo went on to explain, the good king also had to be "living law," priestly interceder for his people before God, and the prophetic possessor of that God-given knowledge that went beyond the uncertainties of merely mortal reason, "for prophecy finds its way to what the mind fails to reach."

Like the sage, Philo wrote, the political leader also had to have command over his passions. [72] Since this true statesman was in a state of Stoic
ἀπάθεια, his true life was lived as a citizen of the cosmopolis, the world-
embracing city of true reason, rather than as a mere slave of the mob in his
own particular nation. [73] The true Law was one and unchangeable, and was
identical with the Logos, natural reason itself. The particular laws of particular nations in fact tended to differ from this universal law due to changes
introduced by covetousness and mistrust. [74] But a truly good king would try
to prevent such distortions from occurring, and would let his laws and decrees and all his public actions be directed by the universal Logos, so that
the state would instead by "piloted by the good pilot, who is right reason
[ὁ ὀρθὸς λόγος]." [75] In this way Moses, Philo's example of the true king,
was spoken of by him in traditional Hellenistic fashion as "Living Law" (νόμος ἔμψυχος), the law of universal reason enshrined in a kingly soul. [76]
In Hellenistic theory, the ruler, as agent of the Logos, was then supposed
to act as a morally reforming force on the lives of his subjects. In the life
of Joseph (whom Philo also uses as an example of true political leadership),
the young Hebrew even while in prison was placed in charge of all the other
prisoners and proceeded to reform them by his preaching of philosophy
and the example of his own life of virtue. The repentant prisoners were
overawed by the light of the Good that they saw in Joseph's person: " 'When
it shines on us we behold as in a mirror our misbehavior and are ashamed.' " [77]

---

[72]As shown for example in Joseph's refusing Potiphar's wife; see Laporte, 25.

[73]Philo, De Iosepho 67, 69, 79. There is a good deal of Stoicism, of course, in
Philo's basically Platonic philosophical system.

[74]Ibid. 28-31, another rather Stoicizing statement.

[75]Philo, Legum allegoriae 3.79-80.

[76]Philo, De vita Mosis 1.162.

[77]Philo, De Iosepho 86-87; see also Goodenough, Politics of Philo Judaeus, 53-54.
Joseph was a man of "divine wisdom" (θείας ἐπιφροσύνης) who proclaimed to
his brothers, "I am of God" (De Iosepho 37, 266). But he was probably not depicted
as a divinized ruler in De Iosepho 174, Goodenough and Dvornik to the contrary.
When the brother said "the inquisitor is no human being, but God or the Logos
or Law of God," the reference was not to Joseph but to the personified Justice
(Δίκη) of God and his providence, mentioned earlier in De Iosepho 170. But see the
arguments of Goodenough, The Politics of Philo Judaeus, 58; and Dvornik, Early
Christian and Byzantine Political Philosophy 2:563-64.

This was the same kind of savior figure whom the pagan political philosophers had tried to portray in their own doctrine of sacred kingship.

Hence one sees in Philo the quasi-divine character of the earthly monarch described in the traditional Hellenistic philosophical language. He used the standard comparison, that the king was to the state as God was to the world.[78] God worked for the good and benefit of the entire world, producing "order from disorder" and "fellowship and harmony from the dissociated and discordant." In turn, "good rulers must imitate [μιμεῖσθαι]" these beneficent works of God "if they have any thought of becoming like God."[79] The good king or emperor did not imitate God by dressing up in costume to look like Heracles with his lion's skin or Apollo with the sun-rays encircling his head.[80] One attained likeness to God by imitating his virtues. Virtue was the true point of contact between the human and the divine. A human monarch could not ever be divine in nature (φύσις) or essence (οὐσία), but if he practiced virtue continually, he could possibly bring his purpose (προαίρεσις) into the divine likeness.[81]

> In bodily substance the king is like any other human being, but in the authority of his rank he is like the God who is over all. For there is nothing on earth more exalted than he. Therefore as a mortal he must not vaunt himself, but as a god he must not give way to anger. For if he is honored as being an image of God, yet at the same time he is fashioned from the dust of the earth, from which he should learn simplicity toward all people.[82]

Philo would not venerate a statue of the emperor Caligula in his synagogue, but in other contexts, as can be seen, he was perfectly capable of

---

[78]Philo, fragment *apud* Eusebius, *PE* 8.14(386c): "for what parents are to children in human relationships, such is a king to a city, and God to the world." Compare Philo, *De specialibus legibus* 4.186-188.

[79]Ἐξομοιώσεως πρὸς θεόν; Philo, *De specialibus legibus* 4.187-188.

[80]As the emperor Caligula tried to do; see Philo, *Legatio ad Gaium* 79, 95.

[81]Ibid. 114.

[82]Philo, fragment *apud* Antonius Melissa, *Sententiae sive loci communes*, Pars II, Sermo 2 (Migne, *Patrologia Graeca* 136, col. 1012bc). See the comments on this passage in Goodenough, *Politics of Philo Judaeus*, 99; Dvornik, *Early Christian and Byzantine Political Philosophy* 2:563.

idealizing the Roman ruler as the "Living Law," the agent of the divine Logos, and the earthly copy of the heavenly grandeur.

This notion of the emperor as the incarnate Law or Logos of God, which appeared in a variety of contexts, both pagan and Jewish, was therefore a widespread and quite commonplace idea in the Roman world during the period of the Early Empire. It was simply a part of the general intellectual atmosphere. [83]

Eusebius, in the fourth century, inherited this Romano-Hellenistic tradition of divine kingship ideology, and once he became convinced that Constantine was sincere in his commitment to Christianity, and was going to be able to control the empire, he linked himself firmly to it. [84] He asserted that Constantine's monarchical rule was the "icon" or image of God's

---

[83]The connection between Eusebius's thought and this preexisting, originally pagan, political philosophy was first pointed out by Norman H. Baynes, "Eusebius and the Christian Empire," in the *Annuaire de l'institut de philologie et d'histoire orientales* 2 (1933-34), *Mélanges Bidez* (Brussels: 1933) 13-18; reprinted in Baynes's *Byzantine Studies and Other Essays* (London: Athlone Press, 1955) 168-72. Baynes based his article on Goodenough's *Political Philosophy of Hellenistic Kingship*, which had appeared only five years previously.

[84]George Huntston Williams ("Christology and Church-State Relations in the Fourth Century," *Church History* 20, 3 [1951]: 3-33; and 20, 4 [1951]: 3-26) argued that Arians and Catholics had quite different notions of the proper relationship between church and state, and that this was in fact closely connected with their differing conceptions of the divine Logos. Catholics defended the independence of the church, while Arians tended to subordinate the church to the state. Williams's position is of importance in the present context, because he included Eusebius among those he called Arians. The same arguments were repeated by Marie Ann Giuriceo, "The Church Fathers and the Kingly Office" (Ph.D. Dissertation, Cornell University, 1955) esp. 168-73. This approach has been criticized very effectively, however, by Per Beskow, *Rex Gloriae: The Kingship of Christ in the Early Church*, trans. E. J. Sharpe (Stockholm: Almqvist and Wiksell, 1962) 317: "Williams' account of the imperial ideology of the Arians is based largely on Eusebius and Themistius. This choice of source-material to some extent shows up the weakness in his argument, since neither was an Arian. Eusebius was a left-wing representative of the school of Origen; Themistius was not a Christian at all. It is not an easy matter to find out what the Arians really thought on these questions, since most of their literature has vanished irretrievably." For further detailed criticisms of Williams's position, see Beskow, 319-24; see also 313-14.

monarchical rule, so that Constantine's lordship was thereby a μίμησις or imitation of the Divine lordship.[85] God's reign was the eternal reality, while Constantine's reign was the shadow cast on the world of historical and temporal process. A basic Platonic dualism shaped the fundamental relationship. The rule of the emperor was patterned "after the archetypal Idea."[86] He was an image of the Logos as the Logos was an image of the Father.[87] The basic form of Eusebius's theory of rulership was the same as that encountered previously in the pagan theorists of the Early Empire. The ruler's divinity for these political thinkers had lain in his imitation (μίμησις) of God's rule; and in particular, the ruler's soul had been said to be a reflection of the divine word or law (λόγος or νόμος).

Of course, Eusebius had to modify these theories in certain places much as Philo had done. The common pagan practice had assumed that the emperor's reflected divinity allowed one to treat him as god on earth in a way that went far beyond Christian or Jewish tolerance. So Eusebius, like Philo, had to deny divine honors to the emperor past a certain point. In the Great Persecution, Eusebius's contemporaries had often fled or died rather than sacrifice to the emperor. However, one immediately remembers that even the Christian emperors continued to preserve a good many of the trappings of Hellenistic sacred kingship. Their court, their palace, and their persons were sacred, and were both spoken of and treated as such.

Eusebius does not seem to use the actual term νόμος ἔμψυχος in referring to Constantine. Presumably the title of Law Incarnate sounded too

---

[85]In Eus. VC 1.5 God gave Constantine "the icon of His own monarchical authority." In Eus. De laud. 1 Constantine received "the icon of the Highest Kingdom," and administered the world's affairs "in μίμησις of God himself."

[86]Eus. De laud. 3. As has been noted in an earlier chapter, the idea of oneness was a key point of correspondence in the political allegory of Eusebius: "our emperor is one, derived from one, the icon of one—the One who is Emperor of All" (De laud. 7.12). Monotheism and monarchy went together as necessarily as polytheism and what Eusebius called polyarchy (the fragmentation of the Mediterranean world into numerous separate warring states). Monarchy was by far the best form of government, "for the polyarchy whose onslaught has its origin in equality of honor, is, instead, anarchy and revolution" (De laud. 3). Eusebius further buttressed his monarchist principles by affirming the hereditary succession of monarchs as a "law of nature" (θεσμῷ . . . φύσεως), VC 1.9.

[87]Eus. De laud. 1.

much like Word Incarnate, and might be regarded as giving Christological honors to the emperor. This was especially a problem, since in Eusebius's Origenistic Christology he most probably followed Origen all the way and put the nexus of the union in the human soul of Jesus, which formed an exact image of the Logos.[88] Origen's Christology was in many ways already simply an adaptation to Christian purposes of the Romano-Hellenistic theory of divine monarchy. Since Constantine as emperor was also an image of the Logos, Eusebius came perilously close in many passages even then to giving him Christlike honors. Likewise, Eusebius does not seem to have made direct use of the Hellenistic royal title Ἐπιφανής, with its implicit notion of full deification, in speaking about Constantine, but he used the term indirectly by speaking of Constantine's victory over the foes of the Church as an "epiphany" of Christ.[89] Presumably regarding an event rather than a person as the epiphany removed the danger of idolatry.

---

[88]Aloys Grillmeier (*Christ in Christian Tradition* [London: Mowbray, 1965] 166) correctly points out that for Origen "the Logos is the image of God, but the soul of Christ is the image of the Logos." Grillmeier argues (180-81) that Eusebius failed to follow Origen on this point, and adopted a Logos-sarx Christology instead, but the references to the soul of Christ in Eusebius cannot be brushed aside simply because they are associated with scriptural quotations. Patristic theology regularly tries to tie its most important Christological points to a handful of key scriptural passages. More important, an oft overlooked but vital Christological passage lies buried in the middle of one of Eusebius's arguments in the *Contra Hieroclem*. Eusebius was arguing about which of the two was the true Divine Man, Jesus or Apollonius of Tyana (chapters 4-5). Then in chapter 6 he describes this true Divine Man as a person who has received, from the "Lord of the entire economy and of gifts of grace . . . an illumination as it were of the light which streams from him." This person, "having cleansed his understanding and dissipated the mist of mortality, may well be described as truly divine, and as carrying in his soul the image of some great god. Surely so great a personality will stir up the entire human race, and illuminate the world of humankind more brightly than the sun, and will leave the effects of his eternal divinity for the contemplation of future ages." In the context of the argument it is clear that only Jesus and not Apollonius could fulfill those criteria. Eusebius seems to have been saying therefore that the divinity of Jesus arose from the illumination of his human soul by God in such a way that the divine light kept the image of God imprinted within that soul. This was basically an Origenistic conception of the divine-human union.

[89]Eus. *HE* 10.8.1.

In a series of allegorical comparisons, Eusebius drew up five parallels between the Logos and the emperor Constantine: The Logos ruled eternally, and analogously Constantine had ruled for a very long time. The Logos ordered the universe according to the Father's will, and analogously Constantine brought the people of his empire to the Logos and made them fit subjects for God's kingdom. The Logos defeated the evil daemons, and analogously Constantine defeated the human enemies of God in battle. The Logos gave knowledge and wisdom to humanity, and analogously Constantine had proclaimed the way of truth to his subjects in order to bring them to knowledge of God. The Logos had opened the gates of heaven to humanity, and analogously Constantine's desire had been to bring every one of his subjects to eventual salvation.[90] Again one sees the typical emphases of Hellenistic kingship theory: The Hellenistic king was to bring cosmic order and harmony down to earth. The Hellenistic king was at least partly turned into a divine savior figure who rescued his people from their sins and returned them to right thought and heavenly obedience. The Hellenistic king was an intermediary through whom the Logos could be planted as a seed on earth, there to blossom and drive out sin, evil, and forgetfulness of humanity's divine origin and destiny.

It was in the context of this Hellenistic political theory that it became important to affirm, not only that Constantine himself was εὐσεβής (pious),[91] but that he was also "a teacher of εὐσέβεια" to all humankind, both by public testimony[92] and by living his own life as a visible paradigm of εὐσέβεια.[93] This idea of the emperor's quasi-religious function as teacher of piety to his people was a part of the Hellenistic political inheritance that caused Constantine and his Christian successors repeated difficulty as they tried to be ideal Hellenistic monarchs in a Christian theological milieu that put enormously greater stress on doctrinal orthodoxy than any pagan cult had ever seen.

When Eusebius portrayed Constantine in one of his most important images as the New Moses, this may possibly have been due to the influ-

---

[90]Eus. De laud. 2.

[91]Eus. VC 1.6; De laud. 9.18.

[92]Eus. VC 1.5.

[93]Eus. VC 1.3-4 (θεοσέβεια seems to mean the same as εὐσέβεια in Eusebius's usage).

ence of Philo, who, as has been seen, treated Moses in his *Life of Moses* as the ideal philosophic ruler of Hellenistic kingship theory. This seems one possible way of explaining why it was Mosaic imagery instead of, for example, Davidic imagery that was chosen in the most important linkages of Constantine with Old Testament political leaders, even though David, to modern eyes at any rate, seems much more kingly than Moses. Constantine as the New Moses was portrayed by Eusebius as the man who came to set God's people free.[94] When the pontoon bridge collapsed at the battle of the Milvian bridge, and Maxentius drowned amidst the flotsam, this was to Eusebius the destruction of Pharaoh's army as it disappeared beneath the churning surface of the Red Sea.[95]

In various kinds of ways, therefore, prevailing Romano-Hellenistic modes of political philosophy exerted an enormous influence on Eusebius's thought about Constantine.[96] Particularly the idea of the emperor's tem-

---

[94]Eus. *VC* 1.12.

[95]Eus. *HE* 9.9.2-8; *VC* 1.38. Dvornik (*Early Christian and Byzantine Political Philosophy* 2:644) points out the connection between Philo's Hellenized Moses (the pattern of all kingly virtues) and the parallel drawn in the *Vita Constantini* between Constantine and Moses. The parallel, Dvornik notes, was used in other ways as well: "The Red Sea passage became a subject for artistic representation . . . , Moses being made to typify Constantine, and the Pharaoh his enemy Maxentius. It is often depicted on the sarcophagi of the fourth century: the many examples found in Rome and in Arles, Constantine's favorite city, testify that the symbolism had become equally popular in the West." See also Erich Becker, "Protest gegen den Kaiserkult und Verherrlichung des Sieges am Pons Milvius in der christlichen Kunst der konstantinischen Zeit," in Franz Jos. Dölger, ed., *Konstantin der Grosse und seine Zeit* (Freiburg i. Br.: Herder, 1913) 155-90.

[96]One could have explored the association between the emperor and the gods, for example, from a number of other directions. Sabine MacCormack ("Roma, Constantinopolis, the Emperor, and His Genius," *Classical Quarterly* 25 [1975]: 131-50) discusses the role of various divine pairings in literature and art between the emperor and his genius, the emperor and his *comes* (such as Sol-Apollo, Jupiter, or Hercules), the emperor and the deified and personified Roma, the emperor and his Tyche, and the emperor and the deified and personified figure of Constantinopolis. She shows how this evolved in the Christian empire into a much more unequal pairing between the emperor and God, where the two are closely associated, but are no longer regarded in any way as being on the same level. See also Arthur Darby Nock, "The Emperor's Divine *Comes*," *Journal of Roman Studies* 37 (1947): 102-16.

poral reign as reflection down on earth of the heavenly and eternal Logos was originally a well-known pagan philosophical idea that Eusebius simply took over. But Eusebius's Christianization of this particular tradition of political thought gave later generations continued access to it, and the Middle Ages and early modern period were thereby able to draw on Plutarch, Seneca, and other such pagan theorists to aid in describing their own Christian monarchies.

However, this influence of Hellenistic kingship theory was joined by another, completely different thread of thought based on Hebraic ideas and particularly on apocalyptic eschatology. In Eusebius's interpretation of Constantine's reign the two worlds of thought were linked firmly: Constantine was the godlike Hellenistic king of the earthly realm, but he was also the man raised up by God at the end of this world to create the Kingdom of the Last Days.

Discussions about eschatology occur frequently when Eusebius is writing about history. One notices first of all the set of lengthy attacks in Eusebius's *Church History* against that particular variety of literalistic apocalypticism called "millennialism" or "chiliasm." It is important to note exactly what Eusebius was condemning. He was denouncing certain people who, he said, preached that there would be a thousand-year reign of Christ on earth ($\dot{\epsilon}\pi\grave{\iota}$ $\gamma\tilde{\eta}\varsigma$, $\dot{\epsilon}\pi\acute{\iota}\gamma\epsilon\iota o\nu$) in a literal, physical kingdom ($\sigma\omega\mu\alpha\tau\iota\varkappa\tilde{\omega}\varsigma$) after the resurrection, in which the good would partake of the pleasures of the body and the lusts of the flesh—a kingdom "with food and things to drink and marriages," "with festivals and sacrifices and slayings of victims," all in a literal, physical fashion right here on earth.[97] Eusebius correctly identifies these beliefs as having their roots in Jewish apocalypticism.[98]

One can easily recognize in Eusebius's description a rather negative account of the extravagant imagery sometimes used to describe the messianic kingdom in that widespread type of early Christian theology that Jean Daniélou called "Jewish Christianity."[99] Irenaeus furnishes a good example of what Eusebius was attacking.

---

[97] Eus. *HE* 3.28, 39.11-13; 7.24.1-3, 25.1-6.

[98] Eus. *HE* 7.24.1.

[99] Jean Daniélou, *The Theology of Jewish Christianity*, trans. J. A. Baker (London: Darton, Longman, and Todd, 1964) esp. chapter 14, "Millenarianism."

The days will come, in which vines will be produced, each one having a thousand branches, and in each branch ten thousand twigs, and on each twig ten thousand shoots, and on each shoot ten thousand clusters, and in each cluster ten thousand grapes, and each grape when pressed will give two hundred and twenty-five gallons of wine. And when one of the saints takes hold of a cluster, another will cry, "I am a better cluster, take me, bless the Lord through me."[100]

Eusebius regarded this kind of millennialism as "mythological" (μυθικώτερα is the word he uses in *HE* 3.39.11). He was scornful in the extreme of Papias, an important representative of these ideas, whom he described as "a man with an extremely small νοῦς."[101] He believed that those biblical accounts that appeared to talk about a millennium had to be read "mystically" (μυστικῶς) and "symbolically" (ἐν ὑποδείγμασι).[102]

Eusebius himself affirmed the natural immortality of the soul, a basic principle of Platonic eschatology that was alien to pure apocalypticism.[103] In a good many passages in Eusebius it seems to be assumed that, when death comes to each human being, his or her soul goes immediately into God's presence without having to wait until the history of this world has run its course.[104] Hence, the dead were spoken of as *already* in heaven.[105] This heaven was a realm of Platonic transcendence, so the only part of the human being that could be taken up into it was the noetic part of the psy-

---

[100]Irenaeus, *Adv. haer.* 5.33.3.

[101]Eus. *HE* 3.39.13. Robert M. Grant, "Papias in Eusebius' Church History," in *Mélanges d'Histoire des Religions offerts à Henri-Charles Puech* (Paris, 1974) 209-13, believes that there was a sharp change between Eusebius's early attitude towards apocalyptic and his later attitude, "that originally Eusebius viewed the Apocalypse as apostolic and had a high regard for the ancient author Papias. Later, however, he doubted the apostolicity of the Apocalypse and explicitly attacked the memory of Papias." More recently, see Grant's treatment of this same issue in *Eusebius as Church Historian* (Oxford: Clarendon, 1980).

[102]Eus. *HE* 3.39.12. This meant allegorical exegesis of course; see *HE* 7.24.2. See also *HE* 7.25.4-6.

[103]The pure apocalyptic position being condemned in Eus. *HE* 6.37.

[104]Eus. *VC* 1.9; 3.46; 4.64.

[105]Ibid. 1.2.

che, [106] which was transformed into "an incorruptible and angelic being."[107]
In this state, the human soul was visualized pictorially as "residing in ethe-
real rest above the vaulted arches of the heavens," clothed in a shining,
flashing robe of light. [108]

A Platonic eschatology required a certain way of life as a consequence:
one had to work to cut loose one's attachments to the visible, corporeal
world so that the soul could rise up unencumbered into the noetic and transcendent realms. "Practice dying," Plato had said (*Phaedo* 67e, 81a), and
Eusebius likewise said that those Christians who set out on the path towards true perfection "appear to die to the life of mortals, bearing along on
earth only the body itself, while in thought the soul is transported into
heaven."[109]

But even though Eusebius spoke of the eschatological character of human existence in Platonic fashion rather than exhorting his listeners to expect the apocalyptic end of the world at any moment, he still believed that
the end of the world would eventually come as a literal historical event. In
his antimillennialist passages Eusebius rejected only the idea of a wonder-
filled thousand-year reign of Christ *on earth*, so that he was involved in no
contradiction when he nevertheless maintained the idea that this present
cosmos would undergo a cataclysmic destruction at some future date in history.

It is possible to establish, in very rough fashion, the approximate date
at which Eusebius expected the end of the world. That there was no lively
sense of it coming in the near future is shown by his vision of a long Constantinian dynasty ruling the Roman empire for generations to come. [110]
Furthermore, the principal purpose for writing history in Eusebius's rationale was to preserve a memory for posterity. [111] Eusebius was counting on
the world lasting for several generations longer at least, in this case so that

---

[106]Ibid. 4.64.

[107]Ibid. 3.46.

[108]Ibid. 4.69, 1.2.

[109]Eus. *DE* 1.8(29b-30b).

[110]Eus. *VC* 1.9.

[111]Among the many passages to this effect, see for example, Eus. *HE* 7.26.3,
32.32; 8.pref.; *VC* 2.23.

there would be a posterity to read his *Church History*! On the other hand, because Jesus had already come, one was already in the last days, at the consummation of this present world-time.[112] A contrast was evident: the Hebrew patriarchs of the pre-Mosaic period had lived at the beginning of this world-time, when everything was fresh and new and growing, while Eusebius thought that his own generation lived at a time when "history was withering away and running down and pushing on towards its final termination."[113] This gives a good idea of the approximate time scale involved: Eusebius thought of himself as about as close to the end of historical time as the patriarchs had been (on the time-scale given in his *Chronicle*) to the beginning. That is, the end of the world was no more than a few centuries away. One might also make a very crude guess about the time-scale, based on Eusebius's identification of the Four Kingdoms in Daniel: he says that they were the Assyrian, Persian, Macedonian, and Roman empires.[114] This Fourth Kingdom was of course the one destroyed in the apocalyptic end of this world. If one assumes that all four exist for very roughly the same period of time, this will give an idea of the possible order of magnitudes involved, that is, time spans measured in centuries rather than decades or millennia. Putting all these clues together, it can be seen that Eusebius regarded the end of the world as reasonably far off—several centuries perhaps, or at least a number of generations away—but that he nevertheless thought of the world he lived in as a world that had already

---

[112]Eus. *DE* 6.15.2 and 8-9(279a and 280ab).

[113]Eus. *DE* 1.9.3-4(30d-31a). Since the beginnings of the faith, Christians had of course frequently tended to regard the end as either immediately imminent or as not too far away. Problems about the delay of the parousia appear in the New Testament itself, and the second-century apologists continued these speculations. Justin, for example, said that the postponement of the end was to allow a further time for repentance of sins (*First Apology* 28). Christianity had to perfect the world before its history could be terminated. In his *Chronographies* (one of the sources of Eusebius's *Chronicle*) Sextus Julius Africanus, in the early third century, had dated the end of this present world and the beginning of the millennial kingdom as coming exactly 500 years after the birth of Christ.

[114]Eus. *DE* 15.fragment 1. (Like Josephus, Eusebius plays with the problems of Danielic numerology, but unlike Sextus Julius Africanus he does not let it affect his periodization of history in any major structural fashion. See Eus. *DE* 8.2(381b-404c), where he interprets the seventy weeks of years in Daniel 9:20-27).

lived most of its history and was now moving through those remarkable events that were to mark its closing days. The fundamental mental attitude was that of having a closed future: perspectives had narrowed, and although there was considerable joy and relief at the prospects for the next few generations (before the dread final time of troubles came), there was also nevertheless no feeling of open horizons, no ebullient enthusiasm over infinite possibilities for future novelty and invention within humanity's historical development on this earth.

When one looks at Eusebius's interpretation of the biblical description of the Last Days, one sees that Eusebius turned it into a sort of "expanded eschatology." That is, the set of predicted eschatological events that the biblical authors generally depicted as taking place over a period of a few years or decades were identified by Eusebius with historical events that were taking place over a time-span of centuries. The fall of Jerusalem in 70 C.E., as the mark of the rejection of the Jews, was turned into an eschatological event by connecting it with a number of passages in the Old and New Testament containing apocalyptic imagery. [115] Likewise, the amazing missionary success of the Church was seen as part of the eschatological drama. [116] The Pax Romana was identified as the predicted eschatological Kingdom of Peace, the very last and greatest of the world empires, to which there would be no imperial successor in this space-time continuum. [117] At the very end, of course, this Kingdom of Peace would change its character com-

[115]In Eus. HE 3.5.4, 7.1, Matthew 24:15 and 24:19-21 are read in the context of the Little Apocalypse in Matthew 24-25. In Eus. HE 3.7.3-6, Luke 19:42-44 and 21:23-24 are read in the context of Luke 19:11, 19:41-44, and 21:5-36 (esp. 21:32). In Eus. DE 2.3.67-73(67ad), Isaiah 2:6 is read in the context of Isaiah 2:2-21. Eus. DE 6.13.3-9 and 12-17(271c-272d and 273ad) treats Micah 1:3-5, while in Eus. DE 8.3.9-15(406b-407b), Micah 3:12 is read in the context of Micah 3:12-4:4.

[116]Eus. DE 2.3.67-73(67ad) interprets Isaiah 2:2-3 and 17-20. Eus. DE 2.3.111-112(75ab) cites Isaiah 11:6 and 9. Eus. DE 6.13.19-20(274bc) reads Isaiah 2:2-3. Eus. Theoph. 3.2 reads Psalm 72:7-8. Eus. Theoph. 4.36 reads Matthew 24:6-14.

[117]Eus. HE 10.1.4-6 reads Psalm 46:8-9. Eus. DE 8.3.9-15(406b-407b) treats Micah 4:1-4. Eus. DE 15.fragment 1 reads Daniel 2:31-45, and Rome is identified as the fourth and final world-empire before the apocalyptic end of the world. Eus. De laud. 16.1-5 and 7-8 refers to Psalm 72:7 and Isaiah 2:4. Eus. Theoph. 3.2 reads Psalm 72:7 and Isaiah 2:4.

pletely, and the Roman empire would become that "Gog"[118] who along with Magog was to fight on Satan's side in the battle of Armageddon.[119] Nevertheless, in the peaceful years remaining before the apocalyptic time of troubles came upon the human race, Eusebius believed that the successive rulers of the Constantinian dynasty, "the saints of the Most High" in Daniel's vision of the Four Beasts, were to reign as the eschatological emperors.[120] It is interesting to compare this idea with the concept of a Golden Age presided over by "the Emperor of the Last Days," which Norman Cohn says played such a major role in medieval European expectations of the apocalyptic end.[121] Eusebius carried this whole method of interpretation to its dubious apotheosis by identifying[122] Constantine's Church of the Holy

---

[118]Eus. *DE* 8.3.5-6(424ac) cites Numbers 24:3-9 (reading "Agag" as "Gog") and Ezekiel 38:3.

[119]Revelation 20:8.

[120]Eus. *De laud.* 3 reads Daniel 7:18.

[121]Cohn traces this motif back to two of the Christian Sibylline oracles, the mid-fourth century *Tiburtina*, and the late seventh-century *Pseudo-Methodius*; Norman Cohn, *The Pursuit of the Millennium*, 2nd ed. (New York: Harper and Row, 1961) 15-20. See also Walter Emil Kaegi, Jr., "Initial Byzantine Reactions to the Arab Conquest," *Church History* 38 (1969): 139-49.

[122]Eus. *VC* 3.33, quoting Revelation 21:2. From the information that has been preserved, this exact motif does not seem to have been used in later liturgical celebrations of the anniversary of the dedication of the church. But similar allegorical comparisons do appear frequently. In the *Itinerarium Egeriae*, the dedication of the Church of the Holy Sepulcher was said to be liturgically linked at that time to the Invention of the Cross and to Solomon's dedication of the First Temple. All three were celebrated on the same day (13 or 14 September). See Egeria, *Diary of a Pilgrimage*, trans. G. E. Gingras (New York: Newman, 1970) chapter 48, with the excellent notes on 254-56 nn485, 486, and 488. In the later liturgy of the Orthodox Church one finds, in the order for the anniversary of the dedication of a church, a troparion linking God's creation of the firmament of heaven to the construction and consecration of the church: "De même qu'en haut tu as produit la splendeur du firmament, tu as aussi produit ici-bas la beauté du saint tabernacle de ta gloire, Seigneur: affermis-le pour les siècles des siècles, et accepte les prières que sans cesse nous t'offrons en lui." 1 Kings 8:22-30 was also used, to establish an allegorical parallel with Solomon's dedication of the First Temple. See Juan Mateos, ed. and

Sepulcher, one of the imperial family's pious building projects, with the descent of the Heavenly Jerusalem in the book of Revelation!

The final time of troubles would involve all the inhabitants of earth in the full paraphernalia of apocalyptic horrors: Antichrist would come for the last time, [123] and then Christ would appear in His Second Coming, as glorious and Godly as His first coming had been humble and human, [124] and Antichrist would be destroyed. [125] The whole material cosmos would disintegrate, including the sun, moon, and stars. [126] The Last Judgment would divide human beings into those who did and those who did not have εὐσέβεια. The first lot would receive eternal life, while the others were condemned to the eternal fire. [127] The blessed would have incorruptible resurrection bodies. [128]

Also in line with a more Hebraic conception of history, Constantine was described explicitly by Eusebius as the man "raised up" by God[129] when He came "with a mighty hand and an outstretched arm"[130] for the salvation of his people. This was an idea really quite alien in spirit to the classical Greek notion of divine action in history. Constantine was therefore "the servant of God,"[131] foreordained by God to his task, for as soon as Constan-

---

trans., *Le Typicon de la Grande Eglise: Ms. Saint-Croix n° 40, xe siècle*, Tome II, *Le Cycle des Fêtes Mobiles*, Orientalia Christiana Analecta 166 (Rome, 1963) 186-87. See also "La dédicace des églises," in A. G. Martimort et al., *L'Eglise en Prière: Introduction à la Liturgie* (Paris: Desclée, 1961) 179-83.

[123]Eus. *DE* 15.fragment 5.

[124]Ibid. 4.1.3(144c), 16.38-40(190bd); 6.15.8-9(280ab); 15.fragment 5. *Theoph.* 4.35.

[125]Eus. *DE* 15.fragment 5.

[126]Ibid. 3.3.14-15(106ab).

[127]Ibid. 3.3.17(106d); 9.15.6-8(453ac); 15.fragment 6; *De laud.* 12.5; *Theoph.* 4.29.

[128]Eus. *HE* 10.4.46; *VC* 3.46.

[129]Eus. *HE* 9.9.1; *VC* 3.1.

[130]A characteristic phrase used by the Deuteronomistic historian (as in Deut. 4:34, 5:15, 7:19, 11:2, 26:8) echoed by Eusebius in *HE* 10.8.19: "with an upraised arm, leading Constantine with His hand." Cf. Eus. *VC* 2.2.

[131]Θεράπων, not δοῦλος (slave). Eus. *HE* 9.9.8; 10.8.19; *VC* 1.12; 2.2; 4.14; *De laud.* 7.11-12.

tius died, Eusebius tells us, "his son Constantine was immediately proclaimed by the armies most perfect Emperor and Augustus, and, long before
them [ἔτι πολὺ τούτων πρότερον], by the All-Ruling Emperor, God
Himself."[132] This idea that the human agent of God in history was precho-
sen by God, and then called to his task, was another fundamental Hebrew
historiographical concept (cf. Jeremiah 1:5).

Eusebius himself put forward as one of his most basic images of the first
Christian emperor that of Constantine the Dragon-Slayer. This motif was
first depicted in an encaustic painting made at Constantine's own direction, portraying the emperor with the Chi-Rho suspended over his head,
and a serpent-like dragon, pierced through with a spear, falling headlong
into the watery primeval abyss.[133] In Eusebius's interpretation the serpent-
monster was of course the symbol of the evil power that was loose in the
world, and the sea was the Abyss of Destruction. This destruction of Satan's power through the agency of Constantine was of course an apocalyptic image, and fitted smoothly into Eusebius's eschatology and the role he
assigned in it to Constantine.

Eusebius did give a partially distorted view of Constantine, though not
for the reason usually assigned. Eusebius's problem was not that he was too
pious and credulous, but that he was too rational. Constantine's religion
was a good deal more primitive than his, so primitive that it embarrassed
him. In his basic personality, Constantine must have been strikingly like
his nephew Julian—a romantic rebel who insisted on flaunting the religion
of the established majority, and also a visionary and a mystic. The two men
were different in that Julian's personal religion was more sophisticated in
some respects, due to his reading in the classics, and more steeped on the
other hand in a credulous trust in divination and fortune-telling. Constantine's religion shortly after the battle of the Milvian bridge seems to have
been some sort of crude mixture of sun worship and partially understood
Christian monotheism. Even as he moved more completely into the Christian orbit, his religion continued to be based on such things as visions, Sibylline oracles, relics of the true cross, and a somewhat overcredulous awe
of rituals like baptism.

---

[132]Eus. HE 8.13.14.

[133]Eus. VC 3.3.

Eusebius was not really comfortable in that kind of religious atmosphere. Hence, in what Eusebius himself regarded as two of the most significant interventions of God in the whole history of Constantine's life, there were no visions or any other kind of miraculous, contranatural intrusions, but instead only chance occurrences that the classical Graeco-Roman historiographical tradition would have ascribed to Fortune. God, not human beings, chose Constantine to be emperor, Eusebius said[134]—but this claim of divine intervention was based upon the observation that Constantius had fathered a great number of children, and that it was only by an act of what a classical Greek would have called Fortune that the one son Constantine happened to be the one present at his father's deathbed.[135] According to Eusebius, the biblical doctrine of God's lordship over history had been vindicated in contemporary history in the eyes of all humanity, even to the greatest doubters—however, it was vindicated *not* by the vision of the cross of light, which Eusebius mentioned almost apologetically,[136] but by the bridge collapsing under Maxentius,[137] an event that a classical Greek would have ascribed to Fortune.

Eusebius was embarrassed by the interpretation Constantine gave to that crucial event in his life. To Constantine, the center of the whole picture had been occupied by the cross of light glittering in the blue Italian sky, and a theophany in which Christ had appeared to his eyes the night after.[138] Eusebius made it very clear that he was repeating this story because the emperor had insisted on its centrality while he was still alive. His protests as to its truth were couched in such a fashion as to make it obvious that he did not expect his educated readers to believe such a tale lightly. We have no way of knowing whether Eusebius actually believed it himself. But Constantine was a man who saw visions with considerable regularity—not just occasionally, but thousands of them![139] In these theophanies God some-

---

[134]Ibid. 1.24.

[135]Ibid. 1.18.

[136]Ibid. 1.28.

[137]Eus. *HE* 9.9.2-8; *VC* 1.38.

[138]Eus. *VC* 1.28-29 and 32.

[139]Eus. *De laud.* 18.1 for the Christian period of his life. And before that there

times revealed future events to him, and plots against his life. [140] At other times, God's revelation told him how to conduct the administration of the empire and frame laws. [141] And perhaps the most striking picture was that of Constantine at war, setting up a small tent outside the fortified camp where his legions were at ease, and praying until a vision of God appeared to him, at which time he would jump up and run to the camp, shouting for his men to draw their swords on the spot and form the battle lines for an immediate attack against the enemy. [142]

One must also not forget that the vision just before the battle of the Milvian bridge had hardly been Constantine's first such experience. Only two years previously, in 310, there had been a vision of Apollo, that is, of the Unconquered Sun, which Constantine had immediately celebrated on the coins he minted. He was a man looking for a faith at the time, the kind of person familiar to us from early Christian history. One is immediately reminded of people like Justin Martyr and Augustine. But Constantine's faith had to be based on visions and miracles. The middle ages would understand him far better than Eusebius did.

Nevertheless, one of the places where the real Constantine did fit into Eusebius's theological framework was in eschatology. The real Constantine was a charismatic, ecstatic prophet and military leader, who set about, with the aid of the defiant bishops of a martyr church newly baptized in its own blood, to build what he and Eusebius both thought would be the truly Final Empire, the Eschatological Kingdom that would reign through

---

had been of course the vision of Apollo that Constantine saw in 310. Sabine MacCormack, "Roma, Constantinopolis, the Emperor, and His Genius," *Classical Quarterly* 25 (1975): 131-50, discusses the pair Constantine-Apollo in the context of other divine pairs or associates; see esp. 139. On Constantine's vision of Apollo, see also the same author's "Latin Prose Panegyrics," in T. A. Dorey, ed., *Empire and Aftermath: Silver Latin II*, 143-205, esp. 165. Also see H. A. Drake, "The Vision of 310," in *In Praise of Constantine*, 20-21.

[140]Eus. *VC* 1.47; *De laud.* 18.3.

[141]Eus. *De laud.* 18.1-3.

[142]Eus. *VC* 2.12-13. Peter Brown, insightfully I believe, regularly includes Constantine in his discussion of Late Antique "holy men." See "The Rise and Function of the Holy Man in Late Antiquity," *Journal of Roman Studies* 61 (1971): 80-101. This point was made also in his 1976 Jackson lectures at Harvard.

the last dying years of a doomed cosmos until the Seven Seals were broken[143] and the final destruction descended on the world. The acts of wild religious fervor that broke out periodically in Western Europe through the course of the Middle Ages (many of them described in Norman Cohn's well-known book, *The Pursuit of the Millennium*) were a natural development of the spiritual inheritance to which all the West fell heir after Constantine's reign.

But Constantine and his successors continued not only the eschatological tradition, they also carried on the Roman and Hellenistic philosophical tradition of monarchy in only slightly modified Christian garb. This was a legacy to the Middle Ages and early modern period as well. When King James I of England in a speech to Parliament in 1610 defended the divine right of kings, and said, "kings are justly called gods for that they exercise a manner or resemblance of divine power upon earth,"[144] we can imagine that Plutarch and Seneca smiled in their graves.

---

[143]Revelation 5ff.

[144]And further, "the state of monarchy is the supremest thing upon earth; for kings are not only God's lieutenants upon earth, and sit upon God's throne, but even by God himself they are called gods" (Speech to Parliament, 21 March 1610, in J. P. Kenyon, ed., *The Stuart Constitution, 1603-1688, Documents and Commentary* [Cambridge: Cambridge University Press, 1966] 12-14, excerpted from *Works*, 529-31). In French documents from the period of Louis XIV, similar statements assert that the king is the special, visible image of God on earth. His unlimited power reflects the divine authority and his words are the proclamations of God. He is a visible divinity. See John B. Wolf, *Louis XIV* (New York: W. W. Norton, 1968) 372-73, for extracts from various French sources from the latter half of the seventeenth century.

CHAPTER 8

Socrates Scholasticus: Origenism, Humanism, and Cosmic Sympathy

Eusebius's historical writings left a lasting impression on the centuries that followed. Perhaps his greatest successor was the tolerant and careful lawyer from Constantinople, Socrates Scholasticus, who wrote, between 438 and 443 C.E., a *Church History* covering events from the accession of Constantine to the year 439.[1] It is one of the classic works of Christian historiography. It dealt with that great period of Christian history that produced such figures as Athanasius, John Chrysostom, and the Cappadocian fathers, and saw the Church embroiled in the long, bitter controversies over Arianism and the beginnings of the dispute over Nestorius. Socrates' work was designed to continue the story of Eusebius's history and bring it down to his own time.

Socrates sorted out the complicated chronology of events as best he could, and enlivened it with anecdotes and an occasional quietly caustic comment about the intolerance of dogmatic bishops and emperors and the willingness of theologians to engage in unbelievably rancorous disputes over minor verbal differences in the wording of doctrines. Socrates was an in-

---

[1] Socrates wrote in *HE* 1. 1-2 and 7. 48 that the beginning point of his history was the proclamation of Constantine as emperor by the legions of Britain (in 306, after Diocletian's abdication in 305) and Constantine's conversion to Christianity in 312. The conclusion to his history was then set at the seventeenth consulate of the emperor Theodosius; that is, in 439 C.E., although this may have been post-dated to correspond with the effective date of the Theodosian Code, promulgated to the East on 15 February 438 but not to take effect until 1 January 439. Since the later *Church History* of Sozomen was dependent on Socrates' history, and the dedication to Sozomen's history was written not long after the summer of 443 (see chapter 9), Socrates must have written between 438 and 443.

teresting personality, who said what he thought regardless of what his readers might think. His history is a refreshing look at the fourth and fifth centuries, and one of the four or five most valuable pieces of history writing from the late Roman period.

Socrates Scholasticus was born ca. 380 in Constantinople, the great Eastern capital, where he spent all his life.[2] He was a layman, a lawyer by profession. This latter fact surely helps to explain why he ended his *Church History* at the precise date which he chose, namely, 439 C.E. The great development in jurisprudence during his career had been the publication of the Theodosian Code, the first official compilation of Roman law, a collection of all general constitutions enacted by the emperors from Constantine down to Theodosius II himself.[3] Book 16 of the Code in particular contained the imperial constitutions concerning religion, which defined theological heresy and orthodoxy and specified the legal privileges of the orthodox clergy and the prohibitions enacted to harass and destroy heretical religious groups.[4] This legislation was inextricably entangled with the history of the doctrinal disputes of the fourth century. The complete Code was promulgated to the East on 15 February 438 to take effect beginning 1 January 439.[5] The latter date was the one taken by Socrates as the termination of his history, so his work therefore encompassed exactly the span of time covered by the constitutions of the Theodosian Code; that is, all events from the accession of Constantine to the effective beginning of the new legal system in 439.[6]

One must suppose that Socrates, as a lawyer in Constantinople, recognized the importance of the emperor Theodosius's great compilation.

---

[2]Compare Socr. *HE* 5.24.

[3]Mommsen's text of the Code has been translated into English in a useful volume by Clyde Pharr, *The Theodosian Code and Novels and the Sirmondian Constitutions* (New York: Greenwood Press, 1952).

[4]For a detailed analysis of this material, see William K. Boyd, *The Ecclesiastical Edicts of the Theodosian Code,* Studies in History, Economics and Public Law edited by the Faculty of Political Science of Columbia University 24, 2 (Whole No. 63) (New York: Columbia University Press, 1905).

[5]*Novels of Theodosius II,* Title 1.3.

[6]The earliest constitutions of Constantine in the Code in fact date back only to 313, when he consolidated his power over the West.

He could even have worked on the project in some secondary role. At Constantinople in 429 Theodosius II had appointed a commission of nine learned men to supervise the project of compiling the code, and had directed them to assemble a staff of experts to carry out the work.

> We are confident that these men [the nine commissioners] who have been selected by Our Eternity will employ every exceptionally learned man, in order that by their common study a reasonable plan of life may be apprehended and fallacious laws may be excluded.[7]

One of the nine commissioners was "the Respectable Theodorus, Count and Master of the Bureau of Memorials."[8] This name is significant because Socrates' *Church History* was written at the request of a man named Theodore, whom Socrates greatly respected for his piety, and to whom he dedicated the work.[9] It is certainly possible that this was the same Theodore, and that Socrates was officially commissioned to produce a historical survey of the theological controversies of the fourth and early fifth centuries to aid the compilers of Book 16 of the Theodosian Code in selecting and interpreting or rejecting the ecclesiastical legislation of the various Arian and orthodox emperors. Socrates could, of course, simply have engaged in his historical researches out of private curiosity. Nevertheless, the connection between the dates of his *Church History* and the dates of the Theodosian Code shows that some juridical interest must have entered into Socrates' historiographical endeavors.

Although he was a layman, Socrates was nevertheless well read in theology. Throughout the pages of his history there occur the names of such figures as Clement, Irenaeus, Julius Africanus, the second-century apologist Apollinaris of Hierapolis, Serapion of Antioch,[10] and above all, the great theologian Origen and other theological writers in his tradition. Socrates' history was filled with Origen's name. He was alternately defended against his attackers and appealed to as the authoritative guide to true Christian

---

[7]*Codex Theodosianus* 1.1.5.

[8]Ibid.

[9]Socr. *HE* 2.1; 6.introd.; 7.48.

[10]Socr. *HE* 2.35; 3.7.

belief.[11] If one wished to know what a scriptural passage truly meant, or what was the true nature of God or Christ, Origen was cited. To Socrates, what one learned from Origen was the true hermeneutics, τὴν ἑρμηνείαν τῶν ἱερῶν γραμμάτων, the key that unlocked all the holy scriptures.[12] He was the teacher who taught "the true philosophy," τὴν ἀληθῆ φιλο-σοφίαν,[13] instead of the mere "dialectics" and "sophistry" that often passed under that name. Allegory was of course the hermeneutical method Ori-gen applied to interpret the scriptures. As Socrates understood this, it meant elevating one's mind to the secret contemplation, the ἀπόρρητον θεω-ρίαν,[14] of the divine reality that was only indicated indirectly by the sur-face, literal meaning of the "mystical discourses."[15] This concept of scripture as symbol and allegory was used by Socrates—as the doctrine of justifi-cation by faith was to be used by other theologians some centuries later—as a means of attacking legalism and ironbound literalism. So, for example, Socrates used allegorical exegesis in HE 5.22 to explain why the Church must allow diversity in Christian ritual observances.[16] The flexibility that the Origenistic allegorical method introduced was part of the reason be-hind the impressive spirit of tolerance that pervaded Socrates' thought.

To defend his master Origen, Socrates leveled extremely sharp criti-cism at the anti-Origenist leader Theophilus of Alexandria, who was ac-cused of using mere "sophisms" to turn simple folk against Origen, and was constantly portrayed in the worst possible light.[17] On the other side, Soc-rates praised throughout his pages the great Origenists of the previous two centuries: Pamphilus of Caesarea, Eusebius of Caesarea (cited in his role

---

[11]For example, Socr. HE 2.21, 35, 45; 3.7, 23; 4.26, 27; 6.13, 17; 7.46.

[12]Socr. HE 4.26. Compare 4.27, τὰ ἱερὰ γράμματα ἑρμηνεύειν.

[13]Socr. HE 4.27.

[14]Socr. HE 3.23 (the Greek phrase occurs twice). The word θεωρία was also used in 5.7, 22.

[15]Λόγοι μυστικοί; Socr. HE 3.23.

[16]See also the comments of S. L. Greenslade, *Schism in the Early Church*, 2nd ed. (London: SCM, 1964) 94-95.

[17]Socr. HE 6.7—τῷ σοφίσματι, τοῦ σοφίσματος—in Socrates, "sophistry" and "dialectic" appear regularly as the oppostite of true φιλοσοφία. See also 6.17.

as a prominent Origenist), Gregory Thaumaturgus, Didymus the Blind, Basil the Great and Gregory of Nazianzus (mentioned in their role as Origenists), and Rufinus the translator of Origen. The name of the great Athanasius was even invoked to defend Origen. [18]

Among this list of prominent Origenists, one of the most important names mentioned was that of Evagrius Ponticus. In *HE* 3.7, Socrates adopted as his own the trinitarian teaching contained in Evagrius's *Monachos*. In *HE* 4.23, Socrates took the highly unusual action, for him, of giving a list of all the works written by Evagrius, and then offered two very long excerpts from Evagrius's writings, an even more unusual practice in his historiographical style. This emphasis upon specifically Evagrian teaching enables one to place Socrates in the context of fourth- and fifth-century radical Origenism.

Evagrius was roughly contemporary with the great figures involved in the first Origenist controversy, the famous dispute that broke out at the very end of the fourth century between Jerome and Rufinus, and Theophilus of Alexandria and the Tall Brothers. [19] (Since he died in 399, Evagrius blessedly missed the bitter events of the peak of the controversy.) He taught a fully developed doctrine of preexistence and apocatastasis: At the beginning, Evagrius said, the pure created intelligences had formed the primitive henad, living in the essential knowledge of God. "Movement" entered, however, and all but one of those intelligences fell from the original unity and became souls. Only Christ remained as the one unfallen intelligence. The second, material creation then gave each fallen intelligence a body, whether angelic, human, or demonic. A return to the original vision of God was possible, however. These fallen intelligences had to rise through the three ascending levels of sensible contemplation (that is, gross contempla-

---

[18]Socr. *HE* 3.7 and 4.27 (Pamphilus); 2.21, 3.7 and 3.23 (Eusebius); 4.27 (Gregory Thaumaturgus); 4.25 (Didymus); 4.26 (Basil and Gregory, and Rufinus); 6.9 (Athanasius).

[19]See Antoine Guillaumont, *Les "Képhalaia Gnostica" d'Evagre le Pontique et l'Histoire de l'Origénisme chez les Grecs et chez les Syriens* (Paris: Éditions du Seuil, 1962) 47-80; Derwas J. Chitty, *The Desert a City: An Introduction to the Study of Egyptian and Palestinian Monasticism under the Christian Empire* (Oxford: Blackwell, 1966) esp. 49-53 on Evagrius's career. On Jerome and Rufinus, see, for example, J. N. D. Kelly, *Jerome* (New York: Harper and Row, 1975).

tion, second natural contemplation, and first natural contemplation) until they had obtained ἀπάθεια and the angelic state. Then, with a final complete purification, the intelligences could regain the essential knowledge of God and the Unity. By the "seventh day" of creation, Evagrius taught, even the demons will have risen through multiple worlds to the level of angels, and be given purely spiritual bodies; Christ will then reign over all rational beings. Finally on the "eighth day" all matter will be abolished, the purified intelligences will regain their original equality with Christ, number and multiplicity will vanish, and the original Unity will be reestablished once more.[20]

Socrates' espousal of Evagrius's teachings made him a more radical Origenist than Eusebius. Socrates in this way also emphasized an element of mysticism largely lacking in the first church historian, who had been much more of a rationalist. Socrates was aware that he was holding a radical position. He knew that he was going against "the many" in championing Origen.[21] He regarded himself quite frankly as belonging to a privileged intellectual set, the small group of people whose philosophical training and greater than ordinary intellectual ability enabled them "to understand the depth of Origen's books."[22]

It seems often to be assumed in our century that ancient allegorical exegesis involved a basically unhistorical approach to the world. But in fact, three of the most important figures in the establishment of Christian historiography—Eusebius, his translator Rufinus, and his continuator Socrates—were all openly avowed Origenists, who publicly fought for and defended their master. It was they who invented the writing of church history. In addition, Eusebius's exhaustive labor putting together the Chronology, the Eusebian Canons, and the work he wrote on biblical geography, indicate a massive amount of pure historical research precisely on the history of the Old and New Testament period—the one area where the allegorical spirit should have most killed his interest in literal historical fact if the allegorical spirit had in fact been basically antihistorical in its bias. In fact, what Origen and his method did was to permit one to say that there

---

[20]Guillaumont, Les "Képhalaia Gnostica" d'Evagre, 37-39.

[21]Socr. HE 6.13.

[22]Socr. HE 2.21.

were historical errors in the Bible.[23] He enabled one to approach biblical history (and therefore any other kind of history) with a free, critical, inquiring spirit.

Therefore instead of reading the church histories written by Eusebius and Socrates in Enlightenment fashion as the triumph of authority over reason[24]—an interpretation that simply does not work—we would do well to consider these histories instead as the creation of the more radical intellectuals among the Christian party, and as part of the ongoing battle between Origenists and anti-Origenists that ran like a submerged turbulence under a large part of Eastern church history during the fourth and fifth centuries.

Not only do we know the basic theological position of Socrates Scholasticus, his basic philosophical position is also clear. He was fundamentally a Platonist.[25] In *HE* 2.35 he invoked the so-called Academic ἐποχή,[26] the skeptical suspense of judgment developed by such Greek logicians as Pyrrho, Arcesilaus, and Carneades in the fourth through second centuries B.C.E., a philosophical position combined with Platonism by the latter two. In its fully developed ancient form, this mode of methodical doubt operated by placing the opposing arguments of differing philosophical schools side by side; in light of the irreconcilable differences that were thereby

---

[23]Origen, *De principiis* 4.2.9; but see also 4.3.4.

[24]See for example the passages on 237-38 of J. B. Bury, *The Ancient Greek Historians* (London: Macmillan, 1909), and on 327-28 of James T. Shotwell, *The Story of Ancient History* (New York: Columbia University Press, 1961), originally published as *The History of History* 1 (New York, 1939).

[25]Socrates Scholasticus referred to Plato as that "marvelous philosopher" among the Greeks (Socr. *HE* 3.23, compare 2.35), but subordinated even Plato to his own namesake, the great Socrates, whom he turned into a rather Christianized philosophic hero. Socrates was the "chiefest" of all the Greek philosophers (3.16 and 23), and is actually called a "Friend of God" (3.23). The members of the great Socratic circle in ancient classical Athens all "recognized that he had thoughts above the merely human" (3.23), but the great philosopher was nevertheless put to death by the Athenians because, we are told, he took the pagan idea of *demons* and "stamped a different face on that coin" (3.16).

[26]Οἱ . . . ἐφεκτικοὶ τῶν φιλοσόφων, "those among the philosophers who practice the ἐποχή."

caused to appear, it declared that no sure human knowledge was possible, only probabilities at best.[27] Socrates Scholasticus seems to have had a peculiar variant of the traditional Academic position, for he supported his position by invoking the name not only of Plato, but also of Plotinus.[28] It was scepticism, therefore, mixed with mysticism, in some broadly Neoplatonic base. This fundamental antidogmatic skepticism also helped contribute to the marvelous spirit of tolerance that was the most outstanding and endearing characteristic of Socrates Scholasticus.

Philosophy in this sense, for Socrates, was therefore good, but mere "dialectic" was bad.[29] The controversies that had shaken the Church for more than a century, Socrates said, were produced by individuals who had fallen prey to the pseudoarguments of dialectic (διαλεκτική)[30] and the love of triumph in disputes (φιλονεικία).[31] Arius had been guilty of that,[32] the

---

[27]For a selection of relevant passages, see C. J. de Vogel, Greek Philosophy: A Collection of Texts 3: The Hellenistic-Roman Period (Leiden: Brill, 1959) 184-230. See also such general works as Edwyn Bevan, Stoics and Sceptics (Oxford: Clarendon, 1913). This Academic skepticism is familiar to us in a later period in the pages of Cicero; it was subsequently picked up from there by Augustine, whom it attracted strongly during the period of his greatest disillusionment; see Peter Brown, Augustine of Hippo: A Biography (London: Faber and Faber, 1967) 79-80.

[28]Socr. HE 2.35: "those among the philosophers who practice the ἐποχή, who expound the ideas of Plato and Plotinus." In addition to Plotinus, one other Neoplatonist was referred to—Porphyry—but unfavorably, because of his famous attack on Christianity, to which Socrates' model, Eusebius of Caesarea, had written twenty-five books in refutation.

[29]Socr. HE 2.35; 3.22-23. By "philosophy" (φιλοσοφία) Socrates Scholasticus meant the thought of men like his namesake Socrates, Plato, Aristotle, Plotinus, the Academics, and Marcus Aurelius, and of course Origen, who taught "the true philosophy" (4.27). It is interesting to note the crucial modification made in the echo of one New Testament text, Colossians 2:8. Διὰ τῆς φιλοσοφίας καὶ κενῆς ἀπάτης becomes in Socr. HE 1.18 ἡ διαλεκτικὴ καὶ κενὴ ἀπάτη, in other words the condemnation of philosophy is altered to a condemnation of dialectic. (The text is quoted in its original, unmodified form in HE 3.16 along with a careful explanation.)

[30]Socr. HE 1.5, 18; 2.2, 35; 4.7; 5.10.

[31]Socr. HE 1.5, 2.2, 3.25, 5.introd., 5.10, 7.32. Compare 1.23, ὡς κατὰ ἀντιπάλων, "as against rivals or adversaries."

[32]Socr. HE 1.5.

Arian controversy had spread throughout the Roman empire for that reason,[33] and the radical Arian Aetius and his disciple Eunomius had been especially notable examples of what happened when dialectic was used in mechanical fashion by men who had not risen above the level of schoolboy philosophical exercises.[34] Nestorius, in the next century, had also gotten too deeply drawn into the *Theotokos* controversy because of his φιλονει-κία.[35] Wise men, like the emperor Jovian[36] and the Novatianist Sisinnius,[37] knew how to recognize disputes of this unprofitable kind in advance, and refused to become involved in them.

An argument that never rose above the level of mere dialectic was an argument only about empty words,[38] a strange battle in the dark[39] in which the disputants strove for precision of language[40] without noetic understanding[41] of what they were talking about. Dialectic alone without any higher understanding was simply another word for sophistry.[42] The sophist exaggerated everything; his pen was for sale, and he would praise a person in one speech and damn him in another, as expediency demanded. Sophistry was a petty art, which worked on the level of schoolboy exercises. It used sneers and ridicule, and pretended that these were rational arguments. Since sophistry was a method of intellectual warfare

---

[33]Socr. *HE* 2.2.

[34]Socr. *HE* 2.35; 4.7. A truly excellent modern study of these two figures is now found in Thomas A. Kopecek, *A History of Neo-Arianism* (Cambridge MA: Philadelphia Patristic Foundation, 1979).

[35]Socr. *HE* 7.32. The modern disputes over the nature of Nestorius's teachings and the character of the textual sources are nicely analyzed in Roberta C. Chesnut, "The Two Prosopa in Nestorius' *Bazaar of Heracleides*," *Journal of Theological Studies* new series 29 (1978): 392-409, which should be consulted before looking at any earlier books or articles on that theologian.

[36]Socr. *HE* 3.25.

[37]Socr. *HE* 5.10.

[38]Socr. *HE* 1.18—κενοφωνίας.

[39]Socr. *HE* 1.23—νυκτομαχίας.

[40]Ibid.—ἀκριβολογούμενοι.

[41]Ibid.—νοοῦντες.

[42]Socr. *HE* 2.35; 4.7.

whose sole object was to defeat the other side, it was by its very nature unfitted for the discovery of truth.[43]

This is the kind of approach to philosophical and theological argumentation that Socrates Scholasticus was actually attacking when he invoked the Academic ἐποχή,[44] and it seems probable that Eunomianism in particular was a principal target.[45] For Socrates (as had also been the case earlier for Basil the Great and Gregory of Nyssa) Eunomianism had been the variety of fourth-century Arianism that presented the real theological challenge. Its syllogisms and tight-knit logic gave its conclusions a frightening appearance of logical inevitability.[46] It is interesting to note that the central error of Eunomius, in the eyes of Socrates, was not his doctrine of the Son's relationship to the Father, but his claim that we could perfectly know and understand what God the Father was in his οὐσία, that is, the claim that we could perfectly know and understand the essential nature of ultimate reality.[47] It was this rather naive and overinflated claim to knowledge that Socrates was undoubtedly condemning above all when he spoke of "sophistry" and mere "dialectics." The Academic ἐποχή, together with a form of Neoplatonic and Evagrian mysticism, was Socrates' attempt to construct a theology with a deeper understanding of the proper goal of human knowledge.

One other statement needs to be made about Socrates' theological position. Though Orthodox and Catholic himself, he had a quite notorious sympathy for the Novatianists.[48] Many Catholics so disliked that rigorist,

---

[43]Socr. HE 3.23, the first part of the chapter, where Socrates was refuting Libanius. The rejection of Christianity by such learned and sophisticated pagans as Porphyry, Julian, and Libanius was set aside by Socrates on these grounds.

[44]Socr. HE 2.35.

[45]Socr. HE 2.35; 4.7.

[46]See J. N. D. Kelly, *Early Christian Doctrines*, 3rd ed. (London: Adam and Charles Black, 1965) 249, and again see the excellent study by Thomas A. Kopecek, *A History of Neo-Arianism*.

[47]Socr. HE 4.7. Compare Kelly, *Early Christian Doctrines*.

[48]See, for example, Socr. HE 1.10, 13 (where the Novatianist holy man and miracle worker Eutychian is called a θεοφιλοῦς ἀνδρός, a "Friend of God"); 2.38; 4.9; 5.10; 6.22 (a whole chapter in high praise of the Novatianist bishop Sisinnius, famous for his witticisms, but also eloquent, a philosopher, skilled in dialectic, and a good exegete of Scripture).

puritan breakaway group that Socrates was apparently courting personal animosity by even using Novatianist sources for his history. He defiantly did so in spite of this, and stated explicitly where his information came from.[49] Socrates' sympathy for the Novatianists arose partly, perhaps, from the record of their common persecution by the Arians.[50] The Novatianists had held to the *homoousios* doctrine along with the Nicene Catholic party, and Socrates' historical researches showed that they had had to pay the price for this during the fourth century on a number of occasions. It seems clear that the fact that the Novatianists held a position identical to that of Catholic Orthodoxy on the *metaphysical* issue of the Trinity[51] was much more important to Socrates than the differing theological doctrines of the *church* held by the two groups. His lack of concern with maintaining uniformity of church rituals[52] went along perfectly with this general attitude. It was a carefully considered doctrine of latitude that Socrates held, however, working within definite bounds and limits, as S. L. Greenslade pointed out.[53] Socrates furthermore held, on the basis of his own historical investigations, that purely intellectual theological issues had not in fact been the determining factors in the rise of the Novatianist movement. When the dispute arose, some sided with Novatian, Socrates said, and some sided with Cornelius, and the decision seemed to be decided by a person's own previous ethos and inclination.[54] Those who liked to sin took advantage of the situation! National character also affected the issue—the Phrygians and Paphlagonians often tended toward fanaticism and moralism, so they swung towards Novatianism easily.[55] Socrates himself had his own definite rigorist tendencies, which gave him more sympathy toward the Novatianist position on church discipline than toward the more lax view that was coming to be taken by many within Catholic Orthodoxy. John Chrysostom's

---

[49]Socr. *HE* 1.13—"I will state precisely who told me this story, and not hide it, *even if I should incur the hatred of some.*"

[50]Socr. *HE* 4.9.

[51]Socr. *HE* 4.9; 5.10.

[52]Socr. *HE* 5.22.

[53]Greenslade, *Schism in the Early Church*, 94-95.

[54]Socr. *HE* 4.28: ἕκαστος κατ' ἔθος εἰς τοῦτο ἔτρεψεν εἰς ὃ καὶ πρότερον μᾶλλον ἐπέκλινεν.

[55]Socr. *HE* 4.28.

pulpit proclamation of mercy, "Approach, though you may have repented a thousand times," drew sharp condemnation from Socrates, who held to the older point of view that only one repentance was permitted after baptism.[56] Of course, even allowing one repentance put Socrates clearly on the Catholic side, since the Novatianists would not have allowed even this.

Moving beyond Socrates' reaction to particular philosophical and theological positions, it is necessary to discuss also his general attitude towards knowledge and culture. The previous century had seen a great struggle between paganism and Christianity to determine who would shape the fundamental institutions of the empire. The pagan extremist Julian reacted in one direction by banning Christians from the Roman educational system.[57] The intolerant Christian emperor Valens, whether deliberately or not, introduced an equally extreme counterreaction when his campaign against the people involved in the tripod episode[58] moved from the execution and torture of those immediately involved into a general antipagan purge with the burning of pagan books (mostly in the liberal arts and jurisprudence) at its focus.[59] Fortunately, the solution that finally prevailed in that century was the kind of middle road represented by works like Basil's *Address to Young Men, on How They Might Derive Benefit from Greek Literature.*[60] Socrates continued this tradition of Christian humanism represented by Basil and the other Cappadocian Fathers.

----

[56]Socr. *HE* 6.21. Cf. Hebrews 6:4-6 and 10:26-31, no repentance after baptism; and Shepherd of Hermas mand. 4.3.3-5, only one repentance after baptism; also the literature particularly on the latter. See also J. N. D. Kelly, *Early Christian Doctrines*, 198-99.

[57]Even a devoted glorifier of Julian like the pagan historian Ammianus Marcellinus was appalled by the action; see Amm. Marc. 22.10.7 and 25.4.20.

[58]Amm. Marc. 29.1.29-32.

[59]Ibid. 29.1.41 and 2.4.

[60]The Cappadocian Fathers with their "Christian neoclassicism" became thereby the great cultural heroes of Werner Jaeger's *Early Christianity and Greek Paideia* (Cambridge MA: Harvard University Press, 1962) esp. 74-75. "They do not conceal their high esteem for the cultural heritage of ancient Greece," but "Christianity through them now emerges as the heir to everything in the Greek tradition that seemed worthy of survival."

Although the crucial phase of the controversy had come shortly before Socrates was born, it was still an issue in some fashion for all of his life-time.[61] In fact, in spite of the Christianization of the empire, the seeds of paganism always lurked under the surface even in the later Byzantine world, and sprouted forth in periodic pagan revivals.[62] Christian historians of the Late Roman and Byzantine empires were therefore never relieved of the   ·
necessity of making some sort of *rapprochement* with the essentially pagan ideas and preconceptions of classical Greek historiography. In this light, it becomes clear why Socrates felt the need to devote a chapter of his his-tory (3.16) to defending the practice of training Christians in the Greek classics. Greek παιδεία, despite its completely pagan character, was for him an object of undisguised admiration, and he therefore insisted that it ought to be retained as the foundation of education even for good Chris-tians.[63] Although the arguments he used in that chapter were in one sense traditional, used previously by other Christian intellectuals,[64] the problem was in no sense a dead issue, and his ideals of a Christian humanism, blend-ing Christian faith and pagan literary education, had to be defended and could not simply be assumed.

---

[61]Compare the experiences, for example, of Socrates' rough contemporary, Augustine. Or, to give other examples, the foundation of the University of Con-stantinople in 425 by the emperor Theodosius the Younger and the closing of the ancient philosophical schools of Athens by the emperor Justinian in 529 show other ways in which the issue of the structure and control of the educational system re-mained a constant problem through this entire period. See H. I. Marrou, "Byz-antine Education," in *A History of Education in Antiquity*, trans. G. Lamb (New York: New American Library, 1956) 452-55; John W. Barker, *Justinian and the Later Roman Empire* (Madison WI: University of Wisconsin Press, 1966) 30, 99-100.

[62]There were famous pagan revivals, for example, in the ninth, the eleventh, and the fifteenth centuries (Marrou, "Byzantine Education," 453).

[63]One should observe that this was a different position from the one taken by the mature Augustine (see for example Peter Brown's comments on the *De doctrina christiana* in his *Augustine of Hippo*, 263-68), or by Jerome, with his famous dream in which he was accused of being "a Ciceronian," not a Christian. Even in the fifth century, Socrates' extremely positive position on the role of the pagan classics in education could not at all be taken for granted.

[64]Socrates quoted Romans 1:18-21 for example, which had been used in a sim-ilar way by Origen two centuries earlier in *Contra Celsum* 6.3-4.

Part of Socrates' own childhood education in Greek παιδεία was carried out under the tutelage of some rather notorious pagans: Helladius, a priest of Zeus, and Ammonius, a priest of the Ape God, who had both participated actively in the great anti-Christian riots in Alexandria in 389 C.E., so actively, in fact, that they both had been forced to leave Alexandria in a hurry, and later had drifted into Constantinople, where they set themselves up as grammarians. There the child Socrates was sent to receive an education. One of the two grammarians, Helladius, boasted that he had murdered nine Christians with his own hands during the great riot.[65] The spirit of traditional Mediterranean paganism was still very much alive in Socrates' time: it was not something one gained only from the pages of a book.

But the books were there too. As a result of his reading of the pagan classics, and his own personal contact with believing pagans, a good many pagan terms crept into Socrates' writing, terms that Eusebius, a century earlier, would never have let touch his page.[66] For example, the words τύχη (Fortune)[67] and μοῖρα (Fate)[68] both occur in Socrates' history. They were used in a fairly innocent manner, perhaps, but they would not have been used at all by Eusebius as a point of principle. Other terms were even more pagan: Socrates suggested that the emperor Julian was slain by the snaky-haired female spirits called the Erinyes.[69] Another kind of classical pagan demon, an Ἀλάστωρ, spelled out the letters ΘΕΟΔ in the famous episode of the magic tripod that foretold the name of Valens's successor.[70] It was also suspected by Socrates that an Ἀλάστωρ was at work on one other occasion.[71]

---

[65]Socr. HE 5.16.

[66]Socrates was of course no pagan in any basic sense. He completely rejected the open paganism of Porphyry, Julian, and Libanius (HE 3.22-23). This was a largely *unconscious* transference of ideas from the omnipresent pagan background in ways that would not have implied to Socrates any basic disloyalty to his Christian faith.

[67]Socr. HE 4.1; 5.25; 7.23.

[68]Socr. HE 6.6.

[69]Socr. HE 3.21.

[70]Socr. HE 4.19.

[71]Socr. HE 7.38.

In this same connection, in Socrates the ability of pagan oracles to predict the future was given slightly more credence than in Eusebius. Like his predecessor, Socrates believed that the great oracular shrines such as the one at Delphi were inhabited by resident demons.[72] But Socrates gave two concrete instances in which pagan oracles supposedly came true: the affair of the tripod just mentioned,[73] and the oracle found inscribed when the walls of Chalcedon were torn down.[74] Eusebius would never have admitted that genuine predictions of the sort claimed to have been made in these two instances could have been made by pagan oracles. It is interesting to note that both these oracles were also mentioned in Ammianus Marcellinus[75]—the pagan historian and the Christian historian were beginning to come onto common ground now. In another case, where there was a purported prediction of Christ's coming by pagan Egyptian priests,[76] Socrates was quite concerned about whether this could truly have happened. But he did not doubt because of any disbelief that pagan oracles could predict the future in general; he doubted because one scriptural text (Col. 1:26) said that the coming of Christ was a special kind of future event that had been "hidden from the aeons and from the generations."

Paganism was therefore still alive. The great issues of pagan historiography were in no sense dead, even though Socrates lived in a world that had been nominally Christianized for more than a century. In particular, as has been noted in previous chapters, the concept of Fortune (τύχη) had lain at the very center of traditional pagan thought about history. Hardly any pagan historian in the Graeco-Roman world could have conceived of writing a history in which the concept of Fortune did not play some role. It would have been just as inconceivable for a Christian, living in that world, to try to write a historical narrative without talking about the power of the unexpected conjuncture to shape the course of events. But because of the pagan religious aura that so often surrounded the figure

---

[72]Socr. HE 3.23.

[73]Socr. HE 4.19.

[74]Socr. HE 4.8.

[75]Amm. Marc. 29.1.29-32; 31.1.4-5. In the latter, there are a few changes in wording.

[76]Socr. HE 5.17.

of Fortune in the late imperial period, the actual word τύχη had become objectionable to Christian ears.

In the early Greek Christian historians of the Eastern Roman empire, one obtained therefore a consistent search for more neutral terms to refer to this commonly recognized fortuitous element in history.[77] In the early fourth century Eusebius picked up some Aristotelian language—used by Aristotle himself in talking about this issue—and re-presented the pagan concept of Fortune in Christian fashion by speaking of τὰ συμβεβηκότα, the "accidents" of history. His successor church historians, however, either did not read the right parts of Eusebius or they rejected this particular gambit, since they chose different terms to use in their own writings. Theodoret, as shall be seen in the next chapter, used a whole series of Fortune words such as συμφορά, εὐκληρία, and δυσκληρία. Socrates (and later, the church historian Evagrius) picked up still another, different thread of Greek thought about Fortune, namely the concept of the καιρός.

Pagan Graeco-Roman historiography had been fascinated with the "key event" and the "critical moment"—the time and the place at which something tiny, like a small decision by a single person, started the giant forces of history grinding and rolling in a completely different direction. The

---

[77]There has been a good deal of scholarly discussion about whether the early Byzantine historian Procopius was a pagan who believed in Fortune or a Christian who believed in a God of providence. See Averil M. Cameron, "The 'Scepticism' of Procopius," *Historia* 15 (1966): 466-82, and *Agathias* (Oxford: Clarendon, 1970); Averil and Alan Cameron, "Christianity and Tradition in the Historiography of the Late Empire," *Classical Quarterly* new series 14 (1964): 316-28; J. A. S. Evans, "Christianity and Paganism in Procopius of Caesarea," *Greek, Roman, and Byzantine Studies* 12 (1971): 81-100; G. Downey, "Paganism and Christianity in Procopius," *Church History* 18 (1949): 89-102. The missing link in these discussions is, I believe, provided by the fourth- and early fifth-century Christian historians, who have not been investigated adequately up to this point. The transition from the pagan concept of Fortune found in pre-Constantinian secular history to the mixed pagan-Christian literary language of the sixth-century secular historian Procopius takes place through the intermediary of the nonsecular, completely ecclesiastical historians of the fourth and early fifth centuries, who first combined Fortune motifs with Christian interpretations of history. They did this in ways that avoided the actual word τύχη, but which in fact incorporated the concept of the fortuitous in terms readily recognizable as such to an ancient reader.

critical moment, the καιρός, was simply another face of Fortune. It was this word καιρός that Socrates seized upon, and gave a novel twist to, by combining it with another ancient idea, the concept of cosmic sympathy.

Socrates did use the word τύχη itself three times,[78] but it was too patently pagan to use often. The word τύχη was never used in the New Testament. Socrates himself records how Julian the Apostate had rather prominently offered sacrifices to the Tyche of Constantinople.[79] Fortune was a goddess portrayed in pagan idols and worshiped in that form. But the word καιρός was an impeccably biblical word—it occurs more than eighty times in the New Testament—that would nevertheless convey to a pagan Greek ear an important aspect of the doctrine of Fortune found in the classical historians. That is, καιρός conveyed the idea of a very special historical situation contrived for a moment by the workings of Fortune.

The word καιρός is used many times through the course of Socrates' history.[80] Evagrius Scholasticus, who carries on the Eusebian tradition of ecclesiastical history in the next century after Socrates, actually personifies Kairos in vivid but bizarre traditional fashion in the pages of his history.

> For the Opportune Moment [ὁ καιρός] is swift of flight: when it is close upon one, it may be secured; but should it once have escaped the grasp, it soars aloft and laughs at its pursuers, not deigning to place itself again within their reach. And hence no doubt it is, that statuaries and painters, while they figure it with a lock hanging down in front, represent the head as closely shaven behind; thus skillfully symbolizing, that when it comes up from behind one, it may perhaps be held fast by the flowing forelock, but fairly escapes when it has once got the start, from the absence of any thing by which the pursuer might grasp it.[81]

Going back to Socrates, then, one can see that when he used καιρός with

---

[78]Socr. HE 4.1; 5.25; 7.23.

[79]Socr. HE 3.11.

[80]Socr. HE 1.6; 2.2, 16-17 twice, 25-26 twice; 3.20; 4.14, 37; 5.introd.; 6.6 three times.

[81]Evag. HE 3.26, compare 6.12. One such statue was the famous one by Lysippus at Sicyon; see Callistratus, Descriptions 6.428-429 K, statue of Kairos; and Greek Anthology, Book 16 (the Planudean Anthology) 275, statue of Kairos.

the verb δράσσομαι (grasp a handful of),[82] the reference is to this same image, that of grasping Kairos by the forelock before he turns his back.

Socrates does make what he believes to be a decisively Christianizing modification in the concept of καιρός by asserting that troubled καιροί come upon the human race, when they do, as a punishment for sins. This contrasts with the common pagan notion of Tyche as a fickle, changeable, *amoral* phenomenon.[83]

An understanding of Socrates' use of the καιρός concept helps to explain another important recurring motif in his history—the notion that troubles in the Church are normally somehow connected with troubles in the State. Socrates discusses this idea at length in the introduction to Book 5 of his history.

> Having set forth to write ecclesiastical history, we mix in with it also those wars which took place at critical moments [κατὰ καιρόν] . . . this we do . . . before all else so that it might be known how, when the affairs of the state have been troubled, the affairs of the churches have been troubled out of sympathy also. For if anyone will observe closely, he will find that evil affairs of state and unpleasant affairs in the churches come to their acme at the same time. For he will find them either moved the same way or following close upon one another. Sometimes the affairs in the churches lead the way; then affairs of state follow in turn; and sometimes the reverse.

Socrates applied this theory in his history in several cases.[84] Most important of all, the nexus connecting troubles in the church with troubles in the state is explicitly said by him to be a καιρός.[85]

This knowledge that the concept of the καιρός is involved keeps one from misinterpreting what Socrates was saying in the passage just quoted. If a modern historian were to write in his history about the close links existing between disputes that took place in the church and disputes that took place within the secular military, political, and social structures of the state, one would immediately look to see if this did not mean an interpretation

---

[82]Socr. *HE* 2.2; 3.20; 4.14.

[83]Socr. *HE* 5.introd.: μὴ ἔκ τινος συντυχίας . . . ἀλλ᾽ ἐκ τῶν ἡμετέρων πλημμελημάτων, "not arising out of some Tyche-like chance, but from our sins."

[84]Socr. *HE* 2.25-26; 6.6; 2.10; 4.3-4.

[85]Socr. *HE* 5.introd. quoted above; see also 2.25-26 and 6.6.

of church history in which socioeconomic factors were depicted as playing a large role in what were ostensibly disputes about matters of theology. But it would clearly be an anachronism to try to read a fifth-century historian in this way. The concept of ideology as merely the passive mirrored image of social and economic forces was not present in Late Roman historiography. It is true that Socrates was well aware, in terms of commonsense political know-how, of the close interrelationship between imperial politics and church affairs. The shrewd observations of the practical politician (he was a lawyer, one must remember) appear frequently in the normal course of his historical narrative: an Arian emperor uses his civil powers to put pressure on the church in various ways; the emperor tries to depose a popular bishop and the bishop's political strength appears as the people of his city riot in the streets; a war takes up all the emperor's attention and ties up all his military forces and this gives his bishops the opportunity to carry out a successful ecclesiastical revolt against his religious policies. Socrates did make observations of that kind frequently, [86] but they did not imply any notion that theology was merely the ideological wrapping of socioeconomic movements, and what is more important, those common sense practical observations about ecclesiastical politics in the Eastern Roman empire were not what he was concerned with in the introduction to Book 5 when he wrote of troubles in the Church as closely connected with troubles in the State.

What Socrates writes at the beginning of Book 5 is that a chart of disrupting historical events in one separate line of historical development (the state) would always tend to peak at the same time as the chart of disrupting historical events in another separate line of historical development (the church). In fact, there is also a third range of phenomena involved, though he does not mention it in that introductory section of his fifth book: the destructive forces of nature (earthquakes, and so forth), which he also believes frequently come to a peak at the same time. [87] The fact that these

---

[86]Socrates is far more sophisticated than Eusebius, at least in his public analysis of events. Eusebius almost never gives any hint of the complexity of the political infighting taking place in affairs of church and state.

[87]As illustrated in, for example, Socr. *HE* 4.3-4, where an earthquake and the sinking and rising of land from the sea occur together with a troubling church council and an attempted imperial coup, all of which are explicitly linked by Socrates. Cf. 4.11.

three different types of phenomena (troubles in the state, troubles in the church, and natural catastrophes like floods, earthquakes, and droughts) supposedly came to a peak at the same time did not imply to Socrates what we today would regard as natural causal connection. It was not even a natural causal relationship between troubles in the state and troubles in the church, as one excellent example from Socrates' imitator Sozomen clearly shows: After describing the way John Chrysostom's followers were persecuted by torture, imprisonment, and confiscation of property in the religious dispute (centering around John himself) that was boiling in Constantinople, Sozomen then went on to show[88] how these troubles in the church were followed by troubles in the state—the Huns invade Thrace, the rough mountaineers of Isauria start making raids outside their mountain region, and Alaric and his Visigoths march into Illyria! There was no natural causal linkage at all—whatever the motivation of the Huns, it was not Christian concern for John Chrysostom's episcopacy. With this vivid example to guide us, we can then turn back to Socrates and see that the natural causal linkages are not shown here either, not only because the causal linkages normally could not be said to have existed by any stretch of the imagination,[89] but also because it was not pragmatic chains of simply earthly causes that were at stake in this matter.

Socrates espoused a doctrine of συμπάθεια, of cosmic "sympathy."[90] When one violin is bowed, the strings of another violin, sitting on a table, resonate with sympathetic vibrations. When disturbances appear in one part of the cosmos, the cosmos is soon thrown out of joint by sympathetic reactions in its other parts. "The times are out of joint, O cursed spite" is not a bad description of what Socrates meant by a καιρός of this sort. There is no need to dwell on the many uses of the idea of cosmic sympathy in the

---

[88]Sozomen, HE 8.25. For an intriguing modern analysis of the attempt to destroy Chrysostom, see Timothy E. Gregory, Vox Populi: Popular Opinion and Violence in the Religious Controversies of the Fifth Century A.D. (Columbus OH: Ohio State University Press, 1979) chapter 3.

[89]For example, in Socr. HE 2.10 we are asked to connect (1) the Council of the Dedication, which took place at Antioch in 341 and tried to put up the first countercreed to the Nicene declaration, (2) raids by the Franks into Gaul, and (3) earthquakes in the East.

[90]Socr. HE 5.introd.: ὡς ἔκ τινος συμπαθείας.

ancient world—Stoic physics,[91] Neoplatonic explanations of astrology and magic,[92] and others—but it will be worthwhile to offer one example from the historical writing of antiquity, to show how this idea had entered into historiographical theory at least in one form long before Socrates' church history. We see this example—one of the clearest—in the sober, scientific and skeptical Thucydides, who offers as proof of the superior magnitude of the Peloponnesian war (compared to all previous wars) among other things the impressive earthquakes, droughts, and eclipses of the sun that took place during its course.[93]

> The greatest achievement of former times was the Persian war, and yet this was quickly decided in two sea-fights and two land-battles. But the Peloponnesian war was protracted to a great length, and in the course of it disasters befell Hellas the like of which had never occurred in any equal space of time. Never had so many cities been taken and left desolate, some by the Barbarians, and others by Hellenes themselves warring against one another; while several, after their capture, underwent a change of inhabitants. Never had so many human beings been exiled, or so much human blood been shed, whether in the course of the war itself or as the result of civil dissensions. And so the stories of former times, handed down by oral tradition, but very rarely confirmed by fact, ceased to be incredible: about earthquakes, for instance, for they prevailed over a very large part of the earth and were likewise of the greatest violence; eclipses of the sun, which

[91]S. Sambursky, *Physics of the Stoics* (London: Routledge and Kegan Paul, 1959) 9, 41-42, 110.

[92]Plotinus, *The Enneads* 2.3.7; 4.4.40. The idea of such a cosmic sympathy was still held in the Western world as late as the English Renaissance. Shakespeare invokes the motif, for example, in both *Hamlet* and *King Lear*, where an act against nature by a monarch (who is still regarded as quasi-divine in England as late as James I) throws the entire times out of joint at all levels (note especially the storm scene in *King Lear*).

[93]Thuc. 1.23.1-3. Cornford (*Thucydides Mythistoricus* [London: Routledge and Kegan Paul, 1965] 102-103) comments on this passage: "Thucydides will not *worship* the inscrutable agencies responsible for convulsions of Nature; but he cannot rule out the hypothesis that such agencies exist and may 'acquire power' to produce the convulsions coincidently with a war in Greece." Thucydides "shows a completely scientific spirit, and also an equally complete destitution of a scientific view of nature."

occurred at more frequent intervals than we find recorded of all former times; great droughts also in some quarters with resultant famines; and lastly—the disaster which wrought most harm to Hellas and destroyed a considerable part of the people—the noisome pestilence. For all these disasters fell upon them simultaneously with this war.

This idea of troubled καιροί and cosmic sympathy also helps explain the full meaning of the concluding lines of Socrates' history (7.48). He prays for peace for both the church and the world, and then explains: "As long as peace continues, those who desire to write histories will find no materials for their purpose." The task of the historian, in Socrates' understanding, is to recount the great cosmic disturbances in which all human and natural affairs are thrown out of joint in worldwide calamity. History is a catalogue of massive human suffering, and consequently, the historian may pursue its study, but must always pray for the return of that cosmic harmony that would bring his own task to an end. This is the peace that will, in the Evagrian doctrine of the last things, eventually extend beyond this world into a mystical reunification of all things, beyond both time and history. The peace of the "eighth day," when all the purified intelligences will regain their original equality with Christ, and matter and multiplicity will vanish, is the ultimate transcendent goal of history. But until then one can at least pray for the cosmic harmony that is the earthly, historical shadow of that eternal peace.

Perhaps the most important place where Socrates concretely applies the theory of καιρός and συμπάθεια is in *HE* 2.25-26. There Socrates' attempt to make the theory of simultaneity of troubles work results in (or at least is accompanied by) a major garbling of the chronology. This can be seen by laying out an outline of the correct chronology[94] and then noting where Socrates departs from it.

337 death of Constantine the Great.

340 death of Constantine the Younger, leaving the empire to his two brothers.

---

[94]Based on Henry Melvill Gwatkin, *Studies of Arianism*, 2nd ed. (Cambridge: D. Bell, 1900), cf. Gwatkin, *The Arian Controversy* (London: Longmans, Green, 1889).

ca. 343 Council of Sardica. (SOCRATES THINKS THIS TOOK PLACE IN 347—SEE HE 2.20. HENCE SOCRATES' STATEMENT IN 2.25-26, THAT THE KILLING OF CONSTANS BY MAGNENTIUS TOOK PLACE "in the fourth year after the council at Sardica." SOCRATES MENTIONS THIS BECAUSE SARDICA RESTORED ATHANASIUS AND ACQUITTED MARCELLUS OF ANCYRA. TO SOCRATES, THIS WAS THE CAUSE OF ATHANASIUS'S TRIUMPHAL RE-TURN FROM HIS SECOND EXILE, AFTER CONSTANS INSISTED THAT CONSTANTIUS HONOR THE FINDINGS OF THE COUNCIL.)

346 Athanasius returned from his second exile—the emperor Constans forced Constantius in the East to let Athanasius return. (SOCRATES WOULD HAVE TO DATE THIS IN OR AFTER 347 BECAUSE OF HIS DATING OF THE COUNCIL OF SARDICA)

350 Constans in the West killed by the usurper Magnentius.

353 Magnentius defeated, commits suicide.

356 Athanasius began his third exile—driven from his see by Constan-tius, he had to remain in hiding until Julian came to the throne. (SOCRATES SEEMS TO THINK THAT THIS TOOK PLACE SHORTLY AFTER 350, **BEFORE** THE DEFEAT OF THE USURPER MAGNENTIUS.)

The way Socrates dated the events, they fell into the form of a great pe-ripety. First came success: in 347 Athanasius triumphed at the Council of Sardica, and, with Constans's backing, returned from his second exile and took control of the church at Alexandria once again. But then in 350 there began a great dramatic reversal. A καιρός occurred in which troubles sprang up simultaneously in various areas of the state and in the church as well. The Persians attacked in the East, and civil war broke out in the West. The emperor Constans was killed by the usurper Magnentius, and then two more men were proclaimed emperor in addition—Vetranio in Sirmium and Nepotian in Rome. In this καιρός, Athanasius's enemies acted. The em-peror Constantius "reversed [μετέστρεφε] all the indulgent proceedings he had so recently resolved on." Athanasius and the other notable sup-porters of Nicaea came under violent attack. For example, Paul, the bishop of Constantinople, was strangled, Lucius of Adrianople died in heavy chains in prison, and Athanasius himself had to flee with a death sentence hang-ing over his head if he were caught. From the great success of 347, Athan-asius was suddenly plunged by this dramatic reversal into terrible defeat. All this was the work of the great καιρός of 350, which disturbed all as-pects of human history due to the phenomenon of cosmic sympathy.

If Socrates had gotten his chronology correct, the thing would not have worked out. But hard facts always seem to be the stumbling blocks that ruin the great attempts to set up theoretical laws concerning the tides of history. In our own time, the great historical theoreticians like Marx and Toynbee have come to grief in the same way.

CHAPTER 9

Sozomen,
Theodoret of Cyrrhus,
and Evagrius Scholasticus:
Other Successors
and Continuators

In addition to Socrates Scholasticus, Eusebius had three other important successors in the centuries immediately following. All three of these
scholars—Sozomen, Theodoret of Cyrrhus, and Evagrius Scholasticus—
left major histories extant. Their works display the further development of
the Eusebian historiographical tradition in the fifth and sixth centuries. Each
in his own way tried to deal with the problem of Fortune in history and
each also wrote in some context about the fall of Rome. Eusebius had held
to a sort of liberal progressivism in which the Christian Roman state was
viewed as the pinnacle of human civilization, the high point of centuries
of historical progress, that would last until the end of the world. The sack
of Rome by Alaric and his Visigoths in 410 C.E., and the disintegration of
Roman central authority in the West in the years following, then inspired
Augustine in North Africa to reinterpret the entire Eusebian understanding
of history.[1] Sozomen, Theodoret, and Evagrius, however, continued to
maintain a basically Eusebian perspective. Augustine's new historical understanding was ignored, and the disastrous events in the Western half of
the empire continued to be treated casually even as late as the end of the
sixth century. It was not until the rise of Islam that the optimism of the

---

[1] Glenn F. Chesnut, "The Pattern of the Past: Augustine's Debate with Eusebius
and Sallust," in J. Deschner, L. T. Howe, and K. Penzel, eds., *Our Common History
as Christians: Essays in Honor of Albert C. Outler* (New York: Oxford University Press,
1975) 69-95.

Constantinian settlement was seriously questioned in the Eastern Roman empire. This rather unconcerned and casual reaction to the barbarization of the West is therefore also worthy of investigation, and must be considered in the case of each of Eusebius's three successors.

Sozomen[2] was a lawyer in Constantinople[3] just as Socrates was, and at about the same time. Unlike Socrates, however, Sozomen was not a native of the great capital city. He came from a Palestinian background. His grandparents, who had lived in the town of Bethelia near Gaza, were converted to Christianity during the first half of the fourth century by Hilarion, the famous Palestinian proponent of the monastic life.[4] The grandparents had to flee during Julian's reign (361-363).[5] Sozomen tells us nothing of his parents, but some of his own early days were spent in that part of Palestine.[6] He himself never entered the religious life, and although he was Christian he always remained very much a layperson—one may note the hint of exasperation with bishops and their politics and disputes that comes out in the introductory remarks to his history.[7] Furthermore, unless these were purely formal protestations, Sozomen explicitly avoided theological questions.[8]

---

[2]Σαλαμάνης Ἑρμείας Σωζομενός is the preferred form of the name according to Bidez and Hansen, GCS text of Sozomen (Berlin: Akademie-Verlag, 1960) lxiv-lxv.

[3]Soz. HE 2.3.10.

[4]Soz. HE 5.15.14-17. Hilarion settled in the wilderness near Gaza in 306 and practiced the monastic life there until ca. 353.

[5]Soz. HE 5.15.14.

[6]Soz. HE 7.28.6: "It is said, and I myself am witness of the truth of the assertion, that when [Zeno] was bishop of the church in Majuma [the seaport of Gaza], he was never absent at morning or evening hymns." See Chester D. Hartranft, introduction to the Nicene and Post-Nicene Fathers translation of Sozomen (Grand Rapids MI: Eerdmans, 1957) 195.

[7]Soz. HE 1.1.15: the various bishops "convened councils and issued what decrees they pleased, often condemning unheard those whose creed was dissimilar to their own, and striving to their utmost to induce the reigning prince and nobles of the time to side with them."

[8]Soz. HE 3.15.10; 6.27.7; 7.17.8. See Hartranft, 195; Bidez and Hansen, xlvi.

He evidently did not come to Constantinople until after 425.[9] He mentions having been present himself at one event that took place in Constantinople during the episcopacy of Proclus (434-446 or 447).[10] One other especially useful date can be established. When the dedication to his church history was written, the emperor Theodosius the Younger had "lately, not long ago" (πρῴην) traveled through Bithynia in the summer on the way to Heraclea in Pontus. This imperial journey was made, according to other ancient sources, in the summer of 443.[11]

Sozomen was a man from a distinctly provincial background, come to the great imperial capital to make his fortune. He was in fact a figure somewhat like the preconversion Augustine: an eager careerist with literary skill, emigrating from the backwaters of empire to one of the great urban centers of power, hoping to make his mark on the world.[12] It can be seen that there were many such men in Constantinople in the first half of the fifth century, for Socrates had described them earlier in his own church history. Whenever the emperor won a victory in battle, "many who were illustrious for their eloquence wrote panegyrics in honor of the emperor, and recited them

---

[9]In *HE* 8.27.5-7, Sozomen refers to Bishop Atticus of Constantinople (d. 425)—his public life, manner, sermon style, and so on—always in terms of information derived from other people. See Bidez and Hansen, *GCS* text of Sozomen, lxv; W. Eltester, in Pauly-Wissowa, Series 2, III A 1 (1927) col. 1240.

[10]Soz. *HE* 9.2.17-18. See A. Güldenpenning, *Die Kirchengeschichte des Theodoret von Kyrrhos* (Halle: M. Niemeyer, 1889) 12; Georg Schoo, *Die Quellen des Kirchenhistorikers Sozomenos* (Berlin: Trowitzsch und Sohn, 1911) 9; Eltester, col. 1240.

[11]Soz. *HE* dedication. 13. See Güldenpenning, *Die Kirchengeschichte*, 12; Schoo, *Die Quellen*, 10; Bidez and Hansen, lxv-lxvi.

[12]When the young Augustine left North Africa and went to Rome and Milan, one remembers that he eventually fell into the attempt to build a political career on his rhetorical skill. A marriage was arranged for him with a rich heiress, and Symmachus, the Prefect of the City and a literary man himself, put his political weight behind Augustine after the young African had performed a speech before him. In the Roman world of that period, as Symmachus himself observed in a letter, "the highroad to office is often laid open by literary success" (*Ep*. 1.20). It was this sort of career, with its prospects of a governmental post, perhaps even a provincial governorship, that Augustine of course later abandoned when he underwent his famous conversion; see the excellent discussion in Peter Brown, *Augustine of Hippo* (London: Faber and Faber, 1967) 69-71, 81, 88, 114.

in public," hoping to catch the imperial notice and receive the imperial reward.[13] Literary activities of this sort were also going on within the court itself, notably in the person of the sophist's daughter Athenais, who became the Empress Eudokia. When the Roman army ended a successful war against the Persians in 422 C.E., Socrates tells us, "the empress herself also composed a poem in heroic verse, for she had excellent literary taste."[14] Almost any armed conflict could be used as a subject. After Gainas the Goth had been defeated in 400, a lawyer named Eusebius Scholasticus

> related the events of it in a heroic poem consisting of four books, and inasmuch as the events alluded to had but recently taken place, he acquired for himself great celebrity. The poet Ammonius has also very lately recited a poem, another description of the same transactions, . . . which made him famous when he displayed it brilliantly before the emperor.[15]

It was a society therefore where public honor and prestige could in fact come to a σχολαστικός who prepared a literary work of this sort, and there were many people struggling for such recognition. Socrates explicitly denied that he himself had written his own church history for such a purpose,[16] but Sozomen, on the other hand, openly stated in his dedication to the emperor Theodosius that he was writing his work to win public recognition and reward from the throne. He praised the emperor's literary judgment.

> And when you preside as ruler of contests and judge of discourses, you are not robbed of your accuracy by any artificial sound and form, but you award the prize sincerely, observing whether the diction is suitable to the design of the composition; so also with respect to the form of words, divisions,

---

[13]Socr. HE 7.21.

[14]Ibid. Among Eudokia's other works were a paraphrase of the Octateuch that she wrote in hexameters and a paraphrase of the books of Daniel and Zechariah. She also wrote a poem about St. Cyprian and put together a composite poem reciting the gospel narrative by judicious selection and juxtaposition of verses from Homer.

[15]Socr. HE 6.6.

[16]Socr. HE 7.22, though in context this clearly may be a merely formal protestation, to give the rhetorical ring of sincerity to the praises he sings of the emperor in the second part of the same sentence.

order, unity, phraseology, construction, arguments, thought, and narrative.

Then, lest he forget, Sozomen reminded the emperor, "You recompense the speakers with your favorable judgment and applause, as well as with golden images, erection of statues, gifts, and every kind of honor." And Sozomen went on to state that the emperor Theodosius surpassed all the rulers of history, including the most famous philomaths and philologues, in his gifts and honors to men of letters.[17]

But Sozomen's history may have become more than just a literary production put together by an unknown but aspiring careerist from the provinces in the hope of bringing his name to the emperor's attention. He also asked the emperor to make the last editorial redactions himself before the history was released to the general public.[18] There is a long history in Roman literature of government-sponsored works designed, in one way or another, to glorify the Roman people and exalt the reigning emperor. The list includes material as diverse as Josephus's history of the Jewish War[19] and Virgil's *Aeneid*. Sozomen may well have been successful in achieving the official recognition he sought. It has been suggested that the lost ending to his history could have been the result of some rather crude editing by the imperial censors before its release as the official court-approved history of the preceding century.[20]

---

[17]Soz. *HE* dedication. 4-7.

[18]Soz. *HE* dedication. 18.

[19]Josephus sent copies of it to Vespasian and Titus, and it became the official government-sponsored and approved history of the war after Titus, now emperor, gave his official seal of approval to the work. Jos. *Vita* 363, *Ap.* 1. 50-51.

[20]Because the final section of the history would have mentioned that it was the Empress Eudokia who had brought the bones of the deacon and protomartyr Stephen back from Jerusalem in 439. But she had had an affair with Paulinus, the Master of the Offices, and had been forced to leave the court in permanent disgrace in 442, thereby making her a person whose name was no longer spoken; see Schoo, *Die Quellen des Kirchenhistorikers Sozomenos,* 6-8. Güldenpenning (*Die Kirchengeschichte des Theodoret von Kyrrhos,* 14-16) believed that Sozomen himself suppressed the ending, but for the same basic reason, fear of offending the court by mentioning the fallen empress's name. The basic theory has been criticized, however, by W.

It should also be said, of course, that Sozomen's history stood far above most of the accounts in heroic meter of the downfall of some particular barbarian chieftain, the poems praising a particular building erected by the emperor, and the other standard pieces of literary favor-seeking that we know from the period, because of the grand scale upon which it was laid out. It was in fact a conception of epic dimension: the glorious history of the Christian empire from its very beginning, on that day when the cross appeared above the sun in the clear Italian skies shortly after noon, to the full flowering of the new civilization under the reign of the emperor Theodosius II. The history was designed to glorify the Christian empire and to exalt the emperor Theodosius and the Christian imperial succession in which he stood, and to that extent, his history was intended to be a sort of Christian prose epic.

There was an ongoing attempt, backed by the imperial court (Theodosius II, Eudokia, and Pulcheria may all have been involved), to produce a Theodosian Golden Age. The University of Constantinople was founded in 425; it was in fact a great university that was still operating a thousand years later when Constantinople finally fell. There were the literary contests and prizes that Socrates and Sozomen described. There was the assembling of the Theodosian Code already mentioned, an ambitious piece of legal scholarship organizing all the imperial constitutions from the time of Constantine onwards. [21] Sozomen hoped to glorify this new Roman resurgence by creating a literary monument to the Christianization of the empire. One conclusion to be drawn from this, of course, is that one will look in vain for any criticism in Sozomen of the beliefs and opinions held in court circles in Constantinople around 443 C.E.

There is a clear relationship of literary dependence between Socrates' *Ecclesiastical History* and Sozomen's. [22] The question of which way the de-

---

Eltester, in Pauly-Wissowa, Series 2, III A 1 (1927), cols. 1240-1241. It has also been hypothesized that Sozomen died just before finishing the history; see Hartranft, introduction to the Nicene and Post-Nicene Fathers trans. of Sozomen, 224, and Günther Christian Hansen, Introduction to the *GSC* edition of Joseph Bidez's critical text of Sozomen.

[21] Sozomen followed Socrates in designing his history so as to cover the period from Constantine to 439 C.E., the date on which the Theodosian Code was to take effect as the law of the land. See Socr. *HE* 7.48; Soz. *HE* dedication. 19.

[22] Bidez and Hansen, *GCS* ed. of Sozomen, xliv-xlv, documents the essential research.

pendence goes is determined by only a single passage, but one that nevertheless seems to decide the issue fairly clearly. Socrates (*HE* 1.10) tells us the anecdote about Constantine saying to the Novatianist bishop at the Council of Nicaea, "Set up a ladder, Acesius, and climb up to heaven by yourself!" Socrates then says, "Neither Eusebius Pamphilus nor any other [οὔτε ἄλλος τις] has even mentioned these things, on the contrary, I heard them from a man," a Novatianist named Auxanon,[23] "who in no way lied, who was extremely old, and said these things about the council as he was giving a narrative." The key statement is the one in which Socrates says that the story has never appeared in a published work before. Sozomen tells exactly the same story (*HE* 1.22), but specifies no source for his information. He merely prefaces the anecdote with a simple "It is said that" (λέγεται). Clearly then, Sozomen's history came after Socrates' work.

The amount of correspondence between the two works is very great. Sozomen apparently made heavy and completely unacknowledged use of a copy of Socrates' history. Eusebius's complaint that the Greeks plagiarized shamelessly and endlessly had once more been proven true—and by someone who claimed to be a successor and continuator of Eusebius! On the other hand, Sozomen did go back and independently make use of the sources from which Socrates had derived his information. Sozomen took an independent look at Rufinus's *Church History*, drew on parts of Eusebius's *Life of Constantine* that Socrates had not used, and also clearly looked at Athanasius's works himself rather than simply copying the material out of Socrates.[24] He did thorough documentary research in the primary sources, as he himself points out at the beginning of his history.

> I shall record the transactions with which I have been connected, and also those concerning which I have heard from persons who knew or saw the affairs in our own day or before our own generation. But I have sought for records of events of earlier date, amongst the established laws appertaining to religion, amongst the proceedings of the synods of the period, amongst the innovations that arose, and in the epistles of kings and priests. Some

---

[23]Socr. *HE* 1.13: "Auxanon, a very aged presbyter of the Novatian church; who when quite a youth accompanied Acesius to the Synod at Nicaea, and related to me what I have said concerning him."

[24]Schoo, *Die Quellen*, 28-39; Bidez and Hansen, xlviii-xlix.

of these documents are preserved in palaces and churches, and others are dispersed and in the possession of the learned.[25]

Sozomen's *Ecclesiastical History* was therefore a genuinely critical piece of historiography in this sense, and on these grounds it is a valuable source of evidence for the history of the period it covered.

In his treatment of the problem of Fortune, Sozomen seems simply to have borrowed from Socrates the idea of καιρός and cosmic sympathy. So, for example, Sozomen devoted a long section of his history to a description of the persecution of John Chrysostom's followers. "Around the same time," he said in the introduction to his next chapter, "as one generally finds happening in the disputes of priests, public affairs also were tried by uproars and disturbance."[26] The chapter went on to describe how the Huns crossed the Danube and invaded Thrace, how the mountaineers of Isauria raided as far as western Asia Minor in one direction and the coast of Syria in the other, and how Stilicho sent Alaric's Visigoths into Illyria to try to create warfare between the realms of the emperors Arcadius and Honorius. As in the work of Socrates, the connection in Sozomen between the disorders in the church and the disorders in the state was not a matter of what one today would call causal linkage; it was a sympathetic reaction of one part of the cosmos to disturbances in some other part.

Sozomen's attitude towards the sack of Rome in 410 is quite interesting. It was regarded as a purely local problem, affecting only the people of that one city, rather than as, with Augustine, a presage of the fall of the entire empire.

> All persons of good sense were aware that the calamities which this siege entailed upon the Romans were indications of divine wrath sent to chastise them for their luxury, their debauchery, and their manifold acts of injustice towards each other, as well as towards strangers.[27]

Sozomen repeated the story, already found in Socrates, that some strange, irresistible inner impulse drove Alaric to the destruction of Rome; in Sozomen the intimation is clear that this was the prompting of God or his

---

[25]Soz. *HE* 1.1.13.

[26]Soz. *HE* 8.25.1.

[27]Soz. *HE* 9.6.

supernatural agents for the express purpose of carrying out the divine judgment. [28] Sozomen was aware that the Roman government's control began to disintegrate after the sacking of the ancient capital, and described in some detail the "many tyrants" who at this time "rebelled against Honorius in the Western government." [29] But the moral of the story, as Sozomen understood it, was that these usurpers all met violent deaths without permanently gaining the throne, while the rightful emperor Honorius successfully passed on his rule to Valentinian III, his sister Galla Placidia's son. All these events thereby showed "that to insure the stability of imperial power, it is sufficient for an emperor to serve God with reverence, which was the course pursued by Honorius." [30]

It should be pointed out that ca. 443 when Sozomen was writing his history, the Vandal Kingdom did control North Africa, but Western Europe was on the other hand restabilized after a fashion under the official rule of the aforementioned Valentinian III. He was considered in Constantinople as legitimate emperor of the West, and had married Eudoxia, the daughter of the emperor in Constantinople (Theodosius II) to whom Sozomen had dedicated his work. It would surely have been impolitic for the history to have expressed any other point of view than the one it did on the fate of the other half of the empire. Nevertheless, Sozomen's interpretation is still important as a guide to the official government position on the situation in the West at that particular stage of the fifth-century crisis. For a number of reasons, therefore, Sozomen's history is a valuable record of events, and in spite of its tendencies merits its status as one of the better histories of the late Roman period.

Contemporary with Socrates and Sozomen, one other great church history was written, that of Theodoret of Cyrrhus. [31] He is perhaps better

---

[28]Ibid., following Socr. *HE* 7.10.

[29]Soz. *HE* 9.11.

[30]Soz. *HE* 9.16.

[31]Note that the references to book, chapter, and section of Theodoret's *Church History* in this present work are to the *GCS* edition edited by Parmentier and Scheidweiler (Berlin: Akademie-Verlag, 1954). The divisions differ considerably from those found in one standard English translation of the *Church History* (that is, the one by Blomfield Jackson in the NPNF series, [Grand Rapids MI: Eerdmans, 1892]).

known as a theologian, but his history is certainly important and valuable enough to have achieved the status of a major work on its own. Theodoret was born at Antioch around 393 and brought up in a pious home in close contact with some of the more austere and famous monks of that area. In his *Historia Religiosa* he left a permanent record of these people, like Peter of Galatia, whom he had admired so much as a child and youth.

He became a monk himself, and in 423 was made bishop of Cyrrhus, a small Syrian city lying back inland, halfway between Antioch and the Euphrates. It was a large episcopal see, with 800 parish churches falling under his supervision.[32] For more than three decades he served as bishop there, strengthening orthodox Christianity in the area and supervising major building projects in Cyrrhus itself, including bridges, porticoes, baths, and an aqueduct. He came to prominence as a supporter of the Antiochene position in the long Christological controversy begun by Nestorius and Cyril of Alexandria.[33] He regarded the Alexandrian position as little better than Apollinarianism (which had also taught the doctrine of one nature in Christ) and as defenseless against many of the subordinationist arguments of Arianism. After the condemnation of Nestorius by the Council of Ephesus in 431, Theodoret continued to defend the two-nature doctrine, and played an important role in obtaining the ultimate victory of that particular formulation at Chalcedon in 451.

At some time between 441 (or 442) and 449, Theodoret wrote his *Church History*.[34] It was a work covering the historical period from 323 to 428 C.E.,

---

[32]Theod. *Epist. Sirm.* 113.

[33]Some of the more recent works on Theodoret's Christological thought include Marijan Mandac, "L'union christologique dans les oeuvres de Théodoret antérieures au concile d'Ephèse," *Ephemerides Theologicae Lovanienses* 47 (1971): 64-96, including a review of some of the major work done on Theodoret over the past hundred years; Jean Chéné, "Unus de Trinitate Passus Est," *Recherches de Science Religieuse* 53 (1965): 545-88, esp. 551-55 on Theodore of Mopsuestia and Theodoret; H. M. Diepen and Jean Daniélou, "Theodoret et le dogme d'Ephèse," *Recherches de Science Religieuse* 44 (1956): 243-48, and the controversy lying behind this interchange of opinions; Kevin McNamara, "Theodoret of Cyrus and the Unity of Person in Christ," *Irish Theological Quarterly* 22 (1955): 313-28.

[34]The date given for the writing of the *Church History* in the common reference works at this time is not correct. See G. F. Chesnut, "The Date of Composition

written as a deliberate continuation of Eusebius's *Church History*.

Eusebius the Palestinian has described the things that happened to the churches, beginning his history with the Holy Apostles, and going up to

---

of Theodoret's Church History," *Vigiliae Christianae* 35 (1981): 245-52, for a detailed account of the arguments that follow, particularly the reasons why Epistle 113 cannot in any way be what it has been supposed to represent. The date of composition commonly given now is 449/450, but this is based solely on the list of his works that Theodoret gives in the letter to Leo the Great after his condemnation at the Robber Council of Ephesus (Theod. *Epist. Sirm.* 113). The problem is that it can be demonstrated very simply that Theodoret was not giving a complete list of his writings there. This forces one to search for dependable *termini* within the history itself. The three latest datable events referred or alluded to in Theodoret's *Church History* are the return of John Chrysostom's remains to Constantinople in 438 (*HE* 5.36.1-2); the accession of the Sassanian king, Yazdgard II, in 438 or possibly 439 (*HE* 5.39.6); and an incident that occurred during the war with Persia in 441 or 442 (*HE* 5.37.5-6a). This sets a *terminus post quem* of 441 or 442 for the date of composition. The *terminus ante quem* is provided by *HE* 5.36.4, which refers to the sisters (in the plural) of Theodosius II. When Marina died on 3 August 449 only Pulcheria among the emperor's sisters was still left living. See Johannes Quasten, *Patrology* (Utrecht: Spectrum, 1963) 3:551; Berthold Altaner and Alfred Stuiber, *Patrologie*, 7th ed. (Freiburg: Herder, 1966) 227; Léon Parmentier, ed., *Theodoret Kirchengeschichte*, xxv-xxvi. Note the warnings against using *Epist. Sirm.* 113 to date Theodoret's works in G. Bardy, "Théodoret," *Dictionnaire de Théologie Catholique* (Paris, 1946) 15, 1:col. 303; and Martin Brok, "Touchant la date du Commentaire sur le Psautier de Théodoret de Cyr," *Revue d'Histoire Ecclésiastique* 44 (1949): 552-56; Brok's valuable article was called to my attention by Professor Jerry Stewardson, for which I am most grateful. See also Henricus Valesius, "Praefatio," in *Theodoriti [sic] episcopi Cyri et Evagrii Scholastici historia ecclesiastica . . .*, ed. and trans. Henricus Valesius (Paris, 1673) B iv obverse and B iii reverse; Güldenpenning, *Die Kirchengeschichte*, 21-25; Blomfield Jackson, "Life and Writings," prefacing his translation of the writings of Theodoret in the Nicene and Post-Nicene Fathers, Second Series, 3:xiii.

For the dating of the events in Persian history, see Arthur Christensen, *L'Iran sous les Sassanides*, 2nd ed. (Copenhagen: E. Munksgaard, 1944) 282-83; R. Ghirshman, *Iran* (Baltimore: Penguin, 1954) 299-300; Franz Altheim and Ruth Stiehl, *Ein Asiatischer Staat: Feudalismus unter den Sasaniden und ihren Nachbarn* (Wiesbaden: Limes, 1954), table 7. It seems correct to reject the reading of events (and the implied dating) given in Otto Seeck's interpretation of Theod. *HE* 5.37.6b; see his *Geschichte des Untergangs der antiken Welt* (Stuttgart: J. B. Metzler, 1920) 6:86-87.

the reign of Constantine, the Friend of God. I shall make the end of that composition the starting point of my own history. [35]

Even though Theodoret was a principal spokesman for the Antiochene party in the Christological controversy, a comparison of his history with Socrates' and Sozomen's does not show many clashes of opinion that could in fact be attributed to his particular theological point of view. One of the few examples might be the differing evaluations Theodoret and Socrates gave of Eustathius of Antioch. Theodoret defended Eustathius in *HE* 1.21.3-9 and presented his accusers as absolute scoundrels who bribed a prostitute to accuse Eustathius of fathering a child she had just borne. Eustathius, it should be remembered, was a thorough Antiochene in his theology, with a Christology somewhat similar to that later taught by Nestorius. Socrates, on the other hand, in *HE* 6.13 condemned Eustathius (along with Methodius, Apollinaris, and Theophilus) because of his opposition to Origen. [36] Eustathius, Socrates said, was one of "a fourfold summation of evil-speakers," all of them "lovers of coarse insults," who spoke of Origen as a blasphemer. [37] This seems one clear instance, therefore, where Theodoret's specifically Antiochene theology helped shape his historical judgment in a simple, direct manner. But there are not too many cases of this sort in his history.

The principal object of theological attack in his work was in fact the Arian movement. Theodoret's *Church History* might almost have been subtitled "An Account of the Arian Controversy." To him, the principal issue facing the church during that century covered by his history had been the conflict between Arianism and Nicene Christianity. To help explain his feeling on this matter, one must remember that during that century, Arian bishops had sat on the Antiochene throne for a full thirty years, from the deposition of Eustathius in 330 until the inauguration of Melitius in 360.

---

[35]Theod. *HE* 1.1.4. The phrase translated "the things that happened" in this passage is in the Greek τὰ συμβεβηκότα. It is possible that Theodoret is deliberately echoing Eusebius's technical terminology here.

[36]See H. M. Gwatkin, *Studies of Arianism*, 2nd ed. (Cambridge: D. Bell, 1900) 77.

[37]As a radical Origenist, Socrates was not of course giving an unbiased account himself.

Furthermore, even though the Council of Constantinople in 381 had decided the hierarchy of the established church in favor of the Nicene faith, Arianism was still a force to be contended with half a century later in Theodoret's own pastoral work.[38] From the point of view of Theodoret, one of the greatest threats raised by the attempt of the Alexandrian school to set up a one-nature Christology was the way in which it undercut the apologetic techniques Theodoret was using to combat Arian subordinationism. When an Arian attempted to apply less-than-divine attributes and activities to the Logos on the basis of certain key scriptural passages in order to deny the full divinity of the Logos, theologians of the Antiochene school could reply that the attributes and activities inapplicable to the divine nature were to be applied to the other of Christ's two natures, the human nature.

It was important to Theodoret therefore to remind his fellow theologians in his *Church History* of the historical importance of the Arian controversy. A two-nature Christology could handle the problems that dispute had raised, he believed, whereas acquiescence to the Alexandrian attempt to force a one-nature Christology on the whole church was a sign of poor historical consciousness and would, if the Alexandrians were successful, plunge the entire church back into the agony of the Arian controversy once again. The writing of a rather pointed history of that earlier conflict was in this way more than a little *indirectly* relevant to Theodoret's participation in the Christological controversy.

Theodoret did not regard the Alexandrian one-nature Christology as Arian. Though he did not devote more than a passage or so to the matter in his *Church History* he did indicate at the appropriate place in the narrative that he felt that the Alexandrian Christology was basically Apollinarian, both in historical origin and in terms of where its own inner logic must necessarily lead it. The key passage was *HE* 5.3.8 (compare 5.9.19-20) where he described the formation of a separate theological party under the leadership of Apollinaris in the latter part of the fourth century, and then went on to say,

> This was the origin of the growth in the Church of the doctrine of the one nature of the flesh and the Godhead, of the ascription to the Godhead of

---

[38]Theod. *Epist. Sirm.* 113.

the passion of the Only Begotten, and of other points which have bred differences among the laity and their priests. But these belong to a later date.

Other than this remark, made in passing, Theodoret's *Church History* was not a direct attack on the Alexandrian Christology. The history comes to its conclusion in 428, mentioning the death in that year of the greatest and most revered theologian of the Antiochene school, Theodore of Mopsuestia, but not the accession of Theodore's student and follower Nestorius in that same year to the patriarchate of Constantinople, which was the start of open hostilities between the Antiochenes and the Alexandrians. Theodoret, a close friend and admirer of Nestorius, had defended him after his deposition at the Council of Ephesus in 431, undoubtedly felt that he had been unjustly treated, and refused to endorse his condemnation until 451. Theodoret had himself nevertheless worked out a delicate compromise between the Antiochene and Alexandrian parties, enshrined in the Formula of Union of 433, which kept a fragile peace intact until 448. One must therefore assume that Theodoret closes his history at the year 428 to avoid having to deal with the Nestorian controversy in its pages, where his words might have undermined the status of the hardwon political compromise contained in the Formula of Union of 433.

Theodoret, like Eusebius, Socrates, and Sozomen, tried to work out a rapprochement between the Christian doctrine of Providence and the doctrine of Fortune found in the pagan historians.[39] Both modes of thought influenced his attitude toward history, as is seen most clearly in a set of letters dealing with two North African refugees who had fled in the face of the Vandal invasion of their homeland. Eight letters (*Epist. Sirm.* 29-36) dealt with a once-wealthy layman named Celestiacus; two letters (*Epist. Sirm.* 52-53) concerned a bishop named Cyprian. This was also the place where Theodoret's reaction to the fall of the Western Roman empire was best displayed. Walter E. Kaegi, Jr., has taken advantage of this to include a care-

---

[39]Theodoret's well-known work, the *De providentia* (*Discours sur la Providence*, trans. with introduction and notes by Y. Azéma, [Paris: De Boccard, 1953]) deals primarily with a refutation of the Epicurean notion of a universe governed by chance, by pointing to the beneficent provisions of the normal natural order. It is therefore not especially relevant to the present inquiry, which is concerned instead with the special providential acts of God in history. Cf. note 15, chapter 3.

ful study of these letters in his general survey of Eastern, Byzantine attitudes toward the collapse of the West.[40]

In these letters one discovers a good deal of Fortune language. Theodoret repeatedly compared the experiences of Celestiacus and Bishop Cyprian to those found in the classical tragedy, that ancient spectacle of Fate and fortune.[41] One common type of tragedy, as Aristotle had explained, dealt with a dramatic reversal in the fortunes of the key figure in the play.[42] In the same fashion, Theodoret spoke repeatedly of the dramatic reversal (μεταβολή) that had struck the North Africans.[43] Since Theodoret was a bishop and official representative of the church, and also a careful theologian, the word τύχη itself never occurred. Other words that referred to Fortune were used instead: the word συμφορά occurred most often,[44] but he also used terms like the pair εὐκληρία and δυσκληρία,[45] which meant good and bad luck respectively in drawing lots (κλῆρος).[46] In Letter 33 one actually sees Fortune personfied under the name of one of these euphemisms for Tyche: "Such is Fortune [ἡ εὐκληρία] among human beings, not willing [ἐθέλουσα] to remain with the same people forever, but in eager haste to pass on to others." Theodoret moreover gave the commonplace warnings about the uncertainty and instability of all "human" things (ἀνθρώπεια), warnings that were a traditional part of classical pagan Fortune language.[47]

But Theodoret differed from the classical historians in the formula he gave for the way in which a human being should react to the ever present

---

[40]In an excellent and helpful book, *Byzantium and the Decline of Rome* (Princeton: Princeton University Press, 1968) see esp. 161-66.

[41]Theod. *Epist. Sirm.* 29 ("the tragedy of Aeschylus and Sophocles"), 33, 34, 53.

[42]Aristotle, *Poetics* 10-11(1452ab). Aristotle called this dramatic reversal a περιπέτεια; in ancient history writers, whether pagan, Jewish, or Christian, the more common word for it was μεταβολή.

[43]Theod. *Epist. Sirm.* 29, 30 (where not only the noun is used, but also the verb form μεταβαλεῖν), 36, 52.

[44]Ibid. 29, 31 (twice), 33, 34, 35, 52, 53.

[45]Ibid. 30, 33.

[46]Ibid. 30, 31, 35.

[47]Ibid. 29, 30, 33, 52.

threat of bad Fortune. The good man or woman should learn piety (εὐσέ-βεια) from trials and troubles.[48] The good person should hymn God during both good times and bad.[49] This sort of attitude on Theodoret's part was clearly a Christian, or at least Stoic, modification of the traditional position.

Theodoret also said that God rewarded those who showed kindness to the victims of Fortune with heavenly gifts,[50] things that "neither words can express nor intelligence understand."[51] This was purely Christian; neither the Stoics, nor Plato, nor Aristotle, nor the classical Graeco-Roman historians spoke that way. Also purely Christian was Theodoret's emphasis upon the universal sinfulness of humankind as something that was part of human nature and made all human beings worthy of destruction at God's hand, even if He were merciful and spared most.[52] Theodoret further raised the fear that God would justifiably bring similar punishment on all those who did not propitiate him and obtain forgiveness for their sins by showing kindness when confronted with the victims of Fortune.[53]

This analysis of Theodoret's ideas is important, because again one notes that, seen from the eastern end of the Roman empire, even at the time of the Vandal invasion of North Africa, the Roman defeats were regarded as only opportunities for general moralizing and, in this case, particular acts of kindness and charity. These events were not regarded as harbingers of the eventual total collapse of centralized government in the Western half of the empire.

The next important church historian in this tradition, Evagrius Scholasticus, lived quite a few years later, after the consequences of the barbarian invasions could, in principle, have been more clearly seen. A brief look at his work will therefore be a logical conclusion to this chapter.

---

[48]Ibid. 31.

[49]Ibid. 29, 30.

[50]Ibid. 33, 52.

[51]Ibid. 30.

[52]Ibid. 31, 32. He uses the participle of the verb πλημμελέω in these passages.

[53]Ibid. 31, 34, 35, 52. In two of these letters (34, 52) participles of the verb πλημμελέω are again used.

From the preface to Evagrius's *Church History*, one can see that by the late sixth century Eusebius, Socrates, Sozomen, and Theodoret had become the great classics of Christian historiography.[54] Evagrius deliberately put himself in their succession, and tried to let the same basic sense of history guide him in his writing. Although other church historians had written, he did not regard them as part of the main succession. He also failed to mention Augustine's work on the Christian understanding of history. In fact, Socrates, Sozomen, Theodoret, and Evagrius make no mention of Augustine's name at any point in their histories; this is a measure of the cleavage that had come to separate the intellectual life of the Eastern and Western worlds.

Evagrius Scholasticus was born in 536/537[55] in Epiphania,[56] on the Orontes river upstream from Antioch, about 80 miles due southeast. He became a lawyer in Antioch, a confidential adviser of the bishop there, and a citizen of such importance that he could afford to flaunt the opinions of the whole city on a major issue[57] and still receive a massive public festival out of city funds when he married for the second time.[58] He completed

---

[54]Evag. *HE* 1.pref.; cf. 5.24.

[55]Evag. *HE* 4.29, combined with date of writing given in 3.33 and 6.24. Until 1981, there was literally no modern, booklength study of Evagrius in any language. Pauline Allen, (*Evagrius Scholasticus the Church Historian*, Spicilegium Sacrum Lovaniense 41 [Louvain: Spicilegium Sacrum Lovaniense, 1981]) has met this need magnificently in a large volume displaying a thorough knowledge of the historian himself and an even more impressive and erudite knowledge of the historical background. On the problem of the date of Evagrius's birth, see Allen, 1.

[56]Evag. *HE* 3.34.

[57]Evag. *HE* 6.7. Evagrius was completely on Bishop Gregory's side in the dispute—he describes him with glowing praise in 5.6. Gregory died before Evagrius wrote the closing chapter of his history (6.24). Pauline Allen, *Evagrius*, 2-3, thinks that Evagrius's position was something more than simply an ad hoc counsel from time to time, that he was in effect one of the two official chief legal counsels to the bishop. She points out the importance of this position since, with the decline of local government, major bishops like Gregory had to deal with army mutinies, represent the Roman government to the Persian empire, and carry on many similar missions for the secular government.

[58]Evag. *HE* 6.8. This was in 588 (see Allen, 3), so Evagrius would have been

writing his history in 593/594,[59] when he was fifty-seven years old.[60] His history extends from the beginning of the Nestorian controversy (soon after Nestorius became patriarch of Constantinople in 428) to the twelfth year of the emperor Maurice,[61] that is, around 593/594, the year in which he wrote the history.[62]

Evagrius had obtained honors from two different emperors for earlier literary productions,[63] but he insisted that this was not the purpose of this history, which was not being sent for the present emperor's official perusal.[64] In fact, Evagrius would hardly have been writing his history for the same reason as Sozomen. Sozomen had been trying to work his way up the ladder of social status and power; Evagrius was already there. He had represented the Patriarch of Antioch before the imperial court in Constantinople. As mentioned before, the city of Antioch, one of the three most important capitals in the eastern empire, had celebrated his wedding with a public festival. He was on social terms with the emperor's mother and father,[65] and thus had already gained entry into that privileged set that had access to the imperial court.

Evagrius's history was like those of his predecessors in admitting a Christianized concept of Fortune into the historical process. A passage in the description of the marriage festival of the emperor Maurice in HE 6.1 shows one way it could be done.

---

fifty-one or fifty-two years old. The first wife died in the recurrent plague he describes in 4.29.

[59] Evag. HE 3.33; 6.24. The date Evagrius uses for the Antiochene era can be checked from information in a number of passages: 4.1, 4, 9. Cf. Allen, 1.

[60] Evag. HE 4:29, in the fifty-eighth year of his life, that is, fifty-seven years old.

[61] Evag. HE 6.24. Cf. Allen, 267.

[62] Glanville Downey, "The Perspective of the Early Church Historians," *Greek, Roman, and Byzantine Studies* 6 (1965): 57-70.

[63] Evag. HE 6.24.

[64] Evag. HE 6.1. But note Pauline Allen's well-phrased warning in *Evagrius*, 245. Evagrius does elaborately flatter the emperor at one point, although obviously not for the same reason as Sozomen.

[65] Evag. HE 5.21.

Damophilus, when writing on the subject of Rome, says that Plutarch the Chaeronean has well remarked,[66] that in order to her greatness alone did Virtue and Fortune [Τύχη] unite in friendly truce. But for myself, I would say that in respect of Maurice alone did Piety and Good Fortune [Εὐδαι-μονία] so conspire, by Piety laying compulsion upon Good Fortune, and not permitting her to shift at all.

Εὐδαιμονία ("prosperity," "happiness," or "good fortune") as an equivalent for τύχη was one of the standard usages of the word in pagan Greek literature.[67] Evagrius did move to Christianize the concept by asserting that the emperor Maurice received this eudaemonistic good fortune or prosperity as a reward from God for his piety (θεοσέβεια).

In HE 6.17 Evagrius explicitly linked the omnipresent role of Fortune in human history to the tragic vision of life seen in the work of the classical Greek playwrights: "The quick-changing ebbs and flows of human life [τὰς ἀγχιστρόφους παλιρροίας τῆς τῶν ἀνθρώπων ζωῆς]" made human existence like "the unstable life of a buskined actor in the tragic drama [τὸν ἀσταθῆ καὶ κόθορνον βίον]."[68]

This tragic vision of human existence on occasion shaped the actual interpretation of major historical events, particularly in the form of the pattern of tragic downfall. In ancient Greek drama, Fortune and human character were often linked together in a typical chain of events that formed the basic plot and structure of the play. Success and prosperity would tempt the tragic hero into an act of hybris in which he would inadvertently bring

---

[66]Plutarch, De fortuna Romanorum 316f-317a and passim.

[67]One can give many instances of such use. Herodotus, for example, wrote at the beginning of his history that he would discuss both good and bad fortune in his work, because life was such "that human prosperity [εὐδαιμονίην] never continues in one stay" (Her. 1.5). The word also occurred in Herodotus's account of Solon's sermon to Croesus on the uncertainty of a world ruled by fortune (Her. 1.32).

[68]In this passage (6.17) the good emperor Maurice recognizes the instability and quick-changing character of human life and so decides to show mercy to his fallen enemy (Khusro II Aparwez, put back on the throne with Roman aid in 591 C.E.). Maurice's behavior in this crucial moment, his recognition of Fortune's power, and the merciful action that flows from it, prevents the situation from developing into the pattern of tragic downfall.

about his own doom. This is of course a commonplace, a truism, of classical dramatic criticism. But this idea was then passed on to the great classical historians, especially Herodotus; and then some centuries afterward, through one route or another, to the later Christian historians also. Although Eusebius never used the idea, it began creeping in immediately with his fifth-century successors. Sometimes it took only the form of simple moralizing statements about someone having been "unable to bear his good fortune with moderation."[69] In other passages a slightly more complicated formula was used. One sudden turn of Fortune seemingly put a person's enemies in his power. He refused to show mercy to them. Then a second turn of Fortune delivered the person into the hands of those very people to whom he had first refused mercy.[70]

Perhaps the best example of the use of this historical model is found in Evagrius, whose description of the career of the emperor Justin II (*HE* 5.1-13) is an almost perfect case of the pattern of tragic downfall. He depicted Justin as a man who was in some ways a good emperor, but who had developed just the sort of tragic character flaws that would be provoked by the power and wealth associated with the imperial throne. Then he showed this overproud recipient of Fortune's favor treacherously murdering the other, not so lucky, contender for the throne—a failure to show mercy to one's defeated foe in the hour of success. The emperor then tempted For-

---

[69]For example, Socr. *HE* 4.35 and 7.10.

[70]This formula was the basis, for example, of Socr. *HE* 2.34 and 5.25, and Theod. *HE* 5.24.10-16. It was also a constituent of the overall plot in Socr. *HE* 3.21, where Julian the Apostate refused mercy to the Persians when at first he seemed to have the upper hand. And in Socr. *HE* 6.5 there were two of these formula plots interwoven. Eutropius was merciless when Fortune was in his favor, but then was kept from obtaining mercy himself, when Fortune turned against him, by his own previous machinations (compare Polyb. 36.13.2). But John Chrysostom was then in turn merciless to Eutropius when Eutropius was the victim of Fortune, and this, along with other similar acts, served as a prelude to John Chrysostom's own downfall in Socrates' account of the matter (*HE* 6. *passim*). These church historians gave positive examples also, as when in Socr. *HE* 7.20 Theodosius the Younger showed mercy and moderation in his dealing with the Persians when the turn of events went his way, or when in Theod. *HE* 5.24.14 Theodosius the Great showed mercy to the troops of the usurper Eugenius when the battle suddenly and unexpectedly turned in favor of the imperial forces.

tune yet again, by starting a campaign against the Persians without showing sufficient foresight. As the Roman predicament grew worse and worse,
he grew blind to reality, "indulging rather the thoughts suggested by his
wishes"[71]—what the ancient tragic dramatists had called "Hope" in the
negative sense.[72] Fortune was ever changeable, and part of learning to be
a human being was learning to expect this. Fortune had put Justin on the
imperial throne, and now Fortune was allowing the Persians to triumph on
every hand. The emperor is unwilling to "bear what had befallen him with
resignation suited to a human being, falls into a state of frenzy, and becomes unconscious of all subsequent transactions."[73] The story ended with
Justin's formal abdication from the throne, and then a recognition scene,
in the manner of an ancient Greek tragedy, in which he finally recognized
the nature of his tragic doom and his own personal responsibility for it. In
a tragic speech that, the reader is told, brought tears to everyone's eyes,
Justin publicly warned his successor.

> Do not let the mere appearance of your clothing lead you into error, nor
> the stage-setting of visible things, by which I was led slowly on, without
> noticing myself, until I became liable to be sentenced to the gravest pen-
> alties.[74]

This was one of the strongest importations of the traditional classical dramatic motifs into history since Herodotus himself. But it indicates the hold
that the tragic vision of the fortuitous still had over the Greek mind.

The most important Fortune concept of all, of course, was the idea of
the καιρός, the "opportune moment," which was already partially discussed in the preceding chapter on Socrates. In Evagrius the idea was even
more important, and it is in this latter historian that one sees the full figure
of Kairos personified, soaring aloft and laughing at those who had let him

---

[71]Evag. HE 5.9, οἰόμενος ὅπερ ἐβούλετο.

[72]F. M. Cornford, Thucydides Mythistoricus (London: Routledge and Kegan Paul,
1965) 167-68.

[73]Evag. HE 5.11.

[74]Evag. HE 5.13; cf. Pauline Allen, Evagrius Scholasticus the Church Historian, 13-
14, 209-26.

slip past, while his long forelock blew in the air stirred by his passage.[75]
This concept of the καιρός played an important role in Evagrius's psychological theories, as can be seen from certain key passages in HE 5.19.
In the virtuous person, he said, "Fortitude and Prudence were the chari-
oteers of the opportune moments [τοῖς καιροῖς], and guided their reins
in whichever direction usefulness ordered." Fortitude and Prudence (ἀνδρεία and φρόνησις) were classical virtues,[76] and Evagrius indicated appropriate vices as their opposite numbers in the same passage: cowardice
(δειλία) could prevent a person from seizing the καιρός when it came;
ignorance (ἀμαθία) produced a person who was overrash (θρασύς) and
leapt in when the moment was not opportune. These were vices because
the virtuous individual might have to engage in a risky venture (κινδύ-
νευμα) when good advice (εὐβουλία) so indicated; whereas on the other

---

[75]Evag. HE 3.26, "For the Καιρός [the Opportune Moment] is swift of flight:
when it is close upon one, it may be secured; but should it once have escaped the
grasp, it soars aloft and laughs at its pursuers, not deigning to place itself again
within their reach. And hence no doubt it is, that statuaries and painters, while
they figure it with a lock hanging down in front, represent the head as closely
shaven behind; thus skillfully symbolizing, that when it comes up from behind
one, it may perhaps be held fast by the flowing forelock, but fairly escapes when
it has once got the start, from the absence of anything by which the pursuer might
grasp it." See also Evag. HE 6.12. There was a famous statue of this sort by Lysippus, described in Callistratus, Descriptions, ed. and trans. A. Fairbanks, LCL, (Cambridge MA: Harvard University Press, 1931) 6.428-429 K. A similar description
is found in Greek Anthology, trans. W. R. Paton, LCL, (Cambridge MA: Harvard
University Press, 1918) 5: Book 16 (the Planudean Anthology) 275, of a statue of
Kairos by Lysippus: "Why dost thou stand on tip-toe? I am ever running. And why
hast thou a pair of wings on thy feet? I fly with the wind. And why dost thou hold
a razor in thy right hand? As a sign to men that I am sharper than any sharp edge.
And why does thy hair hang over thy face? For him who meets me to take me by
the forelock. And why, in Heaven's name, is the back of thy head bald? Because
none whom I have once raced by on my winged feet will now, though he wishes
it sore, take hold of me from behind."

[76]Fortitude was one of the four cardinal virtues for both Plato and the Stoics.
Aristotle also discussed it in Nicomachean Ethics 2.7.2(1107b) and 3.6-9(1115a-
1117b). The other virtue, Prudence, was discussed by Aristotle in Nichomachean
Ethics 6.5.1-13.8(1140a-1145b). The charioteer as psychological metaphor is ultimately derived from Plato; see Phaedrus 246a.

hand, caution (ἀσφάλεια) might dictate a shrinking back from action (ὄκνος) on other occasions. The virtuous person's actions had to be perfectly matched to the καιροί, so that "the slackening and tightening of the lyre-strings of his desires took place in some metre and rhythm."

Pulling all of these different observations together, one can see that Evagrius's whole view of the world was dominated by this brooding sense of the continual shifts and fortuitous changes of events. One moment brought the chance of enormous worldly success, the next brought a chance of catastrophic defeat. The feeling of not being in control was probably heightened in his case by the personal tragedies arising from the plague that had been ravaging the empire off and on for the previous fifty-two years.[77] Evagrius himself had caught it while still a boy, but he had somehow survived. Across the years, however, he had lost his wife and several of his children to it, in addition to many other relatives and old family servants. Not two years before he wrote this history, Evagrius stated with some dismay, one of his daughters and her son had died of the plague. The seemingly random fashion in which death struck its victims in such an epidemic, and the near impossibility, in a prescientific age, of taking practical steps to avoid it, gave a feeling of utter helplessness to those who were compelled to live through it. The concept of a personified, all-ruling Fortune or ever shifting Kairos was a useful mythological way of verbalizing and expressing this feeling.

He recognized this as the view of life once taught by the great tragedians of ancient classical Greece, and only lightly Christianized it by suggesting that personal piety could sometimes lay some force of compulsion upon good fortune. He believed that tragedies as great as those of Oedipus and Agamemnon could, for example, still be written about Byzantine emperors who did not understand that defeat was as much a part of human life as victory. Kairos, the ever changing moment, was therefore acutely real to him, not only as the highly personified work of the sculptor, but also as the fabric itself of human existence. This is why he stressed the psychological attributes of Fortitude and Prudence, which caused the good man or woman to dare bravely or hold back cautiously at the opportune moments. To Evagrius, the real victims of history were those who replaced Fortitude and Prudence with Cowardice and Ignorant Rashness, and went,

---

[77]Evag. HE 4.29.

as a consequence, to a tragic doom. But through all this, the basic sense of history was not all that different from that held by Aeschylus, Sophocles, or Euripides; only a few of the words had been changed.

One can, in fact, see a long-term development taking place in the historiography, both Christian and pagan, of the late Roman period. One must start with Eusebius, at the time when the official Christianization of the empire first began; notions of the fortuitous were already present in his theology of history, but great pains were taken to avoid any overtly pagan language. The pagan historian Ammianus Marcellinus, who wrote later in the same century, acknowledged the existence of Christianity, but kept his own historical interpretations resolutely pagan in both language and substance. One might therefore say that in the fourth century the dividing lines between pagan and Christian historiography were still clearly marked in language, although in substance Christian ideas of history had begun to show signs of adaptations to pagan concepts. In the fifth century, Socrates, Sozomen, and Theodoret openly began using some of the traditional language associated with the pagan understanding of historical existence; references to pagan oracles and pagan avenging spirits occurred, along with talk of the classical tragic drama as normative for the structure of human life.

The two worlds finally came completely together in the mid-sixth-century secular historian Procopius. He has perplexed many modern scholars because he wrote at times as a complete pagan who believed in Fortune while in other passages he wrote as a Christian who believed devoutly in a God of providence.[78] But the development of this mixed pagan-Christian literary language was perfectly understandable in view of the history of the previous two centuries. A culture had been created in which pagan and Christian motifs could coexist side by side, under a government that was officially completely Christian, but which for that very reason had to tol-

---

[78]See for example, Averil M. Cameron, "The 'Scepticism' of Procopius," *Historia* 15 (1966): 466-82, and *Agathias* (Oxford: Clarendon, 1970); Averil and Alan Cameron, "Christianity and Tradition in the Historiography of the Late Empire," *Classical Quarterly* new series 14 (1964): 316-28; J. A. S. Evans, "Christianity and Paganism in Procopius of Caesarea," *Greek, Roman and Byzantine Studies* 12 (1971): 81-100; G. Downey, "Paganism and Christianity in Procopius," *Church History* 18 (1949): 89-102.

erate a wide range of internally contradictory beliefs. Procopius seemed no more jarring to a sixth-century reader than the mixture of pagan and Christian motifs in the frescoes of the Sistine Chapel seemed to a Renaissance man or woman.

Evagrius wrote about forty years after Procopius, and in fact made extensive use of his predecessor's history in writing his own.[79] Coming at this last part of the sixth century, *after* Procopius, gave him a good deal of freedom, because the basic cultural problem had already been resolved. It had now been established that it was perfectly permissible for a Christian literary figure to use a fair amount of pagan material as long as he was careful to state his Christian loyalty as well. As long as a historian of Evagrius's generation was willing to affirm a personal deity as ultimate ruler of the universe, and some element of human responsibility for the outcome of human events, he was free to write as much as he wished about the ever changing καιρός and the tragic downfall of the arrogant ruler.

Evagrius engaged in disputes in the pages of his history with two earlier historians, one Christian and the other pagan. The Christian, Zacharias Rhetor, had been a monophysite, so Evagrius's dispute with him dealt with the question of what had really happened at Chalcedon and during its aftermath. As part of this dispute, the issue was raised about whether Nestorius himself had been alive and present at the Council of Chalcedon.[80] That is, was the heretic condemned in 431 allowed to participate and personally influence the events of 451? The monophysite position was of course that the Chalcedonian decree, with its doctrine of two natures in the incarnate Christ, was an unadulterated expression of the Nestorian Christology.[81] To suggest that Nestorius himself had been present, as Zacharias did, would only make the matter worse.

---

[79]See, for example, Evag. *HE* 4.12-27.

[80]Evag. *HE* 2.2, discussed in Pauline Allen, *Evagrius*, 99-100. Evagrius himself had been brought up as a child in the staunchly Chalcedonian area around Apamea, and retained these sympathies throughout his life (see Allen, 1, 4).

[81]Three of the most recent major works on monophysitism are Roberta C. Chesnut, *Three Monophysite Christologies: Severus of Antioch, Philoxenus of Mabbug, and Jacob of Sarug* (Oxford: Oxford University Press, 1976); W. H. C. Frend, *The Rise of the Monophysite Movement* (Cambridge: Cambridge University Press, 1972); and André de Halleux, *Philoxène de Mabbog: sa vie, ses écrits, sa théologie* (Louvain: Univer-

Then a similar dispute was raised as to whether the monophysite bishop of Alexandria, Timothy Aelurus, had been personally responsible when the Chalcedonian bishop of Alexandria, Proterius, was lynched by a mob.[82] Evagrius went on to accuse Zacharias of "having written the whole work in a state of passion," and claimed that he had deliberately omitted from his history a Chalcedonian counterencyclical written by Basiliscus.[83] Fortunately, a Syriac translation of part of Zacharias's history has survived to the present, so that it is possible to see how events looked from his side as well.[84] Furthermore, it must be noted that Evagrius refers to Zacharias by name as his source of historical information on a number of occasions, so that in spite of his criticisms, he must have trusted Zacharias in general, and was willing to acknowledge his use of him publicly.[85]

The pagan historian with whom Evagrius disputed[86] was Zosimus, a fiercely anti-Christian writer from the turn of the sixth century.[87] Evagrius

---

sitas Catholica Louvaniensis, 1963). Also important is the work on Severus of Antioch by J. Lebon, *Le Monophysisme sévérien: étude historique littéraire et théologique sur la résistance monophysite au concile de Chalcédoine jusqu'à la constitution de l'église jacobite* (Louvain: J. van Linthout, 1909); and Lebon's article "La Christologie du monophysisme syrien," in *Das Konzil von Chalkedon: Geschichte und Gegenwart*, ed. A. Grillmeier and H. Bacht (Würzburg: Echter-Verlag, 1951) 1:425-580.

[82]Evag. *HE* 2.8.

[83]Evag. *HE* 3.7.

[84]Part of Zacharias Rhetor's history was preserved as books 3-6 of a *Syriac Chronicle*. An English translation of the whole work was published as *The Syriac Chronicle Known as that of Zachariah of Mitylene*, trans. F. J. Hamilton and E. W. Brooks (London: Methuen, 1899). A translation of the parts actually by Zacharias had already been privately published separately seven years earlier as *The Ecclesiastical History of Zacharias Rhetor, Bishop of Mitylene*, trans. from the Syriac by F. J. Hamilton (London, 1892).

[85]Evag. *HE* 2.10; 3.5 (twice), 6, 9, 12, 18. Pauline Allen, *Evagrius*, 8-9, discusses Evagrius's use of Zacharias as a source.

[86]Evag. *HE* 3.40-41.

[87]*Zosimi comitis et exadvocati fisci historia nova*, ed. L. Mendelssohn (Leipzig: Teubner, 1887); translated into English by J. J. Buchanan and H. T. Davis as *Zosimus: Historia Nova* (San Antonio TX: Trinity University Press, 1967). The history was written definitely after 498 C.E., and is quoted in another work (the chronicle of Eustathius of Epiphania) that can be dated to the first decades of the sixth century.

could tolerate an ambiguous figure like Procopius quite well. A large part of Book 4 of his church history (chapters 12-27) was taken openly from information contained in Procopius's secular history, and the latter was cited by name as the source. But Zosimus was quite a different kind of figure, a pagan propagandist who was bitterly hostile to Christianity, and argued that the decline of the Roman empire had begun with Constantine's reign, when pagan religious practices were first neglected. It was a consequence of this that the old Roman gods had begun to withdraw their favor. The progressive depaganization of the empire that then occurred over the following century made the gods display their resentment in ever greater ways. Zosimus's history broke off in midnarrative while he was describing the events of that ominous year, 410, the year in which the city of Rome itself was sacked and the ultimate doom of the Western empire was foreshadowed.[88]

This was the same pagan argument that Augustine had had to deal with in his *City of God*, and in looking at Evagrius's reply to Zosimus one can see by comparison, in the most marked fashion, the tremendous difference in the response of someone in the Eusebian tradition.

Evagrius began with certain peripheral matters. Zosimus, in accordance with his anti-Christian *Tendenz* had portrayed Constantine in the worst possible light (Book 2). Evagrius chose two of Zosimus's assertions about Constantine to attack in particular, the first concerning a tax called the Chrysargyrum,[89] the second concerning the deaths of Crispus and Fausta.[90]

But then, addressing Zosimus directly, he proceeded to the central issue. "You, O accursed and totally defiled one, say that the fortunes of the Romans wasted away and were altogether ruined from the time when Christianity was made known."[91] Evagrius then carried through the traditional arguments of the Eusebian tradition: The very rise of the Roman empire itself, back in the first century, was providentially linked to the simultaneous rise of the Christian religion. Furthermore, during the cen-

---

[88]Zosimus's position is discussed in detail in Walter Emil Kaegi, Jr., *Byzantium and the Decline of Rome*, chapter 3, "Zosimus and the Climax of Pagan Historical Apologetics," 99-145, and in Walter Goffart, "Zosimus, the First Historian of Rome's Fall," *American Historical Review* 76 (1971): 412-41.

[89]Zos. 2.38; Evag. *HE* 3.40-41.

[90]Zos. 2.29; Evag. *HE* 3.40-41.

[91]Evag. *HE* 3.41.

turies when pagan emperors sat on the throne, one could give a long, extended list of those who, like Julius Caesar, Caligula, and Nero, had come to bad ends. On the other hand, since the conversion of Constantine, not a single emperor (except Julian the pagan and Valens the persecutor) had been killed by their enemies or assassinated by their friends or had their thrones usurped.[92]

The strange feature about Evagrius's arguments (to modern Western readers) is that he completely ignored the sack of Rome in 410 and the whole century of Germanic migrations into Southern and Western Europe and Northern Africa. But Evagrius's point of view was not ours. As Walter Kaegi puts it in his detailed study of Eastern reactions to the fifth-century barbarian invasions,

> Evagrius simply denies that there had been any decline. He apparently believes that one could safely omit any reference to the fate of the former western Roman provinces. In his eyes, the Roman Empire really comprises the eastern provinces and their capital at Constantinople. . . . Evagrius treats Zosimus' charges as though they were unreal. It seemed an obvious fact to him that the Roman Empire continued to endure and was hardly on the verge of disappearing.[93]

The Byzantinization of the East had produced a basic shift in the late antique world's sense of perspective, in both East and West. In the East itself, the circle of human cultural awareness had shrunk to such a point that a person like Evagrius had horizons not much greater than Herodotus or Thucydides: the alien threat of the Persians was the omnipresent menace

---

[92]Ibid.

[93]Walter Emil Kaegi, Jr., *Byzantium and the Decline of Rome,* 221. Also, one must note Walter Goffart's comments in his article "Zosimus, the First Historian of Rome's Fall." He argues that a profound feeling had developed on the eve of the age of Justinian in certain quarters of the Eastern empire that the Roman empire had in fact fallen from its former heights. Zosimus was only an articulate spokesman for what other people of his time were also feeling. However, Justinian himself "appears to have made deliberate efforts, motivated by religious sentiment, to restore the credibility of the Eusebian conception of history," and it therefore might be argued (drawing some conclusions of my own from Goffart's remarks) that Evagrius held the position he did partly because he was writing in the immediately post-Justinian instead of the immediately pre-Justinian period.

to the East, while Western Europe and North Africa formed a hinterland, over on the West, of only peripheral interest.

This view was partially correct in that the west itself had in fact become a peripheral area by the late sixth century. As Peter Brown describes the cultural relationship, the few

> Byzantine outposts in the West were like mirrors, casting the light of the eastern Mediterranean far into the darkness of early medieval northern Europe. Isolated and grandiloquent, the kingdom of Visigothic Spain nevertheless moved to the rhythms of Byzantine life: its rulers eyed the eastern empire closely as a model and as a potential menace. In northern Europe, every great church was hung with Byzantine silks; liturgical books were written on Byzantine papyrus; relics were cased in Byzantine silverwork; legends and liturgy were of eastern origin. [94]

In addition, Justinian's exploits in the West, which Evagrius had read so much about in Procopius, had apparently shown that the Roman emperor at Byzantium could still assert his authority whenever he wished at any point in the West with only a small band of his highly professional soldiers. The final stages of Justinian's reconquests were in fact only just concluding in the 550s, under the direction of his general Narses. Evagrius must have been a young law student in Constantinople at just about that time, and would have heard proclamations and discussions of the great victories in the capital itself. So Evagrius's comments would have seemed quite credible both to himself and to contemporary Byzantine Christians.

One may easily compare Evagrius's arguments with Augustine's on the same topic. Augustine in his *City of God* had had to deal with pagans who were raising the same charges as Zosimus: "It was my first endeavor to reply to those who attribute the wars by which the world is being devastated, and especially the recent sack of Rome by the barbarians, to the religion of Christ, which prohibits the offering of abominable sacrifices to devils." [95] The immediate occasion, of course, was the sack of Rome by Alaric and his Visigoths in 410, but the conservative pagan Symmachus, who had

---

[94] Peter Brown, *The World of Late Antiquity* (New York: Harcourt, Brace, 1971) 158.

[95] Augustine, *De civ. Dei* 2.2; English translation taken from the work of Marcus Dods (New York: Modern Library, 1950).

gotten Augustine his professorship of rhetoric at Milan many years before, had expressed ideas already moving in that direction back in 384 in a letter he wrote to the emperors stating the pagan position in the famous controversy over the Altar of Victory.

Augustine then moved in his own way to rebut these pagan arguments.[96] First it must be noted that Augustine believed as devoutly as the Eastern church historians that it was God who granted victory and empire.[97] It was God who decided how long every particular war lasted.[98] It was God who put a Nero on the throne, or brought about the defeat in battle of a Radagaisus.[99] But Augustine attacked the idea put forward in the Eastern church histories that the pious Christian emperor was regularly rewarded with success while the impious emperor was punished. He pointed out that this theory did not in fact match up with the actual empirical course of history.

> He who gave power to Marius gave it also to Caius Caesar; He who gave it to Augustus gave it also to Nero; He also who gave it to the most benignant emperors, the Vespasians, father and son, gave it also to the cruel Domitian; and finally, to avoid the necessity of going over them all, He who gave it to the Christian Constantine gave it also to the apostate Julian.[100]

---

[96]For a more complete account, see Glenn F. Chesnut, "The Pattern of the Past," 69-95.

[97]Aug. De civ. Dei 4.17, 33; 5.1, 13, 21; 18.2.

[98]Ibid. 5.22.

[99]Ibid. 5.19, 23.

[100]Ibid. 5.21. Augustine accurately described the sort of success the pious emperor was supposed to obtain in the Eusebian tradition of historiography, then simply pointed out that there had been no actual correlation between Christian piety and this sort of success if one looked back over the long run of history: "For neither do we say that certain Christian emperors were therefore happy because they ruled a long time, or, dying a peaceful death, left their sons to succeed them in the empire, or subdued the enemies of the republic, or were able both to guard against and to suppress the attempt of hostile citizens rising against them. These and other gifts or comforts of this sorrowful life even certain worshipers of demons

Furthermore, the Roman empire was not the *Christian* empire for Augustine in the way it was for the church historians in the Eusebian tradition. For Augustine, the Roman empire was a manifestation of the City of Man, not of the City of God. It was with the cruel kingdom of Assyria that Rome was linked in his philosophy of history. [101] Rome and Assyria represented the two outstanding examples of the attempt of fallen humanity to create a way of life that was fundamentally atheistic in its basic ideals and goals—attempts foredoomed to failure in the ultimate scheme of things, since for Augustine there were no supernatural guarantees that the earthly Roman political system would survive. Quite the contrary.

But there was an even deeper criticism that could be raised against the Eusebian theory of history from an Augustinian viewpoint—namely, that it could turn all too easily into nothing less than an attempt by men and women to manipulate and use God for their own selfish human purposes.

> And this is the characteristic of the earthly city, that it worships God or gods who may aid it in reigning victoriously and peacefully on earth not through love of doing good, but through lust of rule. The good use the world that they may enjoy God: the wicked, on the contrary, that they may enjoy the world would fain use God. [102]

From the present point in time, a millennium and a half later, one can look back and see that Augustine was a better prophet than Eusebius, Socrates, Sozomen, Theodoret, and Evagrius. Western Europe fell into the Dark Ages, a genuine Roman empire was never recreated, and even the mighty Byzantine empire was eventually totally destroyed by the Arabs and the Turks. The ancient Roman imperial government in fact had been given no guarantees of permanent divine support because of its official Christianity.

But from another viewpoint, the attitudes of the fifth- and sixth-century church historians—Socrates, Sozomen, Theodoret, and Evagrius—

---

have merited to receive" (ibid. 5.24). "For the good God . . . gave to the Emperor Constantine . . . such fulness of earthly gifts as no one would even dare wish for. . . . But again, lest any emperor should become a Christian in order to merit the happiness of Constantine, . . . God took away Jovian far sooner than Julian, and permitted that Gratian should be slain by the sword of a tyrant" (ibid. 5.25).

[101] Ibid. 18.2.

[102] Ibid. 15.7.

are important in helping to show why the progressive disintegration of Roman central authority in Western Europe during their period was allowed to occur so casually. These four histories show us that in the governing circles in the major cities of the East there were many people who believed that the empire could never fall. Its Christianity defended it against any ultimate catastrophe to the end of time. The loss of battles, of cities, of entire provinces in the West was brushed aside as a disconnected series of merely temporary setbacks. Or the losses were simply denied, as Eastern horizons shrank and the West became less and less important. As long as the emperor remained a pious, orthodox Christian, it was believed too devoutly that no permanent harm could ever come to the empire. Unfortunately, any nation or people that believes itself to be eternal and invulnerable can bring about its own doom by a refusal to take seriously the progressive signs of a disintegrating position until the final, irreversible injury has already occurred. Only those who know they can be destroyed will act with timely vigor before the dangers they face have grown too great to be overcome.

CHAPTER 10

The Pious Emperor
and the Philosopher-King

In the histories of Eusebius's successors, the emperor had of course become the all-important figure in accounts of both secular and ecclesiastical affairs. It is important to comprehend what these historians expected of their rulers. Their presuppositions about the proper actions and attitudes of a good Christian monarch helped set the tone for a thousand years of medieval history. Particularly, the contrast they drew between the pagan Julian and the pious quasi-monasticism of Theodosius the Younger helped establish an ideal for Christian rulers that shaped the behavior of kings like Edward the Confessor and St. Louis of France, for the entire course of the Middle Ages.

It was Constantine, naturally, who made certain parts of this new understanding of rulership possible. The modern reader, brought up in the knowledge of the King Arthur tales and other similar medieval legends, is apt to miss the truly jarring nature, in a fourth-century Christian context, of the figure of the Warrior of God. For a Christian of that time, publicly glorifying a man of war was something totally new. That was a crucial mutation that had to occur in order to produce the medieval ideal of the good Christian monarch.

Nevertheless, Constantine was very different from his successors. He had been essentially a charismatic figure, a peculiar sort of "holy man" in his own way. [1] Continually guided by ecstatic experiences, he had come as

---

[1] A holy man in the sense used by Peter Brown in "The Rise and Function of the Holy Man in Late Antiquity," *Journal of Roman Studies* 61 (1971): 80-101. In his 1976 Jackson lectures at Harvard, Brown argued further that, by the fourth century, "the *locus* of the supernatural in society had shifted significantly. To a far greater extent than in preceding centuries, it had come to be accepted that the

the new Moses and the savior raised up by God to defeat the forces of the demons. His force of personality had been sufficient to unify the entire quarreling empire and produce successfully a gradual but complete change in the basic religion of this major civilization, without stirring up a deadly counterrevolution in the process. Eusebius had erected an imperial ideology on the basis of Constantine's activity and it became the official statement of the role of the ruler in the new Christian state.

But when this imperial ideology was taken over a century later by the next generation of Eastern church historians—Socrates, Sozomen, and Theodoret—there was produced what could be called, in the well-known phrase, a "routinization of charisma." There was a subtle but major shift in the sense of the language of the imperial ideology when it was transferred from the genuinely charismatic figure of Constantine, bursting onto the scene in a starkly pagan world, to that fifth-century empire when Christianity was all-dominant and the world of the Great Persecution was rapidly disappearing from living memory.

With this in view, therefore, it will be useful to look at Socrates and Sozomen as two typical examples, and list some of the areas of concern that they repeatedly displayed in their historical treatment of the emperors in their works. The links with Eusebius's picture of Constantine will be clear, but so will the vast difference between the virtues of a revolutionary (the first Christian emperor) and those somewhat more pedestrian values held by the rulers of an established order of things (his fourth- and early fifth-century successors).

1. The ruler's temperament was carefully noted. The good emperor was supposed to show mercy and was expected to control his anger. Valens, for example, was criticized severely by Socrates and Sozomen for his cruelty.[2] In this case, pagan historians like Ammianus Marcellinus and Zosimus also made the same criticism. Socrates pointed to Julian's displays of

---

supernatural could be represented on earth by human agents." These human agents, endowed with the attributes of the holy, could appear in any stratum of society, as a desert monk like St. Anthony or even as an exceptional emperor like Constantine. Holy men had replaced holy places as the focus of much popular religious feeling, to a marked degree.

[2]Socr. *HE* 4.19, 34. Soz. *HE* 6.7.9, 8.3, 8.4-5, 35.5-8. Constantius is also portrayed in an ungovernable rage at one point—Socr. *HE* 2.26. This may be contrasted with the description of Arcadius—Socr. *HE* 6.23.

temper as evidence of how far Julian had failed to measure up to that ideal of the philosopher that he had set for himself.[3] Mercy, coupled with control over anger, was one of the standard virtues that had been required of monarchs in the pagan Romano-Hellenistic tradition of divine rulership. One need only think, for example, of Seneca's *De clementia*, addressed to the young Nero. Many other examples could be drawn, from the political philosophy of Plutarch, Diotogenes, and so on.[4] This virtue was also regarded as essential to stable rulership in the classical Graeco-Roman historians, where it had its ultimate historiographical roots in the hybris stories of tragic downfall found in that tradition as early as Herodotus. The latter, in turn, may have developed this as a historical motif under the influence of the tragic dramatist Sophocles, with whom he had some contact.

Socrates' account of Julian's death was therefore built around the theme of hybris, the refusal to show mercy, in the manner of an ancient tragedy.[5] Sozomen's story of Theodosius the Great and the massacre at Thessalonica gave the Greek Christian variant of the classical hybris story, with its happier ending as the preaching of the Word brought repentance, and, from that, a breaking of the tragic pattern.[6]

2. Sozomen was interested in the influence of other people on the emperor's decisions: wives, sisters, priests, bishops, eunuchs, and others.[7] This influence was usually regarded as adverse. The account of the influence of the Princess Pulcheria on Theodosius the Younger[8] was the only significant example in Sozomen's history of a positive influence. The obvious concern here was that the emperor remain as far as possible a neutral arbitrator who would not become involved in factional fights within the government.

---

[3]Socr. *HE* 3.1, 19; 7.22.

[4]Plutarch, *To an Uneducated Ruler* 782bc; Diotogenes in Stobaeus, *Anthologium* 4.7.62 (Hense 269.6). A full discussion of this material appears in chapter 7 of this book.

[5]Socr. *HE* 3.21.

[6]Soz. *HE* 7.25.1-7; see also 7.23.

[7]Ibid. 2.27.1-4; 3.1.3-4, 9.5; 4.2.1, 16.21-17.1; 5.2.15-16, 5.8; 7.6.1; 8.16.1, 20.1-2.

[8]Ibid. 9.1.2-9.

3. So far as his personal religious beliefs were concerned, the good emperor was supposed to be a good Christian, and that meant staying clear of both paganism and heresy. The worst thing was to sacrifice to idols, as Julian did.[9] We are told that Jovian, Valentinian, and Valens were all willing to lose their commissions as officers rather than sacrifice.[10] The nonheretical emperors were regarded as Constantine,[11] Constans,[12] Jovian,[13] Valentinian,[14] Theodosius the Great,[15] Arcadius,[16] Honorius,[17] and Theodosius the Younger,[18] while the emperor Valens was regarded as clearly a heretic.[19] Socrates spoke of Constantius as simply an "Arian,"[20] but Sozomen tried to defend him to a certain extent by arguing that this emperor was only a homoiousian, not an extreme Arian, and by insisting further that the distinction between a homoiousian and a homoousian was not all that great.[21]

4. Socrates praised Constantine, Theodosius the Great, and Theodosius the Younger, because in time of war they put their trust in God and had a basic confidence in him as arbiter of battles.[22] This was regarded as an essential virtue. The manner of Julian's death, on the other hand, pointed out the opposing vice. As was noted this was presented as a classic account

---

[9]Socr. HE 3.1, 11, 17, 20; Soz. HE 5.1.2, 2.2-4, 3.1-2, 4.8; 6.1.1.

[10]Socr. HE 3.13, 22; 4.1; see also Soz. HE 6.6.3-6.

[11]Chosen by God himself—Socr. HE 1.2 and Soz. HE 1.3.1-3.

[12]Soz. HE 3.18.1.

[13]Socr. HE 3.24.

[14]Ibid. 4.1; Soz. HE 6.6.10, 21.7.

[15]Socr. HE 5.6; Soz. HE 7.4.3-6.

[16]Soz. HE 8.1.1.

[17]Ibid.; see also 9.16.1.

[18]For the "pious" emperor see Socr. HE 7.22 and Soz. HE 9.1.2-9.

[19]Socr. HE 4.1; Soz. HE 6.6.10, 7.9-10.

[20]Socr. HE 2.26, 37.

[21]Soz. HE 3.18-19; Cf. 4.13.4-14.7.

[22]Socr. HE 1.2, 18; 5.25; 7.22-23, 43.

of hybris leading to a tragic end.[23] The opposite of faith in God was an arrogant overconfidence in one's own human powers, which was sure to lead to destruction.

5. The good emperor protected the Christians from pagan persecution.[24] Socrates held that such an emperor was even willing to go to war to stop Christians from being persecuted.[25] Julian, the pagan persecutor, was naturally the archexample of a bad emperor.[26] Julian could be held out as proof that the Christians could not live in safety unless there were a Christian emperor on the throne.

6. The church historians emphasized the various ways in which the good emperor Christianized the state. Some of these ways were more symbolic: for example, the cross was put on coins and on the imperial images.[27] Although coinage was always an important vehicle of official propaganda in Roman imperial history, the point here was that the public image of the state should be at least nominally Christian. Julian tried to de-Christianize the state, and as one symbol of this, pagan devices went back on the coinage.[28] Socrates recounted with some disgust that Julian's palace was also filled with what was in effect a new chaplaincy, the pagan philosophers in their palliums.[29]

But Christianization struck other levels too. Socrates claimed that Constantine's army had gone to battle led by a standard in the form of a cross;[30] Jovian went further and, according to Socrates' and Sozomen's story, refused to lead any army that did not profess itself to *be* Christian;[31] Theodosius the Younger, in his role as public head of empire, led all the

---

[23]Ibid. 3.21.

[24]Ibid. 1.1, 2; Soz. *HE* 1.2.2, 6.1, 8.3-4; 2.15.1-5, 34.3; 5.2.1; 6.3.3-4.

[25]Socr. *HE* 1.4; 7.20.

[26]Ibid. 3.12, 13, 14, 17, 18-19; Soz. *HE* 5.2.1, 4.1-9, 5.2-6, 9.11-13, 11.12, 15.1-14, 17.1-12, 18.1, 20.1-3, 20.7; 6.6.3-6.

[27]Soz. *HE* 1.8.13.

[28]Socr. *HE* 3.17; Soz. *HE* 5.17.3-6.

[29]Socr. *HE* 3.1.

[30]Ibid. 1.2.

[31]Ibid. 3.22. Soz. *HE* 6.3.1.

assembled people of Constantinople in hymn singing.[32] Crucifixion was forbidden as a punishment.[33] Judicial business was not permitted to be carried out on Sundays and Fridays.[34] The Roman law was modified to conform with Christian morality.[35] Christians were given government posts.[36] Episcopal courts were given legal power.[37] All of these actions were listed with some satisfaction by Socrates and Sozomen, and here again, Julian was presented as the emperor who tried to reverse this process.[38]

There may have been some anachronism here in some of the details. Christianity did not truly become the established religion of the Roman state until the reign of Theodosius, and the picture Socrates and Sozomen gave of the period before his rule may have exaggerated the swiftness of the Christianization process. But certainly by the early fifth century a state had been created that was officially and publicly Christian—one of the most important religious assumptions that was to be passed on to the Middle Ages.

7. The good Christian emperor was expected to give financial aid to the church.[39] This especially took the form of church building programs and church restoration projects.[40] Julian, on the other hand, was pictured as attacking the church on the economic level.[41] Socrates and Sozomen

---

[32]Socr. *HE* 7.22, 23.

[33]Soz. *HE* 1.8.13.

[34]Ibid. 1.8.11-12.

[35]Ibid. 1.8.6, 9.1-4.

[36]Ibid. 1.8.5.

[37]Ibid. 1.9.5.

[38]Socr. *HE* 3.13; Soz. *HE* 5.3.2, 5.2.

[39]Soz. *HE* 1.8.7, 8.10, 9.5; 3.17.2.

[40]Socr. *HE* 1.2, 3, 9, 16, 17, 28; 2.8; Soz. *HE* 1.8.7; 2.1.1, 3.1, 3.7-8, 26.1-3; 3.17.3; 7.21.5; 8.1.5. On the Princess Pulcheria see Soz. *HE* 9.1.10, 3.1. Financial support for the church eventually came to form a significant part of the Byzantine imperial budget; see André M. Andréadès, "Public Finances: Currency, Public Expenditure, Budget, Public Revenue," in Norman H. Baynes and H. St. L. B. Moss, eds., *Byzantium* (Oxford: Clarendon, 1948) 71-85, esp. 76.

[41]Soz. *HE* 5.5.2-4. Julian also gave extra financial support to non-Christian cults; see Socr. *HE* 3.20, Soz. *HE* 5.3.1-2.

did not mention that the state continued to give its traditional financial support to the pagan cults as well for a long time after Constantine's inclusion of Christianity in the roster of religious organizations receiving state economic aid.

8. Socrates portrayed the good Christian emperors as giving special honor to clergymen and holy men. According to his account, Constantine refused to sit in the presence of the bishops at Nicaea until asked by them to do so.[42] One was told that Theodosius the Younger "had a reverential regard for all those who were consecrated to the service of God; and honored in an especial manner those whom he ascertained to be eminent for their sanctity of life."[43] This latter involved the emperor, according to Socrates, in wearing a very dirty haircloth cloak which had once belonged to a Christian holy man.[44] As can be seen, a rather medieval sense of piety had already begun to take hold. Julian, on the other hand, was shown making fun of Bishop Maris's blindness.[45] Julian's action was regarded as a dangerous flaunting of the powers of the holy in a society where the holy man was playing an increasingly more important role in general piety.

9. The good Christian emperor was expected to attack the pagan cults. This meant closing temples or destroying them or converting them into churches.[46] It also entailed the prohibition of pagan ceremonies.[47] The way in which pagan cult objects were exposed to ridicule or simply put out like museum pieces in public places was recounted with great satisfaction.[48] This was the negative side of the establishment of Christianity by Theodosius; the Christian historian now glorified the forcible suppression of the wor-

---

[42]Socr. *HE* 1.8; see also 1.11.

[43]Ibid. 7.22.

[44]Ibid.

[45]Ibid. 3.12. Julian honored the anti-Christian professional philosophers instead—the palace was filled with men wearing palliums (3.1). When Jovian took over the throne, "the philosophers . . . laid aside their palliums" (3.24).

[46]Socr. *HE* 1.3; 3.24; 5.16; Soz. *HE* 2.5.1-6; 3.17.2-3; 7.15.2-10, 20.1.

[47]Socr. *HE* 1.18; Soz. *HE* 1.8.5-6; 2.4; 7.20.2-4.

[48]Socr. *HE* 1.3, 16.

ship of the old gods. Julian, who tried to support pagan cults in every way, was of course the great counterexample. [49]

10. Sozomen was continually concerned about the conversion of the pagans to Christianity. To him, this was the reason for using Christian symbols in the Roman army, [50] the reason why God brought Constantine to power, [51] the reason why the rise of Arianism was bad, [52] and the reason for anti-Jewish legislation. [53] The good Christian emperor was supposed to conduct affairs in general in such a way that pagans would be led to convert to Christianity. [54] Julian was also described by Sozomen as interested in conversion, but conversion back the other direction, from Christianity to paganism. [55] This was of course part of the heritage of the pagan Romano-Hellenistic philosophy of divine rulership. The good monarch was supposed to be the savior of his people by leading them to the Supreme God. Christianity had merely worked out the logic of this basic assumption in its own religious terms.

11. Throughout the pages of these two church histories occur statements indicating an overwhelming desire for the *unity* of the church. Heretics were regarded as bad, often more because they broke this unity than because they distorted the truth of the faith. When the church became torn by disputes, the good emperor was expected to step in and create the conditions in which the leaders of the church could restore unity. [56] Julian was

---

[49] Ibid. 3.1, 11, 18. Soz. *HE* 5.3.1-5, 5.5.

[50] Soz. *HE* 1.4.2, 8.10.

[51] Ibid. 1.8.2.

[52] Ibid. 1.16.1.

[53] Ibid. 3.17.4-5.

[54] Ibid. 2.3.7-8, 5.1-8, 23.7-8, 34.4; 7.15.7, 20.1-2; 8.1.3-5.

[55] Ibid. 5.1.2, 4.6-7, 5.1, 15.1, 15.8-9, 16.1-15, 17.1-9, 18.1-3, 19.4.

[56] Socr. *HE* 1.7, 8, 10, 23, 24, 25, 27, 35; 3.25, 26; 5.7, 10; Soz. *HE* 1.16.1-5, 17.1, 17.3-5, 19.3, 20.1-2, 25.2-4; 2.1.1, 19.2-6, 21.7, 23.6-8, 28.14; 6.24.4; 9.1.9 (the princess Pulcheria). Constantius did want to have a General Council to bring doctrinal unity to the church, Sozomen believes (4.8.1, 11.2), but it would have been a unity imposed by fear (4.16.1).

presented by Sozomen as a counterexample, deliberately trying to sow discord in the church. [57]

12. The emperors regularly used their civil powers in their dealings with the church. They could act to enforce the edicts of a council. They could exile bishops, expel the losing side of any doctrinal dispute from all the churches, even resort to prison, torture, and death. [58] Both Socrates and Sozomen wanted a certain amount of religious tolerance, and strongly condemned the people in their histories who carried out vigorous religious persecutions. [59] But religious tolerance, to the two church historians, did not mean equal treatment for all sects under the law. It meant something more like that limited tolerance grudgingly conceded to dissenting groups at one point in English church history. All sorts of minor legal harassments could still be applied, such as forcing dissenting groups to meet their conventicles outside the city limits; furthermore, the minority of really extreme heretics was to receive severe punishment; and most of all, no one was to be left in any doubt that the established church was *the* Establishment.

13. The good emperor was not supposed to run roughshod over church councils. Constantius, and especially Valens, were criticized on this ac-

---

[57]Soz. HE 5.5.6-7.

[58]Socr. HE 1.8, 25, 27, 28, 35; 2.13, 16, 27, 37, 44; 4.1, 2, 7, 9, 11, 12, 15, 16, 17, 21, 22, 24, 32, 35; 5.7, 10, 20; 6.15, 18; Soz. HE 1.21.4-5; 2.32.2; 3.7.5-8, 9.1-5; 4.2.1-2, 9.4, 9.9, 11.2-12, 26.2; 6.7.9-10, 8.5-8, 9.1, 10.2, 12.5-6, 12.11, 12.16, 13.3-4, 14.2-4, 16.4, 16.8, 18.1-3, 19.2, 19.6; 7.4.5-6, 5.5, 6.7, 9.5, 12.11-12, 17.1; 8.8.1, 8.5.

[59]For more details, and the larger context of this issue, see G. F. Chesnut, "Radicalism and Orthodoxy: The Unresolved Problem of the First Christian Histories," *Anglican Theological Review* 65 (1983): 295-305. There are many statements in both Socrates and Sozomen condemning particular historical figures who set about a vigorous persecution of heretics; see Socr. HE 2.27; 6.3, 29, 31; Soz. HE 4.26.3-4; 6.12.16. Praise is given to those who either practiced a certain amount of religious tolerance or spoke out in favor of it; see Socr. HE 3.25; 4.1, 29, 32; 5.2, 20; 7.2, 11, 41-42; Soz. HE 2.32.5; 6.6.10, 36.6-7; 7.4.5, 12.12. Julian's occasional acts of what appeared to be religious tolerance are regularly attributed to base motives, see Socr. HE 3.1, 11; Soz. HE 5.4.9-5.1, 5.6-7.

count.[60] Sozomen believed that the truly good emperor let church councils convene and reach decisions in perfect freedom, without making any attempt to influence those decisions, and then wholeheartedly supported the conciliar decrees. He believed that two of the emperors—Constantine and Valentinian—had actually behaved that way in practice,[61] but Socrates was more cynical.

14. There were a number of confrontation stories in Socrates and Sozomen, in which a Christian holy man confronted the emperor and rebuked or warned him.[62] Included in this category was the famous confrontation between Ambrose and Theodosius over the massacre of Thessalonica.[63] The Late Roman historian Peter Brown has pointed out the importance of the holy man in the society of this period.[64] The vast number of miracle stories attached to these figures in the fifth- and sixth-century church histories shows the power and fascination of their mysterious aura. Partly as a heritage from one of his precursors, the notoriously abusive Cynic philosophers, the late antique holy man was expected to display as one of his identifying characteristics a παρρησία or divine boldness of speech that would allow him to say anything to anyone, no matter how powerful that person might be. There were also strong biblical roots to this idea. The Old Testament prophets had been called to proclaim judgment and to shepherd, and the church and its spokesmen were the continuing bearers of that task.[65] But whatever the ultimate source, the very amount

---

[60]Socr. HE 2.7, 13, 16, 26, 29, 34, 37, 41; 4.6; Soz. HE 4.16.1, 19.1-9; 6.7.1-9, 8.4-5, 10.2, 21.7.

[61]Soz. HE 1.20.1-2, 25.4; 2.27.12-13, 31.2-3 (cf. 34.6); 6.7.2, 21.7.

[62]Socr. HE 3.12, and perhaps 18-19; 4.26, and perhaps 32 (though Themistius was certainly not a Christian holy man); Soz. HE 3.20.5-7; 4.11.9-10 and 15.5; 5.4.8-9, and perhaps 19.17-20.4; 6.16.4-6, 18.5-7, 21.4-6, 40.1 and perhaps 36.6-37.1 (Themistius); 7.6.4-6, 23.3, 25.1-13; 8.4.7-10.

[63]Soz. HE 7.25.1-7.

[64]Most recently in Brown's 1976 Jackson lectures at Harvard, *The Making of Late Antiquity*. See also his earlier "The Rise and Function of the Holy Man in Late Antiquity."

[65]Παρρησία was also identified in the New Testament as one of the marks of Christian perfection; see, for example, 1 John 4:17-18.

of space devoted to the lives and actions of these holy men in the church histories shows a change in the character of ancient society. These human bearers of the divine had power that could be felt even politically, and before that power even an emperor had to bow his will.

These fourteen motifs give a nicely detailed picture of the good Christian emperor as he was supposed to be, and of his relationship to the church. The idealized image can be used as a valuable piece of data for the social and intellectual history of the early fifth century. Here one has two educated Christian laymen, Socrates and Sozomen, moving in government and legal circles, expressing their ideas about what an emperor should be now that the empire had been officially Christianized. It is a valuable insight into the all-important transitional period that lay between the pre-Constantinian Roman world and that of the early Middle Ages.

Writing in the next century, Evagrius Scholasticus dealt with a different set of emperors, but the same sort of analysis could be easily performed on his history as well. He singled out seven emperors for special comment: Marcian (450-457) was a good emperor.[66] Zeno (474-475, 476-491) was a bad emperor[67] even though he was at one point apparently aided by the martyr Thecla.[68] But since he was a Christian, not a pagan, emperor, divine providence (according to the Eusebian understanding of history) guaranteed that he could not be permanently overthrown by the usurper Basiliscus.[69] This was part of Evagrius's argument against the pagan historian Zosimus. Anastasius (491-518) was a good emperor,[70] although some criticisms were leveled against him at one point.[71] Justinian (527-565) was,

---

[66]Evag. *HE* 2.1, 8. An excellent and detailed commentary on Evagrius's attitude towards each of the emperors with whom he dealt can be found in Pauline Allen (*Evagrius Scholasticus the Church Historian*, Spicilegium Sacrum Lovaniense 41 [Louvain: Spicilegium Sacrum Lovaniense, 1981]), who gives the full historical context, explaining in each case the biases and causes that produced these particular judgments.

[67]Evag. *HE* 3.1-3, 27.

[68]Ibid. 3.8.

[69]Ibid. 3.41.

[70]Ibid. 3.30, 34, 37-38, 39.

[71]Ibid. 3.42.

interestingly enough, placed among the bad emperors. According to Evagrius, Justinian had an insatiable desire for his subjects' money, was a man of savage brutality, and of course at the end fell into heresy, at which time God's providence took him from the scene.[72] Justin II (565-578) was a bad emperor, who repented publicly, however, after his tragic downfall.[73] Tiberius II Constantine (578-582) was a good emperor,[74] and so especially was Maurice (582-602).[75] In Evagrius's description of all these rulers, one can see the same fundamental understanding of the emperor's role that appeared in the histories of Socrates and Sozomen 150 years earlier.

One can also see showing through, in Evagrius's description of the good emperor Maurice, for example, the old Romano-Hellenistic ideal of the ruler as the image of the divine virtues.

> It was henceforward the settled aim of the emperor to wear the purple and the diadem not merely on his person but also on his soul: for he alone of recent sovereigns was sovereign of himself; and, with authority most truly centered in himself, he banished from his own soul the mob rule of the passions, and having established an aristocracy in his own reasonings, he showed himself a living image of virtue, training his subjects to imitation.[76]

In this passage one even had the traditional motif of the ruler's subjects being brought to salvation by imitating the resplendent virtues of their monarch. In many ways, therefore, the new Christian ideal of the emperor did not really alter the old that much.

But there are some distinctive characteristics of the Christian historians' conception of the emperor that marked them off strongly, in their own understanding of the matter, from their pagan predecessors. This is pointed out extremely well in the contrast that Socrates and Sozomen drew between Julian and Theodosius the Younger. The basic issue was a surpris-

---

[72]Ibid. 4.30, 32, 39-41; 5.1.

[73]Ibid. 5.1-2, 5, 7-8, 9, 11, 13.

[74]Ibid. 5.13, 22.

[75]Ibid. 5.19, 20; 6.1, 2, 17 (reacts wisely when the swing of Fortune puts an enemy in his power).

[76]Ibid. 6.1.

ingly ancient one. Plato had proposed, centuries earlier, that the perfect society could not be established until philosophers became kings. The Romano-Hellenistic philosophy of divine rulership had then enshrined this principle at the heart of its political theory. Only the philosopher-sage could embody the divine Logos or Nomos in his own life. Eusebius had seemed to ratify that basic position in his statement that Constantine's rule on earth was the icon or image of the rule of the divine Logos in heaven. But now, in the fifth century, Socrates Scholasticus raised the first serious question about that basic principle. If Julian were the example, he said, then it was not clear that the true philosopher-king was even possible at all.[77]

To understand the full thrust of Socrates' criticism, one must remember the impact that the Cynic revival of the first century C.E. had had on the popular conception of the philosopher. The word "philosopher" came increasingly to imply a wandering beggar-preacher who wore a beard, donned the distinctive and immediately recognizable "philosopher's cloak" as a sort

---

[77]It can be argued that Julian himself did not claim to be a philosopher-king. F. Dvornik, (*Early Christian and Byzantine Political Philosophy* [Washington DC: Dumbarton Oaks, 1966] 2:664) insists that Julian explicitly rejected any idea of being a philosopher-king, citing the *Letter to Themistius the Philosopher* 266cd. Dvornik himself regards Julian as a reactionary, in politics as well as in religion, who deliberately tried to reject the Hellenistic concept of rulership with its elevation of the monarch in pomp and ritual. He believes that Julian was instead making a deliberate attempt at re-creation of the past, and was trying to return to the modest style of the early Principate. Julian attended the meetings of the senate, for example, and gave speeches there himself (Amm. Marc. 22.7.3, Socr. *HE* 3.1), instead of ordering senators to come to him at the palace and pay court to him while standing before his throne, as was the usual practice in the Late Empire. And Dvornik (2:664-65) gives many other examples of his attempts to revive the ancient prestige and authority of the senate. The main point of Dvornik's argument seems to be that to refer to this sort of behavior as an attempt to play the Platonic philosopher-king is to miss completely the major thrust of Julian's actions. On the other hand, one must assert against Dvornik that Julian's infamous beard, the nature of his friends, and his own philosophical writings give fair ground for regarding him as a person who was deliberately attempting to be a philosopher in the fourth-century meaning of the term. Perhaps the fairest statement would be that, while Socrates Scholasticus tended to blame *all* of Julian's behavior on his undeniable attempt to play the role of a philosopher, in fact Julian may have had additional (and quite different) motives for *some* of his actions.

of uniform, and carried only a walking staff and a knapsack as he traveled. A true Cynic was expected to sleep on the bare ground and eat only the necessary minimum of food. Even philosophers who were not Cynics came to copy some of these practices, such as the beard or the philosopher's cloak, as a sort of badge of office, and Julian's ascetic behavior (and notorious beard) had been in line with such tendencies.[78] Socrates was therefore raising the serious question as to whether the Cynic ideal, the ultimate presupposition lying behind some of Julian's behavior, was an adequate ideal for rulership in the Late Roman empire. The crucial problem for him was the Cynic doctrine of poverty and its special influence on Julian.

Socrates performed this criticism by appealing to another, equally ancient presupposition of the Romano-Hellenistic ruler cult.[79] The ruler, it had been said as far back as the Neopythagorean Diotogenes, should display his "majesty" (Doric form σεμνότας) by his very physical appearance.

> He must wrap himself about with such decorum and pomp in his appearance, his calculations, his inferences, and the character of his soul, as well as in the actions, movements, and posture of his body, that he will put in order those who look upon him, amazed at his majesty, his self-control, and his attitude of decorum. For to look upon the good king ought to affect the souls of those who see him no less than a flute or harmony.[80]

The ruler's aura of divine majesty was an important part, in other words, of his saving work as representative of God on earth. The souls of his subjects were to be lifted out of vice and disorderly passion and brought into

---

[78]Julian defended his philosopher's beard, of course, in the famous *Misopogon*, written against the citizens of Antioch. On the character of Julian's Neoplatonic philosophy and its relationship to his defense of the old pagan gods see Hans Raeder, "Kaiser Julian als Philosoph und religiöser Reformator," *Classica et Mediaevalia* 6 (1944): 179-93.

[79]Socrates also made some ad hoc criticisms of Julian's claim to be a philosopher. For example, Julian had been willing deliberately to embroil the Roman Empire in the suffering and slaughter of a civil war, and he had later written a book in which he had publicly cast ridicule upon the memories of past emperors. Neither act seemed appropriate to the manner of a philosopher, who should be a man of virtue in all things; Socr. *HE* 3.1.

[80]Diotogenes in Stobaeus, *Anthologium* 4.7.62 (Hense 268.5).

self-control and responsible, disciplined citizenship by the very sight of the ruler's awe-inspiring magnificence.

A passage in Xenophon's *Cyropaedia* suggests a possible Persian origin for this Hellenistic idea. The Persian king, he said, attempted to "cast a sort of spell" upon his subjects by wearing robes that concealed any physical defects and made him look more impressive, padded shoes to increase his height, and eye makeup and other cosmetics to improve upon nature's art. The members of his royal entourage were ordered

> not to spit or to wipe the nose in public, and not to turn round to look at anything, as being men who wondered at nothing. All this he thought contributed, in some measure, to their appearing to their subjects as men who could not lightly be despised.[81]

But whatever its origin, this idea had become an accepted part of Romano-Hellenistic political thought by the time of Julian.

In fact, Julian's own historian, Ammianus Marcellinus, gives one of the best examples of the sort of majestic behavior which was expected of the ideal ruler during the Late Empire. When Constantius made his triumphal entry into Rome in 357, Ammianus says,

> he himself sat alone in a golden two-wheeled carriage in the resplendent blaze of shimmering precious stones, whose mingled glitter seemed to form a sort of shifting light. . . . he never stirred, but showed himself as calm and imperturbable as he was commonly seen in his provinces. . . . as if his neck were in a vise, he kept the gaze of his eyes straight ahead, and turned his face neither to right nor to left, but (as if it were a statue of a man) neither did he nod when the wheel jolted nor was he ever seen to spit, or to wipe or rub his face or nose, or move his hands about.[82]

It was this standard of imperial pomp and decorum that Julian violated when he came to the throne.

---

[81]Xenophon, *Cyropaedia* 8.1.40-42; E. R. Goodenough, "Political Philosophy of Hellenistic Kingship," *Yale Classical Studies* 1 (1928): 79.

[82]Amm. Marc. 16.10.6-10; Goodenough, in the passage cited in the preceding footnote, and M. P. Charlesworth, "Imperial Deportment: Two Texts and Some Questions," *Journal of Roman Studies* 37 (1947): 34-38, both compare the passages from Xenophon and Ammianus.

So on the one hand, by the fourth and fifth centuries it had come to be assumed that the philosopher should at the very least dress in simple clothes and lead a simple, self-sufficient life. Hence Julian had, among other things, "expelled the eunuchs, barbers and cooks from the palace" and had in many other ways reduced the number and importance of all the palace functionaries. But this then caused the historian Socrates to complain that "the expulsion of the cooks and barbers is the work of a philosopher but not of an emperor," because by this period the idea of the imperial majesty was no longer commensurate with such behavior. Most people in the empire disapproved of what Julian did, Socrates says, because they felt that the emperor must project an image of authority, by the impressive display of the imperial wealth, that would serve as the symbolic focus of the hopes and fears of the mass of the empire's population. It was felt that "when the amazement produced among the masses by the imperial wealth was brought to an end, it made the emperor's rulership easy to hold in contempt."[83]

Socrates stated categorically that a philosopher would fail to reach his goal if he tried to carry out all the duties of an emperor, and he went on to say that there was only one part of the philosopher's life that an emperor should rightfully try to copy: "It is possible for an emperor to be a philosopher, in so far as he is looking towards self-control [σωφροσύνην]" but that was all.[84] And for all of Julian's claims to be the philosopher-king, on this the only part of the philosopher's life open to him the ease with which he fell into anger caused him to fall short of the mark.[85]

But if the life of the philosopher was not possible for a Late Roman emperor, the life of piety was. In an extremely valuable article written about twenty years ago, Glanville Downey pointed out how, in Christian writings, εὐσέβεια (piety) replaced φιλανθρωπία as the chief of the emperor's official virtues. One could see this clearly, he showed, by contrasting the set of official virtues applied to the emperor by a fourth-century pagan orator like Themistius, with the virtues of the quite different rhetorical tradition that was developed in Eusebius, and especially in Socrates, Sozomen, and Evagrius.[86] In this new Christian tradition, piety was the attribute absolutely required of the good emperor.

---

[83]Socr. HE 3.1.

[84]Ibid.

[85]Ibid. 3.19; repeated in 7.22.

[86]Downey, "The Perspective of the Early Church Historians," Greek, Roman, and Byzantine Studies 6 (1965): 57-70.

It was Theodosius the Younger whom Socrates,[87] and Sozomen as well, chose as their outstanding example of the pious emperor. In their histories he was the great contrast to Julian; he was the one who illustrated the truly Christian ideal. Sozomen's description of Theodosius was especially interesting. To begin with, the emperor's piety (εὐσέβεια) was mentioned repeatedly,[88] but in recognition of the older pagan tradition of praising the emperor chiefly for his beneficence, some mention was also made of his φιλανθρωπία.[89] He also was said[90] to have the virtues of wisdom, fortitude, temperance, justice,[91] self-mastery,[92] greatness of soul, gentleness, and love of honor.[93]

But piety was the most important. Eusebius's key word for describing the fundamental attitude that separated the saved from the damned was elaborated by Sozomen, although in a slightly different direction. The pious mode of conduct was similar to the philosophical in that a kind of asceti-

---

[87]Socr. HE 7.22, 42. One might note that even in Augustine, who was frequently so cynical about rulers of the Earthly City, one finds a rather glowing description, in De civ. Dei 5.26, of the elder Theodosius. One must also note Augustine's list of the virtues proper to an emperor, in what John Neville Figgis (The Political Aspects of S. Augustine's "City of God" [London: Longmans, Green, 1921] 12) called "the famous Fürstenspiegel, the picture of a godly prince," in De civ. Dei 5.24.

[88]Soz. HE dedication.2, 3, 11, 15, and 18; 9.1.2 and 8.

[89]Ibid. dedication.3, 15, and especially 9: "Thus you are a lover of humankind [φιλάνθρωπος] and gentle, both to those near, and to all, imitating [μιμούμενος] the Heavenly King, your ruler, who loves to send rain and to cause the sun to rise and to furnish other things ungrudgingly for both the just and the unjust."

[90]Ibid. dedication.15 gives a long list. Additional virtues are mentioned in HE dedication.18 (σοφία), 12 (ἐγκράτεια), and 9 (πραότης).

[91]These first four were originally Plato's cardinal virtues: σοφία, ἀνδρεία, σωφροσύνη, and δικαιοσύνη; see Plato, Republic, Book 4.

[92]In Stoicism (in Cleanthes' list) the four cardinal virtues were self-mastery (ἐγκράτεια), and, as in Plato, fortitude, temperance, and justice; see Frederick Copleston, History of Philosophy (Westminster MD: Newman, 1959) 1:397.

[93]The last three virtues can be found in Aristotle's Nicomachean Ethics (2.7.7-8, 7.10; 4.3-5): μεγαλοψυχία, πραότης, φιλοτιμία. On greatness of soul in particular, see Wolfgang Haase, "Grossmut," in Historisches Wörterbuch der Philosophie 3:887-99.

cism was common to both. When Sozomen described the way of life that prevailed in the imperial household, he stressed that the daily course of Theodosius's activity was one of both physical and intellectual ἄσκησις, in the full, original meaning of "training," "exercise," or "disciplined practice." During the day he was said to exercise (ἀσκεῖν) his muscles and his skill with weapons; while at night he stayed up long after the servants had gone to bed, learning about politics and military tactics from history books.[94] In his daily training (ἐν ταῖς καθ' ἡμέραν ἀσκήσεσι) Theodosius developed self-mastery (τὴν ἐγκράτειαν) over the passions of the soul and body (τῶν παθῶν τῆς ψυχῆς καὶ τοῦ σώματος).[95] Using this kind of language, Sozomen could easily move back and forth between the ἄσκησις of the Christian monk and the ἄσκησις that produced what the ancient Greek ideal had traditionally regarded as the good athlete or the good soldier. In one short section of the dedication, for example, Sozomen moves easily from Theodosius's piety to his daily athletic exercises to an anecdote displaying his ability to withstand heat and thirst in time of war.[96] Sozomen's ideal emperor was half monk, half soldier. The one word ἄσκησις was used to refer to all parts of the training that would produce an emperor who successfully combined the two.

In the picture that Sozomen drew of life in the imperial household, Pulcheria and her sisters were seen living as nuns within the walls of the palace.[97] Pulcheria was the one who directed the ἄσκησις of the young prince Theodosius. He was taught the military arts by experts who were brought in, particularly in order to learn horsemanship and the handling of weapons.[98] Pulcheria herself then made it her own central task to teach the child piety (εὐσέβεια) in the full Christian sense. In good Byzantine manner she trained him to pray without ceasing. She educated him particularly in the special duties of the Christian emperor: frequent appearances

---

[94]Soz. HE dedication. 7-8.

[95]Ibid. dedication. 11-12. Sozomen uses the word ἐγκράτεια in perfectly acceptable fashion, but in the second and third centuries there had been an over-ascetic heresy called the "Encratite" heresy.

[96]Ibid. dedication. 10-14.

[97]Ibid. 9. 1. 3-4 and 3. 1-2.

[98]Ibid. 9. 1. 6.

had to be made at religious services, special honor had always to be shown to priests and monks, lavish gifts and donations had to be made for the building and decorating of churches. [99]

Finally, as one of the most important parts of the young Theodosius's training, he had to be taught proper "stage presence" for his public appearances. He had to be taught how to move regally in the imperial procession, how to walk and sit down without tripping or ludicrously entangling himself in the glittering robes of state as he took part in the intricate ceremonial of the Byzantine court. Like an actor on the stage he had to learn to play a role continuously: never showing amusement, switching immediately from an aspect of mercy and gentleness to a stern and wrathful look calculated to throw utter fear into the heart of the luckless subject who stood before him. [100]

The ideal Christian emperor had to be as ascetic as a Julian in many ways—the standards of the time did require that[101]—but he also had to produce a display of impassive majesty. This was where Julian had most offended people. He had refused to play this role, of the symbolic, impersonal figure who appeared only at a distance, in the glitter of gold and magnificent robes. Even the pagan Ammianus criticized Julian for that: "He delighted in the applause of the mob, and desired beyond measure praise for the slightest matters, and the desire for popularity often led him to converse with unworthy men."[102] Julian's informality had too much the flavor of a Nero. And the pagan Ammianus, surprisingly enough, praised the Christian Constantius for not lowering the symbolic stature of the imperial office in the way Julian was to do: Constantius "always maintained the dignity of the imperial authority (*auctoritas*), and his great and lofty spirit disdained the favor of the populace."[103]

Rather than replacing or totally supplanting the old pagan understanding of the emperor's role, the new Christian ideal therefore simply added

---

[99]Ibid. 9.1.8.

[100]Ibid. 9.1.7.

[101]See Ammianus Marcellinus, for example, on Julian's asceticism: 16.5.4-5; 21.9.2; 24.4.26-27; 25.2.2, 4.2-3; and *passim*.

[102]Amm. Marc. 25.4.18. Compare 22.7.3-4 and 14.1-2.

[103]Amm. Marc. 21.16.1.

to it and modified it. The truly good emperor, to Socrates and Sozomen at least, would be like their picture of Theodosius the Younger: half a soldier, as was said, and half a monk. [104] Whether rightly or wrongly, they believed that this combination was possible in a way that the combination of a philosopher and a king was not. This importation of the monastic ideal into political theory was bequeathed as a legacy to the Middle Ages. For a thousand years it governed the way people thought about the nature of a truly good ruler. It was different from the earlier Constantinian image: monks were safer because they were part of a stable establishment; people who saw too many visions were not.

It is difficult to know how far most medieval monarchs actually tried to live out any of these more monastically oriented features in practice. The ideal itself was nevertheless built deeply into the structures of medieval thought. There were rulers who did genuinely seem to have tried to govern their lives by it, as best they understood it—figures, for example, like Edward the Confessor, the pious eleventh-century king of England, canonized a century after his death. The medieval life of St. Louis by Jean, Lord of Joinville, gives a detailed picture of a thirteenth-century French king who fit a similar pattern of royal piety. [105] Most Crusader knights were of course affected by the notion that true piety and military valor were compatible, and the basic motif of the pious man of war was developed in yet another direction in the more deeply religious versions of the Arthurian legend and

---

[104]The total picture of the development of Christian attitudes toward warfare is of course a complicated one. Even a century after the conversion of Constantine, many influential Christians still retained a distaste for anything that tended to glorify militarism. Sabine MacCormack ("Latin Prose Panegyrics," in *Empire and Aftermath: Silver Latin II*, ed. T. A. Dorey [London: Routledge and Kegan Paul, 1975] 169-70) observes that many fourth- and fifth-century Christian authors displayed qualms about the imperial panegyric as a genre, because "one of the chief topics . . . was imperial success in war and the practice, by the emperor, of the warlike virtues." In Paulinus of Nola's panegyric on Theodosius, for example, he apparently praised the emperor "because he conquered by faith and prayer rather than by arms" (170-71).

[105]Jean, Sire de Joinville, *Histoire de Saint Louis*, reconstruction of the original medieval text, with accompanying modern French translation, by M. Natalis de Wailly (Paris, 1874).

the quest for the Holy Grail. [106] Even a more ordinary medieval monarch like Louis the Fat had himself moved from his sick bed to a carpet covered with ashes when he realized that he was at the point of death, and regretted that he had not had time to put on the garb of a monk. [107] The Roman emperor Theodosius the Younger was the spiritual ancestor of all these figures, and the ideal that his historians Socrates and Sozomen created in their account of his life and virtues helped to replace the old image of the wise philosopher-king with the new Christian picture of the pious but majestic soldier-monk.

---

[106]See for example (from the Prose *Lancelot*), *La Queste del Saint Graal, roman du XIIIe siècle*, the medieval text ed. Albert Pauphilet (Paris, 1949).

[107]Amy Kelly, *Eleanor of Aquitaine and the Four Kings* (Cambridge MA: Harvard University Press, 1950) 8, citing Auguste Molinier, *Vie de Louis le Gros par Suger, suivie de l'histoire du roi Louis VII* (Paris, 1887) 129.

CHAPTER 11

Toward a Tradition
and Theology
of Christian History

In a number of ways, therefore, the histories of Eusebius, Socrates, Sozomen, Theodoret, and Evagrius helped to mold the ideas of the medieval and early modern period. In the Byzantine world their influence was direct; in Western Europe their histories and the products of their research were made known through the translations and adaptations of Rufinus, Jerome, and Cassiodorus. But directly or indirectly their influence was greatly felt. Perhaps it would be good to conclude by summarizing and giving some additional comments about the distinctive emphases of this historiographical tradition and the way each historian developed and adapted the basic stock of ideas to form his own unified theology of history.

Their basic presuppositions about history and human existence differed from the Augustinianism that formed the other major current of Western Christian thought. The two most formative members of their tradition, Eusebius and Socrates, were both Origenists. This meant that they upheld a doctrine of preexistence and denied the literal account of Adam and Eve and the Garden of Eden. Origenism of their sort also rejected the idea of a future millennial kingdom of Christ on earth and held instead to a more Neoplatonic concept of eternal life in some supercosmic realm. Both Eusebius and Socrates allegorized the Scriptures. But they both took history seriously (whether biblical, ecclesiastical, or secular), and even more importantly they completely assimilated Origen's emphasis on free will. They rejected all attempts to deny this freedom, including the pagan understanding of fate that played such a major role in many of the Graeco-Roman histories.

The kind of Origenism that Eusebius maintained was of an extremely rationalistic sort, but this helped to get the new Christian historiography started on a firm foundation of logical inquiry and respect for fact. For him, the Logos or Divine Reason was the structure of all nature and history. One could therefore analyze history and see the internal logic of its chains of events. The irrational and hence daemonic power of human emotion had intruded itself again and again in the course of history, but the Logos could set the human soul free from the passions and allow it to return again to rationality. The rational soul would then spontaneously turn to God himself in εὐσέβεια, the cosmic hymn of praise.

Eusebius's successors did not completely follow this version of Origenist theology. Socrates' Origenism tended more towards mysticism, and combined a rather skeptical form of Neoplatonism with the radical theology of Evagrius Ponticus. It was the transcendent vision of God that stood for him as the goal of history beyond history. Sozomen and Evagrius reacted quite differently: neither seems to have been much theologically or philosophically inclined, or any rate, beyond supporting what had already been officially defined as orthodoxy, they did not so obviously take sides in more speculative theological and philosophical disputes in their histories. Theodoret, with his Antiochene theology, was actually opposed to many of the Origenistic tendencies. But on the fundamental issues of free will and the human possibility in this life, one can say that Sozomen, Evagrius, and Theodoret all three fell into the Eusebian-Socratean historiographical tradition as well.

Eusebius's successors also did a reasonably good job of upholding his emphasis on careful, documented historical research. Because the universal Logos itself was the structure of human history, historical inquiry for these historians was by its very nature a field for logical investigation. One cited facts and stated causes; one did not appeal to faith to prove a point. Eusebius went further, and became the first ancient historian to cite his sources both verbatim and extensively on a regular basis. He did not put made-up speeches in the mouths of his characters as a typical Graeco-Roman historian did. He was, in this way, the first ancient historian to have anything like a modern historian's conscience about careful quotation of copied material and proper identification of sources of information. The critical use of documentary evidence enabled Eusebius and his successors to go back in history to earlier periods, beyond the memories of living witnesses. (As R. G. Collingwood has pointed out, the classical Graeco-Roman historians had been so tethered to oral tradition that they had done really well only in writing the history of the immediately preceding generation.[1])

It was also a tradition of Christian humanism. Eusebius was famous as the greatest Christian scholar of his period, with encyclopedic knowledge of the Greek classics. His *Praeparatio Evangelica* is still mined for its fragments of ancient Greek works otherwise lost. Socrates also supported the study of the classical authors and argued for their necessary role even in a Christian education. They taught both eloquence and the art of reasoning, he said, and furthermore, "there were many philosophers among the Greeks who were not far from the knowledge of God."[2] One need only read through a few pages of Sozomen, Theodoret, or Evagrius to see the classical allusions and rhetorical devices that were the mark of such a humanistic education.

From their immersion in the classics they had all imbibed a strong feeling for the fortuitous character of human life. For the Graeco-Roman historiographical tradition, just as for the Greek tragic drama, the power of Fortune was an inescapable part of human events. Eusebius and his successors all seem to have believed that the idea of Fortune contained some fundamental truth, even while they were trying to modify it in a Christian direction. Even when the actual pagan word τύχη was avoided, euphemisms crept into their writings instead. For Eusebius, using Aristotelian terminology, there were the συμβεβηκότα or "accidents" of history. For Socrates, Sozomen, and Evagrius there was the concept of ὁ καιρός, the ever changing fortuitous moment, that could raise human beings to the heights of power and then immediately turn and destroy them—whether they were emperors, archbishops, or entire nations—with war, schism, earthquake and pestilence. For Theodoret there were words like συμφορά

---

[1]R. G. Collingwood, *The Idea of History* (Oxford: Clarendon, 1946) 26: "Their method tied them on a tether whose length was the length of living memory: the only source they could criticize was an eyewitness with whom they could converse face to face. It is true that they relate events from a remoter past, but as soon as Greek historical writing tries to go beyond its tether, it becomes a far weaker and more precarious thing. For instance, we must not deceive ourselves into thinking that any scientific value attaches to what Herodotus tells us about the sixth century or to what Thucydides tells us about events before the Pentecontaetia."

[2]Socr. *HE* 3. 16.

and εὐκληρία to describe the uncertainty and instability of all "human" things (τὰ ἀνθρώπεια). This ever changing ebb and flow of good and ill was part of the basic texture of historical existence to these historians, and thus became the one historiographical issue that they had to handle most circumspectly in attempting to produce a Christianized version of classical history writing in the tradition of Herodotus and Polybius.

The balance between Christianity and paganism was an uneasy one. Even the technical metaphysical terminology of a Plato or an Aristotle was in fact pagan, if one wished to push the point, so that there was no practical way one could exclude all non-Christian ideas. The question was more about where to draw the line. That pagan terminology that was more obviously religious was carefully excluded by Eusebius. But in the fifth century, Socrates and Sozomen, who were laymen and perhaps had more freedom in such matters, began to speak more openly of such pagan deities as the avenging Erinyes and Alastores, and of more obviously pagan ideas of Fate, Fortune, and oracles. Possibly as a result of this "opening up" on the Christian side, by the time of Procopius in the early sixth century a mixed pagan and Christian historical vocabulary had developed. Late Roman society had developed an intellectual synthesis between the two worlds somewhat like that of the later Italian Renaissance. Evagrius Scholasticus, who came after Procopius in that same century, was thus freed in theory to mix pagan and Christian ideas in a variety of combinations, but in fact followed a generally conservative pattern not much more open to pagan vocabulary than had been the practice of Socrates or Sozomen.

The idea of the emperor was another important area where traditional pagan beliefs had to be dealt with by the first Christian historians. Eusebius began by asserting that God gave success and prosperity to the good emperor, and by defining the good emperor as one who tolerated Christianity. This was an idea obviously aimed at a world in which the emperor was pagan and the Christians were a helpless minority. With the conversion of Constantine and the growth of Christian power during his reign, more had to be said about the concept of the emperor. Even though he rejected parts of the emperor cult in practice, on the theoretical level Eusebius seems simply to have accepted with little modification the basic philosophical interpretation advanced since Hellenistic times by pagan intellectuals to justify the Hellenistic and Roman ruler cults. The good ruler must imitate God and thereby become the image on earth of the divine Mind and Law.

The fifth-century church historians developed still clearer ideas of what was expected of a good Christian emperor. In particular, the reign of Julian forced them to investigate the old Platonic dictum that a truly good government could not be established until philosophers became kings. The Late Roman understanding of the philosophical life, with its Cynicizing presupposition of the value of philosophic poverty, gave Socrates grounds to declare that the life of a philosopher was completely unsuitable to a Late Roman ruler. In an interesting development from traditional Hellenistic political theory, Socrates insisted that the good ruler must display his awe-inspiring majesty, not only in gravity of personal bearing, but also in ostentatious show of wealth and material splendor. This display of majesty, which was thought unsuitable for a philosopher, was for various reasons not thought to be incompatible with a semimonastic Christian piety. Sozomen developed this idea further with his description of Theodosius the Younger as the ideal Christian monarch, half a soldier and half a monk. This idea of the saintly warrior was to be bequeathed to the Middle Ages with enormous effect.

The idea of Rome itself was a richly developed pagan concept. In dealing with it, the Christian historians rejected the pagan notion of the decline of Rome more firmly than the pagan notion of Eternal Rome. What was in fact introduced and presented as the ideal in all their histories was the concept of a Holy Roman Empire, both Christian and universal. This was handed down to both the Byzantine and medieval European worlds, with great historical consequence.

Rome was for Eusebius the final world empire, which would last until the final time of troubles at the end of the world. For this very reason perhaps, Eusebius's successors, even Evagrius at the end of the sixth century, seem to have been completely unable to believe that Rome could fall to this-worldly German barbarians. Because of its basic theology of history, the Eusebian tradition apparently could not take seriously any imminent fall of the Roman empire in the way that Augustinianism did, and so they either denied that it was falling or simply ignored the fact that it had already fundamentally been destroyed. As a different kind of influence, Eusebius's apocalyptic beliefs may have been indirectly transmitted to the later Middle Ages in the form of chiliastic dreams of an "emperor of the last days" who would bring in the millennial kingdom in the rapidly approaching end of the present world.

In all of these ways, therefore, these five church historians set out a distinctive theology of history. It left its mark on the history of thought in the Western world, and had a strong influence on the Byzantine and medieval European period. The various pieces of this basically Eusebian theology of history were all joined together, moreover, to form a unified view of human history. The Origenism that lay behind the tradition committed it to a strong doctrine of free will and a complete rejection of the Graeco-Roman idea of fate. It was a Christian humanism because human freedom made human decisions and human accomplishments of value in the ultimate scheme of things. Even though they inherited the classical world's dark and brooding view of fortune as the continual upsetter of human intentions, they countered this first with the faith that inner human dignity and freedom could endure even under the most dreadful tribulation, and second with the conviction that God's providence was always ruling over the ultimate outcome of events.

They expanded this fundamentally optimistic and humanistic view of reality to the field of politics as well. Because it was this-worldly, the earthly state could not be a society of angels. The historical world of space and time had to have armies and law courts to exercise coercion when necessary, and men and women in this world had to concern themselves with the production and distribution of such material things as food and drink. But in Platonic fashion, the earthly state and its ruler could be a mirror, reflecting on a lower ontological level the eternal love, grace, and order of God's heavenly rule. The ideal Christian ruler therefore had to display splendor and majesty and be a powerful man of war, because of the requirements of this lower world where the course of history was played out. But he also had to participate, by a private life of almost monastic piety, in the life of the eternal world above. This was the other side of that Origenism and Evagrianism which lay in back of the formative thinkers in this historiographical tradition. History had its own kind of value because it was the reflection of the eternal into the world of time, and by fulfilling itself it would provide a route back to humanity's original unfallen status. But only by preserving and strengthening its vision of that higher level of reality could this present world find its proper law of life and achieve its authentic human possibilities.

Bibliography

TEXTS AND TRANSLATIONS

Ammianus Marcellinus. Ed. C. U. Clark. Berlin: apud Weidmannos, 1910-1915.

_____. Ed. and trans. John C. Rolfe. 3 vols. *LCL*. Cambridge MA: Harvard University Press, 1963-1964.

Aristotle. *De arte poetica liber*. Ed. R. Kassel. *OCT*. Oxford: Clarendon, 1965.

_____. *Ethica Nicomachea*. Ed. I. Bywater. *OCT*. Oxford: Clarendon, 1890.

_____. *Metaphysica*. Ed. W. Jaeger. *OCT*. Oxford: Clarendon, 1957.

_____. *Physica*. Ed. W. D. Ross. *OCT*. Oxford: Clarendon, 1950.

Augustine. *The City of God*. Trans. Marcus Dods. New York: Modern Library, 1950.

_____. *Confessions*. Ed. and rev. W. H. D. Rouse. *LCL*. Cambridge MA: Harvard University Press, 1912.

_____. *De civitate Dei*. Ed. B. Dombart. Leipzig: B. G. Teubner, 1909.

_____. *The Political Writings of St. Augustine*. Ed. and introduction by Henry Paolucci, analysis by Dino Bigongiari. Chicago: Henry Regnery, 1962.

Aurelius, Marcus. Ed. and trans. C. R. Haines. *LCL*. Cambridge MA: Harvard University Press, 1930.

_____. Ed. Ioannes Stich. Leipzig: Teubner, 1903.

Basil the Great. *The Letters*. Ed. and trans. Roy J. Deferrari. 4 vols. *LCL*. Cambridge MA: Harvard University Press, 1926-1934.

Callistratus. *Descriptions*. Ed. and trans. A. Fairbanks. *LCL*. Cambridge MA: Harvard University Press, 1931.

Chronica Minora Saec. IV. V. VI. VII. Vols. 1 and 2. Ed. Theodorus Mommsen. Tomi 9 and 11 of *Monumenta Germaniae Historica: Auctorum Antiquissimorum*. Berlin: Weidmann, 1891-1894.

Cicero. *De re publica, De legibus*. Ed. and trans. C. W. Keyes. *LCL*. Cambridge MA: Harvard University Press, 1928.

_____. *Scripta quae manserunt omnia*. Ed. C. F. W. Mueller, et al. Leipzig: Teubner, 1889-1902.

Codex Theodosianus: Theodosiani libri XVI cum Constitutionibus Sirmondianis et Leges novellae ad Theodosianum pertinentes. Ed. Theodor Mommsen and Paul M. Meyer. 2 vols. in 3. Berlin: apud Weidmannos, 1962.

_____. *The Theodosian Code and Novels and the Sirmondian Constitutions.* Trans. Clyde Pharr. New York: Greenwood Press, 1952.

Dio Cassius. *Cassii Dionis Cocceiani Historiarum romanarum.* Ed. U. P. Boissevain. 4 vols. Berlin: apud Weidmannos, 1895-1931.

_____. *Roman History.* Ed. and trans. Earnest Cary. 9 vols. LCL. Cambridge MA: Harvard University Press, 1914-1927.

Diogenes Laertius. *Vitae philosophorum.* Ed. H. S. Long. 2 vols. OCT. Oxford: Clarendon, 1964.

_____. Ed. and trans. R. D. Hicks. 2 vols. LCL. Cambridge MA: Harvard University Press, 1925.

Diotogenes. Greek text with French trans. in Louis Delatte, *Les traités de la royauté d'Ecphante, Diotogène et Sthénidas.* Paris: E. Droz, 1942.

_____. English trans. in Erwin R. Goodenough, "The Political Philosophy of Hellenistic Kingship." *Yale Classical Studies* 1 (1928): 55-102.

Ecphantus. Greek text with French trans. in Louis Delatte, *Les traités de la royauté d'Ecphante, Diotogène et Sthénidas.* Paris: E. Droz, 1942.

_____. Eng. trans. in Erwin R. Goodenough, "The Political Philosophy of Hellenistic Kingship." *Yale Classical Studies* 1 (1928): 55-102.

Egeria. *Diary of a Pilgrimage.* Trans. G. E. Gingras. New York: Newman, 1970.

Eusebius of Caesarea. *Chronici canones, latine vertit, adauxit, ad sua tempora produxit, S. Eusebius Hieronymus.* Ed. Iohannes Knight Fotheringham. London: H. Milford, 1923.

_____. *Die Chronik: aus dem armenischen übersetzt.* Ed. and trans. Josef Karst. GCS. Leipzig: J. C. Hinrichs, 1911.

_____. *Die Chronik des Hieronymus.* Ed. Rudolf Helm. GCS. Berlin: Akademie-Verlag, 1956.

_____. *Die Kirchengeschichte.* Ed. E. Schwartz and T. Mommsen. 3 vols. GCS. Leipzig: J. C. Hinrichs, 1903-1909.

_____. *De laudibus Constantini.* In the GCS edition of Eusebius's works, vol. 1, ed. I. A. Heikel, 193-259. Leipzig: J. C. Hinrichs, 1902.

_____. *Demonstratio Evangelica.* Ed. I. A. Heikel. GCS. Leipzig: J. C. Hinrichs, 1913.

_____. *The Ecclesiastical History.* Ed. and trans. Kirsopp Lake and J. E. L. Oulton. 2 vols. LCL. Cambridge MA: Harvard University Press, 1926-1932.

_____. *Life of Constantine.* In *Nicene and Post-Nicene Fathers,* second series, vol. 1, trans. E. C. Richardson, 481-559. Grand Rapids MI: William B. Eerdmans, 1961.

_____. *The Martyrs of Palestine*. In *Eusebius Bishop of Caesarea: The Ecclesiastical History and the Martyrs of Palestine*, trans. Hugh Jackson Lawlor and John Ernest Leonard Oulton, 1:327-400. London: SPCK, 1927.

_____. *On the Theophania or Divine Manifestation of Our Lord and Saviour Jesus Christ*. Trans. from the Syriac by Samuel Lee. Cambridge: Duncan and Malcolm, 1843.

_____. *The Oration of Eusebius Pamphilus in Praise of the Emperor Constantine Pronounced on the Thirtieth Anniversary of His Reign*. In *Nicene and Post-Nicene Fathers*, second series, vol. 1, trans. E. C. Richardson, 581-610. Grand Rapids MI: William B. Eerdmans, 1961.

_____. *Praeparatio Evangelica*. Greek text and English trans. by E. H. Gifford. Oxford: e typographeo academico, 1903.

_____. *Praeparatio Evangelica*. Ed. Karl Mras. GCS. Berlin: Akademie-Verlag, 1954-1956.

_____. *The Proof of the Gospel*. Trans. W. J. Ferrar. 2 vols. London: SPCK, 1920.

_____. *The Treatise of Eusebius, the Son of Pamphilus, against the Life of Apollonius of Tyana Written by Philostratus, Occasioned by the Parallel Drawn by Hierocles between Him and Christ*. Greek text and English trans. of Eusebius's *Contra Hieroclem* in Philostratus, *The Life of Apollonius of Tyana*, trans. F. C. Conybeare, 2:485-605. LCL. Cambridge MA: Harvard University Press, 1912.

_____. *Vita Constantini*. In the GCS edition of Eusebius's works, vol. 1, ed. I. A. Heikel, Leipzig: J. C. Hinrichs, 1902.

Evagrius Scholasticus. *Ecclesiastical History*. Ed. J. Bidez and L. Parmentier. Amsterdam: Adolf M. Hakkert, 1964.

_____. *Ecclesiastical History*. In *The Ancient Ecclesiastical Histories of the First Six Hundred Yeares after Christ, Written in the Greek Tongue by Three Learned Historiographers, Eusebius, Socrates, and Evagrius*, trans. Meredith Hanmer. 1577. Reprint, London: Richard Field, 1619.

_____. *Ecclesiastical History*. Trans. anon. London: Samuel Bagster and Sons, 1846.

Galen. *On the Passions and Errors of the Soul*. Trans. Paul W. Harkins. Columbus OH: Ohio State University Press, 1963.

The Gospel of Truth. Trans. and commentary by Kendrick Grobel. Nashville: Abingdon, 1960.

The Greek Anthology. Ed. and trans. W. R. Paton. 5 vols. LCL. Cambridge MA: Harvard University Press, 1916-1918.

Gregory of Nyssa. *Ad Ablabium quod non sint tres dei*. In *Gregorii Nysseni Opera*, ed. Werner Jaeger, vol. 3.1, ed. F. Mueller, 35-57. Leiden: E. J. Brill, 1958.

_____. *An Address on Religious Instruction.* Trans. of the *Oratio catechetica magna* by Cyril C. Richardson. In *Christology of the Later Fathers,* ed. Edward Rochie Hardy, 268-325. Philadelphia: Westminster, 1954.

_____. *Contra Eunomium.* Migne PG 45: 237-1122.

_____. *Contra Eunomium libri.* Ed. Werner Jaeger. In vols. 1 and 2 of the *Gregorii Nysseni Opera,* ed. Werner Jaeger. Leiden: E. J. Brill, 1960.

_____. *Oratio catechetica magna.* Migne PG 45: 9-106.

Gregory of Tours. *The History of the Franks.* Trans. Lewis Thorpe. New York: Penguin, 1974.

Herodotus. *Historiae.* Ed. C. Hude. 2 vols. OCT. Oxford: Clarendon, 1908.

_____. Ed. and trans. A. D. Godley. 4 vols. LCL. Cambridge MA: Harvard University Press, 1961-1966.

Hesiod. *Carmina.* Ed. A. Rzach. 3rd ed. Leipzig: Teubner, 1913.

_____. Ed. and trans. H. G. Evelyn-White. LCL. Cambridge MA: Harvard University Press, 1914.

Hippocrates. Ed. and trans. W. H. S. Jones and E. T. Withington. 4 vols. LCL. Cambridge MA: Harvard University Press, 1923-1931.

Hydatius. *Chronique.* Ed. and trans. Alain Tranoy. Sources Chrétiennes 218 and 219. Paris: Éditions du Cerf, 1974.

Ioannes Stobaeus. *Anthologium.* Ed. C. Wachsmuth and O. Hense. 5 vols. Berlin: apud Weidmannos, 1884-1912.

Irenaeus. *Adversus haereses.* Selections trans. by Edward Rochie Hardy. In *Early Christian Fathers,* ed. Cyril C. Richardson, 358-97. Philadelphia: Westminster, 1953.

Jordanes. *The Gothic History of Jordanes.* 2nd ed., trans., introduction and commentary by Charles Christopher Mierow. Princeton: Princeton University Press, 1915. Reprint, Cambridge, England: Speculum Historiale, 1966.

Josephus. *Opera.* Ed. B. Niese. 7 vols. Berlin: apud Weidmannos, 1885-1895.

_____. Works. Ed. and trans. H. St. J. Thackeray, Ralph Marcus, Allen Wikgren, and Louis H. Feldman, 9 vols. LCL. Cambridge MA: Harvard University Press, 1926-1965.

Julian. *Works.* Ed. and trans. Wilmer Cave Wright. 3 vols. LCL. Cambridge MA: Harvard University Press, 1913-1923.

Justin Martyr. *Die Apologieen.* 2nd ed., ed. G. Krüger. Freiburg i. B. and Leipzig: J. C. B. Mohr, 1896.

Lactantius. *De la mort des persécuteurs.* Ed. and trans. J. Moreau. 2 vols. Sources chrétiennes 39. Paris: Éditions du Cerf, 1954.

Manilius. *Astronomica*. Ed. and trans. G. P. Goold. *LCL*. Cambridge MA: Harvard University Press, 1977.

Nemesius of Emesa. *De natura hominis*. Migne *PG* 40:503-818.

_____. *On the Nature of Man*. In *Cyril of Jerusalem and Nemesius of Emesa*, ed. and trans. William Telfer, 203-453. London: SCM Press, 1955.

Nicolaus Damascenus. *On the Philosophy of Aristotle*. Ed. and trans. from the Syriac by H. J. Drossaart Lulofs. Leiden: Brill, 1965.

Numenius of Apamea. Ed. and trans. K. S. Guthrie. London: G. Bell and Sons, 1917.

Origen. *Contra Celsum*. Trans. H. Chadwick. Cambridge: Cambridge University Press, 1965.

_____. *Contre Celse*. Ed. Marcel Borret. 4 vols. Sources Chrétiennes. Paris: Éditions du Cerf, 1967-1969.

_____. *De principiis*. Ed. Paul Koetschau. In vol. 5 of *Origenes Werke*, *GCS* edition. Leipzig: J. C. Hinrichs, 1913.

_____. *On First Principles*. Trans. of Koetschau's text by G. W. Butterworth. London: SPCK, 1936. Reprint, New York: Harper and Row, 1966.

Philo Judaeus. Works. Ed. and trans. F. H. Colson, G. H. Whitaker and R. Marcus. 10 vols. + 2 supplementary vols. *LCL*. Cambridge MA: Harvard University Press, 1929-1962.

Plotinus. *Opera*. Ed. Paul Henry and Hans-Rudolf Schwyzer. 3 vols. Paris: Desclée, 1951-1973.

Plutarch. *Lives*. Ed. and trans. Bernadotte Perrin. 11 vols. *LCL*. Cambridge MA: Harvard University Press, 1914-1926.

_____. *Moralia*. Ed. and trans. F. C. Babbitt, W. C. Helmbold, P. H. De Lacy, B. Einarson, et al. 15 vols. *LCL*. Cambridge MA: Harvard University Press, 1927- .

_____. *Moralia*. Ed. G. N. Bernardakis. 7 vols. Leipzig: Teubner, 1888-1896.

_____. *On the Face Which Appears on the Orb of the Moon*. Trans. and notes by A. O. Prickard. London: Simpkin, 1911.

_____. *Vitae parallelae*. Rev. ed., ed. C. Sintenis. 5 vols. in 4. Leipzig: Teubner, 1889.

Polybius. *Historiae*. Ed. Theodorus Büttner-Wobst. 5 vols. Leipzig: B. G. Teubner, 1882-1904.

_____. *Historiae*. Ed. Fridericus Hultsch. 4 vols. Berlin: apud Weidmannos, 1870-1892.

_____. *The Histories*. Ed. and trans. W. R. Paton. 6 vols. *LCL*. Cambridge MA: Harvard University Press, 1922-1927.

Porphyry. *De antro nympharum*. Ed. August Nauck. In *Porphyrii philosophi Platonici Opuscula selecta*. Leipzig: B. G. Teubner, 1886.

Procopius. *The Anecdota or Secret History*. Ed. and trans. H. B. Dewing. *LCL*. Cambridge MA: Harvard University Press, 1935.

_____. *History of the Wars*. Ed. and trans. H. B. Dewing. 5 vols. *LCL*. Cambridge MA: Harvard University Press, 1914-1928.

_____. *Opera omnia*. Ed. J. Haury. Leipzig: Teubner, 1905-1913.

Rufinus of Aquileia. *Church History*. Ed. T. Mommsen. In Eusebius of Caesarea, *Die Kirchengeschichte*, ed. E. Schwartz and T. Mommsen, 3 vols. *GCS*. Leipzig: J. C. Hinrichs, 1903-1909.

Sallust. *Catilina, Iugurtha, Fragmenta ampliora*. Ed. A. Kurfess. Leipzig: Teubner, 1954.

_____. Ed. and trans. J. C. Rolfe. *LCL*. Cambridge MA: Harvard University Press, 1931.

Seneca. *Epistulae Morales*. Ed. and trans. Richard M. Gummere. 3 vols. *LCL*. Cambridge MA: Harvard University Press, 1917-1925.

_____. *Epistulae morales*. Ed. L. D. Reynolds. 2 vols. *OCT*. Oxford: Clarendon, 1965.

_____. *Moral Essays*. Ed. and trans. John W. Basore. 3 vols. *LCL*. Cambridge MA: Harvard University Press, 1928-1935.

_____. *Naturales Quaestiones*. Ed. and trans. T. H. Corcoran. 2 vols. *LCL*. Cambridge MA: Harvard University Press, 1971-1972.

Socrates Scholasticus. *Ecclesiastical History*. Trans. A. C. Zenos. In *Nicene and Post-Nicene Fathers*, second series, vol. 2. Grand Rapids MI: William B. Eerdmans, 1957.

_____. *Historia Ecclesiastica*. Ed. W. Bright. Oxford: Clarendon, 1878.

Sozomen. *Ecclesiastical History*. Trans. Chester D. Hartranft. In *Nicene and Post-Nicene Fathers*, second series, vol. 2. Grand Rapids MI: William B. Eerdmans, 1957.

_____. *Kirchengeschichte*. Ed. Joseph Bidez and Günther Christian Hansen. *GCS*. Berlin: Akademie-Verlag, 1960.

Sthenidas. Greek text with French trans. in Louis Delatte, *Les traités de la royauté d'Ecphante, Diotogène et Sthénidas*. Paris: E. Droz, 1942.

_____. English trans. in Erwin R. Goodenough, "The Political Philosophy of Hellenistic Kingship." *Yale Classical Studies* 1 (1928): 55-102.

Stoicorum Veterum Fragmenta. Ed. H. von Arnim. 4 vols. 1903-1924. Reprint, Stuttgart: B. G. Teubner, 1968.

Tacitus. *Annalium ab excessu divi Augusti libri.* Ed. C. D. Fisher. OCT. Oxford: Clarendon, 1946.

———. *Dialogus, Agricola, Germania.* Ed. and trans. W. Peterson and M. Hutton. LCL. Cambridge MA: Harvard University Press, 1914.

———. *Historiarum libri.* Ed. C. D. Fisher. OCT. Oxford: Clarendon, 1939.

———. *Histories* and *Annals.* Ed. and trans. Clifford H. Moore and John Jackson. 4 vols. LCL. Cambridge MA: Harvard University Press, 1925-1937.

———. *Opera minora (Agricola, Germania, Dialogus de oratoribus).* Ed. M. Winterbottom and R. M. Ogilvie. OCT. Oxford: Clarendon, 1975.

Tertullian. *Opera.* Ed. A. Reifferscheid, G. Wissowa, E. Kroymann, V. Bulhart, and P. Borleffs. 4 vols. *Corpus Scriptorum Ecclesiasticorum Latinorum* 20, 47, 70 and 76. Vienna, Prague, and Leipzig: 1890-1957.

Theodoret of Cyrrhus. *Collectio Sirmondiana,* Epistles 1-147. In vols. 2 and 3 of his *Correspondance.* Ed. and trans. Yvan Azéma. Sources Chrétiennes. Paris: Éditions du Cerf, 1964-1965.

———. *Discours sur la providence.* Trans. with introduction and notes by Y. Azéma. Paris: De Boccard, 1953.

———. *Ecclesiastical History.* Trans. Blomfield Jackson. In *Nicene and Post-Nicene Fathers,* second series, vol. 3. Grand Rapids MI: William B. Eerdmans, [1892].

———. *Letters.* Trans. Blomfield Jackson. In *Nicene and Post-Nicene Fathers,* second series, vol. 3. Grand Rapids MI: William B. Eerdmans, [1892].

———. *Religiosa historia.* Migne *PG* 82: 1283-1522.

———. *Kirchengeschichte.* Ed. Léon Parmentier, 2nd ed. rev. by Felix Scheidweiler. GCS. Berlin: Akademie-Verlag, 1954.

Thucydides. Ed. C. Hude. 2 vols. Leipzig: Teubner, 1898-1901.

———. Ed. H. S. Jones, with *apparatus criticus* emended and augmented by J. Enoch Powell. 2 vols. OCT. Oxford: Clarendon, 1942.

———. Ed. and trans. Charles Forster Smith. 4 vols. LCL. Cambridge MA: Harvard University Press, 1921-1930.

Xenophon. *Cyropaedia.* Ed. and trans. Walter Miller. 2 vols. LCL. Cambridge MA: Harvard University Press, 1914.

———. *Hellenica* and *Anabasis.* Ed. and trans. Carleton L. Brownson. 3 vols. LCL. Cambridge MA: Harvard University Press, 1918-1922.

———. *Opera omnia.* Ed. E. C. Marchant. OCT. Oxford: Clarendon, 1900-1920.

Zacharias Rhetor. *The Ecclesiastical History of Zacharias Rhetor, Bishop of Mitylene.* Trans. from the Syriac by F. J. Hamilton. London: printed privately, 1892. (This is a translation of Books 3-6 of the *Syriac Chronicle.*)

──────────. *The Syriac Chronicle Known as that of Zachariah of Mitylene.* Trans. F. J. Hamilton and E. W. Brooks. London: Methuen, 1899. (Only Books 3-6 of this *Syriac Chronicle* are actually by Zacharias Rhetor.)

Zosimus. *Historia Nova: The Decline of Rome.* Trans. J. J. Buchanan and H. T. Davis. San Antonio TX: Trinity University Press, 1967.

──────────. *Zosimi comitis et exadvocati fisci historia nova.* Ed. L. Mendelssohn. Leipzig: B. G. Teubner, 1887.

LITERATURE

Aall, Anathon. *Der Logos: Geschichte seiner Entwickelung in der griechischen Philosophie und der christlichen Litteratur.* 2 vols. Leipzig: O. R. Reisland, 1896-1899.

Aland, Kurt. "Die religiöse Haltung Kaiser Konstantins." In *Studia Patristica* 1, ed. K. Aland and F. L. Cross, 549-68. *Texte und Untersuchungen* 63. Berlin: Akademie-Verlag, 1957.

──────────. "Eine Wende in der Konstantin-Forschung." *Forschungen und Fortschritte* 28 (1954): 213-17.

Alföldi, Andrew. *The Conversion of Constantine and Pagan Rome.* Trans. H. Mattingly. Oxford: Clarendon, 1969.

Allen, Pauline. *Evagrius Scholasticus the Church Historian.* Spicilegium Sacrum Lovaniense Études et Documents 41. Louvain: Spicilegium Sacrum Lovaniense, 1981.

Altaner, Berthold, and Alfred Stuiber. *Patrologie.* 7th ed. Freiburg: Herder, 1966.

Altheim, Franz, and Ruth Stiehl. *Ein Asiastischer Staat: Feudalismus unter den Sasaniden und ihren Nachbarn.* Wiesbaden: Limes, 1954.

Altman, Marion. "Ruler Cult in Seneca." *Classical Philology* 33 (1938): 198-204.

Amand, David. *Fatalisme et liberté dans l'antiquité grecque.* Louvain: Bibliothèque de l'Université, 1945.

Andréadès, André M. "Public Finances: Currency, Public Expenditure, Budget, Public Revenue." In *Byzantium,* ed. Norman H. Baynes and H. St. L. B. Moss, 71-85. Oxford: Clarendon, 1948.

Annand, Rupert. "Papias and the Four Gospels." *Scottish Journal of Theology* 9 (1956): 46-62.

Armstrong, A. H., ed. *The Cambridge History of Later Greek and Early Medieval Philosophy.* Cambridge: Cambridge University Press, 1967.

Arnold, E. Vernon. *Roman Stoicism.* Cambridge: Cambridge University Press, 1911.

Athanassakis, Apostolos N. "Some Evidence in Defense of the Title *Apocolocyntosis* for Seneca's Satire." *Transactions of the American Philological Association* 104 (1974): 11-22.

_____. "Some Thoughts on *Double-Entendres* in Seneca *Apocolocyntosis* 3 and 4." *Classical Philology* 68 (1973): 292-94.

Auerbach, Erich. "Odyssesus' Scar." In *Mimesis: The Representation of Reality in Western Literature*, trans. W. R. Trask, 3-23. Princeton NJ: Princeton University Press, 1953.

Balas, David. "Plenitudo Humanitatis: The Unity of Human Nature in the Theology of Gregory of Nyssa." In *Disciplina Nostra: Essays in Memory of Robert F. Evans*, ed. Donald F. Winslow, 115-31, 205-208. Cambridge MA: Philadelphia Patristic Foundation, 1979.

Baldry, H. C. *The Unity of Mankind in Greek Thought*. Cambridge: Cambridge University Press, 1965.

Baldwin, Barry. "Zosimus and Asinius Quadratus." *Classical Philology* 74 (1979): 57-58.

Bardy, G. "Théodoret." *Dictionnaire de Théologie Catholique* 15, 1 (1946): 299-325.

Barker, John W. *Justinian and the Later Roman Empire*. Madison WI: University of Wisconsin Press, 1966.

Barnes, Harry Elmer. *A History of Historical Writing*. 2nd ed. New York: Dover, 1962.

Barnes, Timothy D. *Constantine and Eusebius*. Cambridge MA: Harvard University Press, 1981.

_____. *The New Empire of Diocletian and Constantine*. Cambridge MA: Harvard University Press, 1982.

Barr, James. *Biblical Words for Time*. Studies in Biblical Theology 33. Naperville IL: Alec R. Allenson, 1962.

Bauer, Walter. *Orthodoxy and Heresy in Earliest Christianity*. 2nd German ed. trans. Robert A. Kraft, Gerhard Krodel, et al. Philadelphia: Fortress, 1971.

Baur, Ferdinand Christian. *Die Epochen der kirchlichen Geschichtschreibung*. Tübingen: Fues, 1852.

_____. *Ferdinand Christian Baur on the Writing of Church History*. Ed. and trans. Peter C. Hodgson. New York: Oxford University Press, 1968.

Baynes, Norman H. "The Byzantine State." In Baynes, *Byzantine Studies and Other Essays*, 47-66. London: University of London, Athlone Press, 1955.

_____. "Constantine the Great and the Christian Church." *Proceedings of the British Academy* 15 (1929): 341-442.

_____. "Eusebius and the Christian Empire." *Annuaire de l'Institut de Philologie et d'Histoire Orientales* 2 (1933-1934), *Mélanges Bidez* (Brussels, 1933): 13-18. Reprinted in Baynes, *Byzantine Studies and Other Essays*, 168-72. London: University of London, Athlone Press, 1955.

_____. "The Political Ideas of St. Augustine's *De Civitate Dei.*" Historical Association Pamphlet 104. London: G. Bell and Sons, 1936.

_____, and H. St. L. B. Moss, eds. *Byzantium.* Oxford: Clarendon, 1948.

Becker, Erich. "Protest gegen den Kaiserkult und Verherrlichung des Sieges am Pons Milvius in der christlichen Kunst der konstantinischen Zeit." In *Konstantin der Grosse und seine Zeit,* ed. Franz Jos. Dölger, 155-190. Freiburg im Br.: Herder, 1913.

Berkhof, Hendrik. *Die Theologie des Eusebius von Caesarea.* Amsterdam: Uitgeversmaatschappij Holland, 1939.

Beskow, Per. *Rex Gloriae: The Kingship of Christ in the Early Church.* Trans. E. J. Sharpe. Stockholm: Almqvist & Wiksell, 1962.

Bethune-Baker, J. F. *The Influence of Christianity on War.* Cambridge: Macmillan and Bowes, 1888.

Bevan, Edwyn. *Stoics and Sceptics.* Oxford: Clarendon, 1913.

Bieler, Ludwig. Θεῖος ἀνήρ: *Das Bild des "göttlichen Menschen" in Spätantike und Frühchristentum.* 2 vols. Vienna: O. Höfels, 1935-1936. Reprint, 2 vols. in 1, Darmstadt: Wissenschaftliche Buchgesellschaft, 1967.

Bischoff, Heinrich. *Der Warner bei Herodot.* Borna-Leipzig: R. Noske, 1932.

Blenkinsopp, Joseph. "Prophecy and Priesthood in Josephus." *Journal of Jewish Studies* 25 (1974): 239-62.

Bowersock, G. W. *Julian the Apostate.* London: Duckworth, 1978.

_____. Review of *Imperium und Polis in der hohen Prinzipatszeit,* by D. Nörr. *Journal of Roman Studies* 58 (1968): 261-62.

Boyancé, Pierre. *Études sur le songe de Scipion.* Bordeaux and Paris: Feret & fils, 1936.

_____. "La religion astrale de Platon à Cicéron." *Revue des Études Grecques* 65 (1952): 312-50.

Boyd, William K. *The Ecclesiastical Edicts of the Theodosian Code.* Studies in History, Economics and Public law edited by the Faculty of Political Science of Columbia University 24, 2 (Whole No. 63). New York: Columbia University Press, 1905.

Braund, D. C. "The Aedui, Troy, and the *Apocolocyntosis.*" *Classical Quarterly* new series 30 (1980): 420-25.

Bréhier, Émile. *La philosophie de Plotin.* Paris: Boivin, 1928.

_____. *La théorie des incorporels dans l'ancien stoïcisme.* 2nd ed. Paris: J. Vrin, 1928.

Brochard, Victor. *Les sceptiques grecs.* Paris: Vrin, 1959.

Brok, Martin. "Touchant la date du Commentaire sur le Psautier de Théodoret de Cyr." *Revue d'Histoire Ecclésiastique* 44 (1949): 552-56.

Brown, Peter. *Augustine of Hippo: A Biography.* London: Faber and Faber, 1967.

_____. *Religion and Society in the Age of Saint Augustine.* New York: Harper and Row, 1972.

_____. "Religious Coercion in the Later Roman Empire: The Case of North Africa." *History* 48 (1963): 283-305.

_____. "Religious Dissent in the Later Roman Empire: The Case of North Africa." *History* 46 (1961): 83-101.

_____. "The Rise and Function of the Holy Man in Late Antiquity." *Journal of Roman Studies* 61 (1971): 80-101.

_____. *Society and the Holy in Late Antiquity.* Berkeley: University of California Press, 1982.

_____. *The World of Late Antiquity: 150-750.* New York: Harcourt, Brace, 1971.

Büchner, Karl. *Somnium Scipionis: Quellen, Gestalt, Sinn. Hermes* Einzelschriften, Heft 36 (1976).

Budge, E. A. Wallis. *Amulets and Superstitions: The Original Texts with Translations and Descriptions of . . . Egyptian, Sumerian, Assyrian, Hebrew, Christian, Gnostic and Muslim Amulets . . . Divination, Numbers, the Kabbalah, Ancient Astrology, etc.* 1930. Reprint, New York: Dover, 1978.

Burkert, Walter. "Hellenistische Pseudopythagorica." *Philologus* 105 (1961): 16-43, 226-46.

_____. *Lore and Science in Ancient Pythagoreanism.* Trans. E. L. Minar, Jr. Cambridge MA: Harvard University Press, 1972.

Burnaby, John. *Amor Dei: A Study of St. Augustine's Teaching on the Love of God as the Motive of Christian Life.* London: Hodder and Stoughton, 1938.

Burns, J. Patout. *The Development of Augustine's Doctrine of Operative Grace.* Paris: Études Augustiniennes, 1980.

Bury, J. B. *The Ancient Greek Historians.* London: Macmillan, 1909.

_____. "Cleopatra's Nose." In *Selected Essays,* ed. Harold Temperly, 60-69. Cambridge: Cambridge University Press, 1930.

Butterfield, Herbert. *Man on His Past: The Study of the History of Historical Scholarship.* Cambridge: Cambridge University Press, 1955.

_____. *Writings on Christianity and History*. Ed. and introduction by C. T. McIntire. New York: Oxford University Press, 1979.

Cadoux, Cecil John. *The Early Christian Attitude to War*. London: Headley, 1919.

_____. *The Early Church and the World: A History of the Christian Attitude to Pagan Society and the State down to the Time of Constantinus*. Edinburgh: T. and T. Clark, 1925.

Caird, G. B. *Principalities and Powers: A Study in Pauline Theology*. Oxford: Clarendon, 1956.

Cameron, A. E. *Circus Factions: Blues and Greens at Rome and Byzantium*. Oxford: Clarendon, 1976.

Cameron, Averil M. *Agathias*. Oxford: Clarendon, 1970.

_____. "The 'Scepticism' of Procopius." *Historia* 15 (1966): 466-82.

_____, and Alan Cameron. "Christianity and Tradition in the Historiography of the Late Empire." *Classical Quarterly* new series 14 (1964): 316-28.

Campbell, Leroy A. *Mithraic Iconography and Ideology*. Leiden: E. J. Brill, 1968.

Cancik, Hildegard. *Untersuchungen zu Senecas Epistulae morales*. Hildesheim: G. Olms, 1967.

Carr, Edward Hallett. *What Is History?* New York: Knopf, 1961.

Caspary, Gerard E. *Politics and Exegesis: Origen and the Two Swords*. Berkeley: University of California Press, 1979.

Cassels, Walter R. "The Purpose of Eusebius." *Hibbert Journal* 1 (1903): 781-88.

Cerfaux, L., and J. Tondriau. *Un concurrent du christianisme: le culte des souverains dans la civilisation gréco-romaine*. Tournai: Desclée, 1957.

Chadwick, Henry. *Early Christian Thought and the Classical Tradition: Studies in Justin, Clement, and Origen*. New York: Oxford University Press, 1966.

_____. *The Early Church*. Harmondsworth, England: Penguin, 1967.

_____. "Philo and the Beginnings of Christian Thought." In *The Cambridge History of Later Greek and Early Medieval Philosophy*, ed. A. H. Armstrong, 133-92; see esp. the chapter about Origen, 182-92. Cambridge: Cambridge University Press, 1967.

Charanis, Peter. *Church and State in the Later Roman Empire: The Religious Policy of Anastasius the First, 491-518*. 2nd ed. Thessalonica: Kentron Byzantinon Erevnon, 1974.

Charlesworth, M. P. "Imperial Deportment: Two Texts and Some Questions." *Journal of Roman Studies* 37 (1947): 34-38.

Chéné, Jean. "Unus de Trinitate Passus Est." *Recherches de Science Religieuse* 53 (1965): 545-88; see esp. 551-55 on Theodore of Mopsuestia and Theodoret.

Chesnut, Glenn F. "The Date of Composition of Theodoret's Church History." *Vigiliae Christianae* 35 (1981): 245-52.

_____. "Eusebius of Caesarea." *Interpreter's Dictionary of the Bible* (Nashville: Abingdon Press, 1976) supp: 295-96.

_____. "Fate, Fortune, Free Will and Nature in Eusebius of Caesarea." *Church History* 42 (1973): 165-82.

_____. "From Alexander the Great to Constantine: Supplying the Context." *Second Century: A Journal of Early Christian Studies* 1 (1981): 43-49.

_____. *Images of Christ: An Introduction to Christology.* Minneapolis: Seabury Press, 1984.

_____. "Kairos and Cosmic Sympathy in the Church Historian Socrates Scholasticus." *Church History* 44 (1975): 161-66.

_____. "The Pattern of the Past: Augustine's Debate with Eusebius and Sallust." In *Our Common History as Christians: Essays in Honor of Albert C. Outler,* ed. John Deschner, Leroy T. Howe, and Klaus Penzel, 69-95. New York: Oxford University Press, 1975.

_____. "Radicalism and Orthodoxy: The Unresolved Problem of the First Christian Histories." *Anglican Theological Review* 65 (1983): 295-305.

_____. Review essay on Eusebius in recent scholarship, Robert M. Grant, Timothy D. Barnes, et al. *Religious Studies Review* 9 (1983): 118-23.

_____. Review of Hydace, *Chronicle,* ed. and trans. Alain Tranoy. *Church History* 45 (1976): 375.

_____. "The Ruler and the Logos in Neopythagorean, Middle Platonic, and Late Stoic Political Philosophy." In *Aufstieg und Niedergang der Römischen Welt: Geschichte und Kultur Roms im Spiegel der neueren Forschung* 2, 16, 2, ed. H. Temporini and W. Haase, 1310-32. Berlin: Walter de Gruyter, 1978.

Chesnut, Roberta C. Review article on *The Rise of the Monophysite Movement,* by W. H. C. Frend. *Anglican Theological Review* 56 (1974): 64-68.

_____. *Three Monophysite Christologies: Severus of Antioch, Philoxenus of Mabbug, and Jacob of Sarug.* Oxford: Oxford University Press, 1976.

_____. "The Two Prosopa in Nestorius' *Bazaar of Heracleides.*" *Journal of Theological Studies* (Oxford) new series 29 (1978): 392-409.

Chitty, Derwas J. *The Desert a City: An Introduction to the Study of Egyptian and Palestinian Monasticism under the Christian Empire.* Oxford: Blackwell, 1966.

Christensen, Arthur. *L'Iran sous les Sassanides.* 2nd ed. Copenhagen: E. Munksgaard, 1944.

Christian, William A. "Augustine on the Creation of the World." *Harvard Theological Review* 46 (1953): 1-25.

Cochrane, Charles Norris. *Thucydides and the Science of History*. London: Oxford University Press, 1929.

Cohn, Norman. *The Pursuit of the Millennium*. 2nd ed. New York: Harper, 1961.

Collingwood, R. G. *The Idea of History*. Oxford: Clarendon, 1946.

Connolly, R. H. "Eusebius *H.E.* v. 28." *Journal of Theological Studies* 49 (1948): 73-79.

Conzelmann, Hans G. "The First Christian Century as Christian History." In *The Bible in Modern Scholarship*, ed. J. Philip Hyatt, 217-226. Nashville: Abingdon, 1965.

Copleston, Frederick. *A History of Philosophy* 1: *Greece and Rome*. Rev. ed. Westminster MD: Newman, 1959.

Cornford, Francis MacDonald. *Thucydides Mythistoricus*. 1907. Reprint, London: Routledge and Kegan Paul, 1965.

Corsaro, Francesco. "Le *mos maiorum* dans la vision éthique et politique du *De mortibus persecutorum*." In *Lactance et son temps: recherches actuelles*, ed. J. Fontaine and M. Perrin, 25-53. Paris: Beauchesne, 1978.

Costa, C. D. N., ed. *Seneca*. London: Routledge and Kegan Paul, 1974.

Cramer, Frederick H. *Astrology in Roman Law and Politics*. Memoirs of the American Philosophical Society 37. Philadelphia, 1954.

Croce, Benedetto. *Theory and History of Historiography*. Trans. D. Ainslie. London: G. G. Harrap, 1921.

Cross, F. L. "The Council of Antioch in A.D. 325." *Church Quarterly Review* 128 (1939): 49-76.

Cullmann, Oscar. *Christ and Time: The Primitive Christian Conception of Time and History*. Rev. ed., trans. F. V. Filson. Philadelphia: Westminster, 1962.

Cumont, Franz. *After Life in Roman Paganism*. New Haven: Yale University Press, 1922.

_____. *Astrology and Religion among the Greeks and Romans*. 1912. Reprint, New York: Dover, 1960.

_____. *Les mystères de Mithra*. 3rd ed. Brussels: H. Lamertin, 1913.

Cuntz, Otto. *Polybius und sein Werk*. Leipzig: B. G. Teubner, 1902.

Daniélou, Jean. "L'apocatastase chez Grégoire de Nysse." *Recherches de Science Religieuse* 48 (1940): 328-47.

_____. *The Theology of Jewish Christianity*. Trans. J. A. Baker. London: Darton, Longman and Todd, 1964.

D'Arms, John H. *Commerce and Social Standing in Ancient Rome*. Cambridge MA: Harvard University Press, 1981.

Daube, David. *Collaboration with Tyranny in Rabbinic Law.* London: Oxford University Press, 1965.

De Decker, Daniel. "Le *Discours à l'Assemblée des Saints* attribué à Constantin et l'oeuvre de Lactance." In *Lactance et son temps: recherches actuelles,* ed. J. Fontaine and M. Perrin, 75-89. Paris: Beauchesne, 1978.

Delatte, Louis. *Les traités de la royauté d'Ecphante, Diotogène et Sthénidas.* Paris: E. Droz, 1942.

den Boer, W. "A Pagan Historian and His Enemies: Porphyry against the Christians." *Classical Philology* 69 (1974): 198-208.

Des Places, Édouard. *Eusèbe de Césarée commentateur: Platonisme et écriture sainte.* Paris: Beauchesne, 1982.

de Vogel, C. J. *Greek Philosophy: A Collection of Texts 3: The Hellenistic-Roman Period.* Leiden: Brill, 1959.

Dhorme, P. "Les sources de la Chronique d'Eusèbe." *Revue Biblique* new series 7 (1910): 233-37.

Dibelius, Martin. "The Speeches in Acts and Ancient Historiography." In *Studies in the Acts of the Apostles,* ed. H. Greeven, trans. M. Ling, 138-85. London: SCM, 1956.

Diepen, H. M., and Jean Daniélou. "Theodoret et le dogme d'Ephèse." *Recherches de Science Religieuse* 44 (1956): 243-48.

Dillon, John M. *The Middle Platonists, 80 B.C. to A.D. 220.* Ithaca: Cornell University Press, 1977.

Dilthey, Wilhelm. *Pattern and Meaning in History.* Ed. H. P. Rickman. New York: Harper and Row, 1961. Originally published in England as *Meaning in History.* London: Allen and Unwin, 1961.

Dinkler, E. "Ticonius." Pauly-Wissowa, *Real-Encyclopädie,* Zweite Reihe 6.1 (1936) 849-56.

Dodds, E. R. "The Ancient Concept of Progress." In his *Ancient Concept of Progress and Other Essays on Greek Literature and Belief,* 1-25. Oxford: Clarendon, 1973.

——————. *The Greeks and the Irrational.* Berkeley: University of California Press, 1951.

——————. *Pagan and Christian in an Age of Anxiety.* Cambridge: Cambridge University Press, 1965.

Downey, Glanville. "Paganism and Christianity in Procopius." *Church History* 18 (1949): 89-102.

——————. "The Perspective of the Early Church Historians." *Greek, Roman, and Byzantine Studies* 6 (1965): 57-70.

Drake, H. A. *In Praise of Constantine: A Historical Study and New Translation of Eusebius' Tricennial Orations.* University of California Publications: Classical Studies 15. Berkeley: University of California Press, 1976.

Dray, William. *Laws and Explanation in History.* Oxford: Oxford University Press, 1957.

Dudley, Donald R. *A History of Cynicism, from Diogenes to the Sixth Century A.D.* London: Methuen, 1937.

Dvornik, Francis. *Early Christian and Byzantine Political Philosophy: Origins and Background.* 2 vols. Washington DC: Dumbarton Oaks, 1966.

Earl, D. C. *The Political Thought of Sallust.* Cambridge: Cambridge University Press, 1961.

Edelstein, Ludwig. *The Idea of Progress in Classical Antiquity.* Baltimore MD: Johns Hopkins University Press, 1967.

Eger, Hans. "Kaiser und Kirche in der Geschichtstheologie Eusebs von Cäsarea." *Zeitschrift für die Neutestamentliche Wissenschaft* 38 (1939): 97-115.

Eltester, W. "Sozomenos." Pauly-Wissowa, *Real-Encyclopädie* 2nd Series 3 A 1 (1927) 1240-48.

Evans, J. A. S. "Christianity and Paganism in Procopius of Caesarea." *Greek, Roman, and Byzantine Studies* 12 (1971): 81-100.

Evans, Robert F. *Pelagius: Inquiries and Reappraisals.* London: Adam and Charles Black, 1968.

Farina, Raffaele. *L'impero e l'imperatore cristiano in Eusebio di Cesarea: la prima teologia politica del Cristianesimo.* Zürich: Pas Verlag, 1966.

Farmer, William R. *Maccabees, Zealots, and Josephus.* New York: Columbia University Press, 1956.

Farrington, Benjamin. *Greek Science.* Harmondsworth, England: Penguin, 1966.

Ferguson, John. *Utopias of the Classical World.* London: Thames and Hudson, 1975.

Figgis, John Neville. *The Political Aspects of S. Augustine's "City of God."* London: Longmans, Green, 1921.

Finley, M. I. "Myth, Memory, and History." *History and Theory* 4 (1964-1965): 281-302.

Foakes-Jackson, F. J. *Eusebius Pamphili.* Cambridge: W. Heffer and Sons, 1933.

Fredouille, Jean-Claude. "Lactance historien des religions." In *Lactance et son temps: recherches actuelles,* ed. J. Fontaine and M. Perrin, 237-252. Paris: Beauchesne, 1978.

Frend, W. H. C. *The Donatist Church: A Movement of Protest in Roman North Africa.* Oxford: Clarendon, 1952.

_____. *Martyrdom and Persecution in the Early Church: A Study of Conflict from the Maccabees to Donatus*. Oxford: Blackwell, 1965.

_____. *The Rise of the Monophysite Movement*. Cambridge: Cambridge University Press, 1972.

Frost, Stanley Brice. *Old Testament Apocalyptic: Its Origins and Growth*. London: Epworth, 1952.

Fuhrmann, François. *Les images de Plutarque*. Paris: published thesis, 1964.

Gager, John G. *Kingdom and Community: The Social World of Early Christianity*. Englewood Cliffs NJ: Prentice-Hall, 1975.

Ganss, Wilhelm. *Das Bild des Weisen bei Seneca*. Schaan: Inaugural-Dissertation, Fribourg, 1952.

Gardiner, Patrick. *The Nature of Historical Explanation*. London: Oxford University Press, 1961.

_____, ed. *Theories of History*. New York: Free Press, 1959.

Gärtner, Bertil. *The Theology of the Gospel of Thomas*. Trans. E. J. Sharpe. London: Collins, 1961.

"Geister (Dämonen)." *Reallexikon für Antike und Christentum* 9, 68-69 (1974-75) 546-797.

Geppert, Franz. *Die Quellen des Kirchenhistorikers Socrates Scholasticus*. Leipzig, 1898. Reprint, Aalen: Scientia Verlag, 1972. First two chapters published separately as *Die Quellen des Kirchenhistorikers Socrates Scholasticus*, I. Teil. Naumburg a. S.: Inaugural-Dissertation, Universität Greifswald, 1898.

Ghirshman, R. *Iran*. Baltimore MD: Penguin, 1954.

Gillman, Ian. "Eschatology in the Reign of Constantine." *Reformed Theological Review* 24 (1965): 40-51.

Giuriceo, Marie Ann. "The Church Fathers and the Kingly Office." Ph.D. dissertation, Cornell University, 1955.

Glover, T. R. *Herodotus*. Berkeley: University of California Press, 1924.

Goffart, Walter. "Zosimus, the First Historian of Rome's Fall." *American Historical Review* 76 (1971): 412-441.

Golden, Leon. "*Katharsis* as Clarification: An Objection Answered." *Classical Quarterly* new series 23 (1973): 45-46.

Goldschmidt, Victor Ernest. *Le système stoïcien et l'idée de temps*. Paris: Vrin, 1953.

Goodenough, Erwin R. *An Introduction to Philo Judaeus*. 2nd ed. New York: Barnes and Noble, 1962.

_____. "The Political Philosophy of Hellenistic Kingship." *Yale Classical Studies* 1 (1928): 55-102.

_____. *The Politics of Philo Judaeus*. New Haven: Yale University Press, 1938.

Gould, Josiah B. *The Philosophy of Chrysippus*. Leiden: E. J. Brill, 1970.

Graeser, Andreas. *Plotinus and the Stoics: A Preliminary Study*. Leiden: Brill, 1972.

Grant, Robert M. "The Appeal to the Early Fathers." *Journal of Theological Studies* new series 11 (1960): 13-24.

──────────. "Early Alexandrian Christianity." *Church History* 40 (1971): 133-44.

──────────. *Early Christianity and Society*. San Francisco: Harper and Row, 1977.

──────────. *Eusebius as Church Historian*. Oxford: Clarendon, 1980.

──────────. *Gnosticism and Early Christianity*. 2nd ed. New York: Harper and Row, 1966.

──────────. "Papias in Eusebius' Church History." In *Mélanges d'Histoire des Religions offerts à Henri-Charles Puech*, 209-13. Paris,. 1974.

──────────. "The Uses of History in the Church before Nicaea." In *Studia Patristica* 11, ed. F. L. Cross, 166-178. *Texte und Untersuchungen* 108. Berlin: Akademie-Verlag, 1972.

Gray, Patrick T. R. *The Defense of Chalcedon in the East (451-553)*. Leiden: E. J. Brill, 1979.

Greene, William Chase. *Moira: Fate, Good, and Evil in Greek Thought*. 1944. Reprint, New York: Harper and Row, 1963.

Greenslade, S. L. *Schism in the Early Church*. 2nd ed. London: SCM, 1964.

Gregg, Robert C., and Dennis E. Groh. *Early Arianism—A View of Salvation*. Philadelphia: Fortress, 1981.

Grégoire, Henri. "About Licinius' Fiscal and Religious Policy." *Byzantion* 13 (1938): 551-60.

──────────. "Eusèbe n'est pas l'auteur de la 'Vita Constantini' dans sa forme actuelle et Constantin ne s'est pas 'converti' en 312." *Byzantion* 13 (1938): 561-83.

──────────. "La vision de Constantin 'liquidée.'" *Byzantion* 14 (1939): 341-51.

Gregory, Timothy E. *Vox Populi: Popular Opinion and Violence in the Religious Controversies of the Fifth Century A.D.* Columbus OH: Ohio State University Press, 1979.

Grillmeier, Aloys. *Christ in Christian Tradition: From the Apostolic Age to Chalcedon (451)*. Trans. J. S. Bowden. London: A. R. Mowbray, 1965.

Groh, Dennis E. "Galilee and the Eastern Roman Empire in Late Antiquity." *Explor* 3 (1977): 78-93.

──────────. "Hans von Campenhausen on Canon: Positions and Problems." *Interpretation* 28 (1974): 331-43.

──────────. "The *Onomasticon* of Eusebius and the Rise of Christian Palestine." In *Studia Patristica*, forthcoming.

Guillaumont, Antoine. Les "Képhalaia Gnostica" d'Evagre le Pontique et l'histoire de l'Origénisme chez les Grecs et chez les Syriens. Paris: Éditions du Seuil, 1962.

Güldenpenning, A. Die Kirchengeschichte des Theodoret von Kyrrhos: Eine Untersuchung ihrer Quellen. Halle: M. Niemeyer, 1889.

Gustafsson, B. "Eusebius' Principles in Handling His Sources, as Found in His Church History, Books I-VII." In Studia Patristica 4, ed. F. L. Cross, 429-41. Texte und Untersuchungen 79. Berlin: Akademie-Verlag, 1961.

Guthrie, W. K. C. Introduction to his edition of Aristotle, On the Heavens. LCL. Cambridge MA: Harvard University Press, 1939.

Gwatkin, Henry Melvill. The Arian Controversy. London: Longmans, Green, 1889.

—————. Studies of Arianism. 2nd ed. Cambridge: D. Bell, 1900.

Haase, Wolfgang. "Grossmut." Historisches Wörterbuch der Philosophie 3: 887-99.

Hadas, Moses, and Morton Smith. Heroes and Gods: Spiritual Biographies in Antiquity. New York: Harper and Row, 1965.

Hadot, P. "Fürstenspiegel." Reallexikon für Antike und Christentum.

Hahm, David E. The Origins of Stoic Cosmology. Columbus: Ohio State University Press, 1977.

Hahn, T. Tyconius-Studien: Ein Beitrag zur Kirchen- und Dogmengeschichte des 4. Jahrhunderts. Studien zur Geschichte der Theologie und der Kirche 6,2. Leipzig, 1900. Reprint, Aalen: Scientia Verlag, 1971.

Halleux, André de. Philoxène de Mabbog: sa vie, ses écrits, sa théologie. Louvain: Imp. Orientaliste, Universitas Catholica Louvaniensis, 1963.

Hampshire, Stuart. Freedom of the Individual. New York: Harper and Row, 1965.

Harnack, Adolf von. History of Dogma. Trans. from the 3rd German ed. by N. Buchanan. 7 vols. in 4. New York: Dover, 1961.

—————. Militia Christi: Die christliche Religion und der Soldatenstand in den ersten drei Jahrhunderten. Tübingen: J. C. B. Mohr (Paul Siebeck), 1905.

—————. Mission and Expansion of Christianity in the First Three Centuries. Trans. James Moffatt. London: Williams and Norgate, 1908.

—————, and A. C. McGiffert. Articles about "Socrates," "Sozomen," and "Theodoret" in the Encyclopaedia Britannica, 11th ed.

Hartshorne, Charles, and William L. Reese. Philosophers Speak of God. Chicago: University of Chicago Press, 1953.

Haussleiter, J. Die lateinische Apokalypse der alten afrikanischen Kirche. In Forschungen zur Geschichte des neutestamentlichen Kanons und der altkirchlichen Literatur 4, ed. T. Zahn, 1-244. Erlangen: A. Deichert, 1891.

Heim, François. "L'influence exercée par Constantin sur Lactance: sa théologie de la victoire." In *Lactance et son temps: recherches actuelles*, ed. J. Fontaine and M. Perrin, 55-74. Paris: Beauchesne, 1978.

Helgeland, John. "Christians and the Roman Army A.D. 173-337." *Church History* 43 (1974): 149-163, 200.

_____. "Christians and the Roman Army from Marcus Aurelius to Constantine." In *Aufstieg und Niedergang der Römischen Welt: Geschichte und Kultur Roms im Spiegel der neueren Forschung*, ed. H. Temporini and W. Haase, 2,23,1:724-834. Berlin: Walter de Gruyter, 1979.

_____. "Roman Army Religion." In *Aufstieg und Niedergang der Römischen Welt: Geschichte und Kultur Roms im Spiegel der neueren Forschung*, ed. H. Temporini and W. Haase, 2,16,2:1470-1505. Berlin: Walter de Gruyter, 1978.

Hicks, R. D. *Stoic and Epicurean.* New York: Charles Scribner's Sons, 1910.

Hinson, E. Glenn. *The Evangelization of the Roman Empire: Identity and Adaptability.* Macon GA: Mercer University Press, 1981.

Höistad, Ragnar. *Cynic Hero and Cynic King: Studies in the Cynic Conception of Man.* Uppsala: C. Bloms boktr., 1948.

Hoven, René. *Stoïcisme et stoïciens face au problème de l'au-delà.* Paris: Société d'édition Les Belles Lettres, 1971.

Hughes, H. Stuart. *History as Art and as Science.* New York: Harper and Row, 1964.

Jaeger, Werner. *Early Christianity and Greek Paideia.* Cambridge MA: Harvard University Press, 1962.

_____. "A New Greek Word in Plato's Republic: The Medical Origin of the Theory of the Θυμοειδές." In *Scripta Minora* 2:309-316. Rome: Edizioni di storia e letteratura, via Lancellotti, 1960. Originally published in *Eranos Rudbergianus* 44 (1946): 123-30.

_____. *Two Rediscovered Works of Ancient Christian Literature: Gregory of Nyssa and Macarius.* Leiden: E. J. Brill, 1954.

Jonas, Hans. *The Gnostic Religion: The Message of the Alien God and the Beginnings of Christianity.* 2nd ed. Boston: Beacon Press, 1963.

Jones, A. H. M. *Constantine and the Conversion of Europe.* London: Hodder and Stoughton, 1948.

_____. *The Later Roman Empire, 284-602: A Social, Economic, and Administrative Survey.* 3 vols. Oxford: Blackwell, 1964.

_____. "Notes on the Genuineness of the Constantinian Documents in Eusebius's Life of Constantine." *Journal of Ecclesiastical History* 5 (1954): 196-200.

_____. "The Social Background of the Struggle between Paganism and Christianity." In *The Conflict between Paganism and Christianity in the Fourth Century,* ed. Arnaldo Momigliano, 17-37. Oxford: Clarendon, 1963.

Jones, C. P. *Plutarch and Rome.* See esp. chapter 12, "The Political Treatises," 110-21. Oxford: Clarendon, 1971.

Jones, Roger Miller. *The Platonism of Plutarch, and Selected Papers.* Menasha WI: G. Banta, 1916. Reprint, New York: Garland, 1980.

Jülicher. "(7) Euagrios Scholasticus." In Pauly-Wissowa, *Real-Encyclopädie* (1907) 6: 833.

Kaegi, Walter Emil, Jr. *Byzantium and the Decline of Rome.* Princeton NJ: Princeton University Press, 1968.

_____. "Initial Byzantine Reactions to the Arab Conquest." *Church History* 38 (1969): 139-49.

Kee, Howard Clark. *Christian Origins in Sociological Perspective: Methods and Resources.* Philadelphia: Westminster, 1980.

Kelly, J. N. D. *Early Christian Doctrines.* 3rd ed. London: Adam and Charles Black, 1965.

_____. *Jerome: His Life, Writings, and Controversies.* New York: Harper and Row, 1975.

Kennedy, G. A. *The Art of Rhetoric in the Roman World,* 300 B.C.-A.D. 300. Princeton NJ: Princeton University Press, 1972.

Kopecek, Thomas A. *A History of Neo-Arianism.* Cambridge MA: Philadelphia Patristic Foundation, 1979.

Krieger, Leonard. "The Idea of Authority in the West." *American Historical Review* 82 (1977): 249-70.

Kurfess, Alfons. "Zur Echtheitsfrage und Datierung der Rede Konstantins an die Versammlung der Heiligen." *Zeitschrift für Religions- und Geistesgeschichte* 1 (1948): 355-58.

Laistner, M. L. W. *The Greater Roman Historians.* Berkeley: University of California Press, 1963.

Laporte, Jean. *La doctrine eucharistique chez Philon d'Alexandrie.* Paris: Beauchesne, 1972.

_____. Introd. to his edition of Philo, *De Iosepho,* 11-41. Paris: Éditions du Cerf, 1964.

Laqueur, Richard. *Eusebius als Historiker seiner Zeit.* Berlin: W. de Gruyter, 1929.

_____. *Polybius.* Leipzig: B. G. Teubner, 1913.

Lattimore, Richmond. *Themes in Greek and Latin Epitaphs.* Urbana: University of Illinois Press, 1942.

Lawlor, Hugh Jackson. *Eusebiana: Essays on the Ecclesiastical History of Eusebius, Bishop of Caesarea*. Oxford: Clarendon, 1912.

——————, and John Ernest Leonard Oulton. *Eusebius Bishop of Caesarea: The Ecclesiastical History and the Martyrs of Palestine* 2: *Introduction, Notes and Index*. London: SPCK, 1928.

Layton, Bentley, ed., trans., and commentary. *The Gnostic Treatise on Resurrection from Nag Hammadi*. Harvard Dissertations in Religion 12. Missoula MT: Scholars Press, 1979.

Lebon, J. "La christologie du monophysisme syrien." In *Das Konzil von Chalkedon: Geschichte und Gegenwart*, ed. A. Grillmeier and H. Bacht, 1:425-580. Würzburg: Echter-Verlag, 1951.

——————. *Le monophysisme sévérien: étude historique littéraire et théologique sur la résistance monophysite au concile de Chalcédoine jusqu'à la constitution de l'église jacobite*. Louvain: J. van Linthout, 1909.

Leeman, A. D. *Aufbau und Absicht von Sallusts Bellum Iugurthinum*. Amsterdam: Noord-Hollandsche Uitg. Mij., 1957.

Lichtenthaeler, Charles. *Thucydide et Hippocrate vus par un historien-médecin*. Etudes d'histoire de la médecine 4. Geneva: Librairie Droz, 1965.

Lilla, Salvatore R. C. *Clement of Alexandria: A Study in Christian Platonism and Gnosticism*. London: Oxford University Press, 1971.

Lind, L. R. "Concept, Action, and Character: The Reasons for Rome's Greatness." *Transactions of the American Philological Association* 103 (1972): 233-83.

Lindner, Rudi Paul. "Nomadism, Horses and Huns." *Past and Present* 92 (1981): 3-19.

Long, A. A. *Hellenistic Philosophy*. London: Duckworth, 1974.

——————, ed. *Problems in Stoicism*. London: Athlone Press, 1971.

Lossky, Vladimir. *Orthodox Theology: An Introduction*. Trans. I. and I. Kesarcodi-Watson. Crestwood NY: St. Vladimir's Seminary Press, 1978.

——————. *The Vision of God*. Trans. A. Moorhouse. London: Faith Press, 1963.

Luibhéid, Colm. *Eusebius of Caesarea and the Arian Crisis*. Dublin: Irish Academic Press, 1981.

Macan, R. W. "Herodotus and Thucydides." In *Cambridge Ancient History*, 5:398-419. Cambridge: Cambridge University Press, 1927.

McArthur, Harvey K. "Eusebian Sections and Canons." *Catholic Biblical Quarterly* 27 (1965): 250-56.

MacCormack, Sabine. "Latin Prose Panegyrics." In *Empire and Aftermath: Silver Latin II*, ed. T. A. Dorey, 143-205. London: Routledge and Kegan Paul, 1975.

_____. "Roma, Constantinopolis, the Emperor, and His Genius." *Classical Quarterly* 25 (1975): 131-50.

McIntire, C. T., ed. *God, History, and Historians: An Anthology of Modern Christian Views of History*. New York: Oxford University Press, 1977.

McNamara, Kevin. "Theodoret of Cyrus and the Unity of Person in Christ." *Irish Theological Quarterly* 22 (1955): 313-28.

Mandac, Marijan. "L'union christologique dans les oeuvres de Théodoret antérieures au concile d'Ephèse." *Ephemerides Theologicae Lovanienses* 47 (1971): 64-96.

Mandelbaum, Maurice. *The Problem of Historical Knowledge*. 1938. Reprint, New York: Harper and Row, 1967.

Markus, R. A. *Saeculum: History and Society in the Theology of St. Augustine*. Cambridge: Cambridge University Press, 1970.

_____. "Two Conceptions of Political Authority: Augustine, *De Civitate Dei*, XIX, 14-15, and some Thirteenth-century Interpretations." *Journal of Theological Studies* new series 16 (1965): 68-100.

Marrou, H. I. *A History of Education in Antiquity*. Trans. G. Lamb. 1956. Reprint, New York: New American Library, 1964.

Martimort, A. G., et al. *L'Eglise en prière: Introduction à la liturgie*. Paris: Desclée, 1961.

Mathew, Gervase. *Byzantine Aesthetics*. New York: Viking Press, 1963.

Meer, F. van der, and Christine Mohrmann. *Atlas of the Early Christian World*. Trans. and ed. M. F. Hedlund and H. H. Rowley. London: Nelson, 1958.

Meinhold, Peter. *Geschichte der kirchlichen Historiographie*. 2 vols. Freiburg: Alber, 1967.

Merlan, Philip. *From Platonism to Neoplatonism*. 3rd ed. The Hague: Martinus Nijhoff, 1968.

Meyendorff, John. *Byzantine Theology*. New York: Fordham University Press, 1974.

Millar, Fergus. *The Emperor in the Roman World (31 BC-AD 337)*. London: Duckworth, 1977.

_____. *A Study of Cassius Dio*. Oxford: Clarendon, 1964.

Milne, H. J. M., and T. C. Skeat. "The Codex Sinaiticus and the Codex Alexandrinus." 2nd ed., as rev. 1963. London: pamphlet pub. by the Trustees of the British Museum, 1963.

Momigliano, Arnaldo. "Introduction: Christianity and the Decline of the Roman Empire." In *The Conflict between Paganism and Christianity in the Fourth Century*, ed. Arnaldo Momigliano, 1-16. Oxford: Clarendon, 1963.

_____. "Pagan and Christian Historiography in the Fourth Century A.D." In *The Conflict between Paganism and Christianity in the Fourth Century*, ed. Arnaldo Momigliano, 79-99. Oxford: Clarendon, 1963.

_____. *Studies in Historiography.* See esp. "The Place of Herodotus in the History of Historiography," 127-42; "Ancient History and the Antiquarian," 1-39; and "Gibbon's Contribution to Historical Method," 40-55. London: Weidenfeld and Nicolson, 1966.

_____. "Time in Ancient Historiography." *History and Theory* Beiheft 6 (1966): 1-23.

Mommsen, Th. "Die älteste Handschrift der Chronik des Hieronymus." *Hermes* 24 (1889): 393-401.

Moore, John M. *The Manuscript Tradition of Polybius.* Cambridge: Cambridge University Press, 1965.

Moreau, Joseph. *L'âme du monde de Platon aux stoïciens.* Paris: Société d'édition "Les Belles lettres," 1939.

Mosshammer, Alden A. *The Chronicle of Eusebius and Greek Chronographic Tradition.* Lewisburg PA: Bucknell University Press, 1979.

Myres, John L. *Herodotus: Father of History.* Oxford: Clarendon, 1953.

_____. "On the 'List of Thalassocracies' in Eusebius." *Journal of Hellenic Studies* 26 (1906): 84-130.

Neugebauer, O., and H. B. Van Hoesen. *Greek Horoscopes.* Memoirs of the American Philosophical Society 48. Philadelphia: 1959.

Nigg, Walter. *Die Kirchengeschichtsschreibung: Grundzüge ihrer historischen Entwicklung.* Munich: C. H. Beck, 1934.

Nock, Arthur Darby. *Conversion.* Oxford: Clarendon, 1933.

_____. "The Emperor's Divine Comes." *Journal of Roman Studies* 37 (1947): 102-16.

Norris, Richard A., Jr. *Manhood and Christ: A Study in the Christology of Theodore of Mopsuestia.* Oxford: Clarendon, 1963.

O'Connell, Robert J. *St. Augustine's Early Theory of Man, A.D. 386-391.* Cambridge MA: Harvard University Press, 1968.

Oliver, James H. *The Civilizing Power: A Study of the Panathenaic Discourse of Aelius Aristides.* In *Transactions of the American Philosophical Society* new series 58,1 (1968).

Osborn, E. F. *Justin Martyr.* Tübingen: Mohr (Paul Siebeck), 1973.

Oulton, J. E. L. "Rufinus's Translation of the Church History of Eusebius." *Journal of Theological Studies* 30 (1929): 150-74.

Outler, Albert C. "Methods and Aims in the Study of the Development of Catholic Christianity." *Anglican Theological Review* 50 (1968): 117-30.

_____. "The Person and Work of Christ." In *A Companion to the Study of St. Augustine,* ed. Roy W. Battenhouse, 343-70. New York: Oxford University Press, 1955.

_____. *Who Trusts in God: Musings on the Meaning of Providence.* New York: Oxford University Press, 1968.

Overbeck, Franz. *Ueber die Anfänge der Kirchengeschichtsschreibung.* Basel: 1892.

Pagels, Elaine Hiesey. *The Gnostic Paul: Gnostic Exegesis of the Pauline Letters.* Philadelphia: Fortress, 1975.

Pasquali, Giorgio. "Die Composition der Vita Constantini des Eusebius." *Hermes* 45 (1910): 369-86.

Patterson, L. G. *God and History in Early Christian Thought.* London: Adam and Charles Black, 1967.

Pears, D. F., ed. *Freedom and the Will.* London: Macmillan, 1965.

Pédech, Paul. *La méthode historique de Polybe.* Paris: Les Belles lettres, 1964.

Person, Ralph E. *The Mode of Theological Decision Making at the Early Ecumenical Councils: An Inquiry into the Function of Scripture and Tradition at the Councils of Nicaea and Ephesus.* Theologischen Dissertationen 14. Basel: Friedrich Reinhardt Kommissionsverlag, 1978.

Pohlenz, Max. *Die Stoa: Geschichte einer geistigen Bewegung.* Göttingen: Vandenhoeck und Ruprecht, 1948-1949.

Popper, Karl R. *The Open Society and Its Enemies.* 4th ed. 2 vols. London: Routledge and Kegan Paul, 1962.

_____. *The Poverty of Historicism.* 2nd ed. London: Routledge, 1961.

Powell, J. Enoch. *A Lexicon to Herodotus.* Cambridge: Cambridge University Press, 1938.

"Providence." *Dictionnaire de Théologie Catholique* (1936).

Quasten, Johannes. *Patrology.* 3 vols. Utrecht and Antwerp: Spectrum, 1963-1964.

Raeder, Hans. "Kaiser Julian als Philosoph und religiöser Reformator." *Classica et Mediaevalia* 6 (1944): 179-93.

Randall, John Herman, Jr. *Aristotle.* New York: Columbia University Press, 1960.

Riedinger, Utto. *Die heilige Schrift im Kampf der griechischen Kirche gegen die Astrologie: Von Origenes bis Johannes von Damaskos.* Innsbruck: Wagner, 1956.

Rist, J. M. *Stoic Philosophy.* Cambridge: Cambridge University Press, 1969.

Rohde, Erwin. *Psyche: The Cult of Souls and Belief in Immortality among the Greeks.* New York: Harcourt, Brace, 1925.

Ross, G. M. "Seneca's Philosophical Influence." In *Seneca,* ed. C. D. N. Costa. London: Routledge and Kegan Paul, 1974.

Rougé, Jean. "A propos du manuscrit du *De mortibus persecutorum.*" In *Lactance et son temps: recherches actuelles,* ed. J. Fontaine and M. Perrin, 13-23. Paris: Beauchesne, 1978.

Rowland, Christopher. *The Open Heaven: A Study of Apocalyptic in Judaism and Early Christianity.* New York: Crossroad, 1982.

Rubin, Berthold. *Prokopios von Kaisareia.* Stuttgart: A. Druckenmüller, 1954.

Sabine, George H. *A History of Political Theory.* 4th ed., rev. Thomas Landon Thorson. Hinsdale IL: Dryden Press, 1973.

Sambursky, S. *The Physical World of Late Antiquity.* London: Routledge and Kegan Paul, 1962.

——————. *The Physical World of the Greeks.* Trans. M. Dagut. London: Routledge and Kegan Paul, 1956.

——————. *Physics of the Stoics.* London: Routledge and Kegan Paul, 1959.

Sandbach, F. H. *The Stoics.* London: Chatto and Windus, 1975.

Scheidweiler, F. "Nochmals die Vita Constantini." *Byzantinische Zeitschrift* 49 (1956): 1-32.

Schoedel, William R. "In Praise of the King: A Rhetorical Pattern in Athenagoras." In *Disciplina Nostra: Essays in Memory of Robert F. Evans,* ed. Donald F. Winslow, 69-90, 199-203. Cambridge MA: Philadelphia Patristic Foundation, 1979.

Scholem, Gershom. *The Messianic Idea in Judaism and Other Essays on Jewish Spirituality.* New York: Schocken, 1971.

Schoo, Georg. *Die Quellen des Kirchenhistorikers Sozomenos.* Berlin: Trowitzsch und Sohn, 1911. First two chapters published separately as *Die erhaltenen schriftlichen Hauptquellen des Kirchenhistorikers Sozomenos.* Inaugural-Dissertation, Universität Münster. Berlin: Trowitzsch, 1911.

Schur, Werner. *Sallust als Historiker.* Stuttgart: W. Kohlhammer, 1934.

Schürer, Emil. *The History of the Jewish People in the Age of Jesus Christ* 1. English ed. rev. Geza Vermes and Fergus Millar. Edinburgh: Clark, 1973.

Schwartz, E. "Eusebius." Pauly-Wissowa, *Real-Encyclopädie* (1907) 6: 1370-1439.

Scott, Kenneth. "Plutarch and the Ruler Cult." *Transactions and Proceedings of the American Philological Association* 60 (1929): 117-35.

Seeck, Otto. *Geschichte des Untergangs der antiken Welt* 6. Stuttgart: J. B. Metzler, 1920.

Sellers, R. V. *The Council of Chalcedon.* London: SPCK, 1953.

Seston, W. "Constantine as a Bishop." *Journal of Roman Studies* 37 (1947): 127-31.

Shotwell, James T. *An Introduction to the History of History.* New York: Columbia University Press, 1922.

——————. *The Story of Ancient History.* New York: Columbia University Press, 1961. Originally published as vol. 1 of *The History of History* in 1939.

Shotwell, Willis A. *The Biblical Exegesis of Justin Martyr.* London: SPCK, 1965.

Shutt, R. J. H. *Studies in Josephus.* London: SPCK, 1961.

Siegfried, Walter. *Studien zur geschichtlichen Anschauung des Polybios*. Leipzig: B. G. Teubner, 1928.

Silver, Abba Hillel. *A History of Messianic Speculation in Israel: From the First through the Seventeenth Centuries*. Boston: Beacon Press, 1959.

Sirinelli, Jean. *Les vues historiques d'Eusèbe de Césarée durant la période prénicéenne*. Dakar: Université de Dakar, 1961.

Spanneut, Michel. *Le stoïcisme des pères de l'église de Clément de Rome à Clément d'Alexandrie*. Paris: Éditions du Seuil, 1957.

Sterns, Indrikis. *The Greater Medieval Historians: An Interpretation and a Bibliography*. Washington DC: University Press of America, 1981.

Stevenson, James. *Studies in Eusebius*. Cambridge: Cambridge University Press, 1929.

Storch, Rudolph H. "The 'Eusebian Constantine.' " *Church History* 40 (1971): 145-55.

Syme, Ronald. *Sallust*. Berkeley: University of California Press, 1964.

—————. *Tacitus*. Oxford: Clarendon, 1958.

Tanner, R. G. "ΔIANOIA and Plato's Cave." *Classical Quarterly* new series 20 (1970): 81-91.

Tatakis, Basile. *La philosophie Byzantine*. 2nd ed. 2nd supplementary fascicule to Émile Bréhier, *Histoire de la philosophie*. Paris: Presses Universitaires de France, 1959.

Taylor, L. R. *The Divinity of the Roman Emperor*. Middletown CT: American Philological Association, 1931.

Tcherikover, Victor. *Hellenistic Civilization and the Jews*. Trans. S. Applebaum. Philadelphia: Jewish Publication Society of America, 1959.

Teetgen, Ada B. *The Life and Times of the Empress Pulcheria: A.D. 399-A.D. 452*. London: S. Sonnenschein, 1907.

Tennant, F. R. *Miracle and Its Philosophical Presuppositions*. Cambridge: Cambridge University Press, 1925.

Thackeray, H. St. John. *Josephus: The Man and the Historian*. New York: Jewish Institute of Religion Press, 1929.

Thesleff, Holger. *An Introduction to the Pythagorean Writings of the Hellenistic Period*. Abo: Abo Akademi, 1961.

Thompson, E. A. "The Foreign Policies of Theodosius II and Marcian." *Hermathena* 76 (1950): 58-75.

—————. *A History of Attila and the Huns*. Oxford: Clarendon, 1948.

Thompson, James Westfall. *A History of Historical Writing* 1. New York: Macmillan, 1942.

Tiede, David Lenz. *The Charismatic Figure as Miracle Worker*. Society of Biblical Literature Dissertation Series 1. Missoula MT: Scholars Press, 1972.

Torrance, Thomas F. *The Doctrine of Grace in the Apostolic Fathers*. Edinburgh: Oliver and Boyd, 1948.

Trevelyan, George Macauley. *Clio, A Muse: and Other Essays*. London: Longmans, Green, 1913.

Tripolitis, Antonia. "Return to the Divine: Salvation in the Thought of Plotinus and Origen." In *Disciplina Nostra: Essays in Memory of Robert F. Evans*, ed. Donald F. Winslow, 171-78, 209-10. Cambridge MA: Philadelphia Patristic Foundation, 1979.

Turner, C. H. "The Early Episcopal Lists." *Journal of Theological Studies* 1 (1900): 181-200.

Le Typicon de la Grande Eglise: Ms. Saint-Croix n° 40, Xe siècle. Tome 2, *Le cycle des fêtes mobiles*. Ed. and trans. Juan Mateos. Orientalia Christiana Analecta 166. Rome, 1963.

Ullmann, Walter. *A History of Political Thought: The Middle Ages*. Baltimore MD: Penguin, 1965.

Valesius, Henricus. Preface to *Theodoriti episcopi Cyri et Evagrii Scholastici historia ecclesiastica . . .* , ed., trans. into Latin, and annotated by Henricus Valesius, B II obverse to C IV reverse. Paris: 1673. Reprinted in Theodoret of Cyrrhus. *Ecclesiastica Historia*, ed. Thomas Gaisford, v-xiii. Oxford: e typographeo Academico, 1854.

Vittinghoff, Friedrich. "Zum geschichtlichen Selbstverständnis der Spätantike." *Historische Zeitschrift* 198 (1964): 529-74.

Vogt, Joseph. *The Decline of Rome: The Metamorphosis of Ancient Civilisation*. Trans. J. Sondheimer. London: Weidenfeld and Nicolson, 1967.

Von Essen, Martin Heinrich Nikolaus. *Index Thucydideus*. Berlin: apud Weidmannos, 1887.

Von Scala, Rudolf. *Die Studien des Polybios* 1. Stuttgart: W. Kohlhammer, 1890.

Wacholder, Ben Zion. *Nicolaus of Damascus*. Berkeley: University of California Press, 1962.

Walbank, F. W. *A Historical Commentary on Polybius* 1. Oxford: Clarendon, 1957.

Wallace-Hadrill, D. S. "The Eusebian Chronicle: The Extent and Date of Composition of Its Early Editions." *Journal of Theological Studies* new series 6 (1955): 248-53.

——————. *Eusebius of Caesarea*. London: A. R. Mowbray, 1960.

Wardman, A. E. "Plutarch's Methods in the *Lives*." *Classical Quarterly* new series 21 (1971): 254-61.

Warmington, B. H. "Aspects of Constantinian Propaganda in the Panegyrici Latini." *Transactions of the American Philological Association* 104 (1974): 371-84.

——————. "The Later Roman Empire." Review article on *The Later Roman Empire, 284-602: A Social, Economic and Administrative Survey*, by A. H. M. Jones. *History* 50 (1965): 54-60.

Weber, Anton. Ἀρχή: *ein Beitrag zur Christologie des Eusebius von Cäsarea*. Munich: Verlag Neue Stadt, 1965.

Wells, Joseph. *Studies in Herodotus*. Oxford: B. Blackwell, 1923.

Wilken, Robert L. *The Christians as the Romans Saw Them*. New Haven: Yale University Press, 1984.

——————. "Diversity and Unity in Early Christianity." *Second Century: A Journal of Early Christian Studies* 1 (1981): 101-10.

——————. *The Myth of Christian Beginnings: History's Impact on Belief*. Garden City NY: Doubleday, 1971.

Williams, George Huntston. "Christology and Church-State Relations in the Fourth Century." *Church History* 20, 3 (1951): 3-33; 20, 4 (1951): 3-26.

Witt, R. E. *Albinus and the History of Middle Platonism*. Cambridge: Cambridge University Press, 1937.

Wolf, Carl Umhau. "Eusebius of Caesarea and the Onomasticon." *Biblical Archaeologist* 27 (1964): 66-96.

——————. "Location of Gilgal." *Biblical Research* 11 (1966): 42-51.

Zeiller, J. "Quelques remarques sur la 'vision' de Constantin." *Byzantion* 14 (1939): 329-39.

Ziegler, Konrat. "Plutarchos von Chaironeia." Pauly-Wissowa, *Real-Encyclopädie* 21 (1951): 636-962. Also published separately as *Plutarchos von Chaironeia*. 2nd ed. Stuttgart: J. B. Metzler, 1964.

Indexes

General Index

Academic skepticism, 181-82, 184

Accidents of history, 12, 41-42, 44-45, 47-51, 59-60, 190, 255. *See also* συμβε-βηκός

Adam and Eve and the Garden of Eden, 68, 89, 253

Aelius Aristides, 74

Aeon. *See* αἰών; Time and eternity

Africanus, Sextus Julius, 167, 177

Allegorical interpretation, 160, 162, 165, 178, 180, 253

Ammianus Marcellinus, 21-22, 27, 35, 186, 189, 222, 232, 243, 245, 249

Anatolius of Laodicea, 116, 118

Angels, 26, 69-71, 91, 99, 104, 107-108, 179-80

Apocalypticism, end of the world, 66-67, 89-90, 94, 128, 142, 164-65, 166-68 (Eusebius's dating of the end), 169-71, 174, 257

Apollinarius, 208, 211

Apollonius of Tyana, 105, 161

Apologists, second-century, 2, 36, 67, 99, 167, 177

Arcadius, 206, 232, 234

Aristotle and Aristotelianism, 2, 11-14, 17, 22, 35, 40-42, 44, 46, 58, 182, 190, 213-14, 220, 247, 255-56

Arius and Arianism, 63, 80, 159, 175, 177, 183-85, 208, 210-11, 234, 238

Asceticism, 3, 139, 146, 166, 244, 247-249. *See also* Monasticism; ἄσκησις

Astrology, 25-28, 30, 34, 37-38, 40, 53, 63, 70, 195

Athanasius, 80, 123, 138, 175, 179, 197, 205

Augustine, xiv, 4-5, 33, 35, 51, 61-62, 68, 90, 94, 97-99, 101-102, 106-107, 122, 140, 173, 182, 187, 199, 201, 206, 215, 225, 227-29, 247, 253, 257

Augustus, 66, 76-78, 83, 88, 137, 228

Aurelian, 70, 78, 117-18, 121, 129-30

Aurelius, Marcus, 91, 182

Basil the Great, 43, 179, 184, 186. *See also* Cappadocian fathers

Byzantine world and Eastern Orthodoxy, 4, 21, 78, 82, 107-108, 140, 169, 190, 213, 221, 226-27, 229-30, 248-49, 253, 257-58

Cappadocian fathers, 59, 175, 186. *See also* Basil; Gregory of Nyssa

Christ, 66, 70, 73, 75-77, 83, 90, 107, 128, 137-38, 170

Christian empire, Eusebius's vision of the, 137-40

Christology, Eusebius and Origen, 161; Evagrius Ponticus, 179-80; fifth-and sixth-century controversy (Antiochene vs. Alexandrian, Chalcedonian vs. monophysite), 208, 210-12, 216, 223-24, 254

Chrysostom, John, 175, 185-86, 194, 206, 209, 218

Church and state, xi, 66, 76, 82-83, 111, 136-39, 192-97 (connected by "cosmic sympathy").

Cicero, 155, 182, 187

Clement of Alexandria, 2, 59, 67, 177

Constantine, xi, 1, 4, 15, 35, 49, 51, 63, 67, 70-71, 73, 78-80, 83, 94, 101, 108, 111-14, 119, 123-25, 131-38, 141-42, 159-63, 169-76, 196, 204-205, 210, 225-26, 228-29, 231-32, 234-35, 237-38, 240, 243, 250, 256

Constantine's sons, 111, 113, 123-25; Constans, 197, 234; Constantine II, 196; Constantius II, 197, 232, 234, 238-39, 245, 249; Crispus, 114, 125, 135, 225

Constantius Chlorus, 136, 170-72

Creation, 36, 48, 57, 65-66, 68, 83, 93, 98

Index of Greek Terms

Index of Modern Authors

Printed in the United States
1505300004B/1-48